Advertising Campaign Strategy
A Guide to Marketing Communication Plans

Second Edition

Donald Parente
Middle Tennessee State University

Advertising Campaign Strategy
A Guide to Marketing Communication Plans

Second Edition

Donald Parente
Middle Tennessee State University

THE DRYDEN PRESS
Harcourt College Publishers

Fort Worth   Philadelphia   San Diego   New York   Orlando   Austin   San Antonio
Toronto   Montreal   London   Sydney   Tokyo

Publisher	Mike Roche
Executive Editor	Bill Schoof
Developmental Editor	Bobbie Bochenko
Art Director	Scott Baker
Production Manager	James McDonald

ISBN: 0-03-021114-x

Library of Congress Catalog Card Number: 99–074298

Copyright © 2000 by Harcourt, Inc.

Address for Domestic Orders
Harcourt College Publishers., 6277 Sea Harbor Drive, Orlando, FL 32887-6777
800-782-4479

Address for International Orders
International Customer Service
Harcourt College Publishers, 6277 Sea Harbor Drive, Orlando, FL 32887-6777
407-345-3800
(fax) 407-345-4060
(e-mail) hbintl@harcourtcollege.com

Address for Editorial Correspondence
Harcourt College Publishers, 301 Commerce Street, Suite 3700, Fort Worth, TX 76102

Web Site Address
http://www.harcourtcollege.com

Harcourt College Publishers will provide complimentary supplements or supplement packages to those adopters qualified under our adoption policy. Please contact your sales representative to learn how you qualify. If as an adopter or potential user you receive supplements you do not need, please return them to your sales representative or send them to: Attn: Returns Department, Troy Warehouse, 465 South Lincoln Drive, Troy, MO 63379.

Printed in the United States of America

9 0 1 2 3 4 5 6 7 8   039   9 8 7 6 5 4 3 2 1

Harcourt College Publishers

The Dryden Press Series in Marketing

Marketing

Avila, Williams, Ingram, and LaForge
The Professional Selling Skills Workbook

Bateson and Hoffman
Managing Services Marketing: Text and
Readings
Fourth Edition

Blackwell, Blackwell, and Talarzyk
Contemporary Cases in Consumer Behavior
Fourth Edition

Boone and Kurtz
Contemporary Marketing WIRED
Ninth Edition

Boone and Kurtz
Contemporary Marketing 1999

Churchill
Basic Marketing Research
Third Edition

Churchill
Marketing Research: Methodological
Foundations
Seventh Edition

**Czinkota, Dickson, Dunne, Griffin,
Hoffman, Hutt, Lindgren, Lusch,
Ronkainen, Rosenbloom, Sheth, Shimp,
Siguaw, Simpson, Speh, and Urbany**

Marketing: Best Practices

Czinkota and Ronkainen
Global Marketing

Czinkota and Ronkainen
International Marketing
Fifth Edition

Czinkota and Ronkainen
International Marketing Strategy: Environmental Assessment and Entry Strategies

Dickson
Marketing Management
Second Edition

Dunne and Lusch
Retailing
Third Edition

Engel, Blackwell, and Miniard
Consumer Behavior
Eighth Edition

Ferrell, Hartline, Lucas, Luck
Marketing Strategy

Futrell
Sales Management: Teamwork, Leadership,
and Technology
Fifth Edition

Grover
Theory & Simulation of Market-Focused
Management

Ghosh
Retail Management
Second Edition

Hoffman/Bateson
Essentials of Services Marketing

Hutt and Speh
Business Marketing Management: A Strategic
View of Industrial and Organizational
Markets
Sixth Edition

Ingram, LaForge, and Schwepker
Sales Management: Analysis and Decision
Making
Fourth Edition

Lindgren and Shimp
Marketing: An Interactive Learning System

Krugman, Reid, Dunn, and Barban
Advertising: Its Role in Modern Marketing
Eighth Edition

Oberhaus, Ratliffe, and Stauble
Professional Selling: A Relationship Process
Second Edition

Parente
Advertising Campaign Strategy: A Guide to
Marketing Communication Plans
Second Edition

Electronic Marketing

Rosenbloom
Marketing Channels: A Management View
Sixth Edition

Sandburg
Discovering Your Marketing Career CD-ROM

Schaffer
Applying Marketing Principles Software

Schaffer
The Marketing Game

Schellinck and Maddox
Marketing Research: A Computer-Assisted
Approach

Schnaars
MICROSIM

Schuster and Copeland
Global Business: Planning for Sales and
Negotiations

Sheth, Mittal, and Newman
Customer Behavior: Consumer Behavior and
Beyond

Shimp
Advertising, Promotion, and Supplemental
Aspects of Integrated Marketing
Communications
Fifth Edition

Talarzyk
Cases and Exercises in Marketing

Terpstra and Sarathy
International Marketing
Eighth Edition

Electronic Commerce

Weitz and Wensley
Readings in Strategic Marketing Analysis,
Planning, and Implementation

Zikmund
Exploring Marketing Research
Seventh Edition

Zikmund
Essentials of Marketing Research

**HARCOURT COLLEGE
OUTLINE SERIES**

Peterson
Principles of Marketing

Preface

Adapting to Change

These are exciting and challenging times. New ideas, new media, and new technology are having a profound effect on the way advertising is conceived, created, and delivered. We are in the midst of a true communications revolution. Changes are taking place seemingly everywhere and everyday. The challenge to educators is to understand exactly what is changing and sort out what is effective and what may be simply a passing trend.

Because of the speed with which many changes take place today, neither educators nor students can afford the luxury of gradually learning about new developments. Technology, especially with respect to the Internet, is swiftly and dramatically changing the way companies are doing business. Companies and individuals that proceed slowly run the risk that their knowledge will quickly become dated. Many changes are translated into buzz words that are used as a li1mus test to discover whether someone is current on the change *du jour.*

It is not enough, however, to identify and understand change, one has to figure out how to thrive in the new marketing environment. Yet, one gets the distinct feeling that many changes are occurring faster than the field's ability to fully evaluate their effectiveness. One common occurrence is that students often readily adopt changes or new approaches faster than their instructors. Students see what's going on in advertising, but usually they do not have the analytical tools or the knowledge to judge whether what they see is effective. Educators, on the other hand, are much more likely to evaluate new developments or approaches in terms of their experience For example, many highly creative image-oriented commercials are widely admired by students. These same ads are sometimes viewed more skeptically by educators, especially when these ads either ignore or are contrary to many of the principles that have been widely accepted over the years. Among advertising practitioners, it's easy to find conflicting opinions about the relative merits of a specific advertising campaign or approach.

We offer no easy solutions. Our approach is to offer a detailed examination of the campaign process with a special emphasis on the analytical and strategic elements that are likely to lead to effective campaigns. We know there will always be advertising that works for reasons that resist analysis. But we do believe that if you understand the concepts that underlie successful advertising, when changes occur in the marketplace you will be in position to better understand and exploit them.

In the first edition of this book, we were sensitive to titling the book Advertising *Campaign Strategy* even though it was clear to us the book was all about *marketing communication strategy.* We pointed out then that the advertising emphasis in the title was more a reflection of tradition than a belief that advertising can or should be prepared apart from other marketing communication tools such as sales promotion or public relations. We believe that the title and the orientation of the book have been well received. We continue to stress that smart companies begin with the premise that they are planning a marketing communication campaign—not an advertising campaign. This assumption not only helps companies avoid any over-reliance on advertising, but it also helps them proactively consider other promotional options as part of a unified selling strategy. Far too often, communication tools, such as sales promotion, direct marketing, and public relations, are merely combined with an advertising program rather than integrated together to produce a seamless selling effort.

Our challenge as educators is to provide conceptual information in a form that is both useable and practical. To accomplish this task, we included numerous examples of the tests, techniques, principles, and procedures that are used in marketing communication, as well as a number of checklists and tips appropriate for a specific area. We recognize there are many ways to achieve a desired end. We know that as situations change, it may be appropriate to also change the approach or the organization.

Highlights of Advertising Campaign Strategy

The goal for this edition was to strengthen the conceptual elements that form the basis of a marketing communication campaign. At the same time, we wanted to make the information in this edition easier to grasp and to apply.

Chapter 1

This chapter introduces the reader to the purpose and scope of the book. After some discussion of the new marketing environment, including post modern advertising, we present some of the core concepts that should be part of the mindset of students as they prepare for the campaign, including market segmentation, the marketing concept, the communication concept, integrated market communications, and a campaign concept. New to the second edition is a discussion about process orientation. We also present the essential elements in a strategic plan and explain how they relate to a marketing communication campaign. To close the chapter, we present a general outline for the campaign.

Chapters 2 and 3

These chapters cover what many people refer to as the situation analysis. Chapter 2 begins with a discussion of how to get ready for the campaign. This chapter focuses on analyzing the company and the consumer. It includes an updated comprehensive discussion on sources of information, including their availability in a typical university library, an extensive discussion of syndicated research sources, and a broad coverage of the tests and techniques that can be used to complete the analyses. Chapter 3 essentially is a continuation of Chapter 2 but focuseson the market, product, and competitive analyses. Both Chapters 2 and 3 provide the principles and tools to make a thorough situation analysis.

Chapter 4

This chapter is basically about setting objectives. We emphasize that setting objectives should evolve logically out of the research foundation. Critical to our discussion of objectives is the importance of brand equity, which we also discuss in greater detail in the next chapter. To lay a foundation for setting objectives, we discuss the nature of problems and opportunities, and how to uncover them. Most of this chapter focuses on setting objectives, including the decision on how to segment the market. To discuss objectives we follow the principles associated with the management-by-objectives (MBO) philosophy.

Chapter 5

This chapter focuses on the development of marketing communication strategy. We look at four interrelated elements: the management of brand equity, the marketing communication expenditure, the positioning of messages, and the targeting and delivery of messages. We devote most of this chapter to an extensive discussion of brand equity. We cover the communication expenditure only briefly, taking the position that this variable is not something students usually can change. We rely on the next three chapters to cover the positioning and targeting aspects of strategy in greater detail.

Chapter 6

This chapter is organized so that the first part of the chapter covers both essential and optional elements in a message strategy. The second part of the chapter focuses on execution, including how to evaluate the creative opportunity, an examination of strategic approaches for message strategy, an approach to developing creativity, and new and traditional approaches to creating advertising.

Chapter 7

This chapter parallels the organization of Chapter 6 in that it also begins with a brief examination of the elements that make up a media plan including objectives, strategy, and tactics. The chapter then proceeds to explain how to implement the basic media decisions: first:, by examining what is involved with setting both quantitative and qualitative media objectives, second, by breaking down media strategy into its essential elements. This chapter finishes with an explanation of how to execute the media strategy.

Chapter 8

From an organizational point of view, we considered merging this chapter with the previous one on media, calling it integrated marketing communications. It obviously would have been too long, so we separated advertising media from other types of marketing communication using Chapter 8 to cover sales promotion, public relations, and direct marketing. We know that most advertising students do not get in-depth exposure to these areas, especially sales promotion and direct marketing, so we provided an extensive discussion of the techniques and tools common to the trade.

Chapter 9

This is a new chapter. We wanted to put in this chapter the extra things that advertisers increasingly are including in their campaigns to give them an edge over the competition. This chapter includes three major sections: 1) special market segments including global, African American, Hispanic, Asian American, and gay/lesbian markets, 2) special message strategies including, multi-tiered advertising, cause-related marketing, green marketing, cross promotions, and 3) special media strategies including advertising on the Internet: non-traditional media options and examples of creative media approaches such as ambush marketing and fresh TV.

Chapter 10

Evaluating the effectiveness of the campaign is the focus of this chapter. We present a comprehensive view of the many tests and techniques that are used to measure a campaign's effectiveness, briefly covering many of the commercial research companies that are involved in this type of testing. Unlike many of the chapters in other books on this topic, this chapter is organized correspondent to when the need for a particular type of research would arise in a campaign. First, we discuss concept testing, then move to in-depth discussions of copy testing, concurrent testing, and post-testing. This chapter was written with the assistance of Michael P. Kalasunas, Director of Research and Planning, J. Walter Thompson.

Chapter 11

This chapter covers the task of putting a plans book together, largely focusing on interpreting and presenting the material covered in the previous chapters. For this edition, we expanded our suggestions about specific points to cover in the plans book, especially in the situation analysis. We also use many of the ideas and advice of various educators around the country who either teach an advertising campaigns' course or work with the AAF competition.

Chapter 12

This chapter focuses on putting together the presentation. This presentation is a comprehensive approach to the most taxing of areas. We are especially appreciative of having Tom Duncan and Sandra Moriarity's outstanding book *How to Create and Deliver Winning Advertising Presentations* as a model. This chapter also includes an extensive discussion of the special problems associated with the National Student Advertising Competition sponsored by the AAF. For this last section, we borrowed heavily from the advice of AAF competition veterans. Lynda Maddox, George Washington University, provided extensive assistance on this chapter.

Acknowledgments

This book is the result of the collective efforts of many people, including my family and colleagues. I would especially like to acknowledge the warm and friendly people at The Dryden Press: Bill Schoof, the acquisition editor who provided much encouragement and support; Bobbie Bochenko, the development editor, who was always readily available to help me solve problems; Roberta Landi, the copy editor who often helped redirect, if not challenge my thinking; the members of the production team: John Haakenson, James McDonald, Scott Baker, Linda Blundell, and Kim Samuels who helped kept this project on track; and Lise Johnson, our product manager, who helped direct our marketing effort.

I would also like to acknowledge and thank Michael P. Kalasunas, the director of research and planning at J. Walter Thompson in Chicago. He provided many ideas for Chapters 2 and 3, while reviewing and helping me edit Chapter 9. Helen Katz, DDB Needham reviewed Chapter 1 on the media and offered many valuable suggestions.

I would also like to thank the many educators who provided advice, often sharing their own particular approach to doing a campaign. Edd Applegate, Middle Tennessee State University, read most of the book and offered much valuable insight. Bruce Vanden Bergh, Michigan State University reviewed and critiqued the first five chapters. Leonard Reid, University of Georgia, thoroughly reviewed Chapters 2 and 3 in the first edition and the effects of his suggestions continue in this edition. Arnold Barban reviewed the chapter on media and made important suggestions on its organization. Sharon Parente provided important professional assistance throughout the book, but especially in the section on using the library. A number of faculty shared with us their views on how to write a plans book for the first edition: Louise Gainey, University of Miami; Roger Lavery, University of Oregon; Howard Cogan, Ithaca College; Tommy Smith, University of Southern Mississippi;

Carolyn Stringer, Western Kentucky University; and Jim Gilmore, Michigan State University. I am also appreciative of the assistance I received from my research assistants: Lisa Parente, Michigan State University; Ryan Hale (who also designed the cover of the book) and Sheri Morris, both of Middle Tennessee State University.

We also received a great deal of assistance from the following practitioners:

From Leo Burnett Co.,: Mike Allen, Jane Spittler, Colin Hall, Cathy DeThorne, Mike O'Neal, Jack Phifer, Carol Fletcher, Rishad Tobaccowala, Josh McQueen, and Lisa Lager.

From SRI International: Rebecca Hollenbeck

From Hull Marketing Research: Bill Hull

From Foote Cone Belding: Dana Anderson and Karen Randolph

From DDB Needham: Mike Horn

From Executive Recruiter: Susan Sedler

From Helen Curtis: Ralph Blessing

From McDonald's Corporation: Roy Bergold and Elizabeth MacAdams

From Quaker Oats: John Blair, Barb Marusarz, and Scott Hughes

From Nielsen Media Research: Ted Duff

From Nielsen North America: Dan Sarullo, Meredeth Spector, and Connie Milbourne

From Burke Marketing Research: Dan Evarrs

From Lintas Marketing Communications: Lou Schultz

From Tatham Euro RSCG: Michael Robinson

Special Acknowledgments to Former Coauthors

Throughout this book I use the pronoun "we" liberally. Part of the reasoning for this is stylistic, but a large part is my awareness of the contributions my former coauthors, Arnold Barban, University of Alabama, Bruce Vanden Bergh, Michigan State University, and Jim Marra, Temple University, have made to this book. Although much of their work has been rewritten, their ideas and influence is profoundly felt.

I am especially indebted to Arnold Barban for his help and encouragement with both the first and second editions. He has been a good mentor and a special friend.

Don Parente
March 1999

Contents in Brief

Contents

Advertising Campaign Strategy
A Guide to Marketing Communication Plans

Second Edition

Donald Parente
Middle Tennessee State University

Chapter 1

Advertising from a Marketing Communications Perspective

Consider Super Bowl Sunday. This is the day an anxious advertising industry awaits the debut of the new ad campaigns. The ads will be interesting, some may be spectacular. These ads come from some of the most creative minds in the world. New technology has given copywriters and art directors the ability to transform the dreamable into the doable. These ads are so interesting they get talked about before *and* after the game. But these ads better be *more* than interesting. At a cost of almost $2 million for a 30-second spot,[1] the ads will have to sell a lot of "product" to recoup the advertiser's investment. The ads have to be effective. But are they?

Effectiveness can be difficult to achieve and hard to measure. Because of the increasing sophistication of the market and the nature of the advertising task, running some of these ads requires a good measure of faith. The public has become advertising savvy and, perhaps, a bit jaded. Not only is the public exposed to countless ads, they are also inundated with promotional messages virtually everywhere they go—from classrooms and ballfields to the restroom at the local pub. Moreover, many companies sell products that have no distinguishing qualities, nothing to set them apart from the competition other than, perhaps, an image or a personality. In the top agencies, creative people are continually challenged to produce ads that are better and more creative than their earlier work—not to mention that of the competition. Writers and art directors are encouraged to think "out of the box," or to be "disruptive." There's a lot of pressure, but the work can be exciting. The last thing many writers want is to become a "hack"—someone who produces prosaic ideas and pedestrian copy.

Truly creative work often exists at the edges of common thinking. The more common the ideas, the less creative, or different the work. Creative thinking involves expanding, contracting, or reshaping the boundaries of the way people normally think. The important thing is to be fresh. Different. Maybe even original. If people expect one thing, surprise them with another. The forces that lead to creative thinking may produce advertising that is entertaining, but not necessarily ads that sell. Among management, similar thinking often leads to changes in philosophy or procedures. As businesses and markets evolve, changes are inevitable. But the changes may not be for the better. MBO, TQM, IMC, EVA, reengineering, disruption, and under-the-radar are only some of the ideas that have created a buzz in the marketing and advertising business. It's likely these concepts do not hold as much promise today as when they were first introduced. It's great to be an instrument of change. But for most people, it's enough to be able to evaluate change, to figure out what works, what doesn't—how to survive and thrive in a changing environment. Evaluating change can be as difficult as anticipating change. Telling people how to evaluate and anticipate change can be almost as difficult as bringing about change—but we do have a few suggestions.

PROCESS ORIENTATION

It can be helpful to think about change as something that occurs within a **process**—something that occurs over a period of time and usually involving many steps. The key to **adapting to change** is to learn what those steps are and how they interrelate to each other. If you concentrate your attention on producing end results, such as an ad, you may end up seeing what you want to see, or believing what you would like to believe about the ad's likely success. If you pay scant attention to how you get results, as markets change, you may not be flexible enough to keep up. Instead, by understanding how all the parts in a process interrelate, when the environment changes, you can better manage change. Whether your understanding is rigorously analytical or based on intuition, when change comes you can better anticipate it, evaluate it, and be an agent for it.

In developed markets, changes have become so widespread and massive that they appear to be coming from all directions simultaneously. Still, there is often an underlying order even in the most complex situations. What makes change so difficult to manage in today's sophisticated market, (as opposed to a textbook), is that the process is *circular.* In textbooks, the steps in a process often occur along a linear time line, so that a campaign might have a beginning and an end. In a dynamic market, especially one characterized by massive change, conclusions and decisions have to be reevaluated seemingly all the time. Markets today change far more quickly than they did as little as ten or fifteen years ago. We think the steps in the campaign process should be viewed as taking place along a spiral path rather than a straight line. This means that by the time you finish analyzing background information and make decisions, it is often time to gather more information and do more analysis. Viewed this way, the campaign development process strives for continuous improvement. We recommend that you think of the campaign as an evolving work, even though for some people (say, students), the process must have a beginning and an end.

We've organized this book as follows:

Chapter 1 covers the mindset necessary to develop and execute a marketing communication campaign.

Chapter 2 and Chapter 3 examine the principles and tools to analyze the background information.

Chapter 4 covers turning problems and opportunities into campaign objectives.

Chapter 5 discusses the development of campaign strategy.

Chapters 6, 7, and 8 explore the ways to execute the campaign strategy through the development of message, media, and integrated communication plans.

Chapter 9 explores the extra but often substantial things that can be done to enhance the marketing communication campaign.

Chapter 10 discusses how to evaluate a campaign.

Chapter 11 examines the way to put together a comprehensive plans book.

Chapter 12 discusses various ways to put together a winning presentation.

Critical to the understanding of this book is the knowledge that each of these chapters is inextricably linked to all the chapters in what we call the **campaign process.** The purpose of this process is to develop a **marketing communication plan.** This plan outlines the activities, ideas, and executions that take place in order to achieve campaign objectives. In marketing plans, the objectives are usually defined in terms of sales or market share. In an advertising plan, the goals may be the same, or the objectives may be set in terms of communication criteria, such as awareness or image. The best plans are strategic in nature, but it doesn't necessarily follow that all plans are strategic. Plans, like strategy, can take place over an extended period of time.

Developing Strategy Within the Process

The key to strategic thinking involves anticipating consumer and competitive responses to a variety of alternative actions and planning accordingly. Generally, the objective of strategy is to give the company a competitive advantage. Strategic thinkers plan for the current time frame and *at least* the foreseeable future. So, a plan that focuses on price deals or coupon offerings is not particularly strategic since most of its effect is likely to be felt only in the short term. On the other hand, an effort to improve or strengthen the image of a brand is likely to have a much more lasting effect. Strategic plans consist of actions that tend to be general in nature as opposed to tactics that are more specific. Another key to effective strategy is to devise a plan that integrates all the activities, ideas, and executions so that they are directed toward achieving common goals. In an integrated plan, the effect of all the actions taken together is greater than the sum of the individual parts. To develop such a plan, think of the campaign as a series of steps or operations, focusing on the interrelationship of the various elements. This is what we call **process orientation.**

OPPORTUNITY AND THE COMMUNICATION REVOLUTION

The field of advertising continues to be in a state of flux. New technology and new media all promise to change the way people conduct business. Corporations that tightened their belts through layoffs and other staff reductions in the early 1990s later concluded that their smaller operations were the right size. As they reexamined, restructured, and reengineered the way they do business, companies learned to operate leaner and, some would say, meaner. The downsizing of the nineties has led to increased opportunities in the new millennium. The traditional progression of junior executives up through the ranks into middle management positions occurred much less often than it had in the past. The result is a sizable opportunity for beginners to advance their careers in advertising. The more the business changes, the greater the opportunity for people who understand the way things really work.

However, advertising operations, whether in an agency or in a department, are relatively small businesses. The opportunities to learn on the job in an informal or formal training program are much less today than they used to be. New hires, especially recent graduates, will need a solid conceptual understanding of the advertising process. Procedures and techniques—the kinds of things students often learn through internships—are less important in a dynamic changing market. Learning the way things are done today is no guarantee the same procedures will be used next year. The people in the forefront of this new era understand that the changes taking place in business are probably more a function of new attitudes and new ways of looking at advertising than a result of new hardware, emerging technology, or new media.

Yet for many people in advertising, the business and its purpose are fundamentally the same as they were a decade ago. This book strives not only to provide a transition between new and older ways of thinking but also to indicate where a traditional approach is still valid. Over the years, advertising practitioners have referred to advertising as a *problem-solving* business. Typically, the problem involves selling a product, although it can also encompass a service or an idea. Very often these problems are solved through an advertising campaign. In the mid-1990s, advertisers became increasingly aware of a whole range of promotional tools from which to choose: from advertising and public relations to sales promotion, infomercials, and event marketing. This author has titled this book *Advertising Campaign Strategy* more out of a sense of tradition than as a reflection of the view that advertising can or should be prepared apart from other types of marketing communication. Consumers tend to view all contacts they have with promotion elements as advertising. From our perspective, advertising is simply one of the various marketing communication tools businesses use to get their messages to consumers.

Advertising is, of course, a business. Practitioners are keenly aware of this fact; their customers, clients, and business associates seldom let them forget it. Intellectually, students and people starting out in advertising are aware that advertising is a business, but their lack of work experience sometimes causes them to lose sight of this fact. Some may even think of advertising as an art—a kind of applied art. Professionals understand that there is an art to using advertising creatively, but it is still a business, an important tool of marketing. Plainly speaking, its usual goal is to help sell products and services. This book, and particularly this chapter, looks at how advertising interrelates with other aspects of marketing. The challenge to the student of advertising is to reconcile the differences between any new advertising practices or thinking and the principles and procedures that have proven effective over a period of years.

THE NEW MARKETING ENVIRONMENT

To fully appreciate how advertising can solve problems, it is helpful to understand the relationship of advertising to other activities in a marketing program. As many authors have noted, to sell a product effectively, it must be the right product, at the right price, at the right place, and with the right promotion. Each element must be in harmony with the other. The marketing environment has changed quite a bit during the past decade. The forecast for the immediate future: *more change*. To be effective in this new environment, a planner needs to reevaluate exactly what it means to have the right product, price, place, or promotion. To be successful, a company should strive to gain a competitive edge. The alternative is to simply "get by." With this approach, the company runs the risk that it may get "passed by." The reality of the marketplace is that even when the elements may not be quite "right," the company still has to figure out a way to capitalize on what it is doing right or it will be forced out of business.

The Right Product

Coming up with the right product has become increasingly more complicated in recent years. At a time when different product and size introductions are on the rise, retailers are trying to streamline operations to get a better grasp on the profitability of everything they sell to improve the bottom line. Scanner data systems allow managers to assess the movement of every product variation, or stock-keeping unit (SKU), in a store. But getting the right product to the store requires an understanding of how consumers and the marketplace are changing.

Traditionally, marketing-oriented companies either asked consumers what they wanted or drew an inference from their behavior. Today, when researchers ask consumers what they want, consumers often don't know. Products in many generic categories have become so sophisticated that they do at least a fair job of satisfying consumers' needs or wants. Because it is often easier for consumers to focus on what they feel they lack rather than on what they want, researchers usually get more information if they ask consumers about their gripes or complaints. So researchers are focusing less on consumers' needs and wants and more on their dissatisfactions with current choices (that is, the consumers' problems).

As consumers become more sophisticated, they seem to be making more decisions on the basis of microissues. Ten or 15 years ago, car manufacturers seemed ambivalent about where consumers set cups or cans in an automobile. Today, this feature often receives prominent attention in automobile ads, whether the car is inexpensive or pricey. Today, researchers and developers focus hard on consumers' problems, no matter how small or seemingly insignificant. Anything to get an edge. Many consumers report they do not have any problems. When this happens, researchers often shift the focus from consumers' problems to consumers' interests. If the researchers can't find any interests worth promoting, the advertisers may try to build psychological value into a product, often by developing a personality or brand image for the product. Increasingly, advertisers promote their products by trying to get consumers to *like* their advertising.

The Right Price

Increasingly, the right price seems to mean the right lower price. The success of Wal-Mart, Home Depot, Target, Toys 'R' Us, and other mass-merchandise retailers continues to exert downward pressure on prices as value-conscious consumers patronize low-price retailers in ever-increasing numbers. Brand-name manufacturers are no longer able to dictate to retailers suggested retail prices. For example, in the early nineties, Eastman Kodak tried suggesting a "minimum advertised price" (MAP) on its premium-priced Royal Gold film, backing it with dealer rebates for all vendors who held the line on the MAP. The idea was to build a generous margin into the price of each roll of film and thus encourage retailers to do more in-store promotions of Kodak film. However, Wal-Mart disregarded the MAP, gave up the dealer rebate, and priced the product lower than the suggested retail price.[2] Wal-Mart competes on the basis of low prices—and competes very well. In the new marketing environment, there seems little companies can do to stem a retailer's inclination to operate on narrow profit margins.

A landmark date in the trend toward operating on a narrower price margin occurred in the spring of 1993. Philip Morris, the consumer products giant, put a 40-cents-per-pack price cut on its full-price brands of cigarettes. By doing so, the company tacitly acknowledged that the consumer trend toward craving lower prices was here to stay. On what some observers refer to as Marlboro Friday, the response on Wall Street was a drop in the share prices of many consumer product companies, from Procter & Gamble and Sara Lee to Coca-Cola and General Mills. Traders seemed to be saying that if Philip Morris could not maintain its price margins with Marlboro, perhaps the number-one brand in the world, then other consumer product companies would also be vulnerable.

The Right Place

A revolution in the marketplace has also affected the way marketers view strategies of place—the right place. An aggressively competitive marketplace has led many companies to get the product to the consumer in ways that would not have been considered in earlier times. McDonald's, long a staunch advocate of the freestanding store, now places restaurants in gas stations, convenience stores, and other nontraditional locations. Consumer product companies are also steadily losing control over decisions within the channel of distribution to the giant retailers. Wal-Mart is legendary for exacting stringent requirements on its suppliers regarding inventory control and shelf facings.

Many companies are also opting to market their products directly to consumers. With the increasing ease and widespread use of computers in business, many companies are amassing sizable databases that enable them to target narrowly defined consumers with a minimum of waste.

Although the Sears general merchandise catalog is dead, the success of specialty merchandise catalogers, such as Lands' End, L. L. Bean, and Victoria's Secret, suggests there will be even more material in the mailboxes of the future. Now that the success of home shopping networks is well established, the prospect of greater interactive shopping, especially through the Internet, promises to ensure that changes in the distribution system will continue in a dramatic fashion. Products such as Christmas trees, apparel, over-the-counter (OTC) medicines, computers, stocks and bonds, Viagra, toys, wine, and groceries are all sold over the Internet. Peapod, an online shopping service, has over 75,000 members in seven cities.[3] Will consumers really pay extra to have their groceries delivered? It's merely a matter of time and habits; they already do for pizza.

The Right Promotion

Coming up with the right promotion in the new marketing environment continues to pose many more questions than we can now answer. Some industry analysts attribute the changes in the advertising business to the splintering of the mass media into narrower interest segments. Much of this effect is the result of developments in the creation of new databases, the growing use of ZIP Code target marketing, and the use of checkout scanners in retail stores to analyze product movement. Simultaneously, there is a proliferating array of new media delivery options. The dizzying activity taking place within the media appears to be driving many of the changes in advertising.

Another viewpoint is that the changes in the advertising business are more a reflection of a powerful but natural evolution of the marketplace as it becomes increasingly sophisticated. Building brand equity has become more difficult, yet perhaps more important, as products in many generic categories approach parity and consumers change their priorities about the importance of various products in their lives. Companies cope with this difficulty in numerous ways. To reach narrower consumer segments, advertisers experiment with new media delivery systems. The motivation to use these options is a function of both the need to fine-tune the message to the specific needs or wants of the consumer and to reach the target efficiently. Some of the ZIP Code marketing systems, such as PRIZM, allow a marketer to zero in on the geographic location of its prime prospects with a minimum of waste. They also enable an advertiser to custom tailor the message to the target market's values and lifestyles.

A countervailing force in the marketplace is occurring as advertisers size up the differentiating characteristics of their products and conclude that there really is not enough opportunity to promote the product on the basis of benefits. They are aware that consumers believe that there are no significant differences among products in many categories and, because of active or hectic lifestyles, it might not matter much if there were. As a result, companies strive to "build the brand." Their approach is to add value—largely intangible— to the brand name so that consumers buy the brand for what they think it represents. This approach often ends up focusing on image, attitude—or simply entertainment.

In late 1992, Coca-Cola jarred the advertising business by announcing that it would use the Hollywood-based Creative Artists Agency (CAA) to create the bulk of its television commercials. This news left its long-time advertising agency, McCann-Erickson, unclear about its future role. Michael Ovitz, chairman of CAA at the time, and one of the most powerful people in the field of entertainment, had easy access to some of the more renowned directors in Hollywood. Many in the advertising community wondered if Coca-Cola would set an example for other major advertisers to focus more on entertainment and less on selling its product. CAA created numerous spots often without copy, jingle, or any unifying theme other than the tagline "Always Coca-Cola."

Advertising Age commissioned two separate studies to gauge the effectiveness of the campaign. The first study[4] attempted to measure "likability" and the second, "persuasibility."[5] Not surprisingly, the campaign scored high on likability, especially a computer-generated spot featuring polar bears; and ranked below average on persuasibility. Was this an effective campaign? It's hard to measure. Large consumer-goods companies like Coca-Cola are able to reach consumers with various messages or imagery at numerous times through traditional media advertising as well as through packaging and signage. Because of this massive exposure, it is extremely difficult to isolate and measure the true effects of a campaign on sales.

One could, however, argue the campaign's effectiveness based on whether likability is a more-or less-important goal than persuasibility. Is persuasibility any better at generating sales than likability? Because of the prominence of Coca-Cola's advertising in the media and the attention it has received in the trade press, this campaign sent mixed signals to advertising practitioners and educators.

One position might be called the David Ogilvy School of advertising after the legendary advertising great. This position holds that there are factors that make some campaigns succeed and others fail. Advertising educators often favor this approach because it acknowledges that there are a lot of principles and guidelines to sound advertising. Another approach to advertising is loosely associated with the West Coast. It features a lot of unconventional, highly creative approaches and techniques, often dramatizing a relationship between people and the product. Success with this approach is more a function of talent or inherent creativity than with what one might read about advertising techniques in a book. While academicians might admire the "West Coast" advertising, it's a lot harder to teach.

Post-Modern Advertising

For lack of a better term, this unconventional approach to creativity might be called **post–modern advertising.** Like post-modernism in art or architecture, it too challenges rationality or convention in its field. Bob Kuperman, president–CEO of TBWA Chiat–Day North America, believes that "persuasion is an art." This is the kind of advertising that "moves people." Unlike science, "its success is dependent on a complex mix of qualities that can be neither measured nor predicted."[6] Steve Hayden, creative director on the IBM account at Ogilvie and Mather Worldwide believes that most consumer buying decisions are based on irrational processes and require irrational advertising to make it work. On the other hand, a rationalist's position is that these ads are "creatively self-indulgent and grossly inefficient."[7]

Two campaigns, one for Nissan and the other for Miller Lite, are widely cited as examples of this new kind of advertising and its inability to produce results. In the summer of 1996, TBWA Chiat–Day produced a highly popular campaign for Nissan Motor Corp. featuring a quirky-smiling Asian character called Mr. K. The advertising "Life is a journey. Enjoy the ride," hardly showed the product, but instead focused on characters such as dogs, birds, and Barbie doll characters. Many critics and creatives loved the campaign.[8] *Time* magazine ranked it number one in the category, "BEST ADVERTISING OF 1996."[9] By Spring of 1997, the company drastically changed its campaign, prodded by dealer complaints who felt the campaign did little to stimulate sales. Reportedly, there was also pressure from the parent company in Japan who was concerned about a decline in sales despite an increase in sales for the overall category.[10] Eventually, the campaign and its apparent lack of results, is thought to have cost both the Marketing Director and the President and CEO their jobs.

In retrospect, there appeared to be two major problems with the campaign. First, the campaign barely showed what the cars looked like. Conventional wisdom is that people really like the way cars look. Second, the campaign tried to associate a funny, exciting, hip image to a line of cars and trucks that many people feel are somewhat conservative—often visualizing a Nissan car in the color black. As this line of thinking goes, the advertising promise did not reflect perceived product characteristics.

The second campaign was produced by Fallon-McElligott for Miller Lite beer. This campaign consisted of several humorous, off-the-wall, and somewhat irreverent spots supposedly produced by an obviously fictitious person named Dick. The campaign was aimed at twenty-somethings and was designed to give the brand a hip image. The ads said almost nothing about the beer or why someone would want to drink it. In one spot, a magician accidentally makes a rabbit disappear and the fur from the rabbit somehow winds up in the armpits of the magician's assistant. A wacky idea, perhaps, but then some beer drinkers have a wacky streak in their personalities. The campaign ran for over a year. In November of 1998, the company announced that the advertising would be "substantially overhauled," if not "scrapped entirely." A distributor in a comment to *Advertising Age* said it differently, the "campaign was a failure."[11]

It is likely there have been many successful examples of both the post-modern approach and the more conventional approach throughout the history of advertising. A big question today is whether advertising needs to be more entertaining, creative, and different to break through a seemingly ever-increasing number of multimedia messages, or whether the principles and techniques that have evolved over the years are still effective. To answer some of these questions, it might be helpful to look at what we call the right attitude.

The Right Attitude

For a company to have the right product, price, place, and promotion, its employees need the right mindset. We call this the **right attitude.** Companies can be successful even though they appear to do many things wrong. The marketplace can be forgiving; a company need not operate at optimum efficiency or effectiveness in order to make a profit. But the marketplace can be brutal in the price it exacts on companies that have to compete against rivals who understand *how to compete.* Listed below are some of the concepts beginners should keep uppermost in their minds as they prepare an advertising or marketing communication campaign:

- The marketing concept

- The communication concept

- The integrated communication concept

- The advertising campaign concept

- A strategic orientation

THE MARKETING CONCEPT

After World War II, many firms adopted what became widely known as the marketing concept. Basically, this is a philosophy of how to do business. The marketing concept provides decisionmakers with a framework for the planning and development of strategies for the right product, price, place, and promotion. Of all the principles associated with this philosophy, consumer orientation is the most important. Implementing this principle can range from a simple focus on the needs, wants, and problems of specific market segments, or it can mean organizing the entire marketing effort to appeal to a single market segment, or niche.

Consumer Orientation

A consumer orientation emphasizes the importance of planning all marketing activities to satisfy the needs, and wants, of consumers. The notion that planning should start with the consumer evolved as the marketplace began to change after World War II. Before the war, firms in the United States were production-oriented. The population was rapidly expanding, and the Great Depression had left many Americans hungry for products. The demand for goods exceeded the supply, and the main concerns of businesses were to produce products quickly, efficiently, and inexpensively. Because of the burgeoning consumer demand, products generally sold well. During the war, much of industry shifted from the production of consumer goods to wartime matériel, suppressing consumer demand artificially. Nevertheless, because of the tremendous demands of war, industry expanded considerably along with increases in technology. Following the war, American firms realized that they had the capacity and the technology to produce more than consumers would demand. The result was rugged, aggressive marketing competition.

The firms that competed best were those that catered to the specific needs and wants of consumers. Developing products became more important than the manufacturing involved in producing them. At first, the idea was simply to give consumers what they wanted rather than what the engineers, designers, chemists, or chefs had in mind when they developed a product. This new orientation produced results, but it became apparent that a firm could neither quite satisfy all potential consumers with one or two products— nor did it have to in order to make a profit. Product diversification increased as firms vied with one another to satisfy the growing sophistication of consumers' needs and wants.

Market Segmentation

Increasingly through the 1970s, many firms realized that in order to satisfy the growing sophistication of consumers' needs and wants, they had to compete through product diversification. Market segmentation, aimed at specific segments of the overall market, became widespread as firms developed, priced, distributed, and promoted a heterogeneous variety of products to heterogeneous groups of consumers (that is, groups that differ from one another on the basis of some common demographic characteristic such as age, income, or ethnicity). This segmentation happened in many products and industries, such as shampoo, cigarettes, beer, coffee, and, at a much later date, automobiles. Firms realized they would be more competitive by dividing up the overall market for the generic product into smaller markets, or segments, often targeting each segment with its own separate brand. Each of these markets represented relatively homogeneous groups whose members were similar on the basis of a characteristic, such as age, income, or lifestyle. Often, they had the same selective tastes and preferences. Companies appeal to these segments by differentiating their product to cater to these special tastes. The combination of increased brand competition, the increasing risks associated with new product introductions, the pressures of more complex market segmentation, and increasingly involved channels of distribution caused these firms to reevaluate their marketing philosophy.[12]

Other firms understood that segmenting the market was not simply a better way to compete, it was the *only* way they could compete. Increasingly, companies began to target smaller and narrower segments of the broad market, often by creating a database consisting of current and prospective customers. To reach narrow target audiences firms sometimes used direct marketing.

At the retail level, stores have for many years offered a fairly narrow product line, especially clothing stores, such as For Petites Only, 5–7–9, and Lane Bryant, which cater to a certain-size woman. In the 1980s and the 1990s, this kind of segmented selling would be increasingly referred to as "niche marketing."

Niche Marketing
Niche marketing usually means more than merely segmenting the market. Niche marketers typically offer only products within a narrow range, but within that range they will

Figure 1-1   The Marketing Concept Era

1950s	1960s	1970s	1980s	1990s
Consumer Orientation		Market Segmentation		Niche Marketing

offer a fairly deep selection. Sometimes they will compete against a more broadly based company, such as a department store, on the basis of quality, as Victoria's Secret does, and other times they will compete on the basis of price, as Office Depot does.

Many of the new breed of retailers, such as Toys 'R' Us, are able to compete on the basis of price, quality, and selection. As a broad-based retailer, Interstate Department Stores nearly went bankrupt. When it decided to focus its concentration on the toys business with which it had been successful, it changed its name to Toys 'R' Us and became a multibillion-dollar company. These category killers, as they are sometimes called, are enjoying spectacular growth and will likely branch out into other areas in the future.

Bed, Bath & Beyond is typical of the new specialty retailers offering domestic goods such as housewares and linens in the home furnishings market. The stores are all superstores, with each retail outlet averaging more than 35,000 square feet. Department stores and small retailers like Linens 'N'Things and the Pottery Barn are its main competition. Its products are a cut above those of mass merchandisers like Wal-Mart and Kmart in terms of selection and the look of the store, but they are usually cheaper in price than those of a department store. By focusing on "Everyday Low Prices" (EDLP), the company has enjoyed tremendous success.

Figure 1–1 provides a rough approximation of the development of the marketing concept over the past 50 years. There are, of course, wide differences in the way companies within an industry apply the marketing concept and, similarly, there are great differences among industries. For example, the cigarette industry applied the principles of market segmentation much earlier than the beer industry. Though it seems that companies will be forced by market pressures to apply marketing concept principles, it does not mean they will end up as niche marketers. The opposite may in fact be the case. As niche marketers become more successful, they will likely broaden their product line. Already this seems to be happening with Bed Bath & Beyond, Toys 'R' Us, and Office Depot.

Marketing concept notions, such as "the consumer is always right" or "give the consumers what they want" have been around for many years. What is different in the new marketing environment is that consumers have access to much more information than ever before. Already 16% of car buyers shop online before visiting a dealership and they're arming themselves with information on dealer costs.[13]

Marketing Integration

To implement marketing concept principles effectively, firms coordinate decisions within the major areas of a firm, such as production and finance, with those of marketing. All activities then become part of a total system to produce want-satisfying products and services. In the process, marketing decisions usually take precedence over those of finance or production. Within marketing, product planning precedes decisions on pricing and distribution for the determination of product policy. The marketing concept philosophy encourages executives in and out of marketing to integrate their decisions and activities for the achievement of common goals. Decisions about product quality, pricing, and distribution are often beyond the authority of advertising planners even though decisions made in nonadvertising areas have a direct influence on the effectiveness of an advertising campaign. Many firms recognize this relationship and involve advertising specialists in marketing decisions at the planning stage.

Other Emphases

The basic principle of the marketing concept is that a firm should marshal its activities toward producing products or services that satisfy existing needs and wants of the consumers. Rather than emphasizing its own resources as its first priority, a company will instead establish giving consumers what they want as its top priority, or as Ford Motor Company likes to say, "Job One." Ford concluded that what consumers want most in a car is quality, and, in the slogan "Quality is Job One," they are telling consumers that it is their highest priority. In this kind of environment, certain other philosophies, or ways of doing business, become common.

Firms tend to be research-oriented. Product development evolves out of consumer research. The needs, wants, and problems of the consumer are ascertained through an objective evaluation of factual data and scientific forecasts. Focus groups, one-on-one interviews, attitude and opinion surveys, lifestyle and ethnographic studies, product-usage observations, sales analyses, consumer complaint feedback, and test marketing are but some of the ways a research-oriented firm gets information about the consumer. In contrast, new product ideas in many firms come from the president or the research-and-development (R&D) staff. They are often intuitive and frequently reflect the views of manufacturing or engineering.

In fields that are driven by technology, it often makes more sense to allow technical people to lead the way because consumers may not be sufficiently sophisticated to know which kind of features are possible in a new product line. In this kind of environment, the focus is less on satisfying needs and wants and more on *exceeding* needs and wants. Computers, telecommunications, consumer electronics, and automobiles are some examples of product categories where in recent years technical people are producing innovations faster than consumers can articulate their want for them.

Another of the principles associated with the marketing concept is the policy that activities should be planned. With the growing sophistication and competitive nature of the marketplace, firms need to anticipate problems, uncover opportunities, and forecast demand. Planned activities are an efficient and effective way to deal with a complex marketplace. A marketing campaign is the execution of a marketing plan. Plans provide direction for all those involved in the marketing effort. It is common for marketing plans to be written. In advertising, the larger agencies deem it almost mandatory in the planning of an advertising campaign.

The advertising firm Batten, Barton, Durstine, and Osborn Worldwide Inc. (BBDO) gives the following reasons a written plan is necessary:[14]

1. It encourages clear and logical thinking.

2. It demonstrates a management approach to advertising by relating media, copy, and art to marketing facts and goals.

3. A written plan offers a factual basis for advertising direction, execution, performance, and appropriation.

4. It provides a complete guide in writing for everyone working on the account, as well as a ready source of information for new personnel joining the client or BBDO.

5. It registers what needs to be done for future improvement and provides an annual benchmark of accomplishment.

6. A plan informs BBDO's top management of an account's goals and progress.

7. It serves as an as-needed policy document for client advertising management to use with other departments, corporate management, and directors.

8. It promotes understanding of, and agreement on, objectives and tactics among both client and BBDO organizations.

THE COMMUNICATION CONCEPT

It is not enough to have the right product, a company has to communicate what is right about the product, even if it's simply an image. Like the marketing concept, the communication concept suggests that all planning begin with consumers. This concept requires the originator of the message to encode information, whether in words or pictures, *in terms of the consumers' needs, wants, interests, or problems*. To be effective, the message creator has to have a solid understanding of the social and psychological makeup of the target market. In other words, a writer has to understand what makes consumers tick so that he or she can better relate to them—the audience.

Failure to interpret a message in terms of consumers' needs, wants, interests, or problems may mean the ad fails to communicate. Either consumers will ignore the ad, not understand it, or may simply feel that the message is not meaningful. Moreover, because of hectic consumer lifestyles and the vast number of messages consumers are exposed to every day, a message may communicate well enough, but may be forgotten unless it is attached to a distinctive advertising property. Motel 6 and Red Roof Inns both offer budget-priced rooms. Part of what makes Motel 6 sound economical is its name—some people still remember when it had rooms priced at six dollars per night. Red Roof Inns gets across its message in a memorable way with a simple slogan: "Sleep Cheap."

The above proposition seems fairly straightforward and sensible. Yet it appears that many ads are developed more from the perspective of the advertiser than from that of the consumer. When this happens, the advertising tends to focus more on the qualities of the product that the advertiser thinks are important but not, unfortunately, on what the potential consumer thinks are important when considering buying the product.

A related and potentially more serious problem occurs when advertising is created without focusing on consumers' needs, wants, and problems but is created instead to look or sound good. Sometimes this is called creativity for technique's sake. An advertisement can be very entertaining, but it may not help sell the product. Every year after awards such as the Addys and the Clios have been given out to the "best" ads, people in the industry will talk about how the best ads did not win. In fact, advertisers often indulge in a sardonic humor contest trying to predict the first award-winning agency that will lose the account for which they had won the award.

Along with a focus on consumers' needs, wants, and problems, the communication concept implies an understanding of what communication can or cannot accomplish. Specifically, communication affects the way people think, believe, or feel. By itself, it is seldom enough to sell the product. Communication, especially advertising, needs to operate in harmony with the other elements in the marketing mix. It is crucial that planners understand precisely the role advertising needs to assume to influence consumer behavior. Because advertising is a form of persuasive communication, its role is often best defined in terms of communication criteria that have the ability to stimulate purchasing behavior, such as awareness, comprehension, attitude, or image.

For example, when Gillette was ready to introduce its revolutionary Sensor razor, it knew that its advertising would have to do more than tell consumers that it was a better razor; it would have to explain to consumers that the razor was better because the blade was mounted on flexible springs that would float along the contours of a person's skin. The approach was so successful that the Gillette Sensor became the number-one nondisposable razor in the world. Gillette learned from its experience in introducing double-edged razor blades in 1971 that sometimes you have to get consumers to understand how something works before they will believe a product claim. Before double-edged razors came along, it is doubtful that many consumers ever gave much thought to the idea of using more than one blade at a time. Gillette worked hard to get consumers to understand why double-edged razors provide a closer shave. Even today, most readers of this book will be able to complete the following sentence Gillette first put in an ad well over 20 years ago: "The Gillette Trac II gives you a closer shave, because the first blade lifts each hair, and the . . ." (If you said "the second blade cuts it off at the skin line," you are right.) In 1998, Gillette introduced the Mach 3 triple-blade razor. Once again Gillette found it necessary to explain how the product delivered on the advertising promise of offering the consumer "a closer shave in fewer strokes."

Deciding on an appropriate role for advertising is of course no easy decision. The advertising planner has to project what the effects of each possible strategy might be on consumers' behavior, for example: Would establishing or increasing brand awareness lead to greater sales? Would it be more effective to reinforce or change the attitude of the consumers? Should advertising try to improve or intensify the image of the product?

It is easier to establish awareness than it is to change consumers' attitudes or get consumers to understand how a product operates. Moreover, there are no guarantees that if these tasks are achieved, they will result in increased sales. Not surprisingly, many advertisers opt for the conceptually simpler tasks of increasing awareness or working with a brand's image. With those approaches, however, advertisers run the risk that the copywriter or art director will become misguided and focus more on the creativity or the technique in the advertisement and less on what would be an appropriate selling message.

INTEGRATED MARKETING COMMUNICATION

The idea that a firm should coordinate, or integrate, all of its communication or promotional activities has been around for well over two decades. What is different in the past 10 years is that firms better understand that to compete in an increasingly sophisticated marketplace, the messages they disseminate must blend together to achieve interrelated objectives. In the past, companies were often content to let an ad agency take care of its advertising, a public relations agency handle the PR, and their own marketing department manage the sales promotion. Very often the advertising would go off in one direction, the public relations program in another, and the sales promotion in still another. Although the efforts might produce interrelated results, a marketer might question whether this is the most efficient and effective way to operate. The integrated concept embodies the idea that all parties involved in a campaign blend their efforts into producing seamless marketing communications.

Propelling the new emphasis on integrated marketing communication are marketers who understand that the old ways of doing business no longer work. Today's marketplace has become increasingly sophisticated. Although academicians have discussed integrating and coordinating elements of the marketing and promotion mixes since at least the 1960s, especially by using what was then referred to as a "systems approach," it has been only relatively recently that the concept has caught on.[15]

As the physical distinctions among brands in many categories become negligible, the role advertising plays in creating a psychological difference has become more important. At the same time, other types of communication may become even more important in stimulating short-term sales, such as sales promotions and direct marketing. Increasingly, the strategy for many large advertisers is to surround consumers with as many points of contact with the brand as is economical. As a result, nontraditional media and other marketing communication tools often take on added importance.

As firms apply the lessons of market segmentation and product differentiation, they target smaller parts of the overall market. As firms speak to consumers with an increasing number of voices, locating the sources of all of a company's communication within the same organization can be more efficient. Typically, there is better communication within an organization than between organizations.

Because of the tremendous increase in communication technologies, marketers need to be flexible to revise strategies and tactics to meet changing situations. It can be more efficient and quicker for all of a firm's messages to come from one organization. *Whether it is more effective is a matter of some debate.*

For some people, the concept of integrated marketing communication sounds better as theory than it works in practice. Locating the sources of a firm's message in one marketing communication company will only make the operation more efficient and effective if each specialized area of that group works harmoniously with each other and avoids the political infighting that sometimes occurs as each unit vies for a piece of the promotional budget. Moreover, advertisers may want more expertise than an ad agency typically possesses. The solution is to go elsewhere. If a frozen food company wants a sales piece for a new product launch, does it want an agency's creative person or someone who is an expert in frozen food? The expert may have 20 years experience at Kroger. The expert will likely know from experience what is likely to motivate the trade people—a key to many new product launches. The agency creative person's experience is generally with consumers.

Not only are advertisers telling agencies they don't want them to handle other types of marketing communication, but frequently they want them to handle only parts of their advertising as well. So an agency may get the media assignment on an account, but not the creative and vice versa. It's also common these days for an advertiser to give creative assignments for the same brand to *different* agencies. The Budweiser frogs were created by DDB Needham in Chicago, but the Budweiser lizards were created by Goodby, Silverstein and Partners in San Francisco. While agencies may suggest that the combined effect of all the messages work best when one source handles everything, ad directors retort that it is *their* job to see to it that all messages are compatible (not the agency's).

Ad agencies, especially the big ones, are also at a disadvantage in terms of cost-effectiveness. Advertisers can often outsource promotional work to suppliers who operate with a lower overhead, particularly in terms of real estate. Other advertisers find that they can maintain direct control at a lower cost over promotional elements, such as direct marketing, sales promotion, and packaging, by locating these specializations within the company. Ad agencies are often located in some of the priciest locations—at least in major cities.

Regardless of the source of each promotional element, the effect of all activities should be synergistic; that is, each individual or unit's activity should be coordinated so that the combined effect of all contributions is greater than the sum of its parts.

THE ADVERTISING CAMPAIGN CONCEPT

The key to successful advertising is planned advertising. One of the better ways to plan promotional activities is through a campaign that interrelates all activities. Advertisements that are interrelated have greater retentive value than a series of different one-shot ads. Consumers remember advertising longer when each advertisement helps support, reinforce, or even intensify the others.

There are both highly visible and unseen aspects to an advertising campaign. To the average consumer, an advertising campaign is simply a series of ads that look or sound alike. To the student or the practitioner, a campaign may involve all the activities that help produce advertisements designed to achieve interrelated goals, such as consumer surveys, brainstorming, or media analyses. Considering this broader range of activities, we define an **advertising campaign** as a series of advertisements, and the activities that help produce them, which are designed to achieve interrelated goals.

This definition works in situations where the advertiser relies exclusively on advertising. However, in many cases the advertiser will broaden its promotional focus to include other types of marketing communication, such as sales promotions, publicity, and direct marketing. A broader focus requires more than a new definition; it also requires a new way of looking at a campaign. Therefore, it may be more accurate to think of an advertising campaign as a marketing communication campaign even though it relies exclusively on advertising as its promotional tool. Notwithstanding, it is likely that the label advertising campaign will stick. Whether you think of it as a marketing communication campaign or the more common advertising campaign, the definition above specifies what it does, but it does not tell what an effective campaign is or does.

CHARACTERISTICS OF AN ADVERTISING CAMPAIGN

The written form of the advertising plan is usually called either the campaign plans book or, simply, the **plans book.** Planning is the process by which one establishes the objectives, strategy, and tactics. The main quality that distinguishes a campaign from merely a collection of ideas and ads is unity. Upon seeing or hearing an ad from a unified campaign, people can tell that it belongs to a family of other ads that have preceded it. To unify a series of ads, there should be some element that weaves a thread of continuity throughout the campaign that ties all the ads together. To be effective, campaigns should be strategic in nature, thereby recognizing that campaigns take place over a period of time and are adjusted and modified to take into consideration a changing situation.

Campaign Continuity

In a sense, all ads for the same product are interrelated inasmuch as they generally try to achieve the same ultimate objective—sell the product. What separates a campaign from a collection of ads is the degree to which each execution is connected. In a campaign, the general plan is to put something in each ad that leaves a similar impression with consumers so that they feel one ad is a continuation of the others. These elements can be something observable (or physical) or something one thinks about (or psychological). In Chapter 6, dealing with message strategy, we'll look at some of the ways to add continuity to a campaign.

Many advertising launches start out as cohesive, coherent campaigns, but somewhere in development, the advertising loses its focus because of weak leadership, poor planning, or executional problems. Inadequate execution can result from a variety of problems, such as lack of talent, deficient work habits, personality problems, or insufficient motivation. Problems with leadership or planning often stem from the wrong kind of orientation. The best campaigns are oriented strategically.

Strategic Orientation

If creative ideas are the heart and soul of a campaign, then strategy is the brain. Strategy is the general plan designed to give the campaign its competitive edge. It is more like an outline than a blueprint. The guidelines that are a part of the plan provide direction over the course of the campaign period. Strategy provides the framework within which all those involved in the campaign should operate. Strategy implies that all members of an organization work as a team toward common goals. Strategic plans result from team members who can anticipate the future and who are able to develop the ideas, operations, and procedures to achieve the organization's goals. A major problem with many strategic plans is that they simply take too long to develop, especially when they are put together by a *committee*. As part of the strategic-planning process, companies need to build into their operations a strict time schedule and a way of limiting discussion of the items in a plan, or they run the risk of what is sometimes called paralysis by analysis. Ten years ago, it was common for firms to talk about contingency plans to describe the course of action a company would implement if the situation changed. Today, markets change so quickly and frequently that one can be sure the situation will change and in ways that are often difficult to anticipate. It is therefore imperative that firms integrate into their strategic plans options that provide sufficient flexibility so firms can respond to changing situations in a timely manner.

Not having a contingency plan can prove costly to a company, as AT&T discovered. In the spring of 1991, MCI instituted its highly successful Friends and Family long-distance calling plan. Within two years, MCI signed up an additional 10 million customers.[16] Initially, AT&T did not respond to the campaign. Eventually, it developed a campaign disparaging MCI's campaign, and in the spring of 1993 it launched a $50-million campaign aimed at luring back customers who had defected to MCI.[17] For the most part it was too late. By 1998, At&T, which had a $54.3-billion lead over MCI in 1991 (a nearly 8:1 lead in sales), saw its sales advantage narrow to $31.6 billion (barely more than a 2.5:1 sales ratio).[18]

While it is easy to talk about strategic plans, it is another thing to deliver them. Advertisers often demand highly creative campaigns—the kind of out-of-the-box thinking that sometimes resists strategic or conceptual analysis. To deal with this potentially conflicting situation, advertisers sometimes assign their advertising requirements to an agency and their strategic planning to a management consultant, such as Andersen Consulting. In response, some agencies, such as Ammirati Puris Lintas, have restructured their agencies to enhance their ability to offer strategic planning—even referring to it as reinventing the ad agency.[19] Some agencies, such as Ammirati, have even been hired in a strategic role. These agencies know that to do this job well they need access to corporate management thinking at a higher level than they *sometimes* have had in the past.

A CORPORATE STRATEGIC PLAN

To understand corporate thinking, you need to understand upper–level management. Since these people are not always available, the next best place to start is with the corporate strategic plan (assuming one exists). There are a number of elements common to all strategic plans, although different disciplines may call them by different names. The management consultants Patrick Below, George Morrissey, and Betty Acomb have taken an in-depth look at strategic planning, and their concept of a strategic plan has the following seven elements:[20]

- Organization mission
- Strategic analysis
- Long-term objectives
- Strategy
- Integrated programs
- Financial projections
- Executive summary

Although these elements are listed here for a strategic corporate plan, they should be an integral part of all ad campaigns. In an advertising or marketing communication plan, they will likely appear in various sections of a plans book. Listed below is a description of each of these elements, with an explanation of how they might be handled in an advertising plan.

1. Organization Mission. An organization mission statement embodies what the organization is concerned with, the purpose of its existence and, perhaps, why the business was started. It is the logical starting point of a strategic plan. In advertising plans, the purpose is to solve marketing and communication problems and to take advantage of opportunities. These points are usually discussed in an analysis of the company that is typically found in a larger section titled "Situation Analysis." Often a company's mission is fairly broad, straightforward, and implied. General Motors' mission is to sell a lot of cars. The Chevrolet division's mission is to provide affordable cars for families. The mission of the Oldsmobile division is unclear. Not surprisingly, the company is struggling.

The company's mission becomes an important aspect of the company analysis insofar as it influences the company's ability to solve its problems or capitalize on opportunities. In some markets the problems may not be easily or readily solved, and the company may be better advised to veer off in a new direction to capitalize on different opportunities. In the 1980s, IBM concentrated on solving the problems associated with its mainframe computer business. As a result, it failed to appreciate fully the market potential of the personal computer and lost its preeminent position in the computer business to other companies that were quicker and more adept at capitalizing on new opportunities.

2. Strategic Analysis. This part is the research foundation of a strategic plan. In an advertising plan, the strategic analysis identifies the critical issues, and the **strategic focal points** that will be addressed by the advertising and marketing communications' strategy. It is normally covered in the situation analysis, which usually consists of an analysis of background information on the company: consumer, market, product, and competition. The purpose of the strategic analysis (or a situation analysis) is to give the company a competitive advantage in information.

3. Long-Term Objectives. Goals, or objectives, are statements about what each unit involved in the campaign would like to accomplish. A corporation's strategic plan tends to be written more for the organization as a whole than for the marketing function, and so they tend to be broadly based and to reflect what the company wants to accomplish over an extended period of time. In contrast, marketing and advertising goals are typically written for no more than a year and are specific. As the marketplace becomes increasingly dynamic, complex, and fast changing in the twenty-first century, it is likely that objectives, whether short-term or long-term, will be set for periods shorter than one year.

4. Strategy. The critical element in any conceptual understanding of strategy is the importance placed on the interrelationship, or interconnectedness, of all the activities planned to achieve a goal. Strategists understand the linkages among actions, between actions and a reaction, or, as is sometimes the case in advertising, between an action and no response. This linkage is what differentiates a strategy from merely a list of ideas or actions. Moreover, a strategist understands that actions, reactions, and responses take place over a period of time. Like a master chess player, a marketing strategist has to forecast each move and countermove in the marketplace. In an advertising plan, there might be marketing, advertising, creative, and media strategies, as well as various strategies associated with other types of marketing communication. The purpose of a strategy is to achieve a goal. The best strategies are competitive in nature, designed to give the company an advantage. Even when a company is content to follow the brand leader and profit on what they leave behind, unless the company finds some advantage, small or large, it runs the risk that it will be forced out of business as consumers determine there is not enough value in what the company sells.

5. Integrated Programs. This aspect of a strategic plan details the cross-functional actions required to implement the strategy and achieve the objectives. In an advertising campaign, these actions are often referred to as tactics or executions, and usually appear in major sections pertaining to the media, creative, or sales promotion strategy. The emphasis on integrated programs underscores the team concept in which each program or activity is designed to work harmoniously with other units in the company.

6. Financial Projections. Financial projections typically involve the financial expectations and the measures used to evaluate the company's performance. In advertising and marketing communication plans, the projections are covered in a number of different ways and places. The actual expenses are normally handled in a section of the plans book dealing with the budget. The sales projections are normally covered under marketing objectives. Profit projections typically are not covered in marketing plans. Measures to assess the financial projections of a marketing communication program may appear if an advertiser prepares the plan. If the plan is prepared by an agency, it is typically omitted. Since around the mid-1980s, agencies have become decreasingly involved in measuring the effectiveness of advertising programs. That function has largely gone over to the advertiser or to outside research firms. Some agency people are delighted to see this responsibility

Exhibit 1-1	Two Approaches to Planning a Campaign

J. Walter Thompson Asks	A Typical Advertising Class Response
Where are we?	Develop a situation analysis.
Why are we there?	Identify problems.
Where could we be?	Identify opportunities.
How could we get there?	Develop message, media, and marketing communication strategy, and tactics.
Are we getting there?	Develop a plan to measure or track the effectiveness of the campaign.

taken over by their clients. As one agency vice president told the author, "It was sort of like grading your own paper."

7. Executive Summary. Although many corporate strategic plans have an executive summary or overview at the beginning, many advertising plans put one at the beginning and frequently a summary at the end of major sections, such as the situation analysis, the creative strategy, or the media strategy.

A CAMPAIGN OUTLINE

There are many different ways to outline a campaign, especially if it is for a marketing communication plan. Essentially, a plan serves as a guide for those who work on the campaign and as a proposal for those who have to have it approved. As a proposal, there are often a number of different approaches to get someone to approve spending what is usually a substantial sum of money. (Generally, it is a good idea to consider any expenditure substantial.)

At the J. Walter Thompson (JWT) agency, planning begins with the answers to five basic questions:

- Where are we?

- Why are we there?

- Where could we be?

- How could we get there?

- Are we getting there?

When the agency gets the answer to the last question, the process starts all over again. At JWT, employees refer to the process as a planning cycle because the process is ongoing. There is a beginning but no real end to the way they plan for an account.

In academic circles, the above questions receive a fair amount of attention, but they usually get labeled differently. Exhibit 1–1 shows how these basic questions tend to be handled in an advertising campaigns class.

Listed in Exhibit 1–2 is the type of outline someone would prepare before undertaking a campaign. This plan lists the steps a company would take in developing a marketing

Exhibit 1-2 An Outline for a Marketing Communication Plan

I. **Introduction or Overview**
II. **Situation Analysis**
   A. Company analysis
   B. Consumer analysis
   C. Market analysis
   D. Product analysis
   E. Competitive analysis
   F. Problems and opportunities (optional)
III. **The Target Market Profile**
IV. **Objectives**
   A. Marketing
   B. Communication
   C. Advertising
V. **Marketing Communication Strategy**
   A. Advertising Strategy
      1. Creative or message strategy
         a. objectives
         b. strategy
         c. tactics or executions (often put at the end of the plan)
      2. Media strategy
         a. objectives
         b. strategy
         c. tactics or vehicles
         d. cost estimates
         e. continuity schedule
   B. Sales Promotion
      1. Objectives
      2. Strategy
      3. Tactics or executions
   C. Public Relations
      1. Objectives
      2. Strategy
      3. Tactics or examples
   D. Direct Marketing
      1. Objectives
      2. Strategy
      3. Tactics or examples
   E. Other (Such as Event Marketing, Infomercials)
      1. Objectives
      2. Strategy
      3. Tactics or examples
VI. **Communication Assessment Measures (Optional)**
VII. **Budget**
VIII. **Summary**

communication campaign. Not all organizations would pursue every step. For example, some companies might not have a direct marketing or public relations plan. These steps will be described in greater detail in following chapters.

Campaign Progress Checklist

At this point in the campaign you should have a solid understanding of the following points:

1. To be successful in a changing environment, you need to understand how advertising works at the conceptual level.

2. Understanding how the elements in a process interrelate increases the likelihood that the end results will be successful.

3. To understand the new marketing environment, you need to know how having the right product, price, place, and promotion has changed in recent years.

4. To produce effective advertising, you need the right attitude or mindset.

5. The marketing concept suggests that all planning be geared toward meeting consumers' needs, wants, interests, or problems.

6. The communication concept suggests that messages should interpret the want-satisfying qualities of the product in terms of consumers, needs, wants, interests, or problems.

7. The integrated marketing communication concept suggests that a firm should coordinate and integrate all of its communication and promotional activities so that they present a unified, seamless message to consumers.

8. The advertising campaign concept suggests that unified, interrelated ads will have a greater effect than the sum of a series of unrelated ads.

9. Successful campaigns are strategic in nature. They provide a general plan, competitive in nature, involving a series of interrelated actions to take place over a period of time. A strategic plan anticipates responses in the marketplace and plans accordingly.

10. Corporate strategic plans are similar to advertising campaigns and should be studied to prepare better campaigns for an advertiser.

Notes and References

[1]Arndorfer, J. B., & Ross, C. (1998, April 13). A-B shells out record price for '99 Super Bowl. *Advertising Age,* p. 1.

[2]Khermouch, G. (1994, April 18) Kodak, Wal-Mart price stand-off is a royal rumble. *Brandweek 35,* p. 6.

[3]Author. (1998, March 16). From soup to nuts. *Newsweek,* p. 77.

[4]Fawcett, A. W. (1993, April 12). CAA ads make big splash with youth, women. *Advertising Age, 64,* p. 1.

[5]Fawcett, A. W. (1993, May 10). CAA's coke ads fall flat on persuasion. *Advertising Age, 64,* p. 4.

[6]Vagnoni, A. (1997, November 17). Creative differences. *Advertising Age,* p. 28.

[7]Vagnoni, A. (1997, November 17). Creative differences. *Advertising Age*, p. 28.

[8]Author. (1996, December 9). Ads hit hot buttons for some, leave others cold. *USA Today*, p. 3B.

[9]Author. (1996, December 23). The best advertising of 1996. *Time*, p. 77.

[10]Author. (1997, March 3). Nissan's 'Mr. K' takes a back seat. *USA Today*, p. 2B.

[11]Author. (1998, November 9). Miller sounds last call for its edgy beer ads. *Advertising Age*, p. 1.

[12]These ideas were first presented to the author by Professor Nugent Wedding at the University of Illinois and exist in John D. Leckenby and C. Nugent Wedding. *Advertising management: Criteria, analysis, and decision making* (Columbus, Ohio: Grid, 1982), chapter 1.

[13]Hamel, G., & Sampler, J. (1998, December 7). "The E-Corporation," *Fortune*, p. 82.

[14]*The advertising plan at BBDO, A handbook for account managers* (New York: Batten, Barton, Durstine & Osborn, Inc., undated).

[15]Robin, D. P., & Harris, C. E., Jr. (1973 Winter). An integrated approach for applying marketing strategy. *Business Ideas and Facts,* pp. 35–40.

[16]Fitzgerald, K. (1993, July 12). AT&T aims to reverse MCI's charge. *Advertising Age,* p. 15.

[17]Lefton, T. (1993, February 22). AT&T intros "I" series discounts. *Brandweek 34,* p. 5.

[18]The best-laid plans push prices down. *Superbrands*, 1992, p. 98. Tobi Elkin, Forecast: more flurries, *Superbrands*, June 5, 1998, p. s58.

[19]Petrecca, L. (1998, November 2). Ammirati 'reinvents' ad agency. *Advertising Age*, , pp. 3, 56.

[20]Below, P. J., Morrissey, G. L., & Acomb, B. L. (1987). *The executive guide to strategic planning.* San Francisco: Jossey-Bass, pp. 9–10.

Chapter 2

The Research Foundation I: Understanding Clients and Buyers

The first place to start in preparing for a campaign is with a pad of paper. While you may prefer to type, the important point is to begin with yourself. What kind of information will you need? Where will you get the information? What do you know about how a campaign fits together? Many beginners go to a library, or head off to a store to observe the product in the marketplace. Not only is this an inefficient way to proceed, it can also be counter-productive. More about this point later.

Professionals are sensitive about how they manage their time. When they search for information, they usually know exactly what they are looking for—even though they may not actually find it. General or undefined searches take up unnecessary time that could be better spent on other assignments. Practitioners seldom have the luxury of "extra time."

DEVELOPING A RESEARCH PLAN

You should work from an **outline**; it will help you organize and manage your time. A plan will help you understand both the information you need, and how to acquire it. As you accumulate information, you should be well on your way to building a research foundation. Professionals usually have their own way of working, but if you are a beginner or a student, consider using the following topics as a rough outline:

- Where to begin the search for information

- How to separate the search into sections

- How to obtain the information

- How to process the information

The Search for Information Starts with the Company

Most professionals can actually start anywhere. Their experience gives them the kind of judgment that allows them to process information in *any* order without biasing the information or ideas that follow. On the other hand, with beginners, first impressions are often lasting impressions. In the classroom, it is not uncommon to hear students generate creative ideas only minutes after receiving a copywriting assignment, and well before they have completed any analysis of background information. Despite being cautioned by the instructor to defer their ideas until they complete a **copy platform** (or **brief**), the same ideas frequently show up in the finished ads. Not surprisingly, the ideas are often off-target and off-strategy.

At the Batten, Barton, Durstine & Osborn Worldwide Inc. (BBDO) advertising agency, it has long been the practice to defer the search for product information until after the prime prospects and their problems have been determined. BBDO's concern is that eager staffers too often immerse themselves in product information before they understand the consumers' needs and wants. By talking first to the designers, engineers, or chemists, they run the risk of assuming that the reasons the R&D people developed the product are the same reasons why consumers buy the product. Companies hope this is true, but frequently it is not.

For example, years ago students in an advertising class did a campaign for Rold Gold pretzels. Very early in the campaign process, the students discovered that pretzels could be differentiated from other snacks on the basis of a health claim—pretzels have far fewer calories and almost no fat compared to other snacks. The students based their message strategy on this finding despite later research that suggested consumers were unlikely to base their purchase decision on the amount of calories or fat contained in pretzels. If the students had deferred their product research until after the consumer research, they might have opted for a message strategy that stressed fun instead of health. Today, research findings might indicate something entirely different. The important thing is to find out.

The BBDO people are applying what academicians refer to as the **marketing concept**, that is, all planning begins with the consumer. However, while we agree with the marketing concept in principle, it is usually more efficient to focus first on the company's problems and opportunities because a firm simply may not want to proceed in certain directions, regardless of what consumers might want.

Separating the Search into Sections

At this stage, it is usually a good idea to divide the search into separate areas. Even though much of the information that is uncovered will apply in several areas, it helps to split up the work so that certain areas are not overlooked. It is much better to get most of the information on the first go-around than to have to go back repeatedly and fill in missing pieces of information. We suggest beginning the search with an analysis of the background information, usually referred to as a **situation analysis.**

We suggest you begin your search in the following areas:

Company analysis
Consumer analysis ⎱ Do these
Market analysis ⎰ together

The order in which you search for information after the company and the consumer/market analysis is not very important. Neither should it be necessary to complete the above analyses before you begin to search for information in the areas listed below:

Product analysis ⎱ Do these
Competitive analysis ⎰ together

Gathering the Information

Information on the company's mission, finances, products, and other matters usually comes from primary sources, such as company executives and staff; and secondary sources, such as magazine articles. It is usually best to start with secondary sources. The information you find can help you develop questions to pursue through primary research. Often, you can anticipate some of your needs for primary research quite early. If so, you should start developing a plan as early as you can.

There are many ways and lots of places to get information. To get the research foundation off on the right footing, it helps if the information is from an objective source. You will probably be tempted to checkout the company on its Web site or in the marketplace through observation and interviews. While these techniques have value, they may be biased. Similarly, you will want to talk to consumers, but it is better to hold off until you can determine the current users of the product objectively. Typically, this means you will start your active search for information in the library.

Processing the Information

Adopting a Competitive Attitude. Getting the information is only half the task. You must also process the findings to provide advantages for the people working on the campaign. This requires the right kind of attitude. The marketplace is very competitive. Copywriters work hard to develop big ideas—approaches that stand out from the competition. Media planners look for unique or special opportunities to deliver selling messages. Buyers look for the most efficient way to send the messages. It's all very competitive. Researchers need to be every bit as competitive as creative and media personnel.

How Much Information Is Enough? You don't have enough information until you can provide campaign planners with information that's better than what the competition is receiving. In many mature product categories, sales increases come primarily from the competition's market share. Competitive researchers strive to furnish planners with an edge by providing information that is current, comprehensive, and insightful.

Analysis versus Description. Comprehensive analyses usually take time, effort, and money. Not all companies (or students) have the resources of their rivals. Therefore, it is worth reemphasizing the importance of searching for information efficiently. Generalized searches often waste time; they tend to be more descriptive than analytical. Descriptive information usually tells people what they already know or could easily find out. An analyst breaks down background information into components, examining the nature and function of each topic to be analyzed and the interrelationships among sections, as you'll see later. Beginners should think like an analyst. For example, as you look for information on the company, you should have a clear understanding of the function of the company analysis, and how this analysis interrelates with the consumer, market, product, and competitive analyses. We will cover these ideas shortly.

Insight Rather than in Sight. The problem with a descriptive analysis is that it usually tells only the obvious. We refer to this treatment as *putting the information in sight*. Even when an analysis is especially comprehensive, most adequate researchers will eventually discover the information. Descriptive information puts the burden of finding value or meaning on the reader (assuming it is a report). The key to doing good research is to interpret the information that is in sight, to provide **insight**. Researchers only gain insight when they clearly understand the inner nature of the object being analyzed. For example, it is not enough to identify the prime prospects and the competition. It is also important to determine why consumers buy the brands they do. This usually requires the researcher to probe beyond what is obvious.

Consider: Why do consumers clip coupons? shop at superstores? drive miles out of their way to buy the lowest-price gas? The obvious reason would be to save money. In the case of Home Depot, it might also be to have access to a wide array of merchandise. Although these may be some of the most important reasons, other obscure, but more profound reasons may be operating. For many homemakers and do-it-yourselfers, saving money is less important for economic reasons than because of how it makes the saver feel. For some consumers, clipping coupons may be less about saving money and more about reinforcing their self-image of being a thrifty homemaker. Similarly, for many do-it-yourselfers, doing home projects is as much about testing one's abilities as it is about saving money. For these people, shopping at Home Depot may help to reinforce an image that the consumer is a smart person.

These suppositions are merely hypotheses. But if you are developing a campaign for Home Depot or a similar advertiser, they might be worth pursuing. The obvious reasons (price, quality, or availability) why consumers buy a product are often the things companies can do very little to change. If the company does not have a clear price or quality advantage, then the company may be lost about how to strategically direct its promotion. Often, it is the obscure or secondary reasons why consumers buy a product that offer the more creative and effective ways to sell a product.

Viewed objectively, a Saturn automobile does not look significantly different from many other cars. But it is clear that Saturn has tapped into a special consumer motive for buying. In the Summer of 1994, 40,000 Saturn owners came to the semirural area around the small town of Springhill, Tennessee, to attend a Saturn homecoming celebration.[1] Was it possible in the short span of a couple of years, that Saturn had achieved the kind of cult status that has been true for cars like Jaguar, Porche, Jeep, or even Mustang? Probably not. What the Saturn owners bought was the Saturn experience. The company correctly identified that many consumers simply wanted, as its slogan said, "a different kind of car" from "a different kind of company," even if that difference came primarily in the form of a change in attitude.

THE SITUATION ANALYSIS

The situation analysis consists of the background information that will be used to develop the campaign. The information should be **organized, structured, detailed,** and **focused.** Typically, the information is typed into a document and then used to develop strategy and tactics. In the business world, this document, or report, is usually put into a loose-leaf binder, signifying that the analysis is ongoing and subject to continual change. Enlightened companies view analyses as part of a research system, instead of the result of a research project. In a class project, the situation analysis is simply the beginning section of a more comprehensive **plans book.**

Organization. There is more than one way to organize a campaign. We recommend organizing in an outline format along simple lines. We delineate campaigns by using sections that cover broad topics like the company, consumer, market, product, and competition. By using broad topics, you can include within a section any analysis that makes sense for that particular situation.

Structure. The situation analysis should be *structured* so that it is clear that the company's problems and opportunities are uppermost in the minds of the people who are performing the analysis. Remember, although you could make a case to conduct the consumer analysis first, company representatives usually feel more comfortable if the company is first.

For each of the sections in the situation analysis, you should assume an *inside–outside* perspective. With an **inside perspective**, you should strive to understand the company's problems from its point of view. However, sometimes company executives are too close to the situation to have an objective viewpoint. Therefore, viewing the company's situation from an **outside perspective** may provide different and valuable information. Similarly, as the analyst, you want to understand, if not empathize—from an inside perspective—how consumers think and feel. If you only view things from the consumer's perspective, however, you may not get an accurate picture of why they buy or do not buy a product. There are fewer subjects about which people are less objective than themselves.

Consider consumers who drink Samuel Adams beer. If you ask them why they choose that particular brand, they will likely give you some paraphrase of the answer "because I like it." If you probe further, they may tell you specifically why their beer choice is superior to other brands, especially the drinkers of Samuel Adams, the best-selling craft-brewed beer. However, in the beer business there is a common saying, "People don't so much drink a brand's beer, as they drink its advertising." This implies that people consume a certain brand of beer more for psychological reasons than physical ones. If so, then the key task of a researcher often involves moving beyond obvious reasons to uncover motives that are more deeply seated. In the case of Samuel Adams, you would want to know how much of the brand's popularity is due to taste, and how much of it is a reflection of the various images consumers have of the brand. In some instances, an inside approach—trying to think like the consumer—works, and in other cases, taking a more detached approach, or an outside perspective, will provide a more objective and accurate answer. We suggest in each analysis you take both an inside and an outside approach.

Detail. The purpose of the situation analysis is to provide a research foundation that can be used to develop strategy and tactics. Because tactics are detailed executions of the overall strategy, it is important to provide creative and media personnel with sufficient detail to fully exploit their opportunities as well as keep their work on target and within the strategy. It is not usually enough to learn that consumers value low prices, fast service, and quality food when they choose a fast-food restaurant. This information does not provide enough useful detail. Research questions should be posed to elicit specific information—how low a price, how fast the service—preferably in quantitative terms. If this information is difficult to obtain, then the questions might be stated to provide information of a relative or comparative nature, such as Company A has higher quality food than Company B.

Focus. It is important that the detail in the situation analysis focuses on identifying problems and opportunities. Detail without focus is merely padding, or information without meaningful significance. For example, the history of the company is an important part of the company analysis, *but only insofar as it sheds light on the firm's current problems and opportunities*. When and how the company was founded is relevant only if it helps to explain recent or current problems and if it helps make clear why the company can take advantage of an opportunity. Problems and opportunities form the basis for setting objectives. All analyses should focus on identifying the particular aspect of the situation that could either prevent the company from achieving its objectives, or enable it to exploit a marketing advantage. These aspects are the company's problems and opportunities, and will be discussed in greater detail later.

Choosing the Analytical Format

There are a number of ways to process the information you collect. Two of the most common are the **SWOT** analysis, and a **Problems and Opportunities** focus. Each approach works well. We don't have a strong preference as to which format you use. Briefly, let's look at the major sections in a SWOT analysis:

Strengths	a firm's marketing, financial, manufactuing, and
Weaknesses	organizational competencies.
Opportunities	a situation, actual or potential, in which a firm can operate profitably
Threats	forces within the environment that threaten profitable operations

Although the SWOT acronym suggests that the analysis begins with an examination of the company's strengths and weaknesses, usually it's the other way around. Typically, the firm analyzes the external environment for threats to its market position and for opportunities it can exploit. These are then evaluated in terms of the company's internal resources, looking at both its strengths and weaknesses. SWOT analyses' findings are then often displayed in chart format. For example, threats may be classified according to their seriousness and the probability that they will occur. Similarly, opportunities may be classified as strong, medium, or marginal.

We use a simple **problems** and **opportunities** approach because it helps to identify where the company is going to have a problem (which is somewhat similar to a threat) or an opportunity. We divide our analysis into the areas mentioned earlier: company, consumer, market, product, and competition. These areas, of course, are part of the situation analysis. The analysis of an area should begin by examining the **critical issues** within the area. For example, the critical issues for most companies are sales and profits. However, for companies breaking into a market, the critical issue may be market share, or more ominously, survival. Sometimes survival is viewed as a temporary hurdle to overcome. For example, civic construction projects can depress a retail store's sales, but the effects are usually short-lived.

A critical issue can also depend on one's perspective. Each fall, a common problem at many division 1A universities is inadequate attendance at football games. At many of these schools, the football program operates very much like a business. From the athletic director's perspective (an inside perspective), the critical issue often involves getting the public to support the team. Entreaties to support the team—"we need your help"—are common. From the public's point of view (an outside perspective), attending a game is not usually about support or school loyalty. It's about enjoyment or satisfaction, something that is likely to be influenced by the quality of the team, the festive atmosphere, or the quality and quantity of restrooms. The athletic administration would like people to attend games because of school or civic loyalty. It's just not very realistic.

In the problems and opportunities approach, the analyst starts by examining critical issues and moves toward uncovering the problems and identifying the opportunities associated with the various critical issues. In Chapter 4, we'll discuss how to turn these problems and opportunities into objectives. The process looks something like this:

Examine Critical Issues → Uncover Problems → Identify Opportunities → Set Objectives

THE COMPANY ANALYSIS

We believe the situation analysis should begin with an analysis of the company. This analysis should consist of some basic ideas of what the company is concerned with and what it represents. The focus in the analysis should be on the company's major problems and opportunities. Whether you are working for the company directly, are with its agency, or are doing this project as a class assignment, it is imperative that you operate on the same "wavelength" as the company. To help you formulate the kind of questions you will ask in your research, try to imagine you are in a marketing staff meeting to review the past year and to make preliminary plans for the upcoming one. What problems would be discussed? What opportunities will the staff talk about? A good company analysis provides a benchmark to keep you from going off on a tangent, pursuing opportunities the company will never consider.

Sales and Profits: A Good Place to Start.

Generally, the problems and opportunities discussed in this type of meeting focus on money, either in the form of sales or profits. For many companies, these are the only issues. Usually money problems are symptomatic of more fundamental problems, especially if you look at sales (or profits) over a period of years. **Trend analyses** often uncover problems that barely show up in a static time frame. A company can have an off-year for many reasons. If sales problems persist for more than a couple of years, it usually points to a weakness in any or all of three categories: the company itself, the industry, or the overall economy. If you start with the money and ask enough questions, the more deeply rooted problems usually emerge, *especially if you look at the company's problems over a period*

Exhibit 2-1   General Motors: Problems and Opportunity Analysis

Question	Answer
What is the basic problem?	Declining sales, eroding share of market, weak profits.
Why?	Consumers increasingly prefer imported cars, especially Japanese.
Why?	Japanese cars have a higher quality image.
Would consumers buy more GM cars if the quality improved?	Not significantly in the short run.
Why?	The problem is as much perceptual as it is real.
Would it help with the image if GM built a completely new car in a newly formed division?	Only if consumers could be convinced the car was made completely different from the old GM ways by a new kind of company.

of time. Exhibit 2-1 presents how you can use an extended line of questions to uncover a company's fundamental problems and to evaluate whether they can become opportunities.

As the decade of the eighties opened, things were not going well at General Motors (GM). Foreign imports had made steady in-roads in the automobile industry, and GM was having difficulty competing, especially against the Japanese automobile manufacturers. Exhibit 2–1 is a simplistic view of how GM might have determined their opportunity to develop the Saturn automobile.

This line of questioning is, of course, simplistic. It merely demonstrates the value of extending a line of questioning to uncover hidden problems and opportunities. In an actual discussion, the participants would need more information both to pose the questions and to answer them. To ask and answer questions intelligently, your research should include information that is both internal and external to the firm.

Internal Information. Essentially, internal information comes from within the firm, although the company may not be forthcoming with the information you need. In some instances, it must be inferred from outside sources. Consider asking the following questions:

- What is the company's mission?

- What is the company's culture like? (laid back? Conservative? progressive?)

- How ambitious is the company?

- How much risk is it willing to incur?

- What is the state of the company's financial, technological, and managerial resources?

- What are the sales trends over the past several years?

- How profitable has the company been?

- Has the company's share-of-market been going up? down?

External Information. This type of information covers the factors or forces outside the firm that influence its problems and opportunities. Consider asking the following questions:

- What has been the sales trend in the industry over the past several years?
- What is the general economic climate? (recession? boom times?)
- Are there any social, cultural, or political conditions detrimental to the future of the company? (changing dress codes? new political administration?)

At this point, the analysis should not be in depth, or you would run the risk that the company's perception of its problems and opportunities would bias the way you look at the consumer. To evaluate the company's problems and opportunities fully, you need to complete the situation analysis, by examining the consumer, market, product, and competition.

Starting the Library Search

A general literature search on the company is a good place to start. You will be looking primarily for articles on the company, but information on the industry or generic category can also be useful. After you have acquired and digested general information, the next step is to focus on specific information about the company. The most informative articles usually come from trade publications, newspapers, and popular periodicals. The articles are likely to be indexed in either print (hard copy) or electronic format.

Using the Library

Libraries serve as both repositories and gateways to vast amounts of information. Exposure to this information is usually obtained from one of the following access points: a reference librarian, an electronic data search, or a print-based index. While a reference librarian may be the most convenient (or easiest) place to start, experienced users usually omit this step. Today, most academic libraries provide access to numerous subscription-based electronic databases in addition to their online catalogs. Electronic searches are often quicker, more comprehensive, and usually offer the searcher the ability to download the information to disk, email it, or to obtain a printed copy. Still, there may be some sources of information that are easier and certainly cheaper to search in a print-based format. In addition, access to some notable sources may not be offered in electronic format by the library, its consortium, or a statewide network. Electronic library databases are typically offered online and in CD-ROM formats.

Online. Academic libraries are increasing their online subscriptions to both specific databases like *ABI/Inform* and to services like the *LEXIS/NEXIS Academic Universe,* which offers access to a collection of electronic resources. Access to these online databases is frequently offered through the World Wide Web and is limited to only those individuals affiliated with the subscribing college or university. Users are expected to perform their own searches with little or no formal training at single or networked public-access computers with assistance from librarians if needed. These Web-accessible online databases and services are the high-quality electronic information products of publishers or commercial information producers *and are not to be confused with free websites that may or may not be reliable or valuable.*

Libraries also maintain transactional accounts with one or more database vendors to provide electronic access to collections of databases that are either too specialized or expensive to justify individual subscriptions. Well-known vendors/services include Dow Jones Interactive, the DIALOG Corporation, STN International, *LEXIS/NEXIS*, and OCLC. These online vendors provide up-to-date access to databases including trade publications, newspapers, directories, government documents, academic journals, as well as other indexes. Check with a librarian to see which services they can access. Because of the charges involved, librarians trained in the vendor's search system typically perform the searches rather than the library user and may pass some or all of the cost onto the requestor. A notable exception is OCLC's *FirstSearch*, which is designed for the general user. Some search services also offer off-hours access to simplified versions for general users.

CD-ROM. Most academic libraries subscribe to a variety of databases on CD-ROM. Typically, CD-ROM databases are searched at the same public-access computers as online databases and may be networked or offered at only a single computer station. Databases on CD-ROM are updated less frequently than online versions and subscriptions often limit the number of simultaneous users.

Indexes

The most comprehensive and detailed information will be found in sources from financial investment information services such as Moody's and Standard & Poor's. Occasionally, there may be books on the specific company, but the information contained in them will probably be dated. Some of the more widely available sources of information are listed below. However, although there is a vast amount of information in indexes, much of it will be of limited value in doing the company analysis. *Students, in particular, will have to piece together a composite picture from multiple sources.*

ABI/Inform. This valuable source indexes articles appearing in over 800 management, marketing, and business journals, including articles on advertising. Each citation includes a 150-word summary of the article. This index is available only online or on CD-ROM from 1970 to the present.

Predicasts F & S Index United States. This is another valuable source that indexes the contents of trade journals, U.S. government documents, newspapers, and special reports for current information on products, industries, and companies. Companion indexes include *Predicasts F & S Index International* and *Predicasts F & S Index of Corporate Change*. This index is available in print and in various electronic formats.

LEXIS/NEXIS Academic Universe. The academic version of *Lexis/Nexis* provides subscribers with unlimited Internet access to a reduced, but still significant number of news, business, legal, government, medical, and reference resources. Subscribing universities receive one password for access to the full service.

Business Periodicals Index (BPI). This well-known index provides author and subject access to approximately 397 English-language business and trade periodicals, the *Wall Street Journal*, and the business section of the *New York Times*. Coverage extends from 1958 to the present. The BPI is available in print, on CD-ROM, and online. The entries do not include summaries making it more difficult to gauge the relevance of cited articles.

Comprehensive Investment Services

Moody's Manuals. The Moody's Manuals series consists of eight volumes that provide financial and operating information on over 30,000 publicly traded domestic and international companies plus 20,000 municipal and government securities (stocks and bonds). The manuals of special interest to advertising students are the *Industrial Manual,* which provides in-depth descriptions of top U.S. industrial companies; the *OTC Industrial Manual,* which provides coverage of approximately 2,700 Nasdaq and OTC companies; and the *OTC Unlisted Manual,* which provides information on approximately 2,000 emerging companies. Each manual is published annually with weekly and bi-weekly *News Reports* serving as updates. Entries typically include a company history, a business description, a list of subsidiaries, and up to seven years of financial statement information. The manuals are available in print, online, and on CD-ROM.

Standard and Poor's Corporation Records. This is similar in content to *Moody's Manuals*, and provides financial information on 11,000 publicly held U.S. corporations in six alphabetically arranged loose-leaf volumes. The company entries are updated annually on a rotating basis. The service is kept up to date with the *Daily News Service* published each business day of the year. *Corporation Records* is available in print and in various electronic formats.

Value Line Investment Survey. This widely consulted loose-leaf investment service provides in-depth evaluative reports on approximately 2,000 companies representing over 40 industries. Each company is profiled in a one-page summary that is updated quarterly on a rotating basis. The entries include a 10–15 year statistical history plus a narrative statement addressing recent developments and future prospects. This source is available in print, online, and on CD-ROM.

Disclosure. The *Disclosure* database contains detailed financial and management information on over 12,000 public corporations. The data are taken from annual and periodic reports filed with the U.S. Securities and Exchange Commission (SEC). This database is available online, on CD-ROM, and is also included in *LEXIS/NEXIS Academic Universe.*

Directories

Million Dollar Directory: Leading Public and Private Companies. This five-volume set published by Dun & Bradstreet provides brief entries for approximately 160,000 leading U.S. public and private companies valued at $500,000 or more. The information includes the Standard Industrial Classification (SIC) code, and estimated sales. The *Million Dollar Directory* is available in print, on CD-ROM, and other various electronic formats.

The Encyclopedia of Associations. This comprehensive directory provides detailed information on nearly 23,000 nonprofit American organizations and international organizations with North American ties. At least 4,000 of these are trade and industry associations. This directory includes the organization's name, address and telephone number, and the name of a chief contact person to whom you can write for more information.

Miscellaneous

Company Reports. Many academic libraries maintain a collection of annual company reports and/or other periodic reports filed with the SEC in paper or electronic formats. Many services, such as *Moody's, Standard & Poor's,* and *Disclosure* contain excerpts from these reports as well. Company information can also be obtained through company Web pages.

Government Documents and the Internet.   Government data of interest to business researchers is now widely accessible on CD-ROM at the library or through the Internet. For example, the extremely detailed economic censuses (e.g., the *Census of Manufacturers*, the *Census of Retail Trade*, the *Census of Service Industries*, and the *Census of Wholesale Trade*) are available on CD-ROM in addition to or in place of the print versions. The economic censuses are valuable in particular for providing demographic information of interest to marketers and are organized by state, county, Metropolitan Statistical Area (MSA), city, census tracts, and blocks.

Free/Fee Information.   Much economic government data can be obtained for free or fee over the Internet. Of particular note among the free Web sources is the *EDGAR Database (http://www.sec.gov/edgarhp.htm)*. This service provides access to financial disclosure filings such as 10Q and 10K reports submitted electronically by public U.S. corporations to the SEC. The database covers from January 1994 to the present. Most government departments support Web pages and make available electronic versions of valuable publications such as the Bureau of Economic Analysis' *Survey of Current Business (http://www.beadoc.gov/pubs.htm)*. The Federal Interagency Council on Statistical Policy sponsors Fedstat *(http://www.stat-usa.gov)*, which offers a one-stop search service for accessing statistics collected by over 70 agencies.

The Department of Commerce's *STAT-USA/Internet (http://www.stat-usa.gov)* service is notable among fee-based government sites. It allows users to search, in one location, business and economic information collected from over 50 U.S. government agencies, as well as providing access to the entire *National Trade Data Bank.* It is accessible at no charge at academic libraries participating in the federal depository program. Government sources available through the Internet enjoy the same reputation for quality as their print versions.

Moving Forward in the Analysis

After you get a good feel for the company's situation, it's time to begin the consumer analysis. Later, as you begin to understand the consumer, you may want to complete the company analysis by observing or interviewing company personnel and getting sales data from within the company. It may seem awkward or contrived to begin the company analysis, and then move on to the consumer analysis, and then come back again to complete the company analysis. Keep in mind that doing research is every bit as much an art as it is a science. The idea is to discover information in such a way that you remain as objective as possible. Once you listen to what company personnel have to say, your thinking may become biased.

CONSUMER ANALYSIS

The distinguishing feature of successful advertising is a persuasive, memorable message. The message can be spoken, printed, or simply implied. The key to developing these kinds of messages is not so much to understand words and ideas, but to understand people. Leo Burnett, like many advertising greats, intuitively knew how to talk to the average person. He was often described as a man of average appearance and voice, who could instantly grasp the "inherent drama," in a product and relate it to consumers in a way that neither talked up nor down to people. In the twenty-first century, the marketing task will be far more complex and competitive than it was as little as 10 to 15 years ago. More than ever, marketing and advertising people need to understand consumers. A good consumer analysis boils down to about five general questions:

- **Who are the consumers?** What characteristics do they have in common?

- **What motivates them to buy?** How do they think or feel about buying things in general, and the generic product or the brand in particular?

- **How do they use the product?** Where? When?

- **What do they look for in a product?** What are their needs, wants, problems, and interests?

- **How do they look at life?** What are their values? What do they like? How do they go about their life daily life routines? How does the product fit into their lives? How are they influenced by others?

Who Are the Consumers?

The prime prospects for most products are usually the people who have consumed the product in the past. While this is not an ironclad rule, it is a guideline that most companies follow. Even though one market segment may be comparable to another in terms of demographic and psychographic characteristics, there may be other factors that influence product usage that are difficult to pinpoint. The simplest way to predict future usage is to look at product usage data. The best place to fish is not necessarily where the fish are, but where the fish are "biting" (feeding).

For example, more hot dogs are sold per capita in the city of Chicago than in any other major metropolitan city in the United States. Hot dogs have long been part of the culture in Chicago, and have been big sellers there for over 40 years. The hot dog of choice is a kosher-style, all-beef product, and is usually sold in a small building specializing in take-out service. The most popular brand is Vienna. Over the past 20 years, entrepreneurs have taken this concept to cities as diverse as Atlanta, St. Louis, Denver, Nashville, and Panama City, Florida. Although these businesses survive, they seldom thrive as they do in Chicago. Why? Because these cities are not Chicago. Apparently, the hot dog does not have sufficient want-satisfying qualities to have anything more than limited appeal. In Chicago, people go out of their way to eat hot dogs because it is something many of them have grown up with. The original reasons why they consumed hot dogs no longer really matter.

Product Usage

Even though you may be able to get information on product usage from trade publications, information will likely be more comprehensive and objective if you consult either *Simmons Media and Markets* published by the Simmons Market Research Bureau (SMRB) or *Mediamark Research Inc.* (MRI). *Simmons* and *MRI,* as they are often called, are the two major syndicated research sources of product-usage information. Each of these services reports on the usage of brands, products, and services in approximately 800 categories. Usage is typically cross-referenced according to various demographic characteristics, including gender, age, education, occupation, geographic location, race, income, and marital status. Figure 2–1 is an example of data that might be found in *Simmons* or *MRI.* How to use (read) the information included in this figure follows.

How to Read Columns A, B, C, and D

Column A refers to the total number of people who bought or used the product that fall into the demographic segment to the left (e.g., there are 18,787,000 adults who used regular cola drinks in the past 12 months).

Column B indicates the percentage of people who bought or used the product that fall into the demographic segment to the left. (e.g., 16.1% of all adults who used cola drinks in the past 12 months are 18–24 years of age).

Column C indicates the percentage of the demographic segment to the left that fall into the user category at the top (e.g., 76.2% of all adults 18–24 years of age used cola drinks in the past 12 months).

The number in column D compares how the demographic segment to the left uses the product to the average usage for all adults. The index number for average usage is 100 and any number above or below 100 indicates above or below average usage (e.g., adults 18–24 years of age were 27% more likely to use cola drinks than the average adult).

To understand consumers, it helps to look at current users. The goal of the analysis is to describe consumers on the basis of common characteristics. These characteristics can then be used to define or delineate a **market segment**. A market segment then becomes the **target audience**, or **target market**, if it is the segment at which the advertising is to be directed. *The targeting decision is a key element of the campaign strategy and should be deferred until all the individual analyses have been completed.* Users are typically described according to the following characteristics:

- demographic criteria

- psychographic criteria

- degree of product/brand usage

- degree of brand loyalty

Figure 2-1 MRI Product Usage Data

REGULAR COLA DRINKS, NOT DIET

BASE: ADULTS	TOTAL U.S. '000	ALL A '000	ALL B % DOWN	ALL C % ACROSS	ALL D INDEX	HEAVY (MORE THAN 7) A '000	HEAVY B % DOWN	HEAVY C % ACROSS	HEAVY D INDEX	MEDIUM (3 - 7) A '000	MEDIUM B % DOWN	MEDIUM C % ACROSS	MEDIUM D INDEX	LIGHT (LESS THAN 3) A '000	LIGHT B % DOWN	LIGHT C % ACROSS	LIGHT D INDEX
						DRINKS OR GLASSES/LAST 7 DAYS											
All Adults	193462	18787000	16.1	76.2	27	36389	100.0	18.8	100	42693	100.0	22.1	100	37289	100.0	19.3	100
Men	92674	60456	52.0	65.2	108	20563	56.5	22.2	118	22808	53.4	24.6	112	17085	45.8	18.4	96
Women	100788	55915	48.0	55.5	92	15826	43.5	15.7	83	19885	46.6	19.7	89	20204	54.2	20.0	104
Household Heads	117223	70193	60.3	59.9	100	22567	62.0	19.3	102	25898	60.7	22.1	100	21728	58.3	18.5	96
Homemakers	120984	69416	59.7	57.4	95	21063	57.9	17.4	93	24757	58.0	20.5	93	23595	63.3	19.5	101
Graduated College	41082	22484	19.3	54.7	91	5223	14.4	12.7	68	8199	19.2	20.0	90	9063	24.3	22.1	114
Attended College	51120	31076	26.7	60.8	101	9571	26.3	18.7	100	11270	26.4	22.0	100	10235	27.4	20.0	104
Graduated High School	65024	40293	34.6	62.0	103	13752	37.8	21.1	112	15053	35.3	23.1	105	11488	30.8	17.7	92
Did not Graduate High School	36235	22518	19.3	62.1	103	7843	21.6	21.6	115	8171	19.1	22.6	102	6503	17.4	17.9	93
18-24	24658	18787	16.1	76.2	127	6873	18.9	27.9	148	6736	15.8	27.3	124	5179	13.9	21.0	109
25-34	41962	29340	25.2	69.9	116	9938	27.3	23.7	126	10559	24.7	25.2	114	8842	23.7	21.1	109
35-44	42970	27052	23.2	63.0	105	8799	24.2	20.5	109	9258	21.7	21.5	98	8995	24.1	20.9	109
45-54	30865	16882	14.5	54.7	91	5498	15.1	17.8	95	6190	14.5	20.1	91	5195	13.9	16.8	87
55-64	21197	10928	9.4	51.6	86	3008	8.3	14.2	75	4102	9.6	19.4	88	3818	10.2	18.0	93
65 or over	31810	13382	11.5	42.1	70	2273	6.2	7.1	38	5849	13.7	18.4	83	5260	14.1	16.5	86
18-34	66619	48127	41.4	72.2	120	16811	46.2	25.2	134	17295	40.5	26.0	118	14021	37.6	21.0	109
18-49	127083	84612	72.7	66.6	111	28605	78.6	22.5	120	29985	70.2	23.6	107	26022	69.8	20.5	106
25-54	115796	73273	63.0	63.3	105	24235	66.6	20.9	111	26007	60.9	22.5	102	23032	61.8	19.9	103
Employed Full Time	107008	66060	56.8	61.7	103	22202	61.0	20.7	110	24218	56.7	22.6	103	19639	52.7	18.4	95
Part-time	17702	11317	9.7	63.9	106	3471	9.5	19.6	104	3634	8.5	20.5	93	4212	11.3	23.8	123
Sole Wage Earner	35152	21837	18.8	62.1	103	7624	21.0	21.7	115	7247	17.0	20.6	93	6965	18.7	19.8	103
Not Employed	68752	38994	33.5	56.7	94	10716	29.4	15.6	83	14841	34.8	21.6	98	13437	36.0	19.5	101
Professional	19050	10549	9.1	55.4	92	2643	7.3	13.9	74	3928	9.2	20.6	93	3977	10.7	20.9	108
Executive/Admin./Managerial	17654	9737	8.4	55.2	92	2724	7.5	15.4	82	3546	8.3	20.1	91	3467	9.3	19.6	102
Clerical/Sales/Technical	36512	21953	18.9	60.1	100	6333	17.4	17.3	92	8273	19.4	22.7	103	7346	19.7	20.1	104
Precision/Crafts/Repair	13368	9241	7.9	69.1	115	3792	10.4	28.4	151	3216	7.5	24.1	109	2233	6.0	16.7	87
Other Employed	38125	25896	22.3	67.9	113	10180	28.0	26.7	142	8888	20.8	23.3	106	6828	18.3	17.9	93
H/D Income $75,000 or More	34245	18306	15.7	53.5	89	4932	13.6	14.4	77	6550	15.3	19.1	87	6823	18.3	19.9	103
$60,000 - 74,999	20204	11765	10.1	58.2	97	3489	9.6	17.3	92	4102	9.6	20.3	92	4174	11.2	20.7	107
$50,000 - 59,999	17746	10582	9.1	59.6	99	2793	7.7	15.7	84	4247	9.9	23.9	108	3542	9.5	20.0	104
$40,000 - 49,999	22067	13613	11.7	61.7	103	4396	12.1	19.9	106	5402	12.7	24.5	111	3816	10.2	17.3	90
$30,000 - 39,999	26072	16835	14.5	64.6	107	5712	15.7	21.9	116	6157	14.4	23.6	107	4966	13.3	19.0	99
$20,000 - 29,999	28213	17172	14.8	60.9	101	5673	15.6	20.1	107	6559	15.4	23.2	105	4940	13.2	17.5	91
$10,000 - 19,999	27851	17536	15.1	63.0	105	5660	15.6	20.3	108	6052	14.2	21.7	98	5824	15.6	20.9	108
Less than $10,000	17063	10562	9.1	61.9	103	3734	10.3	21.9	116	3624	8.5	21.2	96	3204	8.6	18.8	97
Census Region: North East	39112	22674	19.5	58.0	96	5531	15.2	14.1	75	8464	19.8	21.6	98	8679	23.3	22.2	115
North Central	45331	26225	22.5	57.9	96	7454	20.5	16.4	87	10129	23.7	22.3	101	8642	23.2	19.1	99
South	67756	42685	36.7	63.0	105	17137	47.1	25.3	134	14405	33.7	21.3	96	11143	29.9	16.4	85
West	41262	24787	21.3	60.1	100	6268	17.2	15.2	81	9695	22.7	23.5	106	8824	23.7	21.4	111
Marketing Reg.: New England	10174	5399	4.6	53.1	88	1212	3.3	11.9	63	2187	5.1	21.5	97	2000	5.4	19.7	102
Middle Atlantic	32886	19993	17.2	60.8	101	5237	14.4	15.9	85	7204	16.9	21.9	99	7553	20.3	23.0	119
East Central	25885	15869	13.6	61.3	102	4476	12.3	17.3	92	6297	14.7	24.3	110	5096	13.7	19.7	102
West Central	29342	17022	14.6	58.0	96	4899	13.5	16.7	89	6689	15.7	22.8	103	5434	14.6	18.5	96
South East	37012	23433	20.1	63.3	105	10477	28.8	28.3	150	7555	17.7	20.4	92	5401	14.5	14.6	76
South West	21905	13119	11.3	59.9	100	4812	13.2	22.0	117	4466	10.5	20.4	92	3841	10.3	17.5	91
Pacific	36256	21535	18.5	59.4	99	5277	14.5	14.6	77	8295	19.4	22.9	104	7964	21.4	22.0	114
County Size A	79362	47479	40.8	59.8	99	12694	34.9	16.0	85	17342	40.6	21.9	99	17442	46.8	22.0	114
County Size B	57583	35022	30.1	60.8	101	11741	32.3	20.4	108	12599	29.5	21.9	99	10682	28.6	18.6	96
County Size C	27751	17271	14.8	62.2	103	6026	16.6	21.7	115	6438	15.1	23.2	105	4808	12.9	17.3	90
County Size D	28765	16599	14.3	57.7	96	5928	16.3	20.6	110	6314	14.8	21.9	99	4357	11.7	15.1	79
MSA Central City	65429	39738	34.1	60.7	101	12774	35.1	19.5	104	14030	32.9	21.4	97	12934	34.7	19.8	103
MSA Suburban	89768	54174	46.6	60.3	100	15558	42.8	17.3	92	19959	46.8	22.2	101	18657	50.0	20.8	108
Non-MSA	38265	22458	19.3	58.7	98	8056	22.1	21.1	112	8704	20.4	22.7	103	5698	15.3	14.9	77
Single	44200	31388	27.0	71.0	118	10687	29.4	24.2	129	11346	26.6	25.7	116	9355	25.1	21.2	110
Married	112965	65578	56.4	58.1	97	19584	53.8	17.3	92	24360	57.1	21.6	98	21634	58.0	19.2	99
Other	36296	19405	16.7	53.5	89	6118	16.8	16.9	90	6987	16.4	19.2	87	6300	16.9	17.4	90
Parents	67742	44693	38.4	66.0	110	14407	39.6	21.3	113	16211	38.0	23.9	108	14075	37.7	20.8	108
Working Parents	52706	33896	29.1	64.3	107	10816	29.7	20.5	109	12387	29.0	23.5	107	10694	28.7	20.3	105
Household Size: 1 Person	24385	12204	10.5	50.0	83	3737	10.3	15.3	81	4507	10.6	18.5	84	3961	10.6	16.2	84
2 Persons	62064	34562	29.7	55.7	93	9893	27.2	15.9	85	12753	29.9	20.5	93	11916	32.0	19.2	100
3 or More	107013	69604	59.8	65.0	108	22759	62.5	21.3	113	25433	59.6	23.8	108	21412	57.4	20.0	104
Any Child in Household	81486	54301	46.7	66.6	111	17912	49.2	22.0	117	19770	46.3	24.3	110	16619	44.6	20.4	106
Under 2 Years	14735	10288	8.8	69.8	116	3336	9.2	22.6	120	3815	8.9	25.9	117	3136	8.4	21.3	110
2-5 Years	31551	21898	18.8	69.4	115	7374	20.3	23.4	124	7795	18.3	24.7	112	6729	18.0	21.3	111
6-11 Years	38084	24772	21.3	65.0	108	8228	22.6	21.6	115	8712	20.4	22.9	104	7832	21.0	20.6	107
12-17 Years	36369	24064	20.7	66.2	110	7648	21.0	21.0	112	9244	21.7	25.4	115	7172	19.2	19.7	102
White	163736	96296	82.7	58.8	98	29237	80.3	17.9	95	35860	84.0	21.9	99	31199	83.7	19.1	99
Black	22435	15559	13.4	69.3	115	6005	16.5	26.8	142	5186	12.1	23.1	105	4368	11.7	19.5	101
Spanish Speaking	17144	11136	9.6	65.0	108	3859	10.6	22.5	120	4022	9.4	23.5	106	3254	8.7	19.0	98
Home Owned	130597	74041	63.6	56.7	94	20745	57.0	15.9	84	27777	65.1	21.3	96	25519	68.4	19.5	101
Daily Newspapers: Read Any	106786	61743	53.1	57.8	96	18159	49.9	17.0	90	23248	54.5	21.8	99	20337	54.5	19.0	99
Read One Daily	86476	50380	43.3	58.3	97	15300	42.0	17.7	94	18913	44.3	21.9	99	16167	43.4	18.7	97
Read Two or More Dailies	20310	11363	9.8	55.9	93	2858	7.9	14.1	75	4334	10.2	21.3	97	4170	11.2	20.5	107
Sunday Newspapers: Read Any	122411	71481	61.4	58.4	97	21516	59.1	17.6	93	26261	61.5	21.5	97	23704	63.6	19.4	100
Read One Sunday	109654	64560	55.5	58.9	98	19787	54.4	18.0	96	23534	55.1	21.5	97	21239	57.0	19.4	100
Read Two or More Sundays	12757	6921	5.9	54.2	90	1729	4.8	13.6	72	2727	6.4	21.4	97	2465	6.6	19.3	100
Quintile I - Outdoor	38692	22789	19.6	58.9	98	6937	19.1	17.9	95	8216	19.2	21.2	96	7636	20.5	19.7	102
Quintile II	38692	23335	20.1	60.3	100	7907	21.7	20.4	109	8162	19.1	21.1	96	7266	19.5	18.8	97
Quintile III	38695	22922	19.7	59.2	98	7557	20.8	19.5	104	8631	20.2	22.3	101	6734	18.1	17.4	90
Quintile IV	38689	24126	20.7	62.4	104	7454	20.5	19.3	102	8750	20.5	22.6	102	7922	21.2	20.5	106
Quintile V	38694	23197	19.9	60.0	100	6533	18.0	16.9	90	8934	20.9	23.1	105	7731	20.7	20.0	104
Quintile I - Magazines	38688	24460	21.0	63.2	105	7864	21.6	20.3	108	9052	21.2	23.4	106	7545	20.2	19.5	101
Quintile II	38696	23211	19.9	60.0	100	7443	20.5	19.2	102	8394	19.7	21.7	98	7374	19.8	19.1	99
Quintile III	38693	23372	20.1	60.4	100	7087	19.5	18.3	97	8821	20.7	22.8	103	7464	20.0	19.3	100
Quintile IV	38693	22983	19.8	59.4	99	7635	21.0	19.7	105	8435	19.8	21.8	99	6914	18.5	17.9	93
Quintile V	38691	22344	19.2	57.7	96	6360	17.5	16.4	87	7991	18.7	20.7	94	7993	21.4	20.7	107
Quintile I - Newspapers	38695	21667	18.6	56.0	93	5780	15.9	14.9	79	8136	19.1	21.0	95	7751	20.8	20.0	104
Quintile II	38694	21806	18.7	56.4	94	6007	16.5	15.5	83	8327	19.5	21.5	98	7471	20.0	19.3	100
Quintile III	38680	23648	20.3	61.1	102	7942	21.8	20.5	109	8348	19.6	21.6	98	7358	19.7	19.0	99
Quintile IV	38701	25148	21.6	65.0	108	8274	22.7	21.4	114	9405	22.0	24.3	110	7469	20.0	19.3	100
Quintile V	38692	24102	20.7	62.3	104	8386	23.0	21.7	115	8476	19.9	21.9	99	7240	19.4	18.7	97
Quintile I - Radio	38694	24247	20.8	62.7	104	8456	23.2	21.9	116	8146	19.1	21.1	95	7645	20.5	19.8	103
Quintile II	38691	24061	20.7	62.2	103	7607	20.9	19.7	105	9186	21.5	23.7	108	7268	19.5	18.8	97
Quintile III	38692	24569	21.1	63.5	106	7749	21.3	20.0	106	8813	20.6	22.8	103	8007	21.5	20.7	107
Quintile IV	38693	22172	19.1	57.3	95	6443	17.7	16.7	89	8129	19.0	21.0	95	7600	20.4	19.6	102
Quintile V	38691	21321	18.3	55.1	92	6133	16.9	15.9	84	8418	19.7	21.8	99	6769	18.2	17.5	91

Spring 1997

Figure 2-1 *Continued*

REGULAR COLA DRINKS, NOT DIET 1

BASE: ADULTS (193,462,000)	ALL			SHARE OF USERS	SHARE OF VOLUME	VOLUME/ USERS INDEX
	'000	%	UNWGT			
Total Drank in Last 6 Months	116370	60.2	11552			
Kinds:						
Plastic Bottles	53893	27.9	5350			
Glass Bottles	7847	4.1	754			
Cans	66459	34.4	6576			
Brands:						
Canfield	644	.3	89	.4	.2	50
Caffeine Free Classic Coke	6097	3.2	634	3.4	2.2	65
Caffeine Free Coke	4330	2.2	446	2.4	2.5	104
Cherry Coke	9043	4.7	906	5.1	2.2	43
Coca Cola Classic	59875	30.9	6026	33.8	35.5	105
Coke II	2195	1.1	207	1.2	1.2	100
Crystal Pepsi	1463	.8	132	.8	.5	63
Pepsi-Cola	55380	28.6	5286	31.3	37.5	120
Caffeine Free Pepsi	6613	3.4	734	3.7	2.4	65
Cherry RC	665	.3	72	.4	.1	25
RC Cola	6530	3.4	610	3.7	2.2	59
Shasta Cola	2047	1.1	174	1.2	.7	58
Store's Own Brand	9736	5.0	940	5.5	4.3	78
Other	12371	6.4	1187	7.0	8.5	121
Forms:						
Caffeine-free	15554	8.0	1610			
Drinks or Glasses/Last 7 Days						
L None	17200	8.9	1837			
L 1	8339	4.3	973			
L 2	11750	6.1	1238			
M 3	9083	4.7	970			
M 4	8508	4.4	840			
M 5	7718	4.0	727			
M 6	5811	3.0	546			
M 7	11573	6.0	1094			
H 8	2369	1.2	234			
H 9 or more	34020	17.6	3093			
L Total	37289	19.3	4048	32.0	3.5	
M Total	42693	22.1	4177	36.7	23.9	
H Total	36389	18.8	3327	31.3	72.6	

Demographic Criteria. Demographic criteria describe the consumer in terms of variables such as age, gender, income, geographic location, marital status, education, race, and family life cycle. These criteria are easily the most widely used form for describing or defining the target market. This information is relatively easy to measure, and is available from a number of research sources, such as *Simmons* and *MRI.*

Although the value of using demographic criteria to segment the market is obvious for some products, for others it may not provide enough discriminatory power to distinguish between prime and only fair prospects. For example, two groups may be comparable in terms of age, sex, education, and income, but may not have the same propensity to buy ski equipment because they differ in ways that demographic criteria are not able to suggest. To better understand consumers, an analyst will often examine the psychological makeup and lifestyles of consumers to gain insight into other factors that can affect their predisposition to buy. However, when it comes to buying media, planners usually revert to demographic criteria.

Psychographic Criteria. Psychographic criteria include information that is both psychological in nature (such as personality, motivation, and attitude), and sociological in nature (such as lifestyles, activities, and the way people go about their daily routines). Although demographic criteria are relatively easy to measure, psychographic characteristics are not. The data are not likely to be as reliable or valid as demographic information because of the greater difficulty in defining and measuring psychological and sociological constructs. It is usually much easier to measure whether someone is male or female and a high school graduate than it is to measure whether someone is affectionate, liberal, or even something as simple as how often he or she dines out. As a result, much of the psychographic information used in advertising is customized to fit the specific needs of the advertiser. We will discuss two sources of information in this section: (1) *Simmons,* which is widely available, but of limited value, and (2) the *VALS* 2 system, which is widely used, *but not likely to be available in libraries.*

Simmons presents some psychographic information cross-referenced to demographic criteria and media exposure. This information is based on a respondent's self-concept and is collected via personal interview. Basically, interviewers ask consumers to rate themselves with the respect to a group of adjectives according to a 5-point (Likert) scale. Each of the adjectives, such as affectionate, broad-minded, and egocentric, is then cross-referenced with demographic variables, such as age, income, and geographical location. This information is provided on CD-ROM, which is the way most advertisers and agencies access this data. The categories (four to a page) are as follows:

AFFECTIONATE	AMICABLE	AWKWARD	BRAVE
BROADMINDED	CREATIVE	DOMINATING	EFFICIENT
EGOCENTRIC	FRANK	FUNNY	INTELLIGENT
KIND	REFINED	RESERVED	SELF-ASSURED
SOCIABLE	STUBBORN	TENSE	TRUSTWORTHY

To use this information, an analyst first has to determine the demographic makeup of the product users, and then use the above descriptors to help define the market segment.

VALS™ (Values and Lifestyles) is a consumer psychographic system developed by SRI International for segmenting U.S. consumers and predicting consumer behavior. VALS classifies consumers into eight basic groups based on their answers to a battery of

35 attitude items and several demographic questions. (Figure 2–2 presents the VALS typology). Integrating the VALS battery into commercial surveys (for example, VALS is integrated into the *Simmons Survey of Media and Markets*) and into custom questionnaires or focus group screeners allows new product developers and marketers a method for identifying appropriate targets for their products and services. VALS data also provides a method for an integrated marketing approach from new product development to brand positioning and from advertising to media selection.

The VALS system is based on two concepts: self-orientation and resources, and was developed according to VALS, to segment the market and predict consumer behavior. According to *VALS,* consumers are motivated to pursue and acquire products, services, and experiences that provide satisfaction and give shape, substance, and character to their identities. They are guided by one of three powerful self-orientations:

1. *Principle Oriented*—these consumers are guided in their choices by abstract, idealized criteria, rather than by feelings, events, or desire for approval and opinions of others.

2. *Status Oriented*—these consumers look for products and services that demonstrate the consumers' success to their peers.

3. *Action Oriented*—these consumers are guided by a desire for social or physical activity, variety, and risk taking.[2]

The VALS system also suggests that consumers' behavior is influenced by the *resources* they are able to draw on such as income, education, energy level, and self-confidence. Related VALS products include GeoVALS™, providing data on where to find concentrations of the desired target by Zip Code or block group, as discussed in Chapter 3, iVALS ™, used to understand which VALS groups are on the Internet and what they do there, and JapanVALS™, for understanding Japanese consumers.

Other sources of psychographic information are also available, especially on lifestyle. Most of these sources, such as Claritas, Inc., and *SRDS,* use the information in coordination with data on specific markets, as will be discussed in Chapter 3 under "market analysis." *If these sources of information are not available, the researcher will have to collect the information using primary research techniques.* We will discuss some of these techniques later in this chapter.

Degree of Product/Brand Usage.   Another useful way to think of consumers is according to the amount of a product they use. The standard way to classify usage is to categorize consumers into *heavy, medium,* and *light* users. Both *Simmons* and *MRI* report their data on product usage in this manner. Although it may seem obvious that an advertiser would want to target heavy users, this is not an appropriate strategy for all marketers. Aiming at heavy users usually puts a company into direct competition with the market leader. In some categories, such as candy bars or appliances, advertisers can aim at the heavy users, and even if they sell much less than the brand leader, they can still carve out a satisfactory share of the market (niche). In other categories, such as cigarettes, going after the heavy user will pit the company directly up against Marlboro and Newport, the two top brands of cigarettes in the United States. In the case of Marlboro, one of the two or three most powerful brand names in the world regardless of the product category, the competition is especially formidable. When new brands are introduced in the cigarette industry, they usually target the message strategy to the medium and light users. On the other hand, if you have the marketing muscle like McDonald's, you can do as they do and target a number of segments, including super heavy users (SHUs).

Figure 2-2   The VALS Network

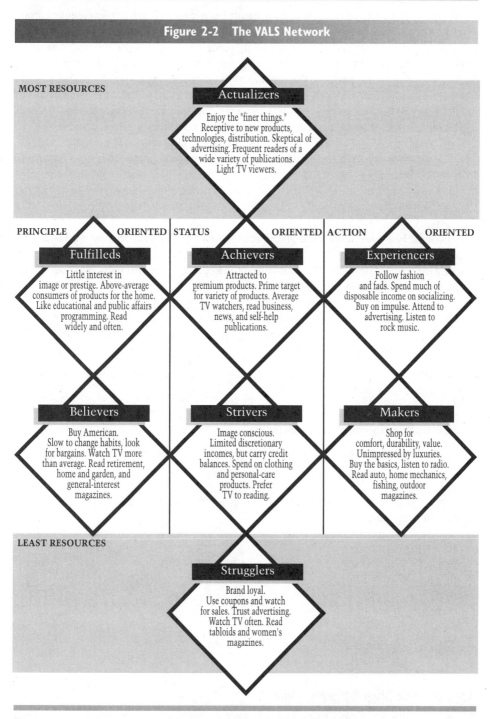

MOST RESOURCES

Actualizers

Enjoy the "finer things."
Receptive to new products,
technologies, distribution. Skeptical of
advertising. Frequent readers of a
wide variety of publications.
Light TV viewers.

PRINCIPLE   ORIENTED STATUS   ORIENTED ACTION   ORIENTED

Fulfilleds

Little interest in
image or prestige. Above-average
consumers of products for the home.
Like educational and public affairs
programming. Read
widely and often.

Achievers

Attracted to
premium products. Prime target
for variety of products. Average
TV watchers, read business,
news, and self-help
publications.

Experiencers

Follow fashion
and fads. Spend much of
disposable income on socializing.
Buy on impulse. Attend to
advertising. Listen to
rock music.

Believers

Buy American.
Slow to change habits, look
for bargains. Watch TV more
than average. Read retirement,
home and garden, and
general-interest
magazines.

Strivers

Image conscious.
Limited discretionary
incomes, but carry credit
balances. Spend on clothing
and personal-care
products. Prefer
TV to reading.

Makers

Shop for
comfort, durability, value.
Unimpressed by luxuries.
Buy the basics, listen to radio.
Read auto, home mechanics,
fishing, outdoor
magazines.

LEAST RESOURCES

Strugglers

Brand loyal.
Use coupons and watch
for sales. Trust advertising.
Watch TV often. Read
tabloids and women's
magazines.

Source: *American Demographics,* July 94, p. 3 © 1994 and VALS, SRI Consulting, Menlo Park, CA, 1998.

Degree of Brand Loyalty. It is usually helpful to get some feel for the amount of brand loyalty in a product category. It is widely believed that during the 1980s, consumers became much more value conscious. One study reported that the percentage of customers who would remain with their brand in the face of competitive price deals changed from 80% to 60% during this period.[4] The amount of brand loyalty displayed by consumers can have a strong influence on both advertising strategy and tactics. Knowing the amount of brand loyalty in the market can help determine whether the brand's core equities are eroding. If so, then the planners have to decide whether to take steps to shore up a brand's equity (to be discussed in Chapter 4) or rely on various pricing and sales promotion tactics.

The most powerful type of brand loyalty measures is behavioral. Both AC Nielsen and Information Resources, Inc. (IRI), measure the extent to which households buy the same brand in two successive time periods. Customers are then divided into new and loyal customers. New customers are further classified according to whether they purchased on a deal or not.[5]

If the analyst does not have access to scanner data, then *an alternative approach is to collect information on consumer buying styles either through primary or secondary research.* One method developed by Leo Burnett is to categorize consumers into four different patterns of brand loyalty and buying strategies.

1. *Long loyals* are committed to one brand regardless of price or any other factor. These numbers are declining and are seen mostly when the purchase is "highly involving." Top-of-the-line cosmetics is a good example.

2. *Rotators* show regular patterns of shifting between preferred brands motivated by variety rather than price.

3. *Dealer sensitives* show a pattern of shifting between preferred brands determined by availability of special offers or incentives.

4. *Price sensitives* follow a decision rule to purchase the cheapest option, regardless of brand.[6]

Simmons reports information on buying style (based on the consumer's self-concept) in the following categories:

BRAND LOYAL	CAUTIOUS
ECONOMY-MINDED	EXPERIMENTERS
PLANNERS	STYLE-CONSCIOUS
CONFORMISTS	ECOLOGISTS
IMPULSIVES	AD BELIEVERS

This information is available only on CD-ROM.

When and How Often Consumers Buy

A common premise in advertising is to advertise in line with existing trends of consumer behavior. Two trends that are especially important to media planners are:

- How often consumers buy the product (that is, the purchase cycle)

- When consumers buy the product (that is, the seasonality)

Media planners use information pertaining to how often consumers buy and when they buy to help them schedule advertising impressions. The most accurate source of information on the purchase cycle and the seasonality of consumer purchases usually come from AC Nielsen's or IRI's product usage audit. An analyst can also access information from trade articles and industry associations.

What Motivates Consumers to Buy

After you have identified current users, it can be helpful to understand what motivates them to spend their money one place and not another. To understand consumers' motivations, you must first understand what factors influence them. Advertisers are always trying to understand why consumers behave the way they do. Over the years, numerous models have been developed to explain the consumer buying process. These models typically explain the process from a consumer's first exposure to an ad, to the actual purchase of the product. These models are explained in most consumer behavior texts, usually under the subheading of *learning hierarchy*, and are widely available in libraries. You may want to consult them.

Trade articles about consumers can provide some insight into what motivates people to buy a product. Other secondary research is unlikely to be of much help. Primary research will probably be your best source of information. We shall discuss some of the techniques later in this section, but first you need to determine which questions to pursue.

One way to organize your understanding of buyer behavior is to examine what consumers think and feel about the product and how they use it. This material in Exhibit 2–2 presents some of the questions you should consider when pursuing your secondary or primary research and will help you organize the kind of information you need to understand about why consumers will or will not buy a product.

The information obtained from these questions will then be used to help determine the campaign's problems and opportunities. These in turn will provide the foundation for setting objectives after all the analyses are completed.

What Consumers Expect in a Product

In the course of conducting consumer interviews, there is often a subtle shift in the focus from how consumers think or feel about a product to *what they would like the product to do for them.* Although some consumers are able to identify quickly how they expect to benefit from using a product, it can take other consumers a while to make this identification. If they do not make this shift, you will have to lead them in this direction, whether you are using a structured questionnaire or conducting a **depth interview**. If you can pinpoint how consumers expect to benefit from a product, then the most direct and effective way to advertise is simply to interpret the want-satisfying qualities of the product in terms of the needs or wants of the consumer.

Determining consumers' needs and wants in the 1950s, 1960s was relatively easy; it has become a lot harder in the 1990s. Today, consumers may not be perfectly satisfied with

Exhibit 2-2 Research Questions to Consider

How consumers think about the product

1. To what extent are they aware of the product, especially the brand name?
2. Do they know about the brand's special features, ingredients, or hidden qualities?
3. Do they understand how the product or brand works?
4. Do they understand the brand's superior qualities?

How consumers feel about the product

1. What is their attitude toward the product category?
2. What is their attitude toward the specific brand?
3. To what extent do they like or desire the product or brand?
4. Do consumers trust the brand to deliver the promised benefits?
5. Do consumers have a preference for this brand?
6. What image or personality do consumers associate with the product or brand?
7. What do consumers feel is this brand's essence?

How consumers use the product

1. How do consumers use the product?
2. Where do consumers use the product?
3. When do consumers use the product?
4. Why do consumers use the product?
5. Are there alternative uses for the product?
6. Under what conditions would the consumer use more of the product?

a product, but it does not necessarily follow that they can articulate exactly what they are looking. It takes some skill on the part of the interviewer to get consumers to reveal enough information to provide insight into why they might buy a product. Consumers typically buy products for the following reasons:

- The product satisfies needs or wants.

- The product helps solve problems.

- The product simply arouses curiosity or interest.

- The consumer likes the brand or its advertising.

Consumers may also buy a product because they like the values or lifestyle depicted in the advertising. However, this insight is more likely to result from an analyst's inference about consumers' values and lifestyles rather than from consumers' explanations of why they buy a product. Consumers may say they are buying the product because of the ads—after interviewers show consumers the advertising—but they don't usually offer that information before.

Needs and Wants. The difference between a need and a want is generally a matter of perspective. Consumers often confuse this difference. A young boy going to a basketball camp may feel he "needs" a pair of Air Jordan shoes to fit in; a young girl may feel she "needs" to diet for similar reasons. Most people would not agree with the boy or the girl. To a researcher, the difference between a need and a want may be a semantic distinction with no practical implications.

Problems. Generally, people's needs and wants are fairly well satisfied with most products. This makes it more difficult to get information from consumers. Even when people are dissatisfied with the results of using a product, they may not be aware of what they want in its place. However, if you ask consumers if they have any gripes about or problems with using the product, the information they reveal can provide just enough insight upon which you can base an advertising campaign or make product improvements. For example, consumer research for Gillette uncovered the useful information that when women cut themselves shaving, they blame themselves. Perhaps, not surprisingly, when men cut themselves, they blame the blade or the razor.

Consumer researchers have to be careful when designing questions that they move beyond simple questions that ask people what they need or want in a product. In the case of companies like Gillette, if researchers ask women what they want in a razor, it is very likely that the women would not know what to tell them. However, Gillette researchers know that women have problems shaving, so in their consumer research they questioned women about how they use their razors.

Researchers found that women usually shave their legs while showering, whereas men mostly shave at a sink. Researchers also knew that when men use a razor, the head of the razor is on top, and the stem is on the bottom. Conversely, when women are showering, the stem of the razor is usually on top and the head of the razor is usually facing down. As a result, the underside of the razor catches the water streaming down from the showerhead, and women commonly complain the razor slips from their hands, especially if their hands are soapy.

Gillette used this information to redesign the Sensor razor expressly for women. Instead of a thin stem, the housing holding the razor was made to fit the palm of a woman's hand. A special rubbery grip, which Gillette obtained from its Parker Pen subsidiary, was attached to the housing. Because Gillette relied heavily on consumer research to develop the product, its print ads are laden with copy reflecting how the Sensor for Women addresses women's problems.[7]

How Consumers Look at Life

Although a substantial amount of information on consumer values and lifestyles is available from syndicated sources, it may not be specific enough to fit the given campaign. Also, the sources are not widely available in libraries. A number of primary research techniques that can be used to get the above information will be discussed shortly. One of these techniques, based on observation, is widely used in advertising and goes by the name **ethnography**. This type of qualitative research is especially helpful in focusing on those aspects of consumers' lifestyle that directly affect the way consumers use a product.

Ethnography. The literal meaning of *ethnography* refers to the description and classification of various cultures and racial groups. In advertising, it pertains more to the observation of consumers as they go about their daily routines. Many of the techniques are borrowed from anthropology. Researchers try to put themselves in the place of consumers by getting as close to them as possible and by trying to simulate an actual purchase decision for a particular product. To learn about the consumer's lifestyle and how they use a product, an interviewer goes to a consumer's environment and observes behavioral patterns and asks questions. As part of the observational process, the interviewer takes photographs.

When conducting research for a food product, for example, an interviewer would ask the consumer questions to reveal his or her eating philosophy and management: Is the family health-oriented? To what extent do family members make trade-offs between foods that are good for them and food that simply tastes good? How does the family rationalize their choices? How much of a family's food intake is consumed on the run? How much is part of a regular sit-down meal? How often does the family dine out?

The interviewer may also accompany the consumer to a supermarket and observe the decision process up close and personal. This process provides the research effort a better understanding of the dynamics and trade-offs consumers make while shopping for a particular product. If an advertiser wants to know what consumers think of a certain restaurant chain, the researcher not only goes to the restaurant to observe consumers, but also goes to one of the restaurants *with* a consumer. This way the researcher can experience firsthand the problems, irritants, and satisfactions from the of the consumer's point of view. The researcher hopes to gain insight by looking for clues and relationships. The idea is to think like a consumer, but interpret like an analyst.

Euro RSCG Tatham, a major advertising agency in Chicago, used ethnographic research (see Exhibit 2–3) to learn how consumers make decisions about frozen entrees. The company learned that consumers have both rational and emotional needs connected to frozen entrees. Consumers classify brands in either a rational category (good for you) or an emotional category (tastes good). Consumers perceive all the nutritional brands, like Healthy Choice, Lean Cuisine, and Weight Watchers, as *nutritional frozen food*. Because these products satisfy rational needs, there was little emotional loyalty to any one brand.

The agency found that when consumers stand in front of a frozen-food case, they "taste bud" shop rather than "brand shop" for frozen entrees. Consumers chose the individual items they know taste good and meet their personal nutritional needs. The challenge for the agency and the advertiser was, first, to interrupt this kind of switching behavior and, second, to secure greater loyalty toward their brand through more emotionally based communications that were more relevant to consumers' needs and that differentiated the company's brand from the others.[8]

Other Qualitative Research Techniques

In addition to ethnography, there are a number of other techniques that can be used to gain insight on consumers. In many ways, the research that is done to develop campaigns is more an art than it is a science. It is quite common to hear advertising people refer to their research as "soft." Technically, this could mean that there were no control groups in an experiment, no systematic manipulation of variables, or the sample was not selected randomly. Usually, it simply means that the analysis is more qualitative than quantitative. The main purpose of qualitative research is to develop insights into how to talk to consumers. Among the heaviest users of qualitative research are agency account planners.

	Exhibit 2-3 A Day in the Life of an Ethnographer

9:00 A.M.	The researcher arrives at the home of a consumer to discuss food. The appointment has been set up by a firm that specializes in recruiting people to participate in consumer research.
9:05 A.M.	After exchanging pleasantries, the interviewer engages the consumer in a discussion of the family's eating philosophy and the way she (or he) manages the cooking and the availability of food for the family. The interviewer asks about the role played by other members of the household in shopping and cooking.
9:15 A.M.	The interviewer asks to see the consumer's cookbooks and any special recipes. A photograph is taken of the books.
9:25 A.M.	The interviewer asks to look in the consumer's pantry and cupboards, carefully noting snack items, national brands, and the proportion of canned to soft-packaged goods. The interviewer photographs the products.
9:35 A.M.	The interviewer asks to look inside the refrigerator, noting the amount of fresh food, the leftovers, and the prominence of national brands. More photos are taken.
9:45 A.M.	The interviewer checks the freezer and inquires about the length of time items have been in there. The proportion of entrées to single-item packages including desserts is noted. More photos are taken.
9:55 A.M.	The interviewer takes photos of the kitchen, especially of gadgets and other labor-saving devices. The interviewer asks to go shopping with the consumer and gives him/her $50.
10:10 A.M.	They arrive at the supermarket, get a cart, and walk down the aisles. The interviewer takes special note of the consumer's interest in fresh produce, bakery items, canned goods, meat, nonfood items, and frozen food. The interviewer observes the consumer's interest in price shopping and the relative importance of store brands to nationally advertised items.
10:40 A.M.	Prior to getting in the checkout lane, the interviewer takes a photograph of the cart. While in the checkout lane, the interviewer asks the consumer to explain the purchase decisions.
10: 45 A.M.	The interviewer says good-bye and prepares to go to the next meeting. Later, back in the office, the consumer's statements will be compared to the photographs and the interviewer's notes.

The Account Planning Revolution

By the early 1980s, a number of U.S. agencies, notably Chiat/Day, adopted a system many British ad agencies were using to manage the flow of information used to develop marketing campaigns. This system is called **account planning.**[9] The account planner's main function is to develop and manage the flow of information using traditional and nontraditional research to uncover special consumer insights that could provide the basis for a message strategy. Account planners work directly with the copywriters and art directors, often sharing responsibility for the creative ideas, instead of apart as traditional researchers have often done. Historically, copywriters have had an aversion to researchers bearing numbers. This in part led some agencies, such as Foote, Cone & Belding, to replace their researchers with account planners. Although account planners use all kinds of information, much of the research effort they manage is qualitative, including **ethnographic studies, one-on-ones, focus groups,** and **projective tests**. The more traditional quantitative research such as surveys, observation, consumer panels and experiments is likely to be done by the advertiser (or a research supplier).

The Role of Qualitative Research

The key to successful qualitative research is to understand both the purpose and the limitations of the various techniques. Qualitative research is usually conducted to *develop* the campaign strategy. It is especially useful in gaining insight on consumers. However, this type of research should not be viewed as a substitute for more rigorous and systematic studies because of the limited size and representativeness of the typical sample, and the difficulty and subjectivity in coding lengthy conversation. Qualitative studies can be useful in providing ideas and in evaluating concepts, ads, and campaigns, but may not be as reliable or valid as a more traditional quantitative study.

Asking Questions. The key to a good interview is to know when and how to ask questions. A good interviewer looks for insight on how the consumer thinks, feels, and acts. The most meaningful information is rarely on the surface. An interviewer must use sensitivity and judgment to ferret out the best pieces of information. Often this information will be used to develop **strategic** and **tactical focal points**. (More about these later.) Interviewers tend to get better with experience; however, If beginners pay attention to the tips in Exhibit 2–4, they should do fine.

One of the main advantages to qualitative research is the opportunity it provides to uncover consumers' underlying thoughts, and feelings, including attitudes, prejudices, biases, and motivations. While it helps to have an experienced interviewer conduct the research, there is a simple technique—called **laddering**— that beginners can use as a tool to link up a product's attributes, or qualities, with the values consumers place on using a particular product.

Laddering. This technique refers to a type of questioning used with depth interviews. An interviewer asks a series of questions designed to trace the relationship between a product's attributes and the value consumers get out of using a product. The technique is based on **Means-End Theory**, which loosely states that consumers use products as the means to achieve various ends. These ends get defined in terms of consumer values.[10] Most consumers respond to a question as to why they use a product, or what they look for in a product, with an answer that focuses on a product's qualities, or attributes. This is a relatively basic or "lower" form of knowledge. However, consumers do not buy products for their attributes, as much as they buy a product for what it can do for them—how it makes them feel. If advertisers can uncover a person's feelings, or how consumers get value out of using a product, they can use this information to develop a message strategy based on emotions rather than on simple product characteristics.

The technique is called laddering because the interviewer keeps asking questions that gradually reveal the relationship between a product's attributes and the value it provides to a consumer. Since an attribute tends to be a physical property, and a value is psychological in nature, the interviewer is moving from a lower form of knowledge to a

Exhibit 2-4   Ten Tips to a Productive Interview

1. **Be yourself.** It is important to make the consumers feel as comfortable as possible. If they sense you are acting in a way that is very different from your normal personality, it could make them feel uneasy. So be yourself—your warm, friendly, serious self.

2. **Briefly tell the consumer about the interview.** Consumers are naturally curious, if not suspicious. Keep the information general but informative. Tell them you are developing an advertising campaign and want their opinions on the product (or category).

3. **Tape record the interview.** After a while interviewees tend to forget about the tape recorder. However, if they see you feverishly taking notes, they may slow down to let you catch up. They may also feel self-conscious.

4. **Give the consumers easy questions to start.** The object is to get the consumers talking easily and naturally. Though the first questions should be easy, they should be open-ended so the interviewee doesn't simply answer the question with a one-word answer.

5. **Avoid leading questions.** If interviewees sense how you might answer a question, they may tell you what they think you want to hear. Be sure to phrase questions without giving any verbal or nonverbal clues as to what your position might be.

6. **Probe. Probe. Probe.** Consumers don't always know why they think, feel, or act a certain way. You'll want to use the word *why* repeatedly to get at deeply seated thoughts and feelings.

7. **Listen carefully to the answers.** Many times inexperienced interviewers will be so busy planning their next question that they will fail to pay attention to details and miss an opportunity to follow up on an important line of questioning.

8. **Make the interviewee work.** Even conscientious interviewees get tired or lazy. After 15 minutes or so, be sensitive to a decrease in the interviewee's attention or interest. Be polite, firm, and persistent. Reward them periodically with positive acknowledgment.

9. **Focus. Focus. Focus.** Interviewers also wear down. Make sure you hear the *last half* of any sentence or phrase.

10. **When finished, say thank you.** It's important you maintain professional standards. Be sure to leave the interviewee feeling positive about the experience.

higher form. In a sense, the interviewer is moving up the "ladder of knowledge" about the product.

Conceptually, the element linking an attribute to a value is a **consequence**. As a result of using a product with certain attributes, consumers usually experience an effect (that is, a consequence). The consumer then interprets this effect in terms of what it means to them (that is, its **value**). These concepts can be further refined. An attribute can be something tangible, or physical (such as flavors, colors, sizes, nutritional ingredients, calories, shapes, and horse power), or it can be something largely intangible, or psychological (such as *sexy* clothing, *funny-looking* toys, *prestigious-looking* automobiles, or *youthful* brand images). Interviewers usually begin their questioning by asking about a product or a brand's attributes.

Consequences can either be functional—more tangible in nature, or psychosocial—more subjective. When the advertising for Silkience shampoo suggests that using the product will leave hair soft, silky, and manageable, it is stressing **functional consequences**. If the advertising stresses how a woman's hair will make people admire her, it is stressing the **psychosocial consequences**. Consequences can also be described from both a negative and positive point of view. Advertisers seldom even imply that using their product will have undesirable consequences, but suggestions that using a competitive product will have negative consequences is a common practice. Advertisers will, however, play up the potential negative consequences of *not* using their product. For example, advertising for Hertz rent-a-cars plays up the negative qualities of a nameless a competitor when they use the tag line, "There's Hertz, and not exactly." In a depth interview, a skillful interviewer will ask consumers why they want to avoid a specific "negative" outcome and then move "up" the means–end chain to questions about positive consequences and eventually about values.

Positive consequences are interpreted in terms of how a consumer **benefits** from using a product. Copywriters put a lot of emphasis on benefits in advertising copy. It is widely believed that consumers buy products more for their benefits than for their attributes. This belief leads some advertisers to *segment* their market, at least in part, in terms of the benefits consumers look for in a product. This approach, called **benefit segmentation**, influences both the message and media strategy. For example, the market for toothpaste consists mostly of consumers who hope to benefit from using a product that prevents cavities, freshens breath, or simply tastes good. Over the years, advertisers have consistently communicated the same general message regarding the benefit they hope to provide to toothpaste users. Some of the benefits and the advertisers that hope to provide them are as follows:

Benefit	↔	**Brand**
Prevents cavities	↔	Crest
Freshens breath	↔	Aquafresh
Tastes good	↔	Aim or Colgate

Students are probably much more familiar with the first two brand/benefit associations because benefit segmentation also influences media strategy. The target market for toothpaste that tastes good is mothers with small children—not college students (even though some college students have small children). Therefore, typical students are much less likely to be exposed to a media message about Aim than Aquafresh.

After the interviewer learns the benefits the consumers are looking for, the questioning can then focus on how the benefits will affect the consumers' state of mind, or **values**.

Some scholars further refine values according to whether they are **instrumental values** (that is, they express preferred modes of conduct and behavior, such as being independent, loving, polite, responsible, or simply having a good time), or they are **terminal values** (that is, they express end states of mind or being such as peacefulness, comfort, self-esteem, security, true friendship, or simply happiness).[11] An experienced interviewer will ladder the questions beginning with inquiries about a brand's attributes and ending with questions that elicit responses that identify the values the respondent hopes to obtain using the product. Figure 2–3 presents the different levels of meaning associated with product usage.

The laddering procedure works best when the interviewer is able to interact with a respondent in a one-on-one situation. With some modification, it can also be used with

Figure 2-3   Levels of Meaning Associated with Product Usage

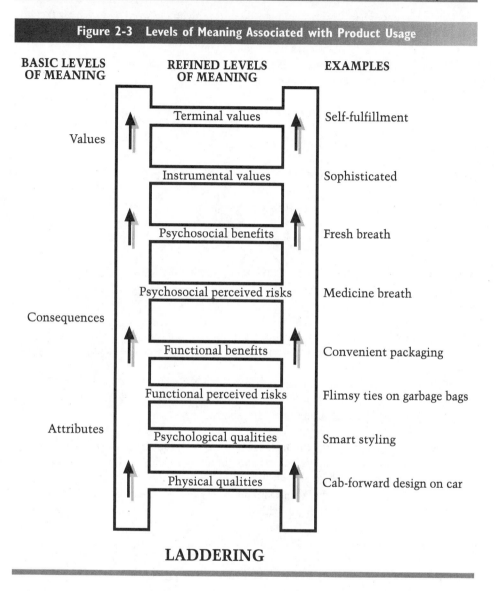

BASIC LEVELS OF MEANING	REFINED LEVELS OF MEANING	EXAMPLES
	Terminal values	Self-fulfillment
Values		
	Instrumental values	Sophisticated
	Psychosocial benefits	Fresh breath
	Psychosocial perceived risks	Medicine breath
Consequences		
	Functional benefits	Convenient packaging
	Functional perceived risks	Flimsy ties on garbage bags
Attributes	Psychological qualities	Smart styling
	Physical qualities	Cab-forward design on car

LADDERING

focus groups. Experienced interviewers use various techniques to elicit distinctions between one level of meaning and another. Respondents may not actually know the answer to a question, or the question may be probing a sensitive area. Sometimes the interviewer can simply redirect the question; other times it maybe helpful to use silence to give the respondent time to think or displace tension. Sometimes it is helpful to change the context of the question from a question involving the interviewee's motives or values, to one involving a third person. Sometimes the laddering procedure will not result in eliciting responses that go beyond consumer benefits.[12]

Often, it is enough to simply begin most questions with the word *why*. Why is that important? Why don't you like that? Why do you think other people will think that? How does that make you feel? What does that mean to you?

The dialogue below presents an example of a laddering technique that was used for a safety razor. The respondent is female.

Interviewer: What do you look for in a razor?

Respondent: One that won't saw my legs off.

Interviewer: What do you mean?

Respondent: I don't like the blades if they're too sharp.

Interviewer: Why?

Respondent: Because I end up cutting my legs up around my knees.

Interviewer: Why?

Respondent: I guess I'm just too impatient. I'm usually in a hurry and half the time I drop the razor and when I go to pick it up I get water in my eyes.

Interviewer: Why do you drop the razor?

Respondent: It just slips out of my hand. It's soapy.

Interviewer: Is it more important to have a razor that isn't too sharp, or would it be better to have a razor that wouldn't slip out of your hands?

Respondent: I guess a razor that won't slip out of my hands. Then I could take more time and do a better job with my legs.

Interviewer: Why is that important?

Respondent: I like the way my legs feel, and I like knowing they look good.

Interviewer: Why?

Respondent: Everybody wants good-looking legs.

Interviewer: Why is that important?

Respondent: It feels good. It just does.

One-on-Ones. The more academic name for this technique is the **depth interview**, but most people in advertising simply call this a one-on-one. This type of interview is generally used when information is going to be difficult to obtain using less-costly techniques such as surveys and focus groups. In these sessions, a trained interviewer interacts with an individual through a variety of loose, unstructured questions. The intent of the interviewer is to uncover hidden meanings, problems, attitudes, motives, and the activities of consumers, while carefully avoiding influencing the respondent. This type of interview is especially appropriate when:

1. a detailed probing of an individual's behavior, attitudes, needs or wants is required;

2. a highly detailed, step-by-step understanding of complicated behavior or decision-making patterns (such as planning the family vacation) are required;

3. the subject matter is of a sensitive or embarrassing nature (such as personal hygiene products);

4. the subject matter is likely to be of a highly confidential nature (such as personal investments);

5. strong, socially acceptable norms exist (such as baby-feeding philosophy) and group interaction may influence responses;

6. the interviews are with professionals (such as finance directors).[13]

Focus Groups. A focus group interview is one of the more useful forms of a depth interview. The typical group consists of from eight to 12 persons, although some major ad agencies report they are using as few as six people. The group' participants are selected and recruited to be representative of the consumer segment thought to be the target audience. The interview generally takes place in a comfortable room, with a trained moderator guiding the discussion. Meetings often last between 1–3 hours; an hour is fairly typical. The session is usually recorded and may even be viewed and videotaped from behind a two-way mirror.

The purpose of the focus group interview is to uncover some of the more hidden thoughts, feelings, and problems consumers have with respect to the product. The moderator follows a prepared rough outline of topical questions to keep the meeting focused on the topic. Moderators take great care not to inhibit discussion. Part of the value of a group interview comes from the interaction of the group's participants. In a productive focus group, participants often make points or ask questions that may not occur to the investigators. Frequently, consumers not only have more answers than investigators, but better questions as well.

Student-directed focus groups sometimes encounter a problem that professionals usually are able to avoid. Experienced moderators know how to subtly steer a discussion to cover all the predetermined topics. Part of the technique involves interjecting a few words, phrases, or short sentences to redirect discussion so that it all appears very natural. This requires the moderator to listen carefully for the right moment to speak. Experience helps, but there is also some skill involved.

Because of a student's lack of experience, he or she is not likely to be as familiar as a trained moderator with the subquestions associated with a topic. This can come across as awkwardness, especially because there is usually some nervousness associated with moderating a focus group for the first time. This problem can be intensified if the student also begins to worry about when to introduce the next question, and how to phrase it so that the transition from one topic to another question is a smooth one.

One solution is to have two student moderators. The first student asks a question and then listens intently for the right moment to introduce appropriate prompting comments. Meanwhile, the other student is following the conversation and mentally preparing for the next general question. When the moment is right, the second student asks the next general question as well as makes the subtle comments that generate the freewheeling atmosphere characteristic of successful focus group interviews. From that moment on, the two students alternate questions.

Projective Tests. This form of qualitative research is another good way to learn about the consumer, but it is also a powerful way to get information about the product so it will be discussed in Chapter 3 under "Product Analysis."

Survey Research

Although qualitative research is very good at generating ideas and providing insight on the consumer, the analyst usually runs a risk that the research findings may not be generalizable to a larger population base. Primarily for this reason, a more rigorous study involving survey research is frequently appropriate.

Survey research tends to imply the use of a questionnaire. The research is usually very structured, quantifiable, and can be administered by less skilled personnel. This type of research is more likely to be administered by the advertiser or a private research company rather than an advertising agency. Among the most popular methods of acquiring data are telephone interviews, personal interviews, self-administered questionnaires, and mail questionnaires.

Telephone Interviews. This technique is particularly useful in studies that require a broad cross section of the population such as a national sample. Its relatively low cost is sometimes offset by the difficulty of keeping individuals talking on the phone longer than 15 minutes. This method has largely replaced door-to-door personal interviews. It is widely used in advertising tracking studies that are designed to assess awareness levels, attitudes, and product usage. According to a survey of 140 corporate marketing research directors, telephone interviewing, especially used in conjunction with a Wide Area Telephone Service (WATS) system, was one of the two most popular data-collection techniques, the other being the mall intercept.[14]

Mall Intercepts. This is the most popular form of the personal interview. Respondents are either interviewed on the spot or escorted to a private area within the mall. Students often use a variation of this technique and interview consumers outside the mall since it is usually time consuming and difficult to secure permission to go inside. Although personal interviews can take place anywhere, including the home, malls offer many advantages. This approach is especially useful when the testing procedure requires getting consumer reaction to visual stimuli such as packaging, name change alternatives, advertising concepts, and advertisements. The interviewer usually works from a questionnaire, and large numbers of consumers can be interviewed in a relatively small period of time. Less skilled personnel can administer the questionnaire.

The major disadvantage of this method is the representativeness of the sample. People who visit shopping malls are not necessarily representative of the rest of the population. On the other hand, mall shoppers are often precisely the cross section of the population many advertisers are interested in reaching. A variation of the mall intercept is the

after-purchase intercept where consumers are interviewed after they have purchased a product.

Self-administered Questionnaires. As a general rule, it is much better to have an interviewer fill out the questionnaire than the consumer. This puts the interviewer in control of the flow of information and reduces the likelihood of misunderstood questions. The interviewer can also control the pacing of questions and answers, thereby helping to ensure that the questions on the second half of a questionnaire receive the same consideration as earlier ones.

There are two basic types of self-administered instruments: a **leave-behind questionnaire,** and a **hand-delivered questionnaire.** With the first type of questionnaire, consumers are invited to fill out a form at some central location, usually a retail store or a restaurant. To work well, some control should be maintained over which respondents fill the form out. The second type of self-administered questionnaire works much better.

With this method, a data collector personally delivers a questionnaire to the home of a preselected respondent who has been offered an incentive. The data collector informs the consumer that the questionnaire will be picked up after a period of time, usually a week. This second step helps to improve the representativeness of the sample, a major problem with self-administered questionnaires. This procedure is the primary method the Simmons Market Research Bureau uses to collect data on product usage, and is especially useful and cost effective when a large amount of information is to be collected.

Mail Questionnaires. This method of gathering data is used primarily because of its low cost. A questionnaire can be mailed to potential respondents, attached to a product in the marketplace, or included within the body of a magazine or newspaper. The main disadvantage of this method occurs with both nonresponses, and the representativeness of the respondents filling out the questionnaire. It is very difficult to determine the extent to which nonrespondents are similar to respondents on the variables that influence product usage, even if you match up both groups on the basis of demographic and psychographic criteria.

This mail questionnaire is actually a variation of the self-administered questionnaire and has many of the same advantages and disadvantages. Some control over nonresponse is gained if the sampling units have been recruited to participate in a consumer panel. National Family Opinion, Research Inc. (NFO) is a leader in this area and uses the mail questionnaire successfully with an active panel base of over 550,000 U.S. households. However, one recurring criticism of panels in general is that even if cooperation can be maintained over panel participants, it is often a more difficult task to get a representative cross section of the appropriate population to join the panel.

This method can be effective if the company offers the consumer a sufficient incentive to complete the questionnaire. To reduce nonresponses, some companies include a product sample with the questionnaire and offer to send the consumer additional coupons upon completion of the questionnaire. Other companies ask customers to fill out mail questionnaires when turning in their warrantee agreements for new product purchases. Companies use this approach as a major source of information in developing a database on their customers. A major variation of the mail questionnaire is the **diary,** which companies use to collect information on consumer purchases. Marketing Research Corporation of America (MRCA) is a company that uses the diary method to monitor the purchasing habits of its consumer panel consisting of 7,500 households.

A Rationale for Conducting the Research in Sequence

There is really no rigid pattern to the order in which professionals conduct their research. However, there may be *some* rationale for students to do their research in the following order:

1. One-on-ones

2. Focus groups and other qualitative studies

3. Surveys

4. More studies as needed

We recommend starting your research with one-on-ones. If you don't have much experience with either the product category or the brand, one-on-ones can give you some depth on how consumers think and interact with the product and/or brand. The background you pick up here can then be used to develop questions for the focus groups or other studies. And the best part for students is that they are a lot more convenient to conduct. After focus group studies are complete, the findings can be used to develop questions for a

Campaign Progress Checklist

At this point in the campaign you should generally be aware of the following points:

1. The most efficient way to begin a campaign is to prepare an outline of the research plan.

2. We suggest doing the background analysis in the following order: company and consumer analyses first, followed by those dealing with the market, product, and the competition.

3. To be competitive, information should be more than descriptive—it should be insightful.

4. Whether you do a SWOT analysis or focus on problems and opportunities, examine the critical issues in the analysis and relate them to problems and opportunities. These will provide the basis for the objectives you set later.

5. In a company analysis, the history of the company is far less important than the history of the company's problems and opportunities.

6. In the company analysis, it's also helpful to look at industry or generic sales trends.

7. It's not only important to know who uses a product or brand, but also why and how they use it.

8. Laddering techniques help uncover how a product's attributes influence the value consumers get out of using a product.

9. One-on-ones and focus group research are a good way to get ideas for strategy and executions, but the findings are not generalizable to the population as a whole.

10. Survey research is a good way to assess the degree to which a finding exists in the overall population, but the results may only be as good as the sample from which the study is drawn.

possible survey. The goal is to get information and ideas from the one-on-ones and focus groups, and then use surveys to assess the extent to which the findings exist among the target audience or the population as a whole. Remember, information obtained from one-on-ones and focus groups is fine for ideas, but it does not mean you can generalize from individuals or small groups to a larger consumer base, such as the target audience. Following the survey research, you will probably want to continue to do research as needed.

COMPLETING THE COMPANY AND CONSUMER ANALYSES

Although this chapter is coming to a close, it does not mean that the company and consumer analyses are complete. Many of the analytical techniques to be discussed in Chapter 3 will shed additional light on the company and consumer. For example, many of the sources of information on the company can and should be used to gain insight on the competition, and many of the techniques recommended for the competitive analysis will also be of value in analyzing the company. It is also worth noting that many of the tests used to evaluate the product say as much about the consumer as they do about the product. In short, although we have separated the situation analysis into distinct sections, the information-gathering efforts described in each section should be used to further the search for insight on the problems and opportunities facing the company. This means that in the event the research foundation is separated into sections and assigned to different members of a team, information should be shared so that each section benefits from the cross-fertilization of the information obtained from other areas.

Notes and References

[1]Serafin, R., & Johnson, B. (1993, October 18). Saturn-alia in Springhill next summer. *Advertising Age, 1*, p. 55.

[2]SRI International, *Values and lifestyles.* Menlo Park, CA: SRI International, 1998.

[3]SRI International.

[4]For more information, see William C. Johnson, Sales promotion: It's come down to "push marketing." *Marketing News* (April, 1998), p. 2.

[5]Curry, D. J. (1993). *The new marketing research systems: How to use strategic database information for better marketing decisions.* New York: John Wiley & Sons, p. 86.

[6]Engel, J. F., Warshaw, M.R., & Kinnear, T. C. (1994). *Promotional strategy: Managing the marketing communications process* (8th ed.) Burr Ridge, IL: Irwin, p. 14.

[7]Koselka, R. (1994, September 12). It's my favorite statistic. *Forbes,* p. 162.

[8]This information is based on written material from Michael Robinson, Research Director, Euro RSCG Tatham.

[9]For more information, see Lisa Fortini-Campbell, *Hitting the sweet spot: The consumer insight workbook* (2nd ed.). Chicago: The Copy Workshop, 1992, pp. 159–170.

[10]Gutman, J. (1982, Spring). A means-end chain model based on consumer categorization processes. *Journal of Marketing, 46*, pp. 60–72.

[11]Milton J. Rokeach as quoted in J. Paul Peter and Jerry C. Olson, *Consumer behavior and marketing strategy* (2nd ed.). Homewood, IL: Irwin, 1987, p. 78.

[12]Reynolds, T. J. & Gutman, J. (1988, February/March). Laddering theory, method, analysis, and interpretation. *Journal of Advertising Research,* p. 16.

[13]Tull, D. S., & Hawkins, D. I. (1987). *Marketing research: Measurement and method* (4th ed.). New York: Macmillan Publishing Co., p. 311.

[14]Dillon, W. R., Madden, T. J., & Firtle,N. H. (1993). *Essentials of marketing research.* Homewood, IL: Irwin, p. 154.

Chapter 3

The Research Foundation II: Market, Product, and Competitive Analyses

THE MARKET ANALYSIS

It is widely understood in the advertising business that the mass market is becoming increasingly fragmented. This change does not necessarily mean that the role of national advertising has diminished. Rather, it underscores the importance of giving extra attention to local markets. One common line used with many variations is "Think globally, but act like a retailer."

The basic purpose of the market analysis is to determine the geographic areas that warrant special attention, either because they are problems or because they are most likely to respond favorably to the company's marketing communication program. In a sense, this section is merely an extension of the consumer analysis. Advertisers treat this topic separately for two reasons: (1) to help organize additional sources of information that focus primarily on geographic data, although they may include demographic and psychographic data; and (2) to help media planners identify geographic areas where they should allocate media dollars. The second point is becoming an important consideration as marketers increasingly narrow the focus of their communication strategy and look for markets that need extra emphasis.

A word of clarification: The term "market" may be used both to indicate a geographic area and as a descriptive term to refer to a population segment, such as a Hispanic market. The words *target market* usually refer to both a population segment and a geographic area.

In some plans, a market analysis would be referred to as a "geographic analysis." That is common and acceptable. We prefer using the word *market* for our section because it connotes a place where sales take place and where consumers live and buy.

Product-Usage Data

The importance of a market is usually determined by the amount of product usage and the number of current users in the area. If this information is unavailable or hard to come by, planners will usually select a market on the basis of the demographic and/or psychographic characteristics of the consumers living in the area. Wherever possible, however, purchase behavior should be used as a predictor of future sales.

A good place to start the analysis is with sales data that are internal to the company. If the company has analyzed its sales geographically, this information is likely to be available from the marketing department. If not, then the task will be far more difficult to accomplish.

The amount and type of information will vary from company to company and usually depend on the research suppliers with whom the company works. For students, the information they can get usually depends on who is providing it and what the sources are willing to share. A student may be limited to what is available in a university library. Unfortunately, many important sources of market information, including share-of-market data, and resource tools, such as AC Nielsen's SCANTRACK and IRI's InfoScan, are not likely to be found in libraries. If the information is available, a common use of the data is to construct index numbers that indicate the relative value of a market.

Index Numbers

Index numbers are widely used measures to indicate a market's sales potential. In this section, we briefly look at three types of indexes: (1) product-usage index numbers cross-referenced by the geographic areas reported by the Simmons Market Research Bureau (SMRB); (2) a buying-power index, usually developed from data in the Sales & Marketing Management Survey of Buying Power; and (3) a brand-development index and its companion, a category-development index.

Simmons Market Research Bureau (SMRB). SMRB provides information on product usage for some 800 brands, products, and services and cross-references them by broad classifications of geographic areas. The areas include nine geographic regions of the country (such as Midwest), four classifications of county size (such as County Size A), three metropolitan categories (such as Metro Central City), and three areas of dominant influence (ADI) categories (such as Top 5 ADIs). The product–usage data are broken down by total usage and the percentage usage accounted for by the geographic segment. Of special interest are the index numbers for the geographic segments that indicate relative product usage. These numbers may be used as a rough predictor of sales potential. Mediamark Research, Inc. (MRI), provides data similar to those of Simmons.

Buying-Power Index (BPI). This index is another handy measure that can be used to help predict sales potential. It is typically developed from data provided by Sales & Marketing Management *Survey of Buying Power* (see below), but can also be compiled from data from a variety of sources. The BPI is a multiple-factor index that uses a number of statistics associated with a market to indicate sales potential. The *Survey of Buying Power* uses population, effective buying income (also called disposable income), and retail sales for its calculations. The *Survey of Buying Power* devotes a page in each issue to take readers step by step through the procedures for calculating a BPI—including how to allocate weights (that is, emphasis) to various factors. Another source for market statistics is SRDS (see below).

Sales & Marketing Management (S&MM). This useful source is available in most libraries, in part because it is relatively inexpensive. It's published monthly, but the most useful issue for market information is the August issue's survey of buying power (see Figure 3–1). This issue provides statistical information on each state, according to Metropolitan Statistical Areas (MSA), counties, and many of the larger cities. Statistics are provided for population, age groups, number of households, effective buying income (EBI), and retail sales for six types of retail stores (food, eating and drinking, general merchandise, furniture/furnishings/appliances, automotive, and drug).

S&MM also produces a special *Survey of Media Markets*. This coverage provides statistics for geographical areas according to designated market areas (DMAs, which are Arbitron's designation for the 211 TV markets). Additionally, S&MM provides a ranking of metropolitan areas for each of 10 retail merchandise lines. Figure 3–1 presents part of a typical page from the *Survey of Buying Power*.

SRDS. In the monthly volumes covering spot radio, spot television, and newspapers, SRDS publishes market information similar to the statistics in the *Survey of Buying Power*. Data are presented for population, households, and effective buying income for the United States, geographic regions, and each state.

Brand Development Index and Category Development Index. The brand development index (BDI) and category development index (CDI) must be calculated using information from various sources. They indicate how well a brand performs in a market relative to the number of people living in the area. So, in an average market, if that market accounts for 1% of the total population, it might be expected to account for 1% of a brand's or a category's total sales. The formula looks like this:

$$\frac{\% \text{ of a brand's total U.S. sales in a market} \times 100}{\% \text{ of total U.S. population in a market}} = \text{BDI}$$

If the index number is greater than 100, it means that the brand is doing above average in this market. If the number is less than 100, the brand is not doing as well proportionally in this market as it is doing in other areas. In either case, the reasons for success in one market or a below-par performance in another should be investigated, if at all possible. A major reason a brand does well is because sales in the generic category are high. To assess this effect, a category development index can be calculated. The formula is as follows:

$$\frac{\% \text{ of a category's total U.S. sales in a market} \times 100}{\% \text{ of total population in a market}} = \text{CDI}$$

If the index number is greater than 100, a preliminary judgment will be that the market is receptive to the product (that is, the category). If the number is less than 100, it does

Figure 3-1 A Typical Page from the Survey of Buying Power

METRO & COUNTY TOTALS

OHIO CON'T.

Population · Retail Sales By Store Group ($000)

METRO AREA COUNTY City	Total Population (000s)	% of Population by Age Group 18-24	25-34	35-49	50 +	House-holds (000s)	Total Retail Sales	Food	Eating & Drinking Places	General Mdse.	Furniture/ Furnish. Appliance	Auto-motive
Lakewood	54.8	8.2	19.4	22.9	25.8	25.1	338,522	64,991	44,851	4,674	10,719	150,984
Parma	85.7	7.0	15.4	20.9	35.2	34.2	945,883	158,370	94,020	150,038	50,088	224,349
GEAUGA	84.4	6.7	12.0	27.1	25.7	28.3	588,814	129,416	57,238	21,003	33,547	169,645
LAKE	223.0	7.6	15.1	25.1	27.1	84.1	2,875,071	400,192	222,278	492,330	157,712	856,478
•Mentor	51.0	6.9	14.2	28.4	23.2	18.3	1,221,020	105,397	75,548	309,425	111,152	310,327
LORAIN	284.3	8.6	14.1	23.7	26.1	100.4	2,521,582	331,666	259,549	362,455	119,750	795,254
•Elyria	56.6	8.8	15.9	22.0	25.6	21.3	867,066	78,880	71,530	278,251	69,964	154,934
•Lorain	70.3	7.9	14.4	20.7	28.1	25.7	346,757	52,356	48,568	9,542	14,697	105,671
MEDINA	140.4	7.2	13.7	27.0	23.5	48.1	1,376,970	179,389	91,698	247,020	36,250	465,925
CLEVELAND-AKRON CONSOLIDATED AREA	2,918.2	8.3	14.4	23.3	28.8	1,123.6	27,697,072	4,185,593	3,116,229	3,150,512	1,563,508	7,260,833
COLUMBUS	1,452.3	10.6	16.8	23.8	23.4	553.7	18,613,646	2,756,537	1,901,801	2,415,498	972,584	4,404,898
DELAWARE	83.2	8.2	13.5	27.6	23.2	29.0	566,457	116,456	51,244	35,932	17,756	191,585
FAIRFIELD	120.2	8.4	13.3	25.3	25.9	42.7	863,584	248,340	93,572	72,867	40,432	204,863
•Lancaster	36.0	8.5	14.2	21.1	31.6	14.6	576,992	172,326	61,533	66,870	32,802	122,386
FRANKLIN	1,016.3	11.5	17.6	23.2	22.5	400.9	15,295,049	2,042,287	1,563,154	2,066,070	860,102	3,535,068
•Columbus	626.3	13.8	19.8	21.5	20.6	255.1	9,853,361	1,146,557	927,191	1,607,290	566,194	1,989,630
LICKING	138.5	8.5	13.9	24.1	27.1	51.3	1,269,661	225,894	120,227	176,756	40,728	321,665
•Newark	45.2	8.3	15.4	20.7	29.6	18.3	517,036	86,747	47,563	90,617	10,355	172,901
MADISON	41.0	9.2	18.1	24.8	23.2	13.2	244,267	47,967	20,212	13,543	2,107	76,884
PICKAWAY	53.1	9.3	17.5	25.4	24.2	16.6	374,628	75,593	53,392	50,330	11,459	74,833
DAYTON-SPRINGFIELD	949.6	9.3	14.4	23.6	27.3	364.2	9,492,745	1,674,100	1,027,133	1,296,576	537,858	2,379,753
CLARK	147.6	8.9	12.7	23.4	29.2	55.5	1,232,185	243,279	127,930	176,741	69,784	288,541
•Springfield	69.8	10.7	13.5	20.9	28.6	27.2	742,961	178,720	86,639	98,740	25,883	173,576
GREENE	139.6	11.8	13.3	24.7	24.4	49.4	1,477,822	252,762	160,648	169,051	33,740	462,384
•Fairborn	28.5	15.7	16.5	20.8	23.7	11.6	385,694	63,086	54,056	42,897	4,156	141,647
MIAMI	97.9	7.5	13.3	24.5	27.9	36.5	940,237	182,122	102,003	112,900	51,422	296,142
MONTGOMERY	564.5	9.1	15.3	23.0	27.6	222.8	5,842,501	995,937	636,552	837,884	382,912	1,332,686
•Dayton	173.9	11.9	15.9	19.6	26.5	69.3	1,037,862	186,805	143,434	123,429	52,062	238,722
Kettering	58.2	7.6	15.4	22.2	33.3	25.2	575,381	96,049	73,249	94,062	41,195	105,968

Effective Buying Income

METRO AREA COUNTY City	Total EBI ($000)	Median Hsld. EBI	% of Hslds: by EBI Group A $20,000- $34,999	B $35,000- $49,999	C $50,000 & Over	Buying Power Index
Lakewood	996,785	32,349	26.3	20.3	25.8	.0202
Parma	1,425,348	37,937	24.0	23.4	31.6	.0351
GEAUGA	1,646,306	47,293	18.9	19.5	46.8	.0333
LAKE	3,855,117	40,415	22.8	22.0	36.3	.0980
•Mentor	944,358	47,479	18.3	21.6	46.7	.0300
LORAIN	4,061,193	35,681	23.1	20.6	30.4	.1007
•Elyria	765,368	30,922	27.4	20.2	22.6	.0240
•Lorain	851,966	27,659	23.3	19.0	20.8	.0197
MEDINA	2,321,430	43,334	20.4	21.2	40.8	.0552
CLEVELAND-AKRON CONSOLIDATED AREA	47,118,450	34,306	22.7	18.9	30.1	1.1214
COLUMBUS	24,473,270	36,402	23.3	19.2	32.7	.6291
DELAWARE	1,672,888	45,468	18.7	19.6	44.3	.0332
FAIRFIELD	1,858,237	36,703	23.3	18.9	33.4	.0418
•Lancaster	472,949	26,683	29.5	17.1	18.0	.0154

Effective Buying Income

METRO AREA COUNTY City	Total EBI ($000)	Median Hsld. EBI	% of Hslds: by EBI Group A $20,000- $34,999	B $35,000- $49,999	C $50,000 & Over	Buying Power Index
FRANKLIN	17,513,716	35,915	23.5	18.9	32.3	.4725
•Columbus	9,678,658	31,847	25.4	19.0	26.0	.2830
LICKING	2,109,291	35,331	23.3	20.6	29.9	.0512
•Newark	631,910	27,710	25.9	18.4	20.5	.0173
MADISON	576,071	35,317	26.4	20.3	30.1	.0129
PICKAWAY	743,067	36,337	23.5	20.6	31.3	.0175
DAYTON-SPRINGFIELD	15,452,712	35,803	22.6	19.5	31.6	.3724
CLARK	2,135,363	32,876	23.6	19.9	26.9	.0518
•Springfield	880,338	25,621	25.0	17.6	18.1	.0248
GREENE	2,406,053	42,854	19.4	19.4	40.6	.0574
•Fairborn	452,326	33,620	22.5	20.5	27.4	.0123
MIAMI	1,615,315	37,743	23.4	20.8	33.2	.0382
MONTGOMERY	9,295,981	34,811	23.0	19.2	30.5	.2250
•Dayton	2,030,326	23,473	24.2	16.1	16.4	.0500
Kettering	1,239,168	39,890	23.3	21.8	35.7	.0262

not necessarily mean that the market is not receptive to the category, but only that the market does not use the product to the same degree as do other markets. This situation calls for further analysis. Is there sufficient distribution in the market? Do the dealers in the market use low, medium, or high levels of promotional support in the market, especially sales promotion? How new is the product to the area? If marketing promotional levels have been weak, it may indicate a marketing opportunity that can be taken advantage of simply through an increase in promotional support. The essential point to understand is that CDIs and BDIs are a way to get you thinking about the relative importance of a market. They should not be used as the only justification for deciding the degree of promotional effort to use in an area.

The next important step is to compare the BDI number to the CDI number. If the BDI is lower than the CDI and both indexes are still greater than 100, that means that the brand and the category are doing well, but consumers are more receptive to competitive brands. This finding is generally perceived as an opportunity because it is usually much easier to get consumers to switch brands than to get them to use a product for the first time. However, it would be a mistake to assume that a high BDI and a higher CDI automatically mean a marketing opportunity. In all cases, the analyst should take a close look at the market and assess the amount of promotional support in a market as well as the history of the market's response to promotions.

Demographic and Psychographic Data

Assessing market opportunities on the basis of product usage is the first step. The next step is to take the demographic and psychographic characteristics of the current users and look for similar characteristics in geographic areas around the country. Generally, the smaller the area you can identify, the more useful the information. *Simmons* and *MRI*, for example, provide demographic information on a regional basis, while some so-called geodemographic companies, such as Claritas, Inc. (with its PRIZM program), and CACI Marketing Systems (with its ACORN Clustering System), provide information on areas as small as block groups (250–550 households), blocks (25–50 households), and ZIP+4s (6–25 households).

Between the geodemographic sources and *Simmons* and *MRI* in terms of value are two syndicated sources of market information that are increasingly available in libraries: The *Lifestyle Market Analyst,* published by SRDS, and the *Sourcebook of ZIP Code Demographics,* published by CACI Marketing Systems.

SRDS's *Lifestyle Market Analyst* is a relatively new source of information. It is becoming increasingly available at university libraries. This source provides demographic and lifestyle information on the DMAs, including county breakouts for the 10 largest DMAs. It includes a profile for each of 68 lifestyle interests, cross-referenced to the 211 DMAs. Figure 3–2 shows how demographic information is presented for the Lincoln & Hastings–Kearney, plus NE market, and Figure 3–3 presents the lifestyle information on Gainesville, FL.

The *Sourcebook of ZIP Code Demographics*, published by CACI, contains statistics on all residential ZIP Codes in the United States. For each ZIP Code, it provides information on population, gender, age distribution, race, people of Hispanic origin, various kinds of household information, and family and household income. The information comes primarily from the U.S. Census, but also includes CACI's own estimates. A statistical summary is provided for each state.

Geodemographic Data

Geodemographic analyses are based on the principle that people who live in the same neighborhood tend to have similar characteristics. There are three major geodemographic

Figure 3-2 Demographic Market Profile from Lincoln & Hastings-Kearney

Lincoln & Hastings-Kearney, Plus, NE

Demographics
Base Index US = 100

Total Adult Population 486,771

Occupation	Population	%	Index
Administrative	60,846	12.5	92
Blue Collar	66,688	13.7	121
Clerical	44,783	9.2	101
Homemaker	67,661	13.9	101
Professional/Technical	112,444	23.1	91
Retired	80,804	16.6	99
Sales/Marketing	22,391	4.6	84
Self Employed	18,011	3.7	148
Student	12,656	2.6	130

Education (1990 Census)			
Elementary (0-8 years)	34,878	8.7	84
High School (1-3 years)	39,689	9.9	69
High School (4 years)	142,318	35.5	118
College (1-3 years)	111,449	27.8	112
College (4+ years)	72,562	18.1	89

Race/Ethnicity			
White	463,893	95.3	131
Black	4,381	0.9	7
Asian	4,868	1.0	29
Hispanic	11,196	2.3	21
American Indian	1,460	0.3	43
Other	974	0.2	200

Total Households 252,056

Age of Head of Household	Households	%	Index
18-24 years old	18,148	7.2	141
25-34 years old	45,370	18.0	95
35-44 years old	52,932	21.0	91
45-54 years old	40,329	16.0	89
55-64 years old	28,986	11.5	92
65-74 years old	31,759	12.6	104
75 years and older	34,784	13.8	137
Median Age	47.4 years		

Sex/Marital Status			
Single Male	45,370	18.0	90
Single Female	55,200	21.9	91
Married	151,486	60.1	108

Children At Home			
At Least One Child	89,984	35.7	103
Child Age Under 2	8,822	3.5	106
Child Age 2-4	23,189	9.2	102
Child Age 5-7	23,441	9.3	102
Child Age 8-10	23,945	9.5	108
Child Age 11-12	17,392	6.9	106
Child Age 13-15	26,970	10.7	115
Child Age 16-18	26,214	10.4	118

Home Ownership			
Owner	169,382	67.2	103
Renter	82,674	32.8	95

Stage in Family Lifecycle	Households	%	Index
Single, 18-34, No Children	29,743	11.8	104
Single, 35-44, "	11,090	4.4	75
Single, 45-64, "	15,627	6.2	70
Single, 65+ "	24,954	9.9	111
Married, 18-34, "	10,586	4.2	100
Married, 35-44, "	6,049	2.4	77
Married, 45-64, "	31,759	12.6	98
Married, 65+ "	32,767	13.0	124
Single, Any Child at Home	19,660	7.8	84
Married, Child Age Under 13	36,800	14.6	102
Married, Child Age 13-18	33,523	13.3	121

Household Income			
Under $20,000	71,332	28.3	108
$20,000-$29,999	42,093	16.7	117
$30,000-$39,999	37,556	14.9	115
$40,000-$49,999	29,238	11.6	105
$50,000-$74,999	44,362	17.6	93
$75,000-$99,999	15,375	6.1	71
$100,000 and over	12,099	4.8	62
Median Income	**$33,374**		

Income Earners			
Married, One Income	59,485	23.6	98
Married, Two Incomes	92,000	36.5	115
Single	100,570	39.9	90

Dual Income Households			
Children Age Under 13 years	26,718	10.6	116
Children Age 13-18 years	26,718	10.6	134
No Children	38,565	15.3	103

Age By Income			
18-34, Income under $30,000	34,532	13.7	122
35-44, "	16,132	6.4	100
45-64, "	19,912	7.9	90
65+ "	42,597	16.9	121
18-34, Income $30,000-$49,999	16,888	6.7	105
35-44, "	16,888	6.7	110
45-64, "	19,660	7.8	108
65+ "	13,107	5.2	118
18-34, Income $50,000-$74,999	8,570	3.4	83
35-44, "	12,855	5.1	89
45-64, "	16,636	6.6	93
65+ "	6,301	2.5	114
18-34, Income $75,000 and over	3,277	1.3	54
35-44, "	6,806	2.7	54
45-64, "	12,855	5.1	70
65+ "	4,285	1.7	106

Credit Card Usage			
Travel/Entertainment	16,132	6.4	49
Bank Card	193,075	76.6	101
Gas/Department Store	59,737	23.7	78
No Credit Cards	48,395	19.2	111

Figure 3-3   Lifestyles Market Profile from Gainesville, FL

Lifestyles
Base Index US = 100

Gainesville, FL

The Top Ten Lifestyles Ranked by Index

Science/New Technology	160	Attend Cultural/Arts Events	127
Career-Oriented Activities	143	Wildlife/Environmental	127
Tennis Frequently	131	Bicycling Frequently	124
Running/Jogging	130	Use an IBM Compatible	124
Science Fiction	130	Use a Personal Computer	120

Home Life	Households	%	Index	Rank	Sports, Fitness & Health	Households	%	Index	Rank
Avid Book Reading	38,001	38.0	106	41	Bicycling Frequently	24,401	24.4	124	22
Bible/Devotional Reading	20,401	20.4	107	114	Dieting/Weight Control	22,101	22.1	94	174
Flower Gardening	32,901	32.9	89	190	Golf	17,701	17.7	86	136
Grandchildren	18,901	18.9	79	201	Health/Natural Foods	19,201	19.2	107	35
Home Furnishing/Decorating	20,501	20.5	83	208	Improving Your Health	24,601	24.6	104	35
House Plants	31,101	31.1	95	183	Physical Fitness/Exercise	40,801	40.8	111	14
Own a Cat	31,601	31.6	117	48	Running/Jogging	15,600	15.6	130	17
Own a Dog	39,701	39.7	112	116	Snow Skiing Frequently	4,700	4.7	59	137
Shop by Catalog/Mail	56,602	56.6	104	75	Tennis Frequently	8,100	8.1	131	13
Subscribe to Cable TV	62,702	62.7	96	146	Walking for Health	28,801	28.8	85	208
Vegetable Gardening	20,901	20.9	84	190	Watching Sports on TV	39,601	39.6	102	74

Good Life	Households	%	Index	Rank	Hobbies & Interests	Households	%	Index	Rank
Attend Cultural/Arts Events	20,701	20.7	127	7	Automotive Work	13,900	13.9	95	191
Fashion Clothing	12,800	12.8	88	131	Buy Pre-Recorded Videos	18,101	18.1	94	177
Fine Art/Antiques	12,500	12.5	107	26	Career-Oriented Activities	13,200	13.2	143	3
Foreign Travel	15,600	15.6	109	31	Coin/Stamp Collecting	6,800	6.8	97	168
Frequent Flyer	21,901	21.9	106	40	Collectibles/Collections	12,200	12.2	88	192
Gourmet Cooking/Fine Foods	19,801	19.8	108	33	Community/Civic Activities	9,700	9.7	92	190
Own a Vacation Home/Property	9,900	9.9	97	83	Crafts	25,501	25.5	95	178
Travel for Business	19,401	19.4	103	56	Current Affairs/Politics	15,900	15.9	100	62
Travel for Pleasure/Vacation	39,701	39.7	93	137	Home Workshop	24,901	24.9	95	188
Travel in USA	35,201	35.2	94	119	Military Veteran in Household	23,401	23.4	92	179
Wines	14,400	14.4	102	48	Needlework/Knitting	12,900	12.9	88	196
					Our Nation's Heritage	5,200	5.2	100	122
Investing & Money					Self-Improvement	19,801	19.8	108	27
Casino Gambling	7,300	7.3	49	194	Sewing	15,700	15.7	98	171
Entering Sweepstakes	17,101	17.1	99	143	Supports Health Charities	19,601	19.6	86	155
Moneymaking Opportunities	11,400	11.4	95	141	High Tech Activities				
Real Estate Investments	6,800	6.8	99	77					
Stock/Bond Investments	17,101	17.1	83	157	Electronics	14,300	14.3	119	9
					Home Video Games	14,300	14.3	102	110
Great Outdoors					Listen to Records/Tapes/CDs	49,701	49.7	108	16
					Own a CD Player	66,402	66.4	108	16
Boating/Sailing	12,400	12.4	114	48	Photography	18,601	18.6	108	39
Camping/Hiking	23,401	23.4	92	149	Science Fiction	12,000	12.0	130	5
Fishing Frequently	27,401	27.4	100	165	Science/New Technology	14,900	14.9	160	2
Hunting/Shooting	12,600	12.6	78	188	Use a Personal Computer	54,702	54.7	120	15
Motorcycles	7,500	7.5	91	164	Use an Apple/Macintosh	9,900	9.9	114	34
Recreational Vehicles	7,900	7.9	84	187	Use an IBM Compatible	51,002	51.0	124	7
Wildlife/Environmental	20,801	20.8	127	13	VCR Recording	18,101	18.1	95	171

computer-programming systems: PRIZM by Claritas, ACORN Clustering System by CACI, and Equifax/National Decision Systems' MicroVision. Each of these systems classifies geographical units of varying sizes according to information obtained from the U.S. Census Bureau. These areas are then delineated using demographic and behavioral data obtained from the U.S. Census, syndicated research sources such as *Simmons* and *MRI*, and the system's own proprietary data-gathering procedures. The systems group areas throughout the United States with similar characteristics into categories so that advertisers can target geographically only those areas that contain their target audience (for example, affluent neighborhoods).

The newest generation of geodemographic systems can be linked to other research databases, including media consumption research, UPC scanner data, consumer panels, and lifestyle typologies (such as VALS). This kind of linkage means that an advertiser could define a target audience in terms of demographic and psychographic characteristics and then identify specifically where these consumers can be found geographically. The primary geographic unit is the postal ZIP Code; hence the use of these systems is often called **ZIP-Code marketing.** We'll examine the oldest and one of the most widely used systems: PRIZM.

PRIZM. This system has been around since the early 1970s and has evolved since then along with the increasing sophistication of the data in the U.S. Census. In the 1990s, Claritas factor analyzed the dozens of demographic and lifestyle variables in the census into six broad categories that represent most of the variance among different neighborhood types. These categories are

Social rank (income, employment, education)
Household composition (age, sex, family type, dependency status)
Mobility (length of residency by owner or renter, auto ownership)
Ethnicity (race, foreign birth, ancestry, language)
Urbanization (population and housing density, such as urban, suburban, small city, town, rural)
Housing (owner/renter status, home values, number of stories)

These six categories are then statistically analyzed to produce 62 so-called neighborhood types. Each of these neighborhood types has been assigned a nickname, such as blueblood estates, executive suites, and pools and patios.[1] PRIZM uses maps and computer software to describe the location of these neighborhood types. The geographical areas are based on a comprehensive, computerized, digitatized street map of the United States that was used in the 1990 census and known by the acronym TIGER (for Topographically Integrated Geographic Coding and Referencing System).

The 62 neighborhood types, or clusters, are also grouped into larger clusters called a social group. Figure 3–4 presents the 15 social groups that represent almost all of the households in the United States.

Each social group is described in words, such as Elite Suburbs. The number under each social group indicates the number of the clusters in each category. For example, the Elite Suburbs, social group S1, consists of five clusters, numbers 01 through 05. Figure 3–5 presents a summary of the demographic and lifestyle characteristics of each of the clusters in this social group. (Note that these are not the five wealthiest neighborhood types.)

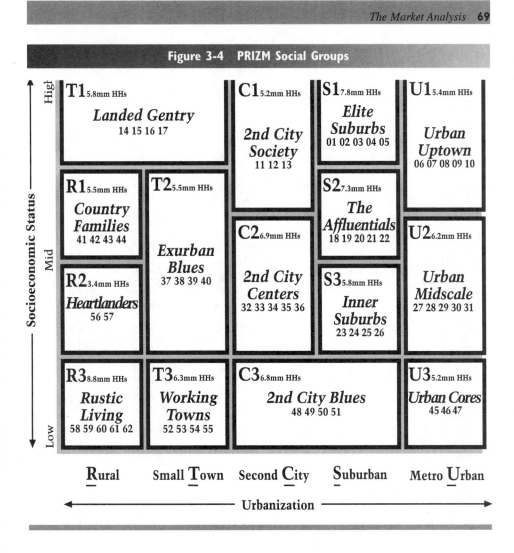

Figure 3-4   PRIZM Social Groups

The ability of the PRIZM system to deliver addressable names and mappable targets at the micromarket level has obvious advantages to advertisers, especially in the planning of media strategy within a larger market. The ability to analyze markets at the microlevel block group or less has also been widely used for fundraising, site selection, and recruiting.[2] Exhibit 3–1 presents the PRIZM neighborhood types.

GeoVals™. SRI Consulting (subsidiary of SRI International) developed GeoVals to allow users of the VALS system, discussed in Chapter 2, to locate concentrations of specific VALS consumers by Zip Code or block group. GeoVALS data can be downloaded into mapping software such as Scan/US or into spreadsheet software, such as Excel. GeoVALS is used most often for direct mail purposes and is also useful for site location applications. Figure 3–6 presents a diagrammatic view of the United States showing the percent of the VALS types in Augusta, Georgia Zip Code 38909. Exhibit 3–2 presents a spreadsheet comparing the distribution of VALS types in several Austin, Texas Zip codes.

Figure 3-5 Characteristics of PRIZM Neighborhood Clusters

PRIZM

	Blue Blood Estates	Winner's Circle	Executive Suites	Pools & Patios	Kids & Cul-de-Sacs
Nickname					
Demographic Caption	Elite Super-Rich Families	Executive Suburban Families	Upscale White-Collar Couples	Established Empty Nesters	Upscale Suburban Families
Cluster Number **Percent of U.S. Households**	**01** 0.8%	**02** 1.9%	**03** 1.2%	**04** 1.9%	**05** 2.8%
Predominant Adult Age Range	35-54	35-54, 55-64	25-34, 35-54	55-64, 65+	35-54
Key Education Level	College Grads	College Grads	College Grads	College Grads	College Grads
Predominant Employment	Professional	Professional	Professional	Professional	White-Collar Professional
Key Housing Type	Owners Single Unit	Owners Single Unit	Owners Single Unit	Owners Single Unit	Owners Single Unit
Lifestyle Preferences	Belong to a country club Own mutual funds $10,000+ Purchase a car phone Watch TV golf Read business magazines	Use a maid/housekeeper Have a line of credit account Eat Brie cheese Listen to classical radio Read travel magazines	Play racquetball Use financial planning services Own a camcorder/video camera Listen to jazz radio Read business magazines	Attend live theatre Own investments $50,00+ Drink Scotch Listen to news radio Read epicurean/leisure magazines	Buy trivia games Have 1st mortgage loan Own a piano Listen to soft contemporary radio Read infant/parenting magazines
Socio-Economic Rank	Elite (1)	Wealthy (2)	Affluent (8)	Affluent (9)	Affluent (10)
Race/Ethnicity	W (A)	W (A)	W (A)	W (A)	W (A)

Legend for Race/Ethnicity Category, first letter indicates key ethnic/racial type, ( ) letters indicate above average concentration.
W=White B=Black A=Asian H=Hispanic F=Foreign-Born

Exhibit 3-1   Prizm Neighborhood Types

Group	Cluster	Cluster Nickname	Group	Cluster	Cluster Nickname
S1	01	Blue Blood Estates	C2	32	Middleburg Managers
S1	02	Winner's Circle	C2	33	Boomtown Singles
S1	03	Executive Suites	C2	34	Starter Families
S1	04	Pools & Patios	C2	35	Sunset City Blues
S1	05	Kids & Cul-de-Sacs	C2	36	Towns & Gowns
Elite Suburbs			2nd City Centers		
U1	06	Urban Gold Coast	T2	37	New Homesteaders
U1	07	Money & Brains	T2	38	Middle America
U1	08	Young Literati	T2	39	Red, White & Blues
U1	09	American Dreams	T2	40	Military Quarters
U1	10	Bohemian Mix	Exurban Blues		
Urban Uptown			R1	41	Big Sky Families
C1	11	Second City Elite	R1	42	New Eco-topia
C1	12	Upward Bound	R1	43	River City, USA
C1	13	Gray Power	R1	44	Shotguns & Pickups
2nd City Society			Country Families		
T1	14	Country Squires	U3	45	Single City Blues
T1	15	God's Country	U3	46	Hispanic Mix
T1	16	Big Fish, Small Pond	U3	47	Inner Cities
T1	17	Greenbelt Families	Urban Cores		
Landed Gentry			C3	48	Smalltown Downtown
S2	18	Young Influentials	C3	49	Hometown Retired
S2	19	New Empty Nests	C3	50	Family Scramble
S2	20	Boomers & Babies	C3	51	Southside City
S2	21	Suburban Sprawl	2nd City Blues		
S2	22	Blue-Chip Blues	T3	52	Golden Ponds
The Affluentials			T3	53	Rural Industria
S3	23	Upstarts & Seniors	T3	54	Norma Rae-ville
S3	24	New Beginnings	T3	55	Mines & Mills
S3	25	Mobility Blues	Working Towns		
S3	26	Gray Collars	R2	56	Agri-Business
Inner Suburbs			R2	57	Grain Belt
U2	27	Urban Achievers	Heartlanders		
U2	28	Big City Blend	R3	58	Blue Highways
U2	29	Old Yankee Rows	R3	59	Rustic Elders
U2	30	Mid-City Mix	R3	60	Back Country Folks
U2	31	Latino America	R3	61	Scrub Pine Flats
Urban Midscale			R3	62	Hard Scramble
			Rustic Living		

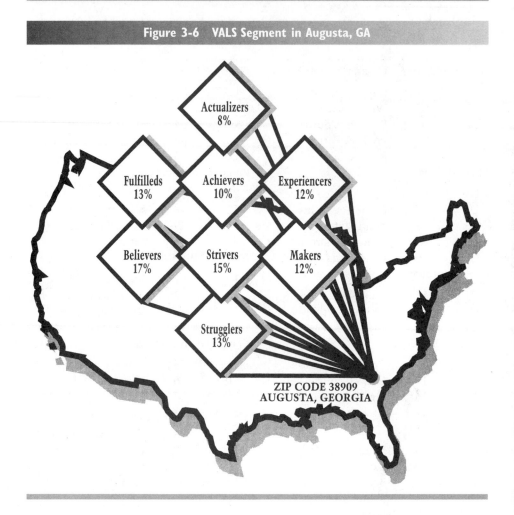

Figure 3-6   VALS Segment in Augusta, GA

PRODUCT ANALYSIS

In the product analysis, the basic questions address how the many aspects of the product match up with consumers' needs, wants, problems, and interests. A product consists of both physical and psychological attributes. Even simple products are surprisingly complex. Is this product the right size? Is it priced right? Is it in the right place? Consumers typically buy a product because of the whole package. They may say they are buying a product on the basis of price, but that is only because they have implicitly accepted that the product has met their minimum standards of quality. The way a product is marketed can have a profound influence on whether consumers believe or feel the product addresses their needs and wants. Perception can be more important than reality. It is up to the analyst to determine both what a product is and how it is *perceived*.

As product categories become more mature, the strategic focus in marketing a product tends to shift from an emphasis on physical qualities to ones that are more *intangible*

Exhibit 3-2   Spreadsheet of Seven VALS Segments

Austin, Texas

ZIP	Post office	County	Actualizer 11.4%	Fulfilled 10.4%	Believer 16.9%	Achiever 14.4%	Striver 12.1%	Experiencer 12.9%	Maker 12.4%	Struggler 9.6%	Adults 189,220,246
	Total U.S. Region Total		11.4	9.9	14.6	11.8	12.9	15.2	14.7	9.4	749,217
78607	Bluffton	Llano	2.6	9.8	40.7	9.2	7.8	5.8	8.0	16.1	25
78608	Briggs	Burnet	7.2	9.3	23.8	6.8	11.7	10.3	13.2	17.8	563
78609	Buchanan Dam	Llano	6.4	12.6	29.2	4.2	9.1	5.9	9.6	23.1	1,246
78610	Buda	Hays	18.3	13.1	10.5	19.9	9.8	11.1	12.8	4.6	6,197
78611	Burnet	Burnet	6.2	10.0	25.8	5.7	10.5	8.9	12.1	20.8	6,684
78612	Cedar Creek	Bastrop	8.9	8.9	18.0	10.5	13.7	12.8	16.9	10.3	6,479
78613	Cedar Park	Williamson	14.4	11.2	11.0	18.0	12.2	13.9	15.0	4.3	18,738

© 1997, SRI Consulting, Menlo Park, CA.

in nature. These intangible qualities are associated with the brand name, or simply, the *brand.* Although consumers buy the package, an insightful analyst will usually think of the product as a whole but break it down into its component parts. The key to organizing the analysis of a product is to look at both the brand, or its psychological qualities; and its physical qualities, which typically include the product's quality, price, distribution, and promotion. Then there are a number of questions to consider:

1. Does the product package have the ability to give consumers what they want (or need, and so forth)?

2. Does the product package promise or address what consumers want?

3. Does the delivery of the product package match up with consumers' expectations?

4. Can the product package exceed consumers' expectations?

5. What is the essence of the brand?

6. Does this essence have value?

7. To what extent is this brand liked?

8. How strong is the brand?

The first three questions tend to focus on potential barriers to a successful marketing program. A product without substance or real want-satisfying qualities is unlikely to be successful over the long term. If a product has special qualities but does not promote them, special opportunities may be lost. Opportunities can be perishable. Promising consumers one thing but delivering another can also lead to a product's diminished effectiveness. Perception is *usually* more important than reality. What gets delivered to consumers is not nearly as important as what they believe they are receiving.

The fourth question focuses more on what the product could be—either real or perceived. This question is the most difficult one to answer—both from the consumers' point of view and from the perspective of a marketing strategist. To get the answer requires imagination on the part of the researcher and the consumer.

The fifth, sixth, and seventh questions have always been important. But for many products, the physical distinctions between one brand and another are not what they used to be. Products are likely to be even more similar in the future than they are now. The day will come when some Coca-Cola knock-off will taste surprisingly like Coke! Companies are increasingly aware that the way to market success is by differentiating the product through the images, personalities, or simply values that are associated with the brand name. This is generally called **building the brand.** The analyst's job is to determine what makes this brand—*this brand* and not some other. The special mental connections that consumers make with a brand, taken as a whole, can be referred to as the **essence of a brand.** Some of the essence is intrinsic to the product the way a BMW's performance characteristics influence the way people think of its drivability. These intrinsic characteristics can be thought of as the DNA of the brand. Other mental connections are the result of the way the brand has been promoted (for example, Marlboro cigarettes) or the way people have experienced the brand (for example, Harley Davidson motorcycles).

Question eight (How strong is the brand?) is the logical conclusion of the preceding seven questions. The answer to this question will provide direction to the development of the *strategic focal point* of the campaign. Brands tend to exert varying degrees of loyalty on consumers. The following is a brand loyalty continuum:

Brand Awareness > Brand Acceptance > Brand Preference > Brand Insistence

Companies want to move consumers across the above continuum toward brand insistence—where consumers will accept no substitutes for the product. Somewhere along the continuum in the area of brand preference and brand insistence is the near ultimate status of the **power brand.** These brands are so powerful that the names alone are worth considerable money to the owners. Coca-Cola. Kodak. Marlboro. Intel. Microsoft. Budweiser. Smuckers. Clinique. The Gap. Steinway. Harley Davidson. Mercedes Benz. Disney World. Heinz. McDonald's. Beanie Babies (probably for a limited time only).

Though companies may desire to own power brands, it is not realistic for most. The analyst's job is to determine the current status of the brand and at least a preliminary assessment of its opportunity to get stronger.

Looking at the Product

To get a full appreciation of what consumers think or feel about a product, it is often helpful to compare it to its competition. In doing a product analysis, it may be useful to perform some aspects of the competitive analysis at the same time. We separate these steps in this chapter primarily to help the reader see how the various parts of the situation analysis fit together and not because we feel they should be done sequentially. There are a number of useful ways to describe a product's qualities: concrete or abstract, physical or psychological, and tangible or intangible. In the advertising business, products are usually discussed in terms of their attributes, which tend to be physical; their functions, which are mostly physical and somewhat psychological; and their images or brand personalities, which are psychological.

Product Attributes

In evaluating a product, it is always helpful to understand how much of a product's want-satisfying qualities are tangible product attributes and how much of a product's qualities are intangible. If a product comes up short in the attribute area, then the solution to the problem of how to market the product is more likely to come from research and development than from marketing. Problems concerning how to market intangible qualities, such as images and brand personalities, can be addressed with advertising and other marketing communication tools. In analyzing a product's more tangible qualities, consider the following:

Product variety
Special designs
Differentiating features
Qualities (hidden and obvious)
Packaging
Sizes

Services
Warranties
Returns[4]

Product Functions

In many product categories, consumers are less interested in a product's attributes, which they don't understand or don't want to understand, than they are in what the product can do for them. In the 1970s, commercials for some antiperspirants said the product contained aluminum chlorohydrate—a technical word, but not beyond the ability of consumers to remember. Today, the active ingredient in Arrid XX antiperspirant deodorant is aluminum zirconium pentachlorohydrexgly. Not surprisingly, all consumers want to know is that it keeps them "extra, extra dry."

Consider paper products. Charmin Ultra bathroom tissue is promoted primarily on the basis of its "Squeezably Soft & Thick" attributes. In contrast, Bounty paper towels have long been promoted on the basis of their absorbency—"The quicker picker-upper." In recent years, ads for Bounty have been emphasizing the towel's strength—"Look! It's Quilted." Of course, it's also possible to emphasize both attributes and functions. Ads for Kleenex Ultra facial tissues emphasize their "extra layer of softness" that provides a "soft, silky feel" to the skin.

For some products, the decision to emphasize an attribute or the function may depend on the target audience. The package of Edge Gel, a shaving preparation targeted for men with sensitive skin, prominently displays the message that the product is "for closer, more comfortable shaves!" Skintimate Shaving Gel for women, like Edge Gel, is formulated for sensitive skin and contains aloe vera. Yet, the Skintimate brand only mentions how the brand functions on the back of the package and in small print. Apparently, women understand the effects of aloe on sensitive or irritated skin better than men. They do not need to be told what effect using the brand might have on their skin.

Brand Personality

People have long projected onto inanimate objects qualities that are normally associated with human beings. This is true for products, and is especially so for branded products. In fact, it is the history of a brand, and all its associations, that often gives a product its distinctive personality. A brand name has value. It can be estimated subjectively through qualitative research or more rigorously in paired comparison tests.

In a research setting, a whole range of questions associated with the brand or the brand personality can be addressed, including those focusing on purchasing intentions and price sensitivity. The research question can be as simple as "Which one do you prefer?" Exhibit 3–3 presents a brand valuation test for a fast-food chicken restaurant using this question in a taste test.

Usually done with matched samples, this type of test is used to estimate the value of the brand name. Presumably, the increased preference shown for Brand A in the second sample (where the brands are named) can be attributed to identifying the chicken as Brand A. This valuation test (or a variation of this test) can be used to determine how much value the brand name adds to the product.

The next step is to understand how the product's attributes and brand personality contribute to its success (or lack thereof). To obtain this information, companies and agencies

	1st Sample	2nd Sample
	Unnamed Chicken	Named Chicken
Brand A (our chicken)	50%	60%
Brand B (the competitor's chicken)	50%	40%

Exhibit 3-3   Brand Valuation: Which Product Do You Prefer?

use a variety of techniques, including some already discussed, such as survey research, one-on-ones, and focus groups, as well as other techniques we will discuss.

Product Testing

One of the best ways to evaluate consumers' thoughts about a product is to give them a product under real-life conditions and ask them what they think of it. Consumer testing focuses on consumers and attempts to understand their wants. Similarly, product testing seeks to understand a product's ability to satisfy a want. For this situation, there are three basic types of testing procedures:

1. Monadic testing presents consumers with one product at a time and requires them to make an evaluation without using any other product for comparison. (When scales are used as the testing instrument, it is sometimes called a noncomparative rating scale.) Monadic tests are designed to mirror real-life situations where consumers do not have competitive products to use as a basis for making comparisons. The idea is that consumers implicitly compare the product undergoing testing with other products they have considered. These tests are widely used in advertising, and examples will be provided shortly.

2. Paired comparison testing presents the consumer with two (or more) products simultaneously, and requires them to make an evaluation. Unlike monadic tests, which focus on the qualities and attributes of the product undergoing testing, paired comparison tests focus on the differences between products. These will be discussed in greater detail in the section on competitive analysis.

3. Projective tests involve a much different way of collecting information about the product. This type of testing comes from clinical psychology. These tests are designed to get respondents to reveal their inner feelings and beliefs by getting them to project their own feelings and beliefs onto some situation that is ostensibly about someone or something other than themselves. Naturally, this is often used to provide information about consumers. We include a description of these tests here because of their value in learning about brand personalities.

Monadic Tests

A wide variety of tests fall into this category. Most of these tests are some variation of a numerical rating scale and involve the measurement of the respondents' predisposition to respond to the product, usually in a favorable or unfavorable way. Some of the more commonly used scales are as follows:

1. Semantic Differential. This is one of the most widely used tests in marketing research. The basic version consists of a series of bipolar adjectives usually separated by a 7-point rating scale. The test can be used to measure both a product's attributes and its image.

Example
Brand X Roasted Chicken Restaurants*

Friendly	___	___	___	___	___	___	___	Unfriendly
Clean	___	___	___	___	___	___	___	Messy
Modern	___	___	___	___	___	___	___	Old-fashioned
Expensive	___	___	___	___	___	___	___	Inexpensive

---

*A variation of this technique uses phrases instead of bipolar adjectives.

2. Stapel Scales. This test is a variation of the semantic differential scale. In this technique, respondents are typically asked to rate a product or a retail outlet according to the intensity of their agreement or disagreement with a product or a phrase. This test is fairly easy to administer and is often used in telephone interviews.

Example
Telephone Interview: Please rate Brand X Roasted Chicken on the following qualities ranging from +5 to −5. (Sometimes a 0 is included as a neutral point, but some researchers feel it is better to make respondents choose a positive or negative value.)

+5	+5	+5	+5
+4	+4	+4	+4
+3	+3	+3	+3
+2	+2	+2	+2
+1	+1	+1	+1
tasty food	nuritious food	good value	distinctive flavor
−1	−1	−1	−1
−2	−2	−2	−2
−3	−3	−3	−3
−4	−4	−4	−4
−5	−5	−5	−5

3. Likert Scales. Respondents are requested to indicate their agreement or disagreement with a series of statements. This is a relatively easy scale to construct and administer. Care should be taken, however, to provide a balance in the number of favorable and unfavorable statements.

Example
Brand X Roasted Chicken Restaurants

	Strongly Agree	Agree	Neither Agree nor Disagree	Disagree	Strongly Disagree
This store has great-tasting chicken.	_____	_____	_____	_____	_____
The counter personnel are unfriendly.	_____	_____	_____	_____	_____
The inside of the store is comfortable.	_____	_____	_____	_____	_____
Roasted chicken is good for you.	_____	_____	_____	_____	_____

4. Purchase Interest. This test requires respondents to indicate on a 5- or 11-point scale the likelihood that they will buy a product or service. The correlation between actual consumer purchases of a product and consumers' indications that they intend to purchase it is less than perfect. Nevertheless, the technique is also called *purchase intent*.

Example
Please answer the following question.
     If roasted chicken was available in your area, how likely would it be that you would purchase it?

_____ Definitely would buy.

_____ Probably would buy.

_____ Might or might not buy.

_____ Probably would not buy.

_____ Definitely would not buy.[5]

5. Likability Scales. These tests are often used when the brand in question is essentially a parity product. In these cases, it is often felt that consumers make brand decisions on how well they "like" a product. The following itemized rating scale is one of a number of tests that can be used to test likability.

Example
Please mark on the following scale how much you like Brand X Rotisserie Chicken.

_____ 100 Superior.	_____ 50 Neutral.
_____ 90 Excellent.	_____ 40 Do not like it very well.
_____ 80 Like it very much.	_____ 30 It's not so good.
_____ 70 Like it quite well.	_____ 20 Do not like it at all.
_____ 60 Like it fairly well.	_____ 10 It's terrible.

Projective Tests

To uncover the more elusive aspects of a brand's personality, many advertising agencies use projective techniques. Trained interviewers coax responding consumers to reveal underlying attitudes, feelings, and motivations by having them project themselves into a situation. Examples of some the more widely used tests follow.

1. Sentence Completion. This technique requires the respondent to complete a series of incomplete statements with the first word or phrase that comes to mind.

Example

The best-tasting pizza usually comes with _____.

The thing I like least about going out to eat pizza is _____.

The thing I like most about eating pizza is _____.

2. Story Completion. This technique is a variation of the sentence completion test. In this test, interviewers tell a respondent the details of part of a story and ask the respondent to fill in the rest.

Example

A man and a woman are walking down the street with their 9-year-old daughter. They stop exactly midway between a Pizza Hut and a KFC restaurant to discuss which one to enter. What are they saying to each other and how does this scene end? _____ (Open-ended question)

3. Word Association. This technique requires respondents to say the first word that comes to mind when they hear a stimulus word. In free word association, only the first word is important. In successive word associations, a series of words is requested. Usually, a neutral word is inserted between the words in which the interviewer is most interested.

Example

Stimulus Word	Word Association	Successive Word Associations		
pizza	_____	_____	_____	_____
Big Foot	_____	_____	_____	_____
inexpensive fast-food	_____	_____	_____	_____
hamburgers (neutral)	_____	_____	_____	_____
healthy fast-food	_____	_____	_____	_____
tasty fast-food	_____	_____	_____	_____

4. Role Playing. A respondent is asked to assume the role of another person or an object. One common technique involves asking the respondent to persuade reluctant customers to buy a product. The techniques that are used tend to reveal the respondent's attitude toward the product and potential customers.

5. Pretend Games. Respondents are asked to imagine the product is an average person, a movie star, a sports figure, or a relative. Typically, the interviewer asks questions about where the people live, the kinds of houses they live in, and their ages. The responses are then used to provide definition to the brand's image or personality.

6. Storytelling. Another technique—popular among account planners—uses story-telling as a way of better understanding what consumers *really* want. It is based on the premise that much of what influences consumers occurs beneath their level of awareness. Storytelling is a way to get people to reveal their inner feelings and thoughts. One of the more popular techniques was developed by Jerry Zaltman at the Harvard Business School. His technique is based on the idea that people think in images, not in words. Product users are directed to collect images from photo albums, catalogues, magazines—virtually any-thing—and produce a collage of these images. These images serve as a metaphor for a per-son's inner thoughts and feelings. Below is a simplified outline of the steps used.

A. Product users are recruited and asked, "What are your thoughts and feelings about buying and using . . ." (the brand or product in question).

B. Users are asked to collect about a dozen pictures.

C. After a week, the subjects are interviewed in an intense two-hour session.

D. With the help of a technician, a collage is computer-generated (that is, a composition of images placed in an incongruous relationship, usually for their symbolic or sug-gestive effect). These new pictures then become windows into the consumers' minds.

Storytelling has been used by duPont to learn about what women *really* feel about panty hose. Previous research, especially focus groups, indicated women hate panty hose and wear them only because they feel they have to. Du Pont, which has a vested interest in panty hose (it manufactures nylon), wondered if there wasn't more to it than that. The women in the study produced images of twisted telephone cords, steel bands strangling trees, and shrink-wrapped fence posts. (Apparently, these women really disliked wearing panty hose.) But there were also conflicting images of a vase of flowers in one collage and a garden hose against a backdrop of a silk dress in another. These images seemed to sug-gest that women had more of a "like–hate relationship" with panty hose. Subsequent in-terviews brought out that women liked the way panty hose made their legs look sexy to men—something they would be unlikely to say in a survey or a focus group. As a result of these findings, hosiery manufacturers and retailers changed their advertising to include im-ages of sexiness, even to businesswomen.[6]

Searching for Product Opportunities

With many of the above tests, the researcher is seeking to understand the extent to which the product's attributes and brand qualities address consumers' needs and wants. Products that match up well with consumers' wants offer a lot of ideas to help shape the strategical and tactical focal points around which the strategy gets developed and executed. Re-searchers can use many of the above tests to predict strategical and tactical opportunities. To identify opportunities with an existing product, a description of the product is often compared to the actual product.

To set up this comparison test, consumers are intercepted in a shopping mall and given a series of tests (such as purchase interest test, a likability test, or a measure of perceived value) asking them to rate the product described on the test (that is, the product concept).

Immediately following these tests, the respondents are given a sample of the product. About a week later they are contacted and asked the same set of questions. The **test–retest procedure** is used to diagnose problems and identify opportunities. If the product does not meet consumers' expectations (that is, it underdelivers), then it may be sent back to research and development for further work. If the product exceeds their expectations (that is, it overdelivers), then this situation is viewed as an opportunity to exploit. This procedure can also be used to compare what the consumer would most like to have in this kind of product (that is, an idealized concept of the product) to the actual product.

Example

Version One	Version Two
Step 1 Rate a description of the product	Rate the idealized **concept** of the product
Step 2 Try the product	Try the product
Step 3 Rate the actual product.	Rate the product again.

. . .

Step 4 Is the product rating in Step 3 better than that in Step 1 (that is, it overdelivers), or worse than that in Step 1 (that is, it underdelivers)?

Evaluating the Rest of the Marketing Mix

To get a complete picture of how the product is matching up with the needs and wants of the consumer, it is necessary to evaluate the rest of the marketing mix: pricing, distribution, and promotion program.

Pricing. Most of the information about consumers' sensitivity to price can be obtained while research is conducted on the product. Care should be taken that consumers' responses are not taken too literally. For example, consumers frequently indicate that a product's price is too high. The key question as to whether or not price is a disadvantage can best be answered by market tests. Companies routinely vary the price of the product in isolated markets while holding other factors constant in order to gauge the effects of a market's sensitivity to price. This procedure is greatly facilitated with the use of scanner (UPC) technology.

Distribution. To understand a product's ability to match up well with consumers' needs and wants, analysis should focus on the extent to which the product is available, in a general sense; and conveniently available, in a specific sense. Judgments can be qualitative and based on simple observation, or quantitative and based on scanner data indicating the percent of the all-commodity volume (that is, the total amount of sales in a given category) that can be accounted for by the outlets handling the company's product.

Promotion. Although it can be helpful to separate advertising from the other forms of marketing communication, the distinction between advertising and sales promotion is increasingly blurred in consumers' eyes. Most of the evaluation in this area comes from consumer research. What do consumers think of the current advertising campaign? What do consumers think about coupons (a form of price discounting)? However, much of what consumers think and feel about the message strategy part of the campaign can be inferred from consumer and product testing, particularly those tests that focus on brand personality. In the past, large advertisers often used sophisticated tracking systems, such as AC Nielsen's Monitor Plus, to monitor the timing, frequency, and content of television commercials. However, AC Nielsen discontinued this service. As a result, advertisers and their agencies use their own proprietary systems to keep track of their rivals' promotional efforts.

Although most of the effects of the creative part of the campaign can be inferred, the media effects should be measured. To do this kind of calculation requires understanding how the media plan will deliver the desired audiences and markets. The success of the plan often depends on how much money is being spent on advertising and whether this amount is sufficient to achieve the advertising objectives. Naturally, companies know how much money they are spending, but if the analyst is a student, then the best source to consult is one of the syndicated sources reporting competitive media expenditures, such as CMR's/Leading National Advertisers Media Watch Multi-Media Service.

COMPETITIVE ANALYSIS

Consumers have a limited amount of purchasing power. What they do not spend on brand X, they will surely spend somewhere else. Even though this statement is not literally true, it is a good position to maintain to keep a company thinking competitively. In other words, a forward-thinking company should always be apprised of its competition, both direct and indirect. A company may be a weak competitor one day, and the next day undertake a course of action that can force its rivals out of business.

To begin a competitive analysis, it is important first to identify the options consumers consider in their purchasing decisions. These options include buying products *that directly compete with each other in the same generic category* and products that only *indirectly compete with each other because they are in different categories.* For example, the direct competition for wine coolers is other wine coolers, but the indirect competition may include wine, clear malt liquor, and specialty mixed drinks. The options also include not buying anything and/or postponing the purchase decision to a later time.

To do a thorough competitive analysis, rival companies and their brands should be understood in as much depth as the analyst's company. In practice, this may not be feasible or practical. At a minimum, companies usually try to get a basic understanding of their rivals' resources and the real and perceived comparative distinctions among the brands that compete with the company's own brands.

Many of the tests and procedures that were discussed in the company analysis (see Chapter 2) and in the preceding description of product analysis are also appropriate here. These procedures include one-on-ones and focus group interviews. Projective tests can also be useful to gain insight into the brand personalities of competitive products. Many of the monadic tests, especially the semantic differential and the Stapel scales, can be used to compare one product to another simply by repeating the test for each competitive brand. This section will emphasize the tests and techniques that are comparative in nature.

Product Comparisons

These evaluations often form the basis for the strategic decisions, especially positioning, that will follow as the campaign develops. We will examine two types of comparisons:

perceptual mapping, which examines where a company or brand fits in consumers' perception of the product category; and attitude scales, which are used to compare one brand or company to another.

Perceptual Mapping

This technique can help the analyst understand how a product is positioned in consumers' minds. Tests to implement perceptual mapping range from a simple technique, which is what we shall discuss here, to more complicated multidimensional scaling techniques that require computer software to calculate.[7]

Perceptual mapping is often used to get a feel for a brand's image. A brand's image is the result of a number of factors, including the physical and functional aspects of the brand, the psychological qualities associated with the brand's heritage, and the totality of all the images associated with competitive brands. A perceptual map helps to define a brand's image by putting it into the context of how consumers perceive the brand with respect to competitive brands. An image takes on a finer shade of meaning when an analyst can see how respondents rate a brand compared to its competition.

A perceptual map shows these distinctions by rating various brands on two dimensions simultaneously. For example, a retail store can be evaluated on the basis of both friendly–unfriendly service and high-quality–low-quality merchandise. Although not all of a brand's image or personality can be explained by two dimensions, this rating usually gives the analyst some feel for how consumers perceive the various brands with respect to each other. In perceptual mapping, the researcher will often choose which dimensions to use with respondents, based on his or her experience. In multidimensional scaling, the testing makes no assumptions with regard to the dimensions that are appropriate for the brands being examined. The dimensions are usually derived from judgments respondents make about the similarity of brands or their preference for the brands based on various attributes or qualities.

Figure 3–7 presents a perceptual map for various performers based on an informal test conducted in an undergraduate class on advertising principles. Naturally, the map would likely look considerably different with an older age group.

Comparative Rating Scales. As we discussed in the section on product testing, one of the basic types of product tests that can be conducted to evaluate the competition is the comparative attitude rating scale.

1. Rank Order Rating Scales. In this test, the respondent is asked to rank order a number of products (or retail stores) on the basis of some specific criterion. The ranking may be on the basis of overall quality, but the criterion is usually a specific attribute or quality.

Example

Please rank the following restaurants from 1 to 5 according to which has the best-tasting chicken. Use a 1 to indicate the best.

_____ Boston Market Chicken

_____ Popeye's

_____ KFC

_____ Church's

_____ Brand X Chicken

Figure 3-7   Perceptual Map of Performances

Perceptual Map

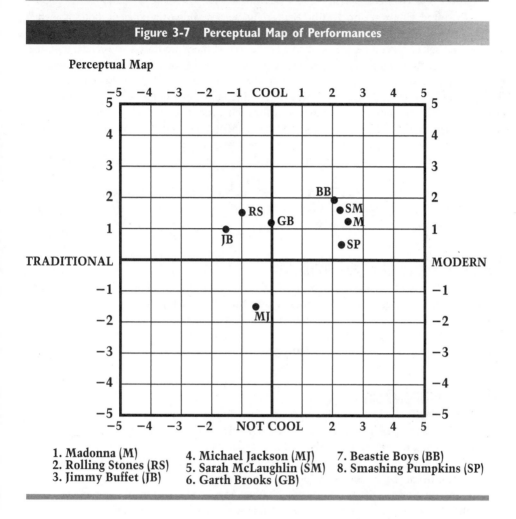

1. Madonna (M)
2. Rolling Stones (RS)
3. Jimmy Buffet (JB)
4. Michael Jackson (MJ)
5. Sarah McLaughlin (SM)
6. Garth Brooks (GB)
7. Beastie Boys (BB)
8. Smashing Pumpkins (SP)

2. Fractionation Rating Scale. The test requires a respondent to rate several products on the basis of some criterion by comparing them to one specific product. Usually, the specific product is the brand leader or the company's brand. The objective of this test is to give the analyst an idea of how similar or different consumers consider the various brands.

Example

If the Brand X Chicken restaurant is assumed to score 100 points on "fast service," how would you compare each of the following restaurants to it?

Brand X Chicken _____

Boston Market Chicken _____

Church's _____

KFC _____

Popeye's _____

3. Paired Comparison Rating Scale. This test is simple in concept, but somewhat complicated to implement. It requires the respondent to compare two products to each other and select one on the basis of some criterion. If there are only two brands, then the testing procedure is a fairly simple one requiring the respondent to indicate a preference for one brand over the other. A comparison is made for each attribute that is thought to be important in the product category. However, if the number of brands in the test is greater than two, then the number of comparisons for each attribute goes up dramatically according to [n(n 2-1)/2]. This means for three brands the number of paired comparisons would be 3 (4 brands = 6; 5 brands = 10); six brands would require 15 comparisons for each rated attribute. To set up this procedure, it might be helpful to consult a marketing research text.[8]

This test can be especially useful when a company is considering two or three versions or recipes of the same product. It is also used when a company believes it may position a brand against a specific competitor.

Double-Checking Prices and Distribution

Analyzing the competition on the basis of price and distribution is fairly similar to the way you analyze the product. You can obtain much of this information as you analyze the product. Because the information will often be obtained in the product analysis, it is usually a good idea to double-check each competitor's prices, and distribution strengths and weaknesses as you would the company in the product analysis.

Promotion Comparisons

To be comprehensive, the competitive analysis should include an understanding of the competition's marketing communications activity. Data on some of the activity may be difficult to obtain; information on advertising is usually more readily available.

Competitive advertising can be divided into information about the message and about the media. Because advertisers no longer have access to the Ad Tracker database that provided information for AC Nielsen's now defunct Monitor Plus service, most analysts (including students) usually construct their own albeit less-sophisticated database. One common method popular among students is to keep a file of all competitive advertising. The print ads can be tearsheets, and the broadcast spots can be brief summaries. Usually it is helpful to do an informal content analysis of ads to track competitive positioning, themes, images, attributes, and objectives.

To get information on competitive media activity, it is possible to systematically monitor the major media. However, this is time consuming and not likely to be comprehensive. The most rigorous approach is to consult one of the syndicated sources of media expenditures, such *as Competitive Media Reporting*'s Leading National Advertisers (LNA). Figure 3–8 presents a partial page from LNA.

The most effective use of this information was summarized by the staff of Media Decisions more than 20 years ago. Although there have been tremendous changes in the media world within the past decade, the information is still very much on target.

1. The expenditure figures can show you regionality and seasonality, and how these factors are changing for all competitive and potentially competitive brands.

Figure 3-8   LNA/Mediawatch Multi-Media Service

LNA/MEDIAWATCH MULTI-MEDIA SERVICE
January - June 1998

CLASS/BRAND $

CLASS/COMPANY/BRAND	CLASS CODE	QUARTERLY AND YEAR-TO-DATE ADVERTISING DOLLARS (000)										
		10-MEDIA TOTAL	MAGAZINES	SUNDAY MAGAZINES	NEWSPAPERS	OUTDOOR	NETWORK TELEVISION	SPOT TELEVISION	SYNDICATED TELEVISION	CABLE TV NETWORKS	NETWORK RADIO	NATIONAL SPOT RADIO
F441 REGULAR CARBONATED SOFT DRINKS		— CONTINUED —										
CADBURY SCHWEPPES PLC (CONTINUED)												
SUNKIST VAR SOFT DRINKS	F441											
COMPANY TOTAL Q1		90.7	—	—	—	90.7	—	—	—	—	—	—
Q2		12.7	—	—	—	12.7	—	—	—	—	—	—
98 YTD		103.4	—	—	—	103.4	—	—	—	—	—	—
97 YTD		240.4	—	—	—	—	—	240.4	—	—	—	—
CAROLINA BEVERAGE CORP												
CHEERWINE SOFT DRINK Q1	F441	24,996.6	159.5	—	17.6	109.6	18,834.6	602.5	2,094.5	3,178.3	—	—
Q2		27,148.0	22.7	—	114.7	104.5	19,346.5	2,274.3	1,523.2	3,761.8	—	0.9
98 YTD		52,144.6	182.2	—	131.7	214.1	38,181.1	2,876.8	3,617.7	6,940.1	—	0.9
97 YTD		50,727.9	75.8	—	42.2	223.8	35,494.0	7,650.0	3,248.8	3,934.5	—	58.8
COCA-COLA CO												
BARQ ROOT BEER SOFT DRINK Q2	F441	41.7	—	—	—	—	—	—	—	—	—	41.7
98 YTD		41.7	—	—	—	—	—	—	—	—	—	41.7
97 YTD		35.7	—	—	—	—	—	—	—	—	—	35.7
CHERRY COKE SOFT DRINK Q2	F441	3,081.7	—	—	—	—	—	3,081.7	—	—	—	—
98 YTD		3,081.7	—	—	—	—	—	3,081.7	—	—	—	—
97 YTD		5,165.4	—	—	—	59.2	1,060.0	4,046.2	—	—	—	—
CITRA CITRUS SOFT DRINK Q1	F441	303.7	—	—	—	—	—	303.7	—	—	—	—
Q2		563.5	76.4	—	—	—	—	487.1	—	—	—	—
98 YTD		867.2	76.4	—	—	—	—	790.8	—	—	—	—
97 YTD		75.2	—	—	—	—	—	75.2	—	—	—	—
COCA-COLA CLASSIC SOFT DRINK Q1	F441	1,597.4	—	—	116.8	58.5	—	1,422.1	—	—	—	—
Q2		4,052.5	—	—	—	354.6	—	3,697.9	—	—	—	—
98 YTD		5,649.9	—	—	116.8	413.1	—	5,120.0	—	—	—	—
97 YTD		627.6	—	—	25.5	24.7	—	577.4	—	—	—	—
COCA-COLA CLASSIC VIGNETTE Q1	F441-8	30,166.2	454.7	—	—	62.2	23,073.4	3,492.2	884.7	2,196.8	—	2.2
Q2		37,382.6	2,540.9	—	—	419.4	19,967.3	9,791.1	2,058.0	2,604.2	—	1.7
98 YTD		67,548.8	2,995.6	—	—	481.6	43,040.7	13,283.3	2,942.7	4,801.0	—	—
97 YTD		56,599.1	1,058.2	—	—	155.9	33,010.8	14,056.4	3,289.8	5,023.2	—	17.8
COCA-COLA OPRY Q1	F441-8	131.7	—	—	—	—	—	122.3	—	9.4	—	—
Q2		2.0	—	—	—	—	—	2.0	—	—	—	—
98 YTD		133.7	—	—	—	—	—	124.3	—	9.4	—	—
97 YTD		13.2	—	—	—	—	—	13.2	—	—	—	—
COCA-COLA SOFT DRINK Q1	F441	15.3	—	—	—	—	—	—	—	—	—	15.3
Q2		15.3	—	—	—	—	—	—	—	—	—	15.3
98 YTD		30.6	—	—	—	—	—	—	—	—	—	30.6
97 YTD		30.6	—	—	—	—	—	—	—	—	—	30.6
COKE SOFT DRINK Q1	F441	178.8	86.3	—	92.5	—	—	—	—	—	—	—
Q2		534.6	322.4	—	204.7	—	—	—	—	—	—	—
98 YTD		713.4	408.7	—	304.7	—	—	—	—	—	—	—
97 YTD		1,188.5	880.0	—	288.6	12.4	—	—	—	—	—	7.5
MELLO YELLO SOFT DRINK Q2	F441	3.0	—	—	—	3.0	—	—	—	—	—	—
98 YTD		3.0	—	—	—	3.0	—	—	—	—	—	—
97 YTD		15.4	—	—	—	15.4	—	—	—	—	—	—
MINUTE MAID ORANGE SOFT DRINK Q1	F441	116.4	—	—	—	—	—	116.4	—	—	—	—
Q2		321.0	—	—	—	—	—	321.0	—	—	—	—
98 YTD		437.4	—	—	—	—	—	437.4	—	—	—	—
97 YTD		713.1	—	—	—	—	—	713.1	—	—	—	—
Q1	F441	0.2	—	—	—	—	—	—	—	—	—	0.2
Q2		0.3	—	—	—	—	—	—	—	—	—	0.3
98 YTD		1.5	—	—	—	—	—	—	—	—	—	1.5

— CONTINUED —

1578

2. The data can give you a market-by-market fix on ad budget size and media mix.

3. You can use the data to spot new product tests and to track new brand roll outs.

4. You can infer from where the money is being spent how competitors view their target audiences, how they profile their brands, and where they seek to position themselves in your marketplace.

5. You can watch spending patterns of the opposition—TV flighting, radio rotation, position practices in magazines, or day of week in newspapers.

6. Once you have complete knowledge of what your "enemies" are up to, you can make better decisions as to where to meet them head-on and when to outflank them.

7. In new-product and line-extension planning, expenditure data are essential to estimate how much it will cost to get into a market, who's already there, and which competitive product types are growing fastest in the new product's market segment.[9]

Campaign Progress Checklist

At this point in the campaign you should generally be aware of the following points:

1. The basic purpose of the market analysis is to identify and understand those geographical areas that are most likely to respond favorably to the marketing communication campaign.

2. A good way to evaluate the relative importance of a market is to look at the amount of product usage and the number of current users in the area.

3. Index numbers are a quick way to assess how a market compares to other markets on the basis of product usage and other demographic variables.

4. Professionals can use geodemographic systems to define their targets in terms of various geographical sizes such as ZIP Codes, postal carrier routes, and blocks.

5. The major purpose of the product analysis is to determine how the product characteristics match up with consumers' needs, wants, and interests.

6. Often, the most important product characteristics are the images, personalities, or values associated with the brand name.

7. To get a complete picture of how the product is matching up with the needs and wants of consumers, it is also necessary to look at a brand's pricing, distribution, and promotion.

8. In analyzing competition, it's important to analyze both the direct competition within the product category, and also indirect competition, which can come from many sources.

9. To thoroughly analyze the competition, rival companies should be understood in as much depth as the analyst's company.

10. An especially valuable way to analyze the competition is to compare media expenditures and creative themes.

11. Following the analysis of the background information, it's often helpful to summarize the problems and opportunities (perhaps in a SWOT format).

Completing the Analysis

The title to this subsection is somewhat of a misnomer because an analysis should be an ongoing process. However, practically speaking, there are deadlines to meet and expense budgets to maintain—research can be expensive. Following the analysis of each of the major sections, there should be at least an informal sense of where the problems and opportunities lie. Frequently, this is a formal procedure. If so, following the completion of all the analyses, you will want to summarize the problems and opportunities. Similarly, if you follow the SWOT format, you'll want to lay out the strengths, opportunities, weaknesses, and threats to provide the basis for decision making, which usually follows soon after the above analyses. We begin to discuss these decisions in the next chapter.

Notes and References

[1] Some of this information is from promotional material by Claritas, Inc.

[2] Curry, D. J. (1993). *The new marketing research systems: How to use strategic database information for better marketing decisions.* New York: John Wiley, p. 255.

[3] This information comes from SRI International fact sheets.

[4] Adapted from Philip Kotler, *Marketing management: Analysis, planning, implementation, and control* (8th ed.). Englewood Cliffs, NJ: Prentice-Hall (1994), p. 98.

[5] For more information on 11-point scales, see William R. Dillon, Thomas J. Madden, and Neil H. Firtle, *Essentials of marketing research.* Homewood, IL: Irwin (1993), p. 279.

[6] Pink, D. H. (1998, April–May). *Metaphor Marketing*, pp. 214–229.

[7] Kinnear T. C., & Taylor, J. R. (1987). *Marketing research: An applied approach* (3rd ed.). New York: McGraw-Hill , p. 536.

[8] Tull, D. S., & Hawkins, D. I. (1987). *Marketing research: Measurement and method* (4th ed.). New York: Macmillan, p. 286.

[9] Do you know your competitive brand data? *Media Decisions* (August 1975), p. 60.

Chapter 4

Equity, Problems, Opportunities, and Objectives

After you finish the background analysis, it's time to reach conclusions and make decisions. However, because the information-gathering function is an ongoing process, all decisions should be revised whenever new information is received. Following the background analysis, the first major conclusion is the determination of how much value there is in either the company's name or in the brands it sells. This value, or equity, can have a significant effect on both the company's problems and their opportunities, which are the second and third conclusions to reach following the analysis.

Now it's decision-making time. The first decision is to define the target market, which is another way of saying where the company expects the business to come from. The problems and opportunities, which influence the delineation of the target audience, form the basis for the setting of the campaign objectives, the next decision at this stage in the campaign process. The campaign objectives, in turn, are then used to provide direction to the rest of the campaign. Organizationally, the campaign should proceed roughly as shown in Figure 4–1.

PURSUING BRAND EQUITY

Businesses do not want consumers to comparison shop. This statement is as true for large firms as it is for small retail operations. Companies may tell consumers they want them to shop around, but they don't really mean it. They would prefer consumers to buy their products or shop in their stores because of what their name represents. These names have value,

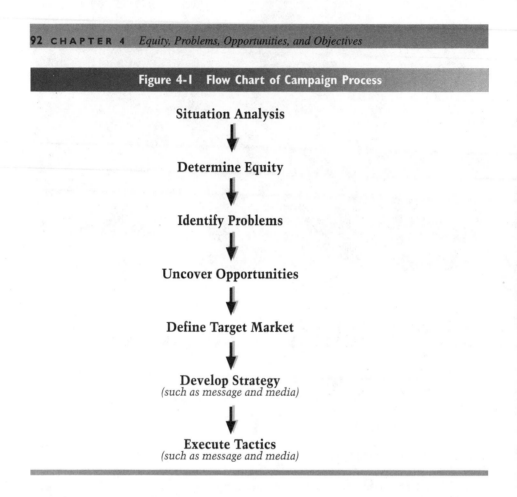

Figure 4-1 Flow Chart of Campaign Process

Situation Analysis

Determine Equity

Identify Problems

Uncover Opportunities

Define Target Market

Develop Strategy
(such as message and media)

Execute Tactics
(such as message and media)

or equity, to a company in the same way that a firm has equity in the assets it owns. After reviewing the background analysis, the analyst should at least have a general idea of how much equity a company currently possesses, and how much it can acquire potentially in the future.

Companies put brand names on products to distinguish them from other products. Naming a product provides consumers with something tangible they can use to associate with thoughts, feelings, and images. If these associations are positive, the advertiser has gained some measure of control over consumers' future purchases and, possibly, over the influence they have with other consumers. These associations provide advertisers with a value they can use to persuade consumers to buy their product. This value is independent of the product's physical or even psychological qualities and is called a product's **brand equity.**

For example, telling someone you own an expensive electric guitar says something about the kind of instrument you own. It might also suggest you are a "cool" individual if you go on to say the guitar is a leading brand such as Gibson instead of a minor brand like Silvertone (that is, a legendary Sears brand). If you expand further and state you have a Les Paul preferred model, many music lovers and musicians would recognize immediately that you own the preferred brand of many legendary rock and blues guitarists and would extend you deferential acknowledgment. Consumers are usually willing to pay the premium price because of the extra value they derive out of owning the Les Paul name. The name has become a company asset.

Avoiding Price Competition

Companies want repeat business for their current products and for their new, improved versions. Most firms do not like to compete strictly on the basis of price. Price competitors often devote so much of their effort to being the low-cost producer that they have insufficient resources left over for product development. This situation can be profitable as long as the firm keeps its costs low. Invariably, firms lose their low-cost advantage, frequently because competitors shift their manufacturing facilities to countries with lower labor costs or because another company has simply found a way to operate more cheaply. Advertisers invest in developing brand equity to avoid price competition, especially as competitive products approach parity. The more value a company can add to its brands, the less likely it will have to compete on a price basis. "Building the brand" can be as important to a company as improving a product's quality.

Competing on the Basis of Quality

Companies also strive to compete through product innovation. This type of competition has become difficult to achieve in many consumer goods categories. Even when a firm is able to develop differentiating qualities for its products, it seldom takes long for the competition to duplicate the product. When Procter & Gamble developed the first soft, chewable cookies, it test marketed them before distributing the product nationally. By the time the product went into national distribution, Nabisco, Keebler, and Frito-Lay all had comparable products in the marketplace.[1]

National brands also face formidable competition from private labels along a variety of fronts. General merchandise retailers, such as Wal-Mart, sell generic equivalents under their own labels. Private-label suppliers, such as Perrigo (which sells personal care and over-the-counter products) and Sovex Inc. (which specializes in cereal knockoffs) continue to encroach into product categories where traditional brands have been dominant. The major brands are also competing against themselves as companies such as Ralston-Purina and Keebler have introduced private-label products into markets in which they are already represented by their major brands. Apparently, they are willing to cannibalize the sales of their own brands because of the perception, "if they don't enter the private-label market, another company will."[2]

Brand Names Remain Important

The result of this multifaceted competition is a dynamic marketplace that redefines the status quo with unprecedented quickness. The traditional notion of carefully and deliberately building brand loyalty through heavy doses of consumer advertising; liberal amounts of sales promotion; and solid, intensive promotion work within the distribution channel has been largely refined by the notion that all of these activities will continue to be important in the twenty-first century—and more—but they will all have to be done much more quickly.

The traditional analogy of building brand equity as a mason builds a wall upon a strong foundation should be reconceived as a hunter sighting a target at point-blank range.

The target is surprisingly difficult to hit because not only is the target moving quickly, so is the hunter. Still, the target can be hit.

Progressive companies understand that achieving brand equity will continue to be an important corporate goal, but they also appreciate that they cannot rest upon past achievements. Successful companies of the future will not build brand equity so much as they will pursue brand equity.

An important function of the situation analysis is to assess the company's brand equity. To both pursue and build brand equity, a successful campaign will have to solve problems and exploit opportunities.

DEFINING PROBLEMS AND IDENTIFYING OPPORTUNITIES

Problem-solving is such an omnipresent aspect of doing business that the management style of some firms seems geared to reacting to problems or, in its more extreme form, crises. These companies seem to be perpetually fighting fires. One of the qualities of a good strategic thinker is the ability to anticipate, so sound strategic planners try to avoid fires by focusing on prevention.

In marketing, **a problem is any barrier or situation that makes it difficult to achieve an objective, whether past, present, or future.** For a company to survive, it must be able to solve its problems and achieve its objectives. In marketing, problems are often discussed in terms of how they relate to sales or market share. Perhaps the most common cause of marketing problems is communication, or its more commercial version, promotion. Of all the variables in the marketing mix, promotion is the easiest to manipulate.

There are only so many things one can do with the price, distribution, or product line. It is impractical to keep changing these elements every week, month, or even year. With promotion—especially advertising—there are new messages, changes in media, and changing audiences to consider continually. Because of the complexity inherent in the promotion area, many of the marketing problems can be traced to communication or message problems. Is the company transmitting the most persuasive message? Is the chosen medium the most cost efficient? To what extent are consumers aware of the products? Some of the marketing problems may be traced also to difficulties with distribution, pricing, or product development. If so, the reader may want to consult one of the many books on marketing management for more details.[3]

If a company is very good at solving its problems, it can turn them into marketing opportunities. For a company to be a leader in its field, it must be able to consistently capitalize on its opportunities. **An opportunity is a situation or a circumstance that can potentially give the company a marketing advantage.** Opportunities are based on assumptions that a company both wants to take advantage of a situation and *can.* Listed in Exhibit 4–1 are some classic examples of companies that were able to transform a marketing problem into an opportunity.

Sometimes the difference between a problem and an opportunity depends on how one looks at a situation. The thick consistency of Heinz ketchup can be viewed as either a problem or an opportunity. Persons who correctly see opportunities where others see only problems are viewed as good leaders. When leaders see opportunity where others cannot, they get elevated to visionary status.

Not surprisingly, problems can't simply be transformed into an opportunity merely by taking an optimistic attitude. Factors internal and external to the firm can have a significant bearing on the extent to which a firm can capitalize on its opportunities.

Exhibit 4-1	Viewing a Problem as an Opportunity

Product: Arm & Hammer baking soda

Problem: Its use for cooking limits its market potential.

Opportunity: Develop new uses for the product (for example, as a freshener in refrigerators and freezers).

Product: Miller Lite beer

Problem: Male heavy drinkers perceive low-calorie products as not very masculine.

Opportunity: Associate the product with very masculine men.

Product: Heinz ketchup

Problem: Product pours too slowly for some users.

Opportunity: Associate slow pouring with richness.

Product: Smuckers jelly and jam

Problem: Has a funny sounding name.

Opportunity: Suggest that the quality must be especially good to overcome the funny name (™With a name like Smuckers it has to be good).

External Factors

A number of conditions under which a firm has little control can often have a profound influence on a firm's ability to take advantage of an opportunity. The political and legal environment, especially in foreign countries, can make it difficult and sometimes next to impossible for firms to get even the simplest venture started.

The cultural and social conditions of a state, region, or country are usually so pervasive as to make it inadvisable for firms to buck existing trends. McDonald's understood that when opening restaurants in India, a country where most of the people do not eat beef, it would have to operate significantly differently than it does in the United States. One difference in India is that McDonald's sells vegetable-based burgers. Similarly, what might sell well in Nashville may not do well in Seattle. It does not take a sophisticated market research study to predict that grits are not likely to do as well in the Northwest as they do in the Southeast, no matter how much promotion they receive.

It is also wise to look at economic conditions. Introducing an expensive product during a recession may be possible but probably not as easy as during a period of economic expansion.

Internal Factors

In evaluating whether or not to pursue an opportunity, a firm needs to be careful to differentiate between a vision and a dream. In marketing, the word *visionary* has come to refer to someone who sees an opportunity and understands whether the company has sufficient resources to take advantage of it. Dreamers also see opportunities, but they are unrealistic about a company's ability to develop and execute successful strategies to see the dream come to fruition. To pursue opportunities, firms usually need adequate resources in three major areas: finance, production, and marketing.

Financial Resources

To compete even on a local level, companies are often best advised to have sufficient capital resources to initiate action and to sustain the activity over a period of time. Many small-business owners underestimate the cost of doing business. For example, restaurants selling pizza can get by with a relatively small overhead as long as they restrict their sales to within the store. If they expand their business to include home delivery, they require considerably larger financial resources. To speed up the baking of the pizza, which it will have to do in order to be competitive, the operation will probably require a conveyor oven, which sells for around $25,000. To get a decent return on the total investment, the company will likely have to draw business from an area larger than its current customer base.

With this kind of investment, the company runs the risk of getting in over its head, particularly when it faces the prospect of significant promotional expenses. The small pizza operation that thought it would be able to compete on the basis of word-of-mouth publicity is faced with financial demands it is unable to meet. Businesses like this can and do lose a lot of money. On a national scale, financial requirements become even more important.

Production Resources

Thinking up new product concepts or services is a lot easier than producing the product or implementing the service. As the saying goes, "The devil is in the details." In the fast-food business, many people will tell you that operational details, including management, doom more restaurants than the product concept. New product ideas do not become opportunities unless the company has sufficient resources to ensure that a quality product gets produced at a competitive cost. In the short run, the firm needs managerial expertise, technological competence, and physical facilities. In the long run, the firm can acquire or buy these things, but opportunities generally do not last over an extended period of time.

Marketing Resources

The Ford Motor Co. was reputed to be one of the most dominant companies in the history of the world. Yet many of the readers of this book think of Ford as the number-two automobile company behind General Motors. The difference is that Henry Ford's genius was in his ability to marshal production resources to sell cars, and the genius of Alfred Sloan of General Motors was in marketing. Henry Ford's myopic view that the company only sell black automobiles regardless of consumer wants is nearly unthinkable today. It underscores the importance of having marketing-savvy people in decision-making positions.

OPPORTUNITIES

Following the analysis of the background information (see Chapter 2 and Chapter 3), it should be apparent where opportunities exist in each of the areas analyzed: the company and its resources, the consumer, the market, the product (including its price, distribution, and promotion), and the competition. The opportunities within the consumer area should receive prominence. The classic mistake is to confuse what the company would like to sell to consumers with what consumers want to purchase. When seeking out opportunities, the focus generally should be on ways to increase sales. There are four basic ways to increase sales:

1. Get current users to continue using the brand.

2. Get current users of the brand to use more of the product.

3. Find new uses for the product.

4. Get new users for the brand.

Retaining Current Users. This should be the foundation on which all strategy aimed at stimulating demand is based. Generally, it's cheaper and easier to convince someone to buy something they are already using. This much is obvious. However, it is important to remember that competitors actively try to persuade consumers to switch brands. This is frequently accomplished by undermining consumers' loyalty to a brand. Brand leaders especially will often remind consumers that they are making the right decision by purchasing their brand. For example, Hertz is the category leader in rental cars. It likes to remind its consumers that even though there are other rent-a-car companies that are cheaper, "There's Hertz, and not exactly" (the tagline in a campaign it used in 1998).

Getting Current Users to Use More. Increasing product use by current users is also a popular way to expand sales. The Hanes Her Way sports bra is now promoted for every day use following company research that showed that the surge in girls' athletics is causing the demo to request the garment for everyday use. The National Fluid Milk Processor Promotion Board with its "Got milk?" campaign encourages people to drink three glasses of milk a day (knowing most adults do not). The Michigan Dental Association reminds the public, "Don't be six months late for your six-month checkup." Advertisers sometimes urge consumers to use more of a product encouraging them with price deals such as buy one get one free (BOGO). Or they may rely on point-of-purchase ads urging consumers to buy a bigger size—"Just Super size it" (McDonald's). Another way to get consumers to use more of a product is to find new uses for the product.

Finding New Uses for a Product. This is accomplished relatively easily with a food product by developing new recipes. The pages of *Family Circle* and *Woman's Day* are filled with numerous ideas on how to use existing products in new, if only slightly different, ways. Arm & Hammer Baking Soda has successfully persuaded consumers to put this product, which was developed for use in baking, in refrigerators to absorb odors. Now it encourages consumers to sprinkle the powder on rugs before vacuuming and on cat litter boxes to prevent odors.

Finding New Users. This is a lot like prospecting for gold. A good place to begin is to look at places where you have already been successful. Next, you'll probably want to look where the other companies have found success. At this point, you'll want to evaluate how much profit you can make searching for gold where it has already been found, or whether it is economically justifiable to start looking at new places. In advertising, you prospect for new users by identifying characteristics that current users possess in common, such as demographic and psychographic variables. One problem with this approach is these variables may not have the same sales predictive power in a new market as they had in the old market.

When seeking ways to expand sales, consider opportunities associated with the following:

- Changing consumers' needs, wants, or interests

- Changing consumers' lifestyles

- Emerging markets in the United States

- Emerging markets overseas

- Established markets overseas

- Product advantages

- Service strengths

- New technologies

- Pricing advantages

- Distribution strengths

- Marketing and promotional strengths[4]

One of the most important opportunities to identify is where the business is going to come from. This opportunity, of course, refers to the **target audience,** or **target market.** This decision helps provide the foundation upon which the campaign is built. Some planners make the mistake of defining the target market immediately following the consumer analysis. This decision should be deferred until all the analyses are complete to be sure the company has sufficient resources to satisfy the consumers' needs, wants, or interests.

The Target Market Decision

Engel, Warshaw, and Kinnear discuss three basic options with regard to this decision: undifferentiated marketing, differentiated marketing, and concentrated marketing.[5] The **undifferentiated market** essentially treats the audience as one mass market. A company must use sufficiently broad but still fairly dramatic creative appeals to be effective with so many diverse subgroups in this overall category. As the marketplace has become increasingly competitive, this approach has decreased in use because rival firms undercut it by targeting a subgroup in the market with a focused and usually more effective appeal. A variation of this option is to target only the largest segment of the overall market, usually the so-called heavy half.

The **differentiated market** is probably the most widely used option today. With differentiated markets, companies may (1) divide the market into segments (usually called primary, secondary, and tertiary markets); (2) identify a target audience, or market, and refer to target groups within that category; or (3) simply call all targets market segments. Cigarette companies have long used a segmented market approach, as do many companies that offer multiple brands in product categories where the products are similar. A good part of the early success of General Motors can be traced to its strategic decision to divide the overall car market into segments and to develop products that catered to the differentiated market segments.

The **concentrated market** is also referred to as a **market niche.** This option assumes that a firm will achieve more success targeting a smaller segment in the overall market than by competing directly against the market-share leader in all segments. The niche marketer runs a risk by conceding the largest segment of the market to another, usually larger company. The market-share leader that has built up brand equity over a broader base may decide to confront the niche marketer head-on with a new product. The leader would be trading on its brand equity to acquire market share from the smaller market while maintaining the same market share in the larger segments. Gatorade, the leader in the sports drink market, undoubtedly realized that once Coca-Cola and Pepsi Co. decided to enter the sports beverage market, share erosion was all but inevitable because of the substantial brand equity associated with the Coke and Pepsi brand and their extensive distribution systems.

Delineating the Target Market

It is important to be sensitive to how information about the target market will be used. Creative people look for insight into the consumer to help them develop and craft persuasive messages; media planners and buyers look for some special piece of information that they can use to deliver these messages efficiently or creatively. At the early stage in the campaign, the determination of the target market is done largely in outline format. Later, the creative and media personnel will use the information discussed in the consumer analysis (see Chapter 2) and their own thinking to define the target audience or market in greater detail. Typically, the target market should be defined, or delineated, considering at least some of the following criteria:

- Demographic variables

- Psychographic variables (including lifestyle)

- Product usage (heavy, medium, or light)

- Brand loyalty

- Benefit segmentation

- Consumers' needs and wants

- Consumers' interests

- Consumers' problems

- Consumers' motivations

SETTING OBJECTIVES

After the target market has been defined, the next step is to translate the opportunities into objectives. Setting objectives is one of the key decisions in any campaign, and it is also one of the hardest. First, planners should determine what advertising, or any other form of communication, can accomplish that will lead to sales. Increase brand awareness? Change in image? Better understanding of how the product works? Next, they need to be specific about the desired level of awareness or understanding, or what kind of an image they want the changed image to be.

Most businesspeople will tell you that their objective in advertising is to sell the product. They may also look at you in a peculiar fashion as though you have been in an ivory tower too long if you fail to recognize what for them is fairly obvious. A standard academic response is to agree that the ultimate goal is to generate sales but add to that the importance of understanding the communication effects that need to be accomplished for sales to result.

One analogy looks at the football coach who enters the locker room at half-time as he prepares to address his team, which happens to be losing. What does he tell them? Try harder. Concentrate. Most modern coaches know that this type of old-style motivational speech can actually produce counter-productive results with the team becoming overly tense or tight. Coaches know that they have to be prepared with a full analysis of the situation before they enter the locker room. If the basic problem is that the team is not completing enough passes, then the coach needs to determine the reason why and whether any coaching adjustments can be made to correct the situation. Is the offense too predictable? Are the offensive linemen not giving the quarterback enough time? The coach's message to the players must address the specific problem.

The solutions to the team's problems are a lot like the objectives one can set for an advertising campaign. There are many different things one can try to accomplish, but individually the achievement of one goal is unlikely to guarantee winning or sales. So the coach might suggest to the offensive coordinator to mix up the offense more, have the receivers run different patterns, change blocking assignments. Put in a new quarterback. Or the coach can do what a lot of advertisers do: Keep trying, keep the faith, and hope things will work out.

Setting objectives is a discipline that presents many problems. In addition to trying to measure objectives, some people feel that the process of researching, determining, and writing the objectives takes more time than they can afford. Others worry that setting specific objectives may make them more accountable than they would prefer. Setting and writing objectives can be difficult. Aside from generating sales, creating awareness, improving images, and generating sales leads, executives often feel unsure about what else they can say. Some of the problems with understanding objective setting are due to semantic confusion, but most of the difficulty results from an inadequate understanding of the various principles that underlie the setting of objectives. Most of the principles in the following section have evolved out of George Odiorne's classic work on management by objectives (MBO).[6]

Definition of Objectives

An **objective is the desired end of an action—what one expects to accomplish.** In MBO terminology, an objective is an effectiveness standard. In an advertising or marketing campaign, all of the strategies and tactics—including creative ideas—are designed to achieve certain results. These results are the objectives, although a practitioner may not refer to them as that.

Some authors, Russell H. Colley in particular, distinguish between an objective and a goal; an objective is general or long term in nature, and a goal is specific or short term in nature.[7] Most advertising texts do not make this distinction; they simply suggest that objectives should be specific. Therefore, in the interest of clarity and simplicity, the terms "goal" and "objective" will be used interchangeably, unless otherwise indicated, to represent a desirable, specific end. When the desired end is general or broad in nature, words such as *long run, long term, broad, general,* or *ultimate* will precede the terms "objective" and "goal" to add precision to their meaning.

Function of Objectives

An objective is established to provide an individual, a group of individuals, or a unit in an organization (such as a department) with direction in a problem-solving situation. The setting of objectives serves to communicate to all those charged with the responsibility of achieving the objectives exactly what is expected of them. Logically, an objective should be set so that if it is achieved it will solve some problem or aspect of a problem. The achievement of an objective may also provide evidence that the firm is capitalizing on an opportunity.

An objective is also established to provide for accountability. Objectives serve as standards against which the output or performance of a person or a unit can be evaluated. In the production area of a firm, setting objectives is a long-established practice. For example, in many factories, production goals (sometimes referred to as quotas) are established for individuals and departments. In the production area it is relatively easy to set objectives because the output is tangible.

In advertising, it is often difficult to establish a direct causal relationship between advertising and sales because advertising is only one of many variables influencing sales. People disagree about the nature of objectives in advertising. Some say objectives should be stated in terms of sales; others want objectives defined in terms of communication effects, such as awareness or attitude shift.

Marketing versus Advertising Goals

Most advertising is basically designed to sell a product or service. However, people do not automatically buy a product after they are exposed to an ad. First, they have thoughts or feelings about a product, and then they buy it (or not buy it). Advertising and other types of marketing communications directly affect consumers' mental processes. Advertising can be thought of as a stimulus that produces a response or an effect.

If the objective is to provide direction to the strategist, then it must indicate specifically what thoughts or feelings an ad should evoke. These thoughts and feelings can be defined in terms of communications criteria, such as awareness and attitude. In other words, if advertising can stimulate an awareness or a favorable attitude in a consumer, then these effects may trigger a purchase response. Therefore, it makes little sense to set sales as an objective for advertising because these communications effects *precede* sales.

The effects that intervene between advertising and sales are usually the goals that advertising, or any other type of marketing communication, should strive to accomplish. These goals, indirect in nature, can be thought of as communications objectives. In most situations, advertising objectives should be formulated as communications objectives.

There are exceptions to this advice. New procedures are being developed and refined with scanner technology that increasingly allow a researcher to isolate the particular effect of advertising on sales. These procedures combine data from consumer panels with information from both in-home and retail scanners of UPC-coded items. The consumer data include information on broadcasting and print exposure, sales promotion activities, and price information. Because the data on media exposure, sales promotion, pricing, and product usage all come from the same sample, it is called **single-source data.** The two largest systems, SCANTRACK from AC Nielsen and InfoScan from Information Resources, Inc. (IRI), have been discontinued. These systems reportedly were expensive and time-consuming. It will be interesting to see whether these systems or similar ones are used in the future, given the potential single-source data systems have in tying a direct causal relationship between advertising and sales.

In some types of direct marketing, researchers are also able to trace a sale to a specific advertisement. However, unless an advertiser uses a single-source system, it is usually easier to evaluate the effectiveness of advertising by measuring the achievement of communications goals than by measuring sales.

Even with single-source data, there are still numerous unmeasured variables that can affect a sale. The effects of advertising frequently interact with a consumer's response to a product's quality, price, service arrangements, and distribution to produce a combined effect that stimulates a sale. Some uncontrollable variables are also at play, such as the economic and political environment, competitive activity, and even the weather. Thus, it is often difficult to isolate the effect of advertising on sales, particularly because advertising often affects sales over a lengthy period of time. Therefore, advertising objectives formulated in terms of communications criteria provide a better measure of accountability than objectives formulated in terms of sales.

Still, it is hard to convince many people that sales are not the relevant measure. Some advertisers would rather define advertising objectives in terms of sales because they have difficulty accepting the value of using communications criteria for their advertising objectives. We then suggest using communications criteria as the core elements in the creative objectives. Until measurement problems linking advertising to sales are overcome (including expense), planners should consider setting advertising objectives in terms of communications criteria. These criteria should be formulated to provide a critical link tying advertising to sales.

Planning the Objectives

To devise an effective strategy, the planner must determine precisely the role that advertising and related communications play in the purchase decision. This role is sometimes called the **communication task.** Over the years, there have been a number of attempts to conceptualize the effects of communication and to relate them to consumer behavior. Implicit in these efforts is the notion that consumers pass through a number of stages on their way to a purchase decision.

Colley in his so-called DAGMAR approach (an acronym for Defining Advertising Goals for Measured Advertising Results) suggests there are five steps through which a brand must climb to gain acceptance: unawareness, awareness, comprehension and image, attitude, and action.[8] Robert Lavidge and Gary Steiner suggest six steps: awareness, knowledge, liking, preference, conviction, and purchase. Their model, which has received wide exposure, further examined the sociopsychological underpinnings of each of these steps.[9]

Each of these models discusses psychological constructs such as attitude, knowledge, and comprehension. These constructs exist within consumers' minds, where they are, of course, not directly observable and therefore difficult to measure. Just as Colley and Lavidge and Steiner do not see eye to eye on the abstract and complex nature of these concepts, there are other differing opinions about the importance of the various communication criteria discussed in these models and their effect on influencing sales. There are also differing opinions about whether consumers need to pass through each phase on the way from awareness to a purchase decision: Must consumers understand how a product operates before they make a purchase? How important is liking the product (or a commercial)? How important is the brand image versus the physical qualities of the product?

The answers to these questions are important because they provide the core elements of a campaign's objectives. The answers are probably also beyond the scope of this book. What seems more probable is that advertising practitioners determine that a communication effect, such as awareness or image, is needed to stimulate sales. Whether or not it is a stage in a hierarchical sequence of steps is less important.

Communication Tasks

Advertising plays an important part in stimulating sales. It may be helpful to think of each communication task as consisting of both a communication effect and an action word that indicates what is supposed to be done with respect to the effect. For example, awareness is a common communication effect. But simply saying that the advertising task is to generate awareness may not provide clear direction to creatives. It may also be a mistake if awareness is not the problem.

During the debate over the effectiveness of the Nissan "Enjoy the ride" campaign, comments in the trade papers indicated that the campaign was an awareness campaign. Was this a problem? Even if its top-of-mind awareness was low, do prospects for this type of car buy the first name they think of? Maybe for a soft drink, or a can of beer, people order the first brand that comes to their minds, but for a $20,000 automobile probably not.

The first step in determining objectives is to figure out which communication effect is likely to predispose the target audience to buy. For Nissan, the campaign was also designed to give the car an exciting—perhaps even—hip image. However, it's similarly hard for cars and people to appear as something they are not—and more important, what people believe they are not. Think of a Nissan and you're likely to think of a black car (unless you own one of a different color). Though the "Mr. K" campaign was fun and entertaining, people still think of a Nissan as a practical car. The follow-up campaign has focused more on product attributes that reflect the car's quality and engineering.

Once you determine the particular effect you want the campaign to achieve, the next step is to determine what you would like to see happen with respect to the desired effect. Pepsi Cola has been fairly successful at getting across the idea that it is a modern, if not hip, drink for young-minded people. Pepsi sells a lot of soft drinks with this image, even if it is not as much as they would like. Since this image works, the communication task shouldn't be to change or even reinforce this image (remember, Pepsi would like to sell more). Their task is to *intensify* this image. For other campaigns, words such as *establish, maintain, increase,* or *change* are action words that indicate the desired status of the effect the campaign is designed to achieve. So one might increase or establish awareness, change an image or attitude, maintain or increase brand preference. One could also set as a goal increasing the levels of trust or liking in a brand. Exhibit 4–2 includes some common communications effects and associated action words.

Exhibit 4-2 Objectives and Their Action Words

Desired Communication Effect	Action Associated with Effect
Awareness (top-of-mind) (brand) (specific product qualities) (of ingredients) (the omission of ingredients)	Establish, maintain, or increase.
Comprehension or understanding	Establish, maintain, or increase.
Conviction or believability	Establish, maintain, increase, or reinforce.
Trust	Establish, maintain, increase, or reinforce.
Attitude	Establish, maintain, reinforce, or change.
Image	Establish, maintain, reinforce, change, or intensify.

Writing the Objectives

Communication objectives should be put into a written operational format. This step facilitates communication by providing a common set of short-term, intermediate, and long-term goals to guide decision making. It also establishes standards that clearly indicate the basis on which a campaign will be evaluated. By communicating the objectives in writing, the likelihood of a misunderstanding or misinterpretation of what is expected is reduced and possibly eliminated.

The task of writing objectives, however, is not easy. It takes skill, care, and a thorough understanding of the principles that underlie the setting of sound objectives. Ten criteria to consider in planning and writing objectives follow.

A CONCEPTUAL FOUNDATION FOR SETTING OBJECTIVES

The principle that objectives should be specific and measurable is well established in advertising literature. However, students and practitioners may still encounter a number of problems unless they consider the following criteria.

Unit Oriented. Objectives should be set for each unit in an organization that performs a task in a business environment. In advertising, the relevant tasks generally are associated with the marketing, advertising, creative (message), and media areas, as well as other types of marketing communication, such as sales promotion and public relations. Even though one person or department may be responsible for decisions in more than one area, it is helpful to set separate objectives for each area. A typical campaign report should include marketing, advertising, creative, media, and marketing communication objectives as long as there are strategies and tactics in place to achieve the goals.

Exhibit 4-3 Linking Objectives

1. *Corporate objective:* to increase the rate of profit from 5 percent to 7 percent of sales by the year 2000.
2a. *Financial objective:* to secure $10 million in capital to finance the construction of a new production facility within the next six months.
2b. *Production objective:* to produce 100,000 cases of Fruit Juicy by the end of the first quarter.
2c. *Marketing objective:* to increase sales of Fruit Juicy 300 percent compared to the previous year by the end of the year.
3. *Advertising objective:* to establish top-of-mind awareness in 70 percent of the target market by the end of October 2001.
4a. *Creative objective:* to establish in the minds of the target market an association between the trade character, JUICE MAN, and Fruit Juicy.
4b. *Media objective:* to reach 85 percent of the target market by the end of the year.
4c. *Sales promotion objective:* to get 20 percent of the target market to play the tropical sweepstakes game during the first quarter.

Objectives should not be set for a unit unless that unit (or department) can achieve the desired result independently. A common mistake is to confuse marketing goals with advertising goals. For example, "to sell X number of units" is clearly a marketing objective because selling a product requires a combination of various activities, such as those associated with product quality, price, distribution, and promotion, that are not normally under the control of the advertising unit. Objectives should be set so that the tasks necessary to achieve the goals are clearly the responsibility of a specific unit.

A staff member working within a unit or area deserves to be rewarded not only for his or her contribution to a unit but also on the unit's contribution to the organization even if the overall effort may be a failure. Formulating objectives that are unit-oriented helps to provide for each unit's accountability.

Unit Linked. All efforts that are oriented toward goals should be linked with one another. The creative plan and the media plan in an advertising campaign each has its own set of objectives, and these objectives should be compatible. These goals must be directly connected to an advertising objective that in turn is tied into a marketing objective. Similarly, marketing goals must be compatible with production goals and finance goals and directly linked to corporate goals. Suppose, for example, the firm Acme's New World Drinks had recently introduced a beverage. Exhibit 4–3 illustrates how its corporate goals might be linked to advertising goals.

In an actual campaign, a number of objectives would be written for each unit; the examples in Exhibit 4–3 illustrate how objectives link together. From this perspective, one can see how the objectives of an advertising campaign are usually linked to sales even though a sales figure is not established as an objective of the advertising effort.

The linking of objectives avoids overlap, a situation in which two units are responsible for accomplishing the same thing. **Overlap** often occurs when a goal like increasing sales is written as both a marketing and an advertising objective. **Underlap** occurs when no unit is assigned the responsibility of achieving a result, as sometimes occurs with sales promotion. The marketing unit may expect the advertising unit to develop the program and vice versa. Writing objectives that are unit linked should avoid overlap and underlap.

Output-Oriented. Many written statements of the objective incorrectly focus on an activity, or input, rather than on the desired result, or output. In other words, the strategy and tactics are confused with the objective. For example, part of a creative approach may be to use an appeal to consumers' desires for safety as part of the overall message strategy. An input-oriented objective might read, "to associate Brand X with safe or security-inspiring situations"; an output-oriented objective would rephrase the statement to read, "to develop within the target market a feeling that Brand X is a safe product." Both statements have approximately the same meaning, but input-oriented statements focus on what it takes to achieve a desired result, which is part of the strategy; whereas an output-oriented statement is the desired result of an activity. Focusing on the desired result rather than the activity is a better indication of advertising effectiveness because the purpose of a campaign is to achieve results. Output-oriented statements are expressed in a way that lend themselves to evaluation.

Time Bounded. An advertising campaign is usually completed within a specified period of time, frequently one year. The progress made in the campaign should be reviewed at various points during the campaign. Objectives should reflect an expectation that specific results will be achieved by specific dates. For example, one might set as an advertising objective, "to achieve brand awareness for brand X fruit drinks in 50% of the target market within the first three months of the campaign" (or by a specific date). A second objective might be to achieve 70% awareness by the end of the second three-month period. Time-bounded objectives establish benchmarks that allow a campaign to be evaluated, or tracked, over a period of time. Increasingly, objectives are likely to be set for periods shorter than one year due to rapidly changing market conditions.

Realistic. Objectives in this category should neither be overambitious nor underambitious—they should be attainable. Some executives may set their objectives at levels they do not expect to achieve but just to give them something to shoot at. These are sometimes called **stretch objectives.** In MBO terminology this situation is an overload, a condition that presents definite problems when trying to evaluate the effectiveness of a unit. Unrealistic objectives only indicate what the planner would like to achieve, not what can be achieved. Even worse, if a firm is using the objective-and-task method of determining the size of the advertising budget, it will set the objectives and then figure out the cost of achieving them. Unrealistically high objectives may increase the budget out of proportion to the value received in achieving the goals. An underload exists when a firm sets its objectives at a level so low that they can be achieved with little or no effort. Unrealistic objectives fail to communicate exactly what is expected from the advertising effort.

Common Effectiveness. Certain responsibilities relating to effectiveness are common to most units. Such responsibilities as to organize, to plan, to reach the target market efficiently, or to be creative, or to do the best job for the least amount of money are standards of effectiveness referred to as common effectiveness. They are usually an implicit part of a standard job description. An employer or client expects these standards to be maintained by an employee or an agency. Establishing these standards as objectives is only stating the obvious.

Singularity of Purpose. For purposes of clarity and ease of evaluation, each objective should be worded so that only one result is associated with each statement. For example, a message strategy may be designed to get prospects to associate "economy of operation" and "high quality" with a particular brand. Is this one objective or two objectives? Having separate objectives prevents the confusion that may occur when only half of a dual objective is achieved. Objectives that are stated in paragraph form or objectives that include three or four desired results in one statement will eventually have to be separated in the evaluation phase of campaign. Otherwise, the researcher ends up having to clarify the results by saying, "We achieved this part of the objective but not that part." It is wiser and more efficient to separate multifaceted goals into distinct goals at the beginning of a campaign rather than at the end.

Measurable. If an objective is to provide accountability, it must be measurable. Problems with measurement account for much of the reluctance to quantify objectives. Measuring communications criteria is still an imprecise science. Many decisionmakers undoubtedly feel that there is no sense in quantifying objectives if the measurement techniques are weak. Notwithstanding, even when measurement problems are too difficult to overcome or too costly to resolve, it is still advisable to quantify objectives whenever possible because quantification adds precision to the sense of direction a campaign must follow.

Although it is possible to quantify objectives for the major decision-making areas in advertising, quantifying objectives in the creative area may not make as much sense because of the subjective nature of many message variables (such as image and attitude). Because the specific relationship between these communications criteria and a marketing goal (such as sales) is seldom precisely known, it is no wonder that copywriters and art directors often experience uneasiness when the "quant jocks" evaluate their work. A secondary problem could also occur if the copywriters take measurement too seriously and develop ads that score high on tests but not so well in the marketplace. Similarly, insisting that all media objectives be quantified may place unwanted restraints on creative media planners (see Chapter 7).

An inexperienced decisionmaker, and in particular students, may regard attempts to quantify objectives as strictly arbitrary and usually just guesstimates. Students may be correct if inexperienced evaluators are doing the work. Talking about such things as establishing new levels of awareness is difficult unless the planner knows what the existing levels are. As one becomes more experienced, quantifying objectives becomes more realistic and meaningful.

Inexperienced decisionmakers can use the following process to help develop precision in quantifying advertising objectives.

1. Estimate the marketing objectives either in terms of sales or share-of-market.

2. Determine the specific role advertising should play in the overall marketing mix.

3. Set the appropriate advertising (or communication) objectives. If the budget has not been set, it becomes primarily a matter of determining what it will cost to achieve the

objectives (measured by estimating media costs). If the budget has already been set, then the decisionmaker compares the cost of achieving the media objectives to the size of the budget. If there is a difference, then some revision of the media objectives would have to take place (or there would have to be an increase or decrease in the size of the budget).

4. Revision of the media objectives should be followed by corresponding revisions of the advertising and marketing objectives. Most beginners and students underestimate how many times objectives need to be revised. In fact, all objectives may need to be in a continuous state of revision until the planning of the advertising campaign is completed. When the planning is completed, the objectives should remain firm, though not necessarily etched in stone.

Specific. Formulating specific objectives helps provide a sense of direction for the unit and establishes benchmarks against which the unit's effectiveness can be evaluated. Using words such as *increase, maximize, satisfy*, or *optimize* without specific quantification is vague and leads to problems in evaluating the campaign. For example, if the advertising objectives are stated as "to maximize (or increase) awareness," what is the standard of success? To make everybody in the market aware of the brand or only as many people as would be economically practical? Writing specific objectives helps avoid these measurement problems.

Exhibit 4-4   Questions to Assess the Soundness of Objectives

1. Is this something my _____ (insert marketing, advertising, creative, media, or the like) plan can accomplish by itself without underlap or overlap? (Is this unit oriented?)
2. Is this objective linked to an objective in another unit, area, or department? (Is this unit linked?)
3. Is this sentence a statement of a strategy or tactic, or is it something I want my _____ (insert marketing, advertising, creative, media, or the like) plan to accomplish? (Is this output oriented?)
4. Is there a specific date by which I expect to achieve this goal? (Is this time bounded?)
5. Is this objective realistic, and attainable, or is it overambitious or underambitious (Is this realistic?)
6. Is this objective something I would expect of every_____ (insert marketing, advertising, creative, media, or the like) plan? (Is this common effectiveness?)
7. Is this objective too complex? Can it be separated into a number of simpler objectives? (Does this have singularity of purpose?)
8. Can we measure this objective? (Is this objective measurable?)
9. Is this objective as specific as it can be? (Is it specific?)
10. Is the value of this objective to the_____ (insert marketing, advertising, creative, media, or the like) plan commensurate with the cost of accomplishing it? (Is this cost-effective?)

Cost Effective. Objectives should always be planned with the idea in mind that they are worth achieving. Because of the difficulty in relating the achievement of communications criteria to sales, it is easy to overlook the cost of achieving the goal. Unless some type of marginal analysis or return on investment is employed, the planner must remember that the process of setting objectives is still the result of executive judgment. Some objectives may be too expensive to accomplish.

Testing for Sound Objectives

During the planning stage or after the objectives have been written, it is helpful to test their soundness by asking the questions listed in Exhibit 4–4 for each objective. Following each question, in parentheses, is the aspect of each objective that is being evaluated.

Campaign Progress Checklist

At this point in the campaign you should generally be aware of the following points:

1. Following the background analysis, the first major conclusion reached is to determine the amount of value, or equity in the brand.
2. In assessing the company's problems and opportunities, a high priority should be given to developing brand equity (that is, building the brand).
3. Part of an advertiser's success in building brand equity depends on its ability to solve problems. The best strategists anticipate problems before they occur.
4. Creative thinkers are sometimes able to turn problems into opportunities.
5. The ability to exploit a weakness depends on more than creative thinking, it requires a thorough analysis of the company's internal and external resources.
6. The targeting decision is one of the most important decisions in the campaign and should be deferred until the analysis of all the background information is complete.
7. The target audience (or market) can be delineated in many different ways.

A key decision is to figure out which criteria are most likely to influence purchasing decisions.

8. The decisions about which problems to solve or opportunities to exploit will form the basis for the campaign objectives. These in turn will provide the direction for the campaign to follow.
9. Marketing or sales goals should be distinguished from communication objectives, which should be set using various communications' criteria.
10. Identifying the key communication task that will lead to the achievement of marketing goals requires the identification of the desired effect (such as awareness) and the action taken with respect to the effect (such as reinforcement).
11. Using sound principles for writing objectives helps provide clear direction for people working on the campaign. It also helps managers evaluate the effectiveness of the campaign.

REVIEWING THE DECISIONS

After the objectives are set, the marketing communication strategy can be developed. Before moving on, it is sometimes helpful to review all key decisions. The most important of these decisions is the definition of the target audience. The target may consist of a single segment of the overall population of consumers, or it may consist of multiple segments, as in primary and secondary targets. These segments should be the prime prospects for the company's products.

The next decision is really a set of decisions. It involves setting the objectives. At this stage, the marketing objectives should be fairly firm, but the advertising objectives can still be fairly flexible. Later, after the media strategy and tactics have been decided, the advertising objectives can be firmed up. However, firming up the objectives does not imply that they can't be revised if new information changes the situation. Even in a speculative presentation it's a good idea to acknowledge that if the situation changes so too should the objectives.

Both the marketing objectives and the advertising objectives should reflect the problems and opportunities that were uncovered in the situation analysis. Of the many problems and opportunities, special attention should be paid to the amount of value, or equity, associated with the company's brand names. Once the target market, or audience, has been identified and the objectives set, the next step is to determine strategic focal points around which the campaign strategy will be focused.

Notes and References

[1] Heller, M. (1985, January). The great cookie war. *Madison Avenue, 27*, p. 100.

[2] Warner, F. (1993, February 1). Going private: Keebler heads into private label after disastrous 1992. *Brandweek, 1*, p. 6.

[3] Kotler, P. (1994). *Marketing management: Analysis, planning, implementation, and control* (8th ed.). Englewood Cliffs, NJ: Prentice-Hall.

[4] For additional information on opportunity analysis, see Robert J. Hamper and L. Sue Baugh, *Strategic market planning.* Chicago: NTC Business Books (1994), Chapter 5.

[5] Engel, J. F., Warshaw, M. R., & Kinnear, T. C. (1994). *Promotional strategy: Managing the marketing communications process* (8th ed.). Burr Ridge, IL: Irwin, p. 162.

[6] Odiorne, G. S. (1965). *Management by objectives: A system of managerial leadership.* New York: Pitman, p. 204.

[7] Colley, R. H. (1961). *Defining advertising goals for measured advertising results.* New York: Association of National Advertisers, p. 6.

[8] Colley, pp. 37–38.

[9] Lavidge, R. J., & Steiner, G. A. (1961, October). A model for predictive measurements of advertising effectiveness. *Journal of Marketing,* vol. 25, pp. 59–62.

Chapter 5

Building the Marketing Communication Strategy

These days, it seems if you phone a large agency or advertiser, instead of an individual, you're likely to get voice mail. If you persist and get through to a secretary, you may hear that the person you called is in a meeting. Why so many meetings? What could all these people be discussing? One answer is that they're analyzing research, discussing objectives, or plotting strategy and tactics. When they're finished, they do it all over again. Unlike a textbook, where once something is discussed the readers move on to the next chapter, in advertising, once you've thought something through, you have to rethink it—and then re-think it all over again. Revision is a way of life.

If you are working on a campaign while you are reading this book, you should understand that as you consider strategy options in this chapter, you may want to go back and redo your research, rethink your target market, and reset your objectives. You may not want to revisit everything, just some of it. In the business world, a dynamic market dictates that a campaign be updated continually to meet changing conditions. Beyond that, revision is simply part of a normal process of fine-tuning your work to produce professional results.

THINKING ABOUT STRATEGY

Advertising or any communication strategy should not be created in a vacuum. Only *after* an analysis of the situation and a systematic delineation of the problems and opportunities is it time to make decisions. These decisions should evolve out of careful analysis. If the problems and opportunities can be determined with insight, decisions about defining the target audience and setting the objectives evolve naturally. The next step is to think about strategy. Strategy is all about identifying the actions that will give the brand a competitive edge. It is general in nature and takes place over a period of time. A good strategy anticipates consumer responses and competitive reactions to the actions of the company.

At this point in the campaign process, strategy basically focuses on message content and the ways in which the message gets delivered. However, strategy can consist of more than creative and media decisions or, for that matter, more than decisions involving sales promotion, direct marketing, and public relations. Strategy can also be about funding, managing, and evaluating a campaign. Thinking strategically should permeate all aspects of the campaign. At the heart of all strategy, however, are the messages that consumers receive. Let's consider some of the ideas and decisions that form the base upon which the message strategy is developed. We call this base the **strategic foundation.**

BUILDING A FOUNDATION FOR THE DEVELOPMENT OF STRATEGY

The strategic foundation consists of the following four elements:

- The management of brand equity

- The positioning of messages

- The funding of the marketing communication program

- The targeting and delivery of messages

The strategic foundation provides the core elements of the campaign strategy that will eventually be developed, expanded, and refined by creative and media personnel. At the center of each element should be a **strategic focal point** around which the subsequent strategies revolve. These focal points evolve directly from the research foundation. Once you determine which problems need to be solved or opportunities pursued, you should then translate these perceptions into objectives. Keep in mind the problems you identify must be solvable and the opportunities realistic. The promise you make in an ad must reflect product characteristics, or the advertising is simply not believable and a waste of money. Part of the purpose of setting objectives is to provide direction for the people working on the campaign. The direction objectives provide, becomes the strategic focal points for the various strategies (such as message, media, and sales promotion) that get developed in the campaign.

Consider Lee jeans. In the eighties and early nineties, this brand was promoted as "the brand that fits." Their advertising generally consisted of spots focusing on young women having difficulty putting on jeans that were tight and the problems they encountered as a result. Naturally, the ads suggested that these problems wouldn't occur with Lee jeans. Since the Lee brand of jeans is a looser fitting jean, the advertising promise reflected real product characteristics. The looser-fitting image, promoted at a time when styles tended toward tight jeans, meant a less-than-stylish image. Yet the product sold fairly well because it did satisfy a real need in the marketplace. In the late nineties, jeans in general tended to fit looser and easier, providing more competition for the Lee brand in terms of product characteristics (that is, a looser fit). Unfortunately for the Lee brand, it continues to carry the less-than-stylish image. The decision to promote product characteristics instead of focusing on more intangible qualities, such as image, often poses a significant problem to planners. When a brand loses its differentiating characteristics, it may have to start over in terms of building the brand. Ideally, the planner would do both, although this is not always easy to accomplish.

Strategy works over a period of time, both during a campaign and from one campaign to another. Separating short-term from long-term effects is a matter of judgment. But it is necessary in order to evaluate comprehensively the effectiveness of a campaign and to plan for future ones. Strategically, each of the above four elements has both short- and long-term ramifications that can influence strategy profoundly. Short-term interests are usually about stimulating sales. Long-term interests are about adding value, or equity, to the brand or company name. This largely intangible value is generally referred to as **brand equity.** This chapter focuses on the decisions involving the management of brand equity. Most of what we have to say about the message and media components of the strategy is discussed in subsequent chapters.

Brand equity considerations, the first element in the strategic foundation, are easily the most important part of a communication strategy. If a brand loses its equity, it may not survive. Too often campaigns are short term in nature, overly concerned with boosting sales quickly. Often management needs to be educated about the strategic importance of building the brand over the long run. The campaign objectives should reflect the relative importance of building the brand versus merely emphasizing product qualities. Nevertheless, it's usually a good idea to rethink how the value in the brand name will be handled, or managed, during the campaign period.

Until recently, McDonald's Corporation did little research to measure the effectiveness of its advertising. Apparently, the company believed it would be too difficult to evaluate its numerous ads by measurement. The bulk of McDonald's advertising is designed to reinforce the brand's core equities: family, good-tasting food, value, fast service, convenience, and cleanliness. These words all reflect ideas and values that are easy to understand but difficult to measure, especially considering the effects a McDonald's commercial has over an extended period of time. McDonald's is now conducting research in this difficult area, not because it has become easier but because it is even more convinced of the strategic importance of managing the brand's equity.

Positioning, or the way the firm presents the brand in its various forms of communication, is the second element in the strategic foundation. It can be planned to achieve short- or long-term effects. Sometimes it can do both. When McDonald's advertises a promotion tied to Barbie dolls and Beanie Babies, ostensibly it is advertising for the short term. The toys are presented as fun and exciting and only available for a limited time. However, by presenting the toys in a wholesome family environment, the company is also reinforcing one of its core equities and enhancing the value of the brand over a much longer period of time.

Decisions about the advertising **expenditures** make up the third element in the strategic foundation. Although very important, we decided not to discuss this in detail because these tend to be more corporate decisions than marketing or advertising ones. Their relevance is particularly minor in a typical advertising campaigns' class where the size of the advertising/marketing communication budget is frequently predetermined.

Expenditure decisions do, however, have both short- and long-term ramifications. The appropriation decision is of long-term strategic interest. To compete in some categories, a firm must be able to marshal sufficient financial resources. On the other hand, budgetary decisions about how to allocate money are short-term operational decisions only indirectly concerned with long-range strategic planning.

The elements of the strategic foundation that deal with positioning and targeting directly influence the development of message and media strategy. These concepts will be covered in greater detail in Chapter 6 (on message strategy), Chapter 7 (on media strategy), and Chapter 8 (on related marketing communications).

The targeting decision, the fourth element in the strategic foundation, can also have both short-term and long-range ramifications. On a daily basis, targeting decisions usually devolve to questions about the efficiency with which the media is delivering messages to target audiences. Of more strategic concern, targeting focuses on the extent to which the messages are delivered to the right target. In 1990, Oldsmobile began a clever and still memorable 18-month campaign to reposition the brand to appeal to a younger market. It was called "This is not your father's Oldsmobile." The consumers' response was clear: "Oh yes it is!" The problem wasn't so much the advertising as it was the product. General Motors was trying to distinguish the Oldsmobile from its other brands and models, mostly Buicks, by giving it a more youthful image. Consumers liked the advertising. They just didn't believe it.

Let's look at each of the four elements of the strategic foundation in some detail.

MANAGING BRAND EQUITY

Brand names have value, or equity, and are an asset every bit as important as the mortar and brick in a company's building. Like an investment property, brand equity must be managed. Brand equity is all about the value—implicit and explicit—in the company's names and symbols. A company's names and its associations can have a significant effect on whether consumers buy the product. Consumers buy brands as much for intangible qualities as they do for physical ones. Budweiser beer is aged in beechwood, but it is doubtful this means as much to the typical consumer of Budweiser beer as its claim, "the king of beers," or its association with Clydesdale horses. A company's branding opportunities must be cultivated and nurtured, its position in the market reinforced and intensified, and its problems dealt with by protecting and defending the brand from any situation that would undermine its status in the marketplace.

David A. Aaker, in his widely influential book *Managing Brand Equity*, discusses five categories of largely intangible assets and liabilities upon which brand equity is based:

1. Brand loyalty

2. Name awareness

3. Perceived quality

4. Brand associations

5. Other proprietary assets such as patents, trademarks, characters, and channel relationships[1]

Brand Loyalty

Establishing, building, reinforcing, and intensifying brand loyalty are easily the most important aspects of managing brand equity. There is an axiom in marketing that suggests it is easier to keep customers than to get new ones. Consumers fall into routines and will

Exhibit 5–1   The Leading Brands

Product	1925	Position in 1985	Position in 1994	Position in 1998
Bacon	Swift	Leader	Number 3	Number 3
Biscuits	Nabisco	Leader	Leader	Leader
Breakfast cereal	Kellogg	Leader	Leader	Leader
Cameras	Kodak	Leader	Leader	Leader
Chewing gum	Wrigley	Leader	Leader	Leader
Chocolates	Hershey	Number 2	Leader	Leader
Mint candies	Life Savers	Leader	Number 2	Leader
Razors	Gillette	Leader	Leader	Leader
Shortening	Crisco	Leader	Leader	Leader
Soap	Ivory	Leader	Number 5	Number 6
Soft drinks	Coca-Cola	Leader	Leader	Leader
Soup	Campbell	Leader	Leader	Leader
Tea	Lipton	Leader	Leader	Leader
Tires	Goodyear	Leader	Leader	Leader
Toothpaste	Colgate	Number 2	Number 2	Leader

Sources: For 1925 and 1985 data, the source is Thomas S. Wurster, "The Leading Brands: 1925-1985," Perspectives (Boston: The Boston Consulting Group, 1987). Quoted in David A. Aaker, Managing Brand Equity; 1994 data courtesy of Information Resources, Inc (IRI); 1998 data is derived from information supplied by IRI and Responsive Database Services, Inc.

often buy a product simply out of habit, especially if they are satisfied. The cost of acquiring new customers is typically greater than that expended on maintaining existing ones. Existing customers also help expand demand by promoting the product through word-of-mouth publicity. If a company takes the proper steps to satisfy its customers, it is amazing how loyal consumers can be to a brand. Exhibit 5–1 compares the leading brands of various products in 1925 with the leaders in 1985, 1994, and 1998. With only a few exceptions, the leaders today are the same as they were in 1925 and 1985.

Simply being a leader, however, is no guarantee of long-term success. The saying "The bigger they are, the harder they fall" applies to companies as well as to giants. Eastern Airlines, a category leader in the 1970s, is no longer in business. Not all companies can be the leaders in their field. Enlightened companies understand that brand loyalty doesn't automatically follow brand-share leadership. As Figure 5–1 illustrates, firms seek to gain control over consumers by moving them along a continuum beginning with brand awareness and ideally ending with brand insistence.

Brand awareness can range from a point where consumers are barely familiar with the brand name to a point at which the brand is the first word that comes to the consumer's mind when the product category is mentioned. Simple brand awareness is only a very mild form of control whereas top-of-mind awareness can be a distinct advantage, particularly in a generic category where the differences among products are slight. In some consumer

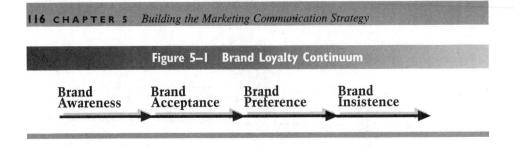

Figure 5–1 Brand Loyalty Continuum

Brand
Awareness

Brand
Acceptance

Brand
Preference

Brand
Insistence

groups or areas of the country, a brand may have high top-of-mind awareness because the brand name is used generically.

In Tennessee, a lot of Coca-Cola is sold to people who use the word *coke* as a generic equivalent for soft drinks. Several years ago, a young man asked the author's daughter to pick up a couple cases of "cokes" for a picnic. When she arrived at the park with two cases of Coca-Cola, the young man asked her why she hadn't bought any Pepsi, which was his favorite. Uncharitably, she laughed. Later, he conceded that from time to time he was served Coke simply because it was the first word that came to his mind, and, to him, it really didn't matter very much.

Most consumer brands fall into the classification brand acceptance. Consumers typically find several brands in product categories satisfactory and appear willing to base their purchase decisions on a sale price or a coupon. Increasingly, the nationally advertised brands are discovering that consumers are extending their level of acceptance to include many store brands and private-label merchandise.

Brand preference is a measure of loyalty that most companies would like their brands to achieve. A brand can achieve leadership in a category even when it is only preferred slightly. Budweiser is clearly the number-one beer in the United States, a position that reflects the preference consumers have for the brand. How strong is this preference? Even though many beer drinkers claim to "love" their Bud, it is highly likely that they would quickly order some other brand if Budweiser was unavailable.

Budweiser does not have brand insistence that is the ultimate level of brand loyalty. Brand insistence means that consumers will *take no substitutes*. So, if a store is out of Budweiser, it's out of beer. Schlitz used a variation of this line in the 1970s: "When you're out of Schlitz, you're out of beer." It's a nice line that speaks of a highly desirable state of brand loyalty, but as legend has it, it was originally spoken by a Budweiser beer salesman. Apparently, after ordering a Budweiser and learning that the bar was out of his brand, he cried, "When you're out of Bud, you're out of beer." A copywriter at Leo Burnett reportedly heard the line and used it in the Schlitz campaign. Unfortunately for Schlitz, nice line that it was, it did not save the brand from declining from the second best-selling beer to a point where it is virtually out of the beer business.

Perhaps the ultimate level of brand insistence has been attained by Harley-Davidson. Not only will potential buyers wait months to purchase the brand, but buyers belong to owners' clubs, attend Harley Davidson rallies, wear shirts with the company logo, and tattoo their bodies with the brand name. Obviously, it is unrealistic to expect this kind of loyalty for the average product. A key part of the background analysis is to determine what level brand loyalty is realistic to attain.

Cultivating Brand Loyalty. The key to developing brand loyalty is to get consumers to make an emotional attachment to the company or its brands, or both. Companies that consistently produce products better than their competitors have a much easier time developing this emotional bond. However, a better product is often a matter of opinion and a function of perspective. In the 1990s, many companies cultivate brand loyalty by *extending* the marketing concept—by giving people not only what they want but also "more": more attention, more recognition, more satisfaction—in short, more value.

Estée Lauder is a company that has built its success on the idea that for many women the experience surrounding the purchase of cosmetics is as important as a product's physical attributes. Selling cosmetics is tricky, partly because you're selling a product that people don't really need. (The author freely recognizes there are readers who would dispute this point.) Estée Lauder, the legendary founder of the company, knew that the way to get customers to buy more than they probably needed was to make each customer feel special. In a typical high-end department store, "beauty advisers," "consultants," and "analysts" try to build a relationship with customers by getting physically close to them in a relaxed and nonthreatening way. To do this, salespeople lightly place their fingers on a woman's forehead, smooth lotion on her cheeks, or apply gloss to her lips. To reinforce the special feelings it provides to its customers, the company spends almost a billion dollars, or nearly 30% of sales, on advertising and promotions. This approach has been so successful that in 1998 Estée Lauder controlled over 45% of the cosmetic market in U.S. high-end department stores. Seven of the top 10 prestige makeup products (mascara, lipstick, foundation, etc.) belong to Estée Lauder. Of the top 10 prestige skin-care products, eight are Estée Lauder brands.[2] Some companies attempt to formalize this approach by giving it a special name: **relationship marketing.**

Relationship Marketing. The key to developing a relationship with consumers is attitude. The firm must be willing to provide extra value to consumers in return for greater brand loyalty. This is a simple paraphrase of the Stuart Smalley pop psychology saying of the 1980s: "If you want to be loved, give love." Many brands maintain substantial amounts of brand equity without resorting to warm and fuzzy marketing, but many companies find that a more caring consumer-oriented approach is good for business. As the differences among products appear to be getting smaller each year, companies search long and hard for ways to provide extra value to consumers.

Companies can forge a positive relationship at all three stages of a consumer's experience with a brand: (1) before the purchase, (2) while the consumer is using the product, and (3) after a customer has stopped using or purchasing the brand. Pepsi Cola and Nike are two advertisers that make extensive use of the relationship concept.

For years, Pepsi has invited consumers to join the Pepsi generation using a fun, even funky, approach. Its message is simple: If you're conservative or stodgy, drink Coke. If you're hip, join us. In recent years, Nike has segmented its approach to selling athletic shoes. To reach men, it uses a traditional campaign with famous athletes, like Michael Jordan, often in humorous situations. To appeal to women, it shows the product less than in its advertising for men, if it appears at all. Instead, the ads use a lot of empathic copy to discuss, if not celebrate, what it is like to be a woman, especially one who works out. The implied message is simple and subtle: "We understand real women. If you're in the market for a pair of shoes, who understands your needs and wants better than Nike?"

Companies that use the relationship marketing approach understand that making the sale is only part of the transaction. Consumer satisfaction can be a transitory thing. What satisfied a consumer yesterday, happened yesterday. Consumers are continually exposed to all kinds of promotions. Consumers who sign up with MCI receive regular calls from the company checking whether they are satisfied with the service.

Saturn prides itself on being a different kind of a company. From its inception, Saturn has worked hard to demonstrate its commitment to being sensitive to the way consumers like to be treated. General Motors (GM) literally bet a large part of its future on this division. If they couldn't get it right there, then they might not have been able to get it right anywhere.

First, the company trained its dealers to work with the salespeople so they were less pushy and more laidback. Next, GM cooperated with the media in letting them know about the delays on the production line, which were to make sure each car was just right. Then, when a car broke down in a far-off place like Alaska, hundreds of miles from a dealer, a repairperson was flown in at the expense of GM to fix it.

Saturn also inaugurated an owners club. These clubs are not uncommon in the auto industry; Saab, Corvette, Mustang, Jeep, and Porsche are only some brands that have had clubs for years. Usually, the cars in these clubs are sporty, foreign, or expensive. Saturn had none of these qualities. Saturn used these clubs as a base to plan its "homecoming" celebration. The company mailed out 700,000 invitations to attend a "homecoming" celebration in Spring Hill, Tennessee, about an hour's drive from Nashville.[3] Amazingly, 30,000 people paid $34 per ticket to attend the festivities and take a tour of the factory, some arriving in caravans from Florida, California, and even Taiwan. Why? Is it the car? Not likely. Evidently, people liked the attention and recognition and a chance to attend a gigantic party (tame as it was). People bought the Saturn experience as much as they bought the car.

Companies are also beginning to understand the importance of pursuing a relationship with customers after they stop buying. Terry Vavra, in his book *After-Marketing*, argues that some of a company's best prospects are the consumers who no longer buy the company's products or services. He gives three reasons.[4] First, there is a wealth of information to be learned from previous customers: Were they dissatisfied with the product or service? Did they switch for a lower price? Have they simply moved on to new interests or wants in their lives?

Second, it is often cheaper to get back old customers than to acquire new ones. Many firms have accumulated a considerable database of previous customers. Instead of purging files of inactive customers, it may be less expensive and easier to retarget old customers than to launch a campaign aimed at winning new ones.

Third, with the information obtained from old customers, a firm can often fix the problems that led customers to buy elsewhere. Consumers who purchased from a company more than once probably have residual positive feelings about a company even after they go elsewhere. In developing campaign strategy, consider prospecting for new business with old customers. It may be possible to rekindle the warmth associated with an old relationship.[5]

Staples, an office supplies store, builds its database of customers by offering them membership cards that entitle them to a special discount. These cards enable the store to track purchase behavior; identify monthly patterns, including responses to various promotions; and detect whether each customer has decreased or stopped purchasing. With this information, Staples is able to mount marketing-oriented countermeasures aimed at regaining business.[6]

Exhibit 5–2   Names and Common Associations

Crest	fights cavities
JiffyLube	fast service
Wal-Mart	low prices
Jerry Lewis Telethon	Muscular Dystrophy Association
Nashville	country music
Uno's, Due's, and Gino's	deep-dish pizza
Baskin Robbins	31 flavors
Budweiser	king of beers

It is becoming increasingly obvious to companies that employing a consumer-oriented approach can pay big dividends in terms of sales. In developing campaign strategy, it is important to identify the company's consumer-friendly attitudes and policies so these can be publicized and promoted. In the Saturn case, where the company flew someone hundreds of miles to fix a consumer's car, the company carefully documented (filmed) these events for promotions; it's not enough for a company to care—the consumer has to know it cares.

Name Awareness

Awareness is an aspect of brand loyalty, but it is important enough as a tactical and strategical concern to merit special attention. Simple awareness by itself does not contribute much to brand loyalty. However, without awareness there can be no loyalty. This premise may be why awareness seems to be the primary objective of so much advertising. In a survey of more than 3,000 directors of advertising designed to look at the way decisionmakers set objectives, more directors stated "awareness" as an advertising objective than any other criterion.[7]

Awareness and Value. David Aaker suggests that awareness contributes to a brand's equity in at least four ways:

1. A name provides an anchor to which you can attach other associations.

2. A recognizable name provides a sense of familiarity that people usually like.

3. A well-known name signals that there is substance and commitment behind it.

4. A well-known name signals that others have found the brand worth considering.[8]

Exhibit 5–2 presents a list of names with some common associations. If you are familiar with the names, you will probably make similar associations. If you are unfamiliar with a name, you may not have a clue as to where the association is coming from. Of course, familiarity doesn't always generate good feelings; sometimes it breeds contempt, as the saying goes. Even in cases where there are negative associations, however, people may be willing to pay attention to the names because they assume others have.

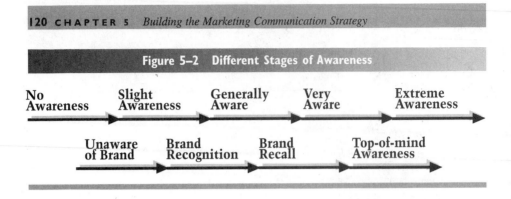

Figure 5–2 Different Stages of Awareness

No Awareness → Slight Awareness → Generally Aware → Very Aware → Extreme Awareness

Unaware of Brand → Brand Recognition → Brand Recall → Top-of-mind Awareness

Stages of Awareness. Awareness can vary on a continuum from no awareness to extreme awareness. However, this is not how it tends to be measured. Figure 5–2 presents a continuum of the different stages of awareness. Below the first line is another continuum displaying how these stages of awareness get measured conceptually. The distinction between stages of awareness and measurement can be important for both strategical and operational purposes.

Using a commonsense approach to discussing strategy, you may simply say that you would like consumers to be very aware of the brand name. When the copywriters and media buyers devise their plans to achieve this aim, however, they may have differing ideas about what "very aware" means. To avoid this confusion, a planner may suggest a more specific goal, such as "We would like X% of our target market to be able to recall the brand name." Brand recognition is the weakest form of awareness, and is measured simply by asking respondents, usually by phone, if they recognize any of the names an interviewer mentions. Recall is measured by asking respondents to name a brand within a product category without any prompting or aid. Both recognition and recall are memory tests. Many planners do not feel comfortable using memory tests both for methodological reasons and because the evidence is not compelling that high scores on a memory test translate into increased sales.

Top-of-mind awareness is basically measured in one of two ways: (1) Respondents are asked to indicate the first word that comes to mind when prompted by a product category, or (2) top-of-mind status is simply assigned to the first brand mentioned in a recall test.

Top-of-Mind Awareness. Top-of-mind awareness can be a distinct advantage to a brand in certain categories. It usually helps to be the first name considered for impulse items and products in categories where many of the brands are comparable in quality and have achieved brand acceptance. Pizza is often an impulse item. Pizza is also a good example of a product category in which many brands have achieved brand acceptance. Even bad pizza seems to sell, sometimes well. In many markets, when people think about delivered pizza, instead of saying, "Let's order pizza," they simply say, "Let's call Domino's (or Pizza Hut)." Is this because Domino's makes great pizza? Probably not. Over the years, Domino's has invested substantial sums of money in building its equity, so that when consumers think of delivered pizza, they think of Domino's first. Domino's might not hold such a preeminent position in consumers' minds if its products were more expensive, if the quality differences among the national brands were greater, or if consumers had a more discerning palate.

The "uncola" campaign for 7-UP is a reflection of the strategic importance advertisers place on top-of-mind awareness. In the early 1970s, 7-UP uncovered in its consumer research the not-too-surprising information that consumers were consistently mentioning either Coca-Cola or Pepsi first in any top-of-mind awareness test. What bothered 7-UP most about these findings was that the pattern was also true for consumers who preferred 7-UP over Coke and Pepsi. No doubt marketers at 7-UP agonized over sales that were lost simply because consumers thought of one of its competitor's brand names first. So for more than 20 years, 7-UP has periodically run the "uncola" campaign in a largely unsuccessful attempt to get consumers to stop automatically thinking of a cola when they want a soft drink.

In the campaign process, it is important to determine whether awareness is the problem that is keeping the brand from achieving its objectives. Often, it's not. The Nissan "Life is a journey. Enjoy the ride" campaign was said to be an awareness campaign, but awareness was not the problem.

Perceived Quality

An image of quality is an important part of brand equity. Once you have a quality image, it becomes an asset that is an integral part of brand loyalty. Achieving this image can be an elusive goal. Companies with substantial R&D functions learn early in their work that there is more to an image than what one sees. R&D people use the qualities that consumers find desirable in competitive products as a benchmark for their own product. Then they try to produce a product that is better than the one in their specifications (specs). If a company can come up with a comparable or even superior product, it's won only half the battle. The rest of the job is convincing consumers.

Al Ries and Jack Trout in their book, *The 22 Immutable Laws of Marketing,* suggest that "marketing is not a battle of products, it's a battle of perceptions."[9] The best product will not automatically become the market leader. It's not how good a product is; it's how good people believe it is. The magazine *Consumer Reports,* which rates the quality of products, provides ample evidence nearly every issue that the highest-rated products are not necessarily the brands with the largest market share.

What makes a quality desirable can also be a matter of opinion. In California, consumers prefer smaller, crisper-handling cars; whereas in the Midwest buyers prefer cars that are bigger and more comfortable to drive. What makes a quality desirable can also be a matter of which company has the best chance to get its image registered with consumers. Apparently, once consumers get an impression or image of a person, product, or place, they tend to keep that image and its associations for a long time. Ries and Trout argue that it is "better to be first than it is to be better. It's much easier to get into the mind first than to try and convince someone you have a better product than the one that got there first."[10] As evidence they cite a number of famous firsts and some not-so-famous seconds. Exhibit 5–3 lists some of their examples along with some of ours.

It is hard to know why the first company to make an impression has such an advantage over other companies. One guess is that when consumers become satisfied with a brand, they have little motivation, reason, or incentive to pursue further information. For example, Whitehall Labs was the first company to take advantage of the Food and Drug Administration's approval allowing ibuprofen to be sold as an over-the-counter drug. In its early advertising, it introduced Advil as the same pain reliever that consumers had been

Exhibit 5–3	Famous Firsts	
Famous Event or Product	**Famous First**	**Not-So-Famous Second**
First person to fly solo across the Atlantic	Charles Lindbergh	Bert Hinckler
First cellophane adhesive tape	Scotch	3-M
First person to walk on the moon	Neil Armstrong	Buzz Aldrin
First sport drink	Gatorade	Unknown
First President of the United States	George Washington	John Adams
First flight	The Wright brothers	Alberto Santos Dumont
First black baseball player	Jackie Robinson	Larry Doby

buying under the prescriptive name Motrin. Later, when Upjohn (now Upjohn-Pharmacia) decided to market its own drug as the over-the-counter brand, Motrin IB, consumers did not flock to the "real thing." Apparently, they were satisfied with Advil. Consumers' perception of Advil's quality is sufficiently high to ward off competition from brands that are equivalent and, in many instances, cheaper. In 1998, Advil was the number-one selling brand of ibuprofen.[11]

Influencing the perceptions consumers have of a product is a challenging task. It is a planner's job to indicate which perceptions should be reinforced or intensified and which should be changed. Obviously, changing consumer perceptions of a brand can be difficult. It is a lot easier to establish a perception for a new brand, or to modify a perception of an established brand, than it is to change the consumer's perception of a brand to something significantly different. In the Nissan "Enjoy the ride" campaign, rather than suggesting the car was exciting or even hip, it would have been much easier to get across the idea that a Nissan car was dependable and well engineered.

Brand Associations

Companies also actively manage the equity in a brand through associations with its proprietary names. Associations can influence perceptions, increase brand awareness, and build brand loyalty. The type of associations companies promote can be almost infinite in scope. In short, the associations consumers make with a brand influence how they think and feel about a product. Some of the more common associations are with celebrities, places, characters, ideas, or words.

The use of celebrities to endorse a product or simply appear in a commercial is widespread. Sales of Gatorade increased significantly when Michael Jordan signed on to appear in the company's ads. The target market, overwhelmingly male, related to the line "Be like Mike."

Other products find positive associations with geographic regions, states, and cities. Jimmy Dean Breakfast Sausage and Bryan sausage both play up their southern heritage while Northern Bathroom Tissue associates with the North. Louisiana Hot Sauce and generic products such as California raisins, Idaho potatoes, and Washington State apples associate with states. Cities are also popular associations. There's Old Milwaukee beer, L.A. Gear sportswear, K.C. Masterpiece barbecue sauce, Philadelphia Brand cream cheese, OshKosh clothing, and Raleigh, Winston, and Salem cigarettes. Do these associations have value? Some appear to have more value than others. Apples grown in the state of Washington and potatoes from Idaho do taste better than ones grown in Tennessee. But the association of cream cheese with Philadelphia, or clothing with OshKosh, Wisconsin probably does not lend a similar amount of value.

Companies also associate with characters. The characters can be animated, such as the Green Giant and the Keebler elves; or live, such as the Maytag repairman and Mikey, the little boy who said he liked Life cereal.

When the Mikey campaign was first run in the early 1980s, it featured two adolescent boys trying to decide if they should eat a bowl of Life cereal. The boys decided to give it to their younger brother, Mikey, as an acid test because Mikey "doesn't eat anything." When the camera zoomed in on Mikey's cherubic face joyously eating the product, his brothers made advertising history by exclaiming, "He likes it." As soon as the people at Quaker Oats, parent company of Life cereal, saw the commercial, they knew it was magic. They rushed the spot on the air without pretesting it, something they rarely did. Later, Quaker Oats tested the commercial, and it did poorly both in terms of the communication measures the company was using and in its sales impact. Consumers could recall the ad but had difficulty recalling the brand advertised. Someone at Quaker came up with the brilliant idea of putting "Mikey's" picture on the Life cereal package and announcing that this was "Mikey's cereal." During the first 18 months following the start of Mikey advertising, sales increased 25%. Today Mikey is a young adult who regularly appears on talk shows.

Competing against a corporate giant is rarely easy. Competing against a company with the size and history of AT&T must be especially daunting. AT&T spends nearly $500 million on media expenditures[12] and over the years has built up considerable brand equity. Part of its equity is based on consumers' confidence in AT&T's technological abilities. Consumers are generally aware that the U.S. phone system is the envy of the world, and AT&T largely gets the credit. To break into this market, both MCI and Sprint have been aggressive price discounters. Both companies realize that eventually they will need to compete on some basis other than price. To get into this market, both companies have been essentially buying market share with price discounts. To stay in this market, MCI has been relying on a number of innovative marketing promotions.

Sprint has also launched a number of marketing initiatives, but it has also spent substantial sums of money to build brand equity by associating its name with an idea. The idea is simple: Sprint has invested in an extensive network of fiber-optic cable. Its reception is so clear, "you can hear a pin drop." The message is designed to allay consumers' concern that the telephone reception on Sprint might be inferior to that of AT&T. The pin association is presented both visually and orally, and for the most part represents an investment to produce short-term sales as well as long-term equity. The problem with this association is that today, unclear reception is not the problem it once was. As a result, consumers probably don't put all that much value in the pin drop association.

Simple word associations can be so strong that a single word or two can be indelibly associated with a brand in the minds of consumers. Budweiser is known as the king of beers. It's a powerful association, and it belongs to Budweiser. Even if it weren't trademarked, a company would be foolish to try and use it. There simply wouldn't be any credibility. Consider the following: "Pabst, the king of beers" or "Stroh's, the beer of kings." Or how about "Miller Genuine Draft: the royalty of bottled beer." In fact, by its association with royalty, Budweiser has preempted the use of all terms that denote royalty. It's unlikely there will ever be a "prince of beers" and certainly not a "queen of bottled beer."

Consider the following associations:

Ivory	floats
Domino's	delivers
Lee's	fit
Michelin	cares
The Club	protects
John Deere's	run

How about two words:

Charmin	squeezably soft
Avis	tries harder
Crest	fights cavities
Allstate	good hands
Energizer	still going
Johnson & Johnson's baby shampoo	no tears

The best word associations are probably those that communicate the message in a word or two. Sometimes a word or two will be used less for its literal associations and more for the associations it stimulates. In the mid-1990s, a story, perhaps apocryphal, was circulating within the Chicago advertising community. Four executives from a top-10 ad agency were quitting the business to enter the microbrewed beer business. Their chief asset was an association. Allegedly, they were going to call their beer Naughty Boy. The copy and visuals would be simple: Two attractive women walk up to a bar. The first woman says, "I'll have a Naughty Boy." The second woman leans forward and with emphasis says, "Make that two Naughty Boys." Tacky? A gratuitous use of sex appeal? Probably. But it might be a powerful use of an association (or so the executives thought), even for the beer business. As the beer business shows signs of fragmenting into smaller segments, or niches, this kind of ad could build awareness. (Gratefully, the brand does not exist today.)

As good as some associations are, their value in maintaining brand equity may be limited over a long term. As advancements continue in the field of computer software, other companies may take over Apple's "user friendly" association. An association based on a physical quality may be more difficult for a company to maintain once its product loses its distinctness.

The fact that Ivory soap floats has nowhere near the value today as it did when it was introduced by Procter & Gamble in 1881. At the time, floating soap did not exist. A worker accidentally fed air into a mixture of soap, and the company was unaware of its buoyant properties until customers tried to reorder the "floating soap."[13] Today other soaps float, and people take more showers. Times change.

A bigger potential problem occurs when a company voluntarily gives up its associations before they have lost their effectiveness. A maxim in the agency business is that clients usually get tired of a strategy or slogan long before it loses its effectiveness. Clients may simply be eager to try new ideas, or may feel the agency is not doing enough to earn their compensation. There is also a temptation to capitalize on the equity in a brand by entering a new category.

In 1993, Miller Lite was the second best-selling brand of beer, Budweiser was easily first, and Coors Light and Bud Light both came in a distant third. In 1991, Miller changed its advertising campaign in an attempt to close up the considerable distance between Budweiser and Miller Lite with a new campaign that used the tagline "It's it and that's that." They were trying to suggest that consumers were drinking Miller Lite for itself and not because it was a beer with fewer calories. The message simply wasn't credible. Taste may be subjective, but do any beer drinkers actually prefer the taste of a thinner (light) beer to a full-bodied (regular) beer? It was a nice idea, but the opportunity simply wasn't there. In 1994, Bud Light overtook Miller Lite as the second best-selling brand of beer.[14] By 1998, Bud Light had a $6.6 billion sales lead despite media expenditures for Miller Lite totaling almost as much as those of Budweiser and Bud Light combined.[15]

Of course, there may be many reasons why the Miller brand has not done well, but it is clear that the advertising for Miller Lite in the 1990s has not generated the kind of sales the company would have liked. An important part of strategy development is determining which brand associations are worth reinforcing or intensifying and which brand associations are worth changing or pursuing. In the case of Miller Lite, they may have given up on their "taste great less filling" campaign too soon. In the case of Nissan, perhaps they should have waited until their cars were perceived as exciting before they tried to promote this brand association.

OTHER PROPRIETARY BRAND ASSETS

Another important part of a brand's equity is assets (or liabilities), such as patents, trademarks, characters, and channel relationships.

Patents and Trademarks. Many companies have exclusive ownership of distinctive assets that contribute to a brand's equity. Until late 1993, Monsanto owned the patent rights to aspartame, a sweetener the company branded under the names Equal, when sold in packages, and Nutrasweet, when used as an ingredient in other products. Many people thought that after the patent ran out other companies would enter the market with a cheaper generic equivalent, which would also be aspartame. These people forgot the lessons learned with Tylenol.

Many companies can easily duplicate acetaminophen, the generic name for Tylenol, but consumers won't buy very much of it. Tylenol is not only far and away the best-selling brand of acetaminophen, but sales of Tylenol are 60% greater than those of the next best-selling, over-the-counter pain reliever, Advil. Doctors rarely recommend acetaminophen; they simply say Tylenol.[16]

Similarly, Monsanto shrewdly managed its asset so that even after it no longer owned the patent, the brand was still protected. Monsanto set up a separate company, The Nutrasweet Co., to manage the brand and give it corporate identity. It invested heavily in advertising and required the thousands of products that use Nutrasweet as an ingredient to list the brand name and its symbol on their labels. The only way a new company could compete would be on price, and even then it is likely that Monsanto would meet any competitor's low price. A competing company would have to overcome both consumer loyalty to the Equal brand and resistance within the production areas of companies reluctant to change their advertising and packaging to reflect the absence of Nutrasweet. As a result, no *significant* competition to Nutrasweet appears on the horizon.

Characters can also be used to manage the equity in a brand. Putting Mikey's face on the box of Life cereal and Morris's picture on the outside of a can of cat food can stimulate sales in the short term and have lasting effects over an extended period of time. The effects can also be permanent.

Characters. In 1950, the Minnesota Valley Canning Company changed its name to the Green Giant Company to reflect its use of the Green Giant character in its advertising. The giant first appeared in the company's ads in 1925, hunchbacked and looking like a "fugitive from a Grimm's fairy tale." Later it evolved into an amiable character, somewhat obscure but most of all imaginary. Leo Burnett added the word Jolly to a proof of a *Ladies Home Journal* ad, and the company has kept the word in its vocabulary ever since.[17]

Channel Relationships. The relationship within the channel of distribution is another important influence on a brand's equity. This relationship, along with the various messages consumers receive from other marketing communication tools, directly influence the image of the company, which in turn influence brand loyalty, perceptions of quality, and brand associations. For example, salespeople put a high premium on the value of their contacts. Frequently, it's not what you know or what you have to sell as much as it is who you know and how much people like working with you. Personal relationships can be very important. Over time, a network of relationships tends to become institutionalized. Companies within a channel of distribution get accustomed to working with certain suppliers. New vendors may require company employees to learn new product specifications, new procedures, and new contacts within their organization. If the company uses any of the supplier's equipment, as often is the case with vending operations, changing suppliers can be a significant inconvenience.

Channel relationships are important, but also the extensiveness of the channel networks can be a positive influence on what consumers and channel members think of a brand. Gatorade is the number-one sport drink with substantial brand equity, but when Coca-Cola entered the market with Powerade and Pepsi with All Sport, Gatorade had reason to be nervous. Both Coca-Cola and Pepsi have substantial resources to spend promoting their products and extensive distribution networks that can make their products available in many locations that are not available to Gatorade. These networks add value to the brand's image because consumers and dealers know Coca-Cola and Pepsi are considerable forces to be reckoned with in the marketplace.

- In the early 1990s, United Airlines ran a commercial that touched upon the importance of personal relationships. The spot used a slice-of-life dramatic approach featuring a CEO addressing his employees in a serious tone of voice. The company had lost a major customer apparently because the company "no longer knew who we were." In the spot, the CEO passes out plane tickets (presumably from United Airlines) and urges his executives to get to know the customers better. In 1997, United Airlines fired its longtime ad agency, Leo Burnett. What happened to the long-term relationships? Not much, as the story goes. The people in the key decision-making positions at United Airlines hadn't been with the company nearly as long as the company had been with the agency. While the relationship between an advertiser and its agency may be important, the company was more concerned with the relationship

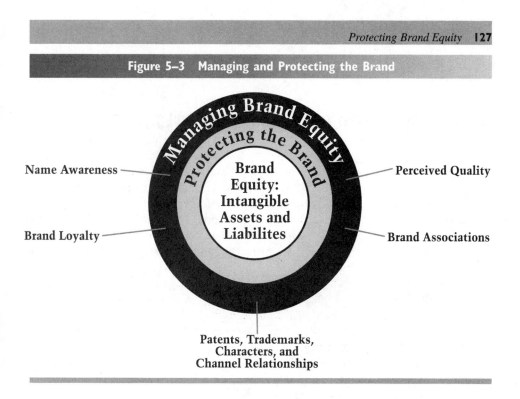

Figure 5–3   Managing and Protecting the Brand

between itself and consumers. The long-time campaign for United Airlines, "Fly the friendly skys of United," focused on the positive aspects of flying. The new United "Rising" campaign focuses on customers.[18]

A critical part of the strategy-building process is to assess the amount of value there is in the company's proprietary assets, such as its patents, characters, and channel relationships. Although these assets can get old and lose their value to the firm, once a company stops promoting them, they may not be able to get them back should they later decide they made a mistake.

PROTECTING BRAND EQUITY

Underlying the development of all communication strategy should be an understanding that the protection of the brand name is of paramount importance. Whereas managing brand equity is part of the strategic foundation that is used to build the marketing communication strategy, protecting brand equity is a philosophy that pervades all strategic and tactical thinking.

Brands can be a fragile asset for a company. Consider the current status of once-proud names, such as Pan Am, Miller Highlife, Schlitz, Wordstar, Foster Grant, and White Cloud. A brand can be a strong player one year and next to nowhere within a few years. At the local level, businesspeople need to work hard to shore up the erosion of their company names. If all the local hardware or garden supply store has to offer is merchandise and equipment, then it surely will be squeezed out of business by Wal-Mart and other mass merchandise retailers.

Through all the steps in building the strategic foundation and while pursuing its strategy and tactics, companies need to be sure that their names are protected. Figure 5–3 presents a diagrammatic view of the relationships involved in managing and protecting brand equity.

SHORT-TERM THINKING VERSUS LONG-TERM INVESTMENT

Much has been written about the differences between Japanese and American businesses. American firms tend to pay more attention to short-term performances because it influences the company's stock prices whereas Japanese companies seem more concerned about success over the long haul. The performances of many brand managers in the United States are evaluated on a quarterly basis. If sales haven't reached marketing goals toward the end of a quarter, many managers will run price promotions, such as trade discounts, consumer rebates, coupons, and price reductions. These promotions eat into profit margins and send a not too subtle message to consumers: Our position is not very strong, they seem to say, so we're lowering prices. If you can't buy now, wait around; we'll probably lower them again. Price promotions undermine consumers' confidence in their perceptions of the brand's worth. The value in having a brand with equity is that consumers are generally willing to pay a premium for a strong name.

Investing in advertising to build a brand's equity or keep it from eroding is a lot more difficult to measure than short-term behavioral effects, such as coupon redemptions, price promotions, or 1-800 inquiries. Focusing on brand equity is more long term in nature because the effects of advertising to build a brand tend to accumulate over an extended period of time. But long term may be interminable to brand managers working their way up the corporate ladder. It is easier for them to document their accomplishments with something that is easily measured than it is with something that can be as vague and difficult to measure as brand equity. New technology, especially check-out scanners, allows managers to track even minor sales downturns and bump them up with price oriented promotions. Though this practice may be to the brand's long-term detriment, the availability of technology makes the temptation hard to resist.

WHO PROTECTS THE NAMES?

If brand managers cannot be relied on to protect the brand's long-term interest, whose responsibility is it? The answer should be everyone's, but in most companies that's not the case. Most companies consider it easier to measure short-term effects than long-term effects, and the results make a decisionmaker's position more defensible and less subject to the demanding scrutiny of a client or supervisor. Much of what is written about setting and writing objectives, including what we have written, works better with short-term effects.

At a minimum, the protection of the brand should be the responsibility of the marketing director and the advertising director. In 1981, McDonald's replaced its advertising agency, Needham, Harper Worldwide, with the Leo Burnett Co. This move stunned the advertising business because Needham had won numerous awards for its creative efforts, and *Advertising Age* had named it the "Advertising Agency of the Year for 1977." Sales were doing fine at McDonald's, but according to insiders, McDonald's had posed a number of marketing questions to Needham, which usually responded with more creative executions. What McDonald's wanted was more insight on strategic planning. In what directions should they take the brand? How might they capitalize on the brand's equity without undermining its value? McDonald's was thinking long term, and Needham was focusing on short term.

The transition from Needham to Burnett appeared to be smoother than it really was. Although Burnett did provide the desired marketing information, the early Burnett ads were not consistent with the way McDonald's had been promoted. McDonald's had to educate Burnett about McDonald's approach to protect the brand equity. As we've mentioned, until 1993, McDonald's had used little to no research to measure the effectiveness of its advertising and acted largely according to its judgment. With a major retail operation like McDonald's, you can often see the effects of an ad or campaign in the marketplace the day after a new campaign begins. Although you may not be able to statistically validate its effects, an experienced manager can make a reasonable judgment. Fortunately for McDonald's, they have had that kind of judgment. In 1997, McDonald's replaced Burnett with DDB Needham (same company, different name). Sales had been flat for a number of years and in a management shakeup at McDonald's, a decision to replace Burnett as the lead agency on its account (Burnett did retain some business) sent a signal that the company was moving decisively to boost its flagging sales.

On the agency side, the guardianship of a brand's equity should nominally belong to the account executive (AE). However, AEs are a lot like brand managers in that they are so involved in day-to-day details, such as checking copy, approving coupons, and reviewing media schedules, that they too run the risk of sacrificing long-term equity for short-term performance. Account supervisors, who rank higher than an AE, should do a better job of focusing on brand equity because they are likely to be more experienced than an account executive and are less involved with day-to-day details.

Perhaps, in recognition that building brand equity is a long-term strategic concern, many agencies are putting more people into positions where their main responsibility is strategic planning. And in recognition, perhaps, that their agencies are not doing the job, advertisers are hiring outside consultants to help them with brand strategy and/or hiring a second agency to help them build the brand.

SPELLING OUT BRAND PROTECTION

Protecting the equity in a brand can be viewed as either a core element in a strategic plan or as a mind-set that should pervade all aspects of any campaign. We prefer to assume that protection of the company's names should be of paramount importance in all activities and need not be spelled out in a firm's marketing plan. Protecting equity is somewhat different from managing brand equity. Protecting equity implies a defensive strategy, whereas managing equity suggests a proactive strategy. A company that is trying to build brand X for Acme Mfg., for example, may recommend an action that could damage the brand or the company name. To manage Acme's equity, someone might interject, "That's not Acme" (meaning, that's not the way we do things around here) or "That's not the brand X way" (meaning, that's not the way we do things for the brand either). Usually, on a day-to-day basis, the questions that come up deal more with managing than protecting brand equity.

However, when a public-relations disaster occurs, companies often adopt a circle-the-wagons approach, in which they try to protect the brand name from all sides. In 1990, traces of benzene, a toxic liquid, were found in Perrier bottled water, forcing a global recall of all supplies of the company's bottled water. At the time, Perrier was the brand leader with more than a 50% market share. There appeared to be little that could be done to protect the brand. Consumers assumed the problem was in the company's product because benzene, a carcinogen, had entered the water in the production process.[19] Nearly three years later, the Perrier brand had sunk to less than a 4% market share, ranking number eight in the bottled-water category, according to Nielsen.[20] By 1994, the best-selling brand of bottled water continued to be a product sold by the Perrier Group of America, only the brand name was Arrowhead instead of the company's best-known name, Perrier.[21] In 1998, the top-selling brand of bottled water was Poland Spring, another Perrier brand.[22] In other words, the only way Perrier could find to manage the crisis was to concentrate on another name and let the Perrier name drop. Although there may not have been much the company could have done, it is possible to manage these crises effectively.

In 1993, reports came out of Seattle, Nashville, and New Orleans that syringes were found in cans of Pepsi and Diet Pepsi. Within days, Pepsi Cola put together a team of 11 high-ranking executives to handle the crisis. It took out ads in more than 200 local newspapers as well as national publications such as the *New York Times* and *USA Today* to reassure consumers that it was "simply not logical to conclude that a nationwide tampering had occurred" based on the production process and other factors. Within days, the media were generally reporting that the stories were probably a hoax. Later research showed no significant effect on sales.[23]

Determining the Right Strategic Focus to Build the Brand

A brand can't rest on past laurels. If it can be improved, it should strive to do so, or the competition will pass it by. Increasingly, leading marketers are selling off their second-tier brands to concentrate on the top performers in their portfolios.[24] However, some brands are limited in their potential to physically improve. Procter & Gamble may try to persuade consumers that "new improved" Tide is an improvement over an older version, but the typical "improvement" is very slight, if even noticeable.[25] Part of the challenge to a strategic planner is to figure out how to add value to a brand by reinforcing or building brand equity. Of the five elements that influence brand equity, each of these generally require different emphases or focus. An important decision in the development of the campaign strategy is to determine the strategic focus, or focal points, for the rest of the brand team to follow.

Brand awareness is not a problem for Campbell Soup. Perceptions of quality may be a problem, but the company is limited in what it can credibly tell consumers. Campbell Soup is good soup, but great soup it probably is not. As a result, the advertising for Campbell Soup often focuses on brand associations that are designed to reinforce brand loyalty. One common theme involves getting consumers to remember the warm fuzzy feelings they had when Mom gave them warm Campbell Soup soup on a chilly day. The nostalgia associated with simpler times, the comforting memories of a loving parent, all add value to what is basically a simple, and even bland product.

Positioning the Message

Positioning is the next important element of the strategic foundation. It is highly interrelated with the management of brand equity. In a broad sense, positioning refers to the way advertisers try to get consumers to think or feel about their products in relation to some context, such as an emotion or an experience. Calvin Klein, for example, wants consumers to feel an emotional connection to Obsession perfume. Ray Kroc, one of the co-founders of McDonald's, always reminded his people that "McDonald's sold more than the hamburger, they sold the experience the hamburger was wrapped in."

Consumers seem to have a perceptual map in their minds that places, or positions, one product in relation to something else. In a narrower use of the positioning concept, that something else is the other brands in the market, and consumers compare brands consciously or subconsciously according to their similarities and differences. When a company tries to influence what consumers think of a brand with respect to its competition, this kind of positioning is called **competitive positioning.**

Chevrolet, for example, is usually thought of as a family car; Volvo as a safe, durable car; and Cadillac as a luxury car. Consumers also make fine distinctions within subcategories. Cadillacs are not simply luxury automobiles; they are also cars that have a more traditional image, conveying status and prestige, a car that might be purchased by a banker or a small-business owner. In contrast, a Lexus has a more contemporary luxury image, a car you might expect an investment counselor or a CEO of a midsize company to own.

Positioning reflects the decisions that companies make to intentionally influence the images and associations that consumers have of their products and, sometimes, even those of the competition. For example, Pepsi would like consumers to believe that it is a product for hip, young-minded people. In contrast, it likes to portray Coca-Cola as an older, more conservative, and somewhat stodgy brand.

In Chapter 2 and Chapter 3, we discussed some of the procedures and tests you can use to determine consumers' perceptions of a brand. A goal of many of these activities is to determine and understand a brand's image or personality. This information can then be used to change, reinforce, or intensify the image. The brand's image or its personality can be the result of many factors, including advertising, pricing policies, signage, packaging, and, of course, the want-satisfying qualities of the product. Positioning is action-oriented. It's what companies do to influence what people think or feel. A brand or a company's image takes time to establish, but once it is implanted on the consumers' perceptual map, it remains firmly established—sometimes even when the company would like to see it changed.

Sears has long had the reputation as a seller of quality merchandise, especially for appliances and hardware. However, in the 1980s it was having a difficult time dealing with two major problems. Its merchandise, especially soft goods, was often perceived as slightly too conservative. Sears was also being undercut badly by discount merchandisers such as Wal-Mart. In some stores, nearly half of all revenue was generated by items on sale.

In the spring of 1989, Sears changed its pricing structure to a policy featuring fewer sale items and everyday low(er) prices (EDLP) on most items. Sears achieved some success with this move but, after an initial spurt in business, stores were allowed to run more sale items. Over the years, Sears had trained its customers to expect sale items; that was part of the consumers' perception of how Sears operates. Despite heavy promotion announcing the new plan, Sears relented, and its pricing policy began increasingly to resemble the old structure.

Sales continued to be a problem. In 1993, Sears restructured its clothing and apparel lines, updating them with a more contemporary look. It then introduced the lines with the very successful advertising campaign, "Come see the softer side of Sears."[26] Sears has been successful with the repositioning of its image because the restructure was not a complete change, but merely an update, which consumers have accepted.

Positioning decisions are strategic in nature and provide the direction for a campaign to follow. Competitive positioning usually implies that the company is willing to sacrifice some component of the overall market to be more effective within a narrower focus. Pepsi positions its brand as a drink for young people, or those who think young. It's willing to sacrifice an appeal to the "older" market. However, Pepsi does quite well with its "limited" appeal. After all there are a lot of people who think they are young.

Positioning a Product

Various authors have noted that there are at least seven different ways to position a product:

1. By product characteristics or customer benefits. (Lee jeans is the "brand that fits.")

2. By a price–quality relationship. (Sears is a "value" store.)

3. By use or application. (Cortaid Cream "relieves itches.")

4. By product user. (Trix "are for kids.")

5. By product class. (Dove is not just a soap, but is a cleansing product for dry skin.)

6. By cultural symbol. (Harley-Davidson, "Born in the U.S.A.")

7. By competitor. (Avis positions itself with Hertz.)[27]

After the basic positioning strategy has been determined, it is up to the copywriters and the art directors to execute a message strategy with creative tactics. The development of the message strategy and tactics will be covered more extensively in Chapter 6.

THE MARKETING COMMUNICATION EXPENDITURE

The decision about how much money to allocate for marketing communications is simple in concept but complicated in practice. This decision is of strategic interest because it has a profound influence on the way a company can compete. Companies compete both in terms of the quality and the quantity of the messages they disseminate. The size of the advertising budget, usually called the appropriation, can influence the creativity involved in the message strategy. It may have an even greater impact on media. Although creativity can flourish independently from expenditures, media exposure cannot. One common viewpoint is expressed as follows:

Share of media expenditures
equals
Share of media voice
equals
Share of mind and heart
equals
Share of market.

Of course, this view only works within a certain range of expenditures. Beyond a certain level of expenditures, each additional dollar spent on advertising or promotion is unlikely to generate sufficient sales to cover expenses and still contribute to net profit. It is relatively easy using marginal analysis to understand the relationship between advertising expenditures and sales in retrospect; it is a lot more difficult to predict this relationship in advance.[28] Determining the optimum amount of money to spend for advertising may be one of the most difficult tasks facing advertising and agency planners.[29]

A complete discussion of all the variables that can influence the appropriation and how to determine the optimal level of expenditures is beyond the scope of this book. Such a discussion would include modeling procedures using multiple regression analysis to explain and predict the relationship between advertising and sales over time.

The typical reader of this book does not usually deal with these issues, and the size of the budget is usually a given in advertising campaigns classes. Agencies, also, do not usually determine the advertising appropriation but receive it from their clients. It is, however, important that the amount of money allocated to marketing communications be appropriate for the expected tasks: solving problems and exploiting opportunities. To provide a rough idea about how these decisions are made, we'll look at some traditional methods for determining the appropriation and some of the factors that influence their size.

Traditional Approaches to Determine the Appropriation

A number of widely used methods appear in advertising textbooks. It is important to understand that a company doesn't necessarily use one method. It is more likely that companies use a combination of methods.

All You Can Afford

The use of this method appears to be on the decline. The chief advantage of this method is that it is simple and, for companies of limited resources, may be the only option. Its main disadvantages are lack of a rational basis for the decision and insufficient resources to generate enough advertising exposure to stimulate an impact in the marketplace. In 1975, San Augustine and Foley found that this was the second most widely used method by large advertisers.[30] In 1981, Patti and Blasko reported that this method had fallen to the sixth position in popularity.[31] Still, approximately 20% of the respondents reported using this method. Many companies reported using more than one method. It is likely that many companies started out using another method and wound up using this one due to budgetary constraints.

Percentage of Sales

This widely used method involves multiplying past or anticipated sales by a certain percentage to determine the amount of money to be appropriated for the marketing communication budget. This percentage can be obtained from a variety of sources: industry contacts, trade associations, trade publications, government data, conferences, and conventions. This method is an especially useful one if the decisionmaker's expertise does not lie within the area of marketing or advertising. If the percentage used as the multiplier is typical of successful firms in the field, then this method is likely to be a good one, depending on the degree to which the advertiser is similar to other companies. Its main disadvantage is that sales are usually used to determine the advertising expenditure. When sales are high, the advertising budget will be high. When sales are low, the budget will also be low. Logically, the situation may require the exact opposite, especially when sales are low.

Competitive Parity

This method uses the competition's expenditures as a benchmark against which the company determines its strategy. Companies use this approach for at least two reasons: First, a company may assume that if the competition is successful, it must know what it is doing, including appropriating the best amount for a budget; and second, a company may feel that it needs to match the competition's expenditures to be competitive.

The limitations of this method vary according to how similar the companies in the category match up. Companies that appear to be similar from afar may have significant differences when scrutinized up close.

Objective and Task

This approach is the most logical method, but it is probably also the most difficult one to use. It is used by nearly two-thirds of the largest advertisers.[32] To use this method, a planner first defines specific objectives. The next step involves determining the various tasks required to achieve the objectives. The last step, also the easiest, involves estimating the cost of implementing the tasks.

This approach is logical because it links marketing communication expenditures to the achievement of specific goals. If the objectives are defined in terms of behavioral objectives such as sales, then the first step, defining objectives, is relatively easy, but the second step is difficult, determining the marketing communication tasks that will likely achieve the objectives.

In the case of sales goals, many of the marketing communication tools, such as advertising, could influence sales. Determining which variable had which effect often leaves a gap in the linkage between sales goals and a specific communication tool, such as advertising or sales promotion. To solve this problem, some advertisers define their communication objectives (at least their message-oriented ones) in terms of communication criteria, such as top-of-mind awareness or attitude change. This makes the link between the objectives and the communication tasks much clearer. It still leaves difficult questions pertaining to the degree to which the achievement of communications criteria, such as attitude change, will result in the achievement of marketing goals, such as sales.

Although the objective and task method is more complicated than many of the other approaches, it attempts to deal with questions the other methods leave unanswered. In 1975, one study of large advertisers reported that only 12% of the companies used the method.[33] By 1981, a similar study indicated that the percentage using this method had increased to 62%.[34] In 1983, a related study of computer-based advertising budgeting practices of large advertisers reported that 80% of companies used this method.[35]

It's ironic that the most popular approach to determining the size of a marketing communication budget is likely one that is never included in industry surveys—*historical precedent*. Companies often base their budgets on what they spent the previous year.

TARGETING AND DELIVERING THE MESSAGE

Targeting is the last element of the strategic foundation. In its broadest sense, targeting the message involves both the people to whom the message is aimed and the means by which the message gets delivered. At this stage in the development of a campaign, the target market has typically already been determined. Nevertheless, during the development of strategy, new opportunities may present themselves that call for either a reexamination or a

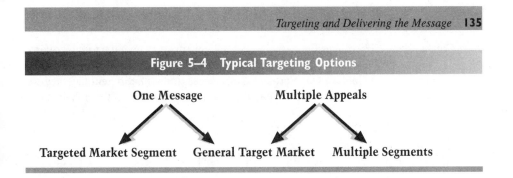

Figure 5–4   Typical Targeting Options

One Message   Multiple Appeals

Targeted Market Segment   General Target Market   Multiple Segments

modification of the target market. This is another example of how the development of a campaign can be an ongoing process.

For example, when Coca-Cola hired CAA out of Hollywood to produce television commercials, it was looking for breakthrough advertising. Coca-Cola's strategy was simple: Hire famous, highly creative film directors to produce highly creative television commercials. The spots were often highly creative, very visual, and mostly unrelated except for the tagline "Always Coca-Cola." Although the campaign was criticized for not having enough continuity, the company's response was that it used different spots to appeal to different market segments.[36]

Whether this strategy was in place before the spots were produced is moot for this discussion. It is easy to argue that the decision to determine the target audience, or markets, should be made before the strategy and tactics are determined; however, it is also common and strategically sound to modify the positioning and targeting strategies as new opportunities develop.

The targeting decision usually ranges from a point where a company will use one message, or appeal, for all consumers to a point at which the company uses separate messages for different market segments. Figure 5–4 presents typical targeting options.

When a company makes a decision to position its message against a specific competitor, it logically follows that it will be segmenting at least part of the market. By influencing consumers to think of a product in a certain way, the company, in effect, is implying not to think of the product in a different way. When Pepsi positions its products as youth-oriented, it is targeting its messages to segments of the overall population who are young, who think young, or who would like to be young.

Companies that use one message to appeal to a mass audience tend to have brands that are used across broad demographic categories, such as Wesson oil, Hunt's tomato paste, and Nabisco saltine crackers. To be successful with this approach, the message should be general or diffuse enough to allow a variety of consumer groups to read into it a benefit that appeals to them. Campbell Soup's "Good for the body, good for the soul" campaign was an example of this type of message. This approach usually works best for the market leader in a category. Campbell Soup sells more than 50% of all canned soup. As product categories become increasingly competitive and as the products within the generic class approach parity, companies usually opt for a strategy positioned around a message that appeals primarily to a portion of the overall market.

Companies that use multiple messages to target multiple market segments tend to be large companies. In many cases, these companies are simply applying the marketing concept to an increasingly fragmented market. In the "Always Coca-Cola" campaign,

Coca-Cola used a variety of musical formats, such as rock, rap, and country, to send different messages to various segments with the same general, low-keyed theme: No matter what's going on, Coca-Cola is always around. To be successful with different messages, a company must be sure to tie each message into the brand's core equities, as Coca-Cola does.

Developing a Marketing Communication Mix

There has been a great deal written in recent years about the importance of integrating the components of marketing communication into a marketing communication mix. Surprisingly, there has been very little written about how much of the marketing effort or budget should be devoted to advertising and how much to other types of marketing communications. Companies offer little insight. The same company that will divulge proprietary information off the record will seldom provide any usable information about how it allocates money to different types of promotion. Generally, companies say they use judgment based on experience. Other times they will indicate they use marketing mix or advertising and marketing (A and M) models, but "they are proprietary." These models may be sophisticated, but the usual impression companies give is that the models are rudimentary or even crude.

A Media-Oriented Approach. One approach to determining the marketing communication mix is to view each type of communication as a means of delivering messages or impressions to consumers. Each promotional tool can then be evaluated in terms of its ability to *efficiently* generate exposure for the brand. Values can be assigned to the importance of traditional media criteria, such as cost efficiency, competitive share of voice, and optimal reach and frequencies, and an allocation model can be constructed. There are at least a couple of problems with this approach. Some forms of marketing communications, such as sales promotion and public relations, are difficult to measure. Any type of quantitative analysis would only be as good as the measurements. However, the main problem with this approach is that it is difficult to integrate a value for message content into a quantitative model.

A Message-Oriented Approach. Some scholars have argued that it is wrong to evaluate media channels in terms of vehicle exposures. Instead, promotional tools should be evaluated on the basis of the information they communicate. Therefore, each medium, or type of marketing communication, can be looked at in terms of its ability to effectively deliver certain types of information. For example:

Network television	delivers a strong brand identity.
Brochures	deliver specific information.
Radio	reminds consumers to act.
Yellow Pages	move consumers to specific buying locations.
Public relations	provides information that is more highly credible.
Infomercials	provide in-depth persuasive information.
Store displays	stimulate action at point of sale.[37]

Both the media- and the message-oriented approach require substantial amounts of judgment. Although it is possible to do a mathematical model to apportion amounts of money to marketing communication tools, expectations of a rigorous approach probably await further research developments. In-depth coverage of marketing communication strategy and tactics will be covered in Chapter 8.

Advertising Media Strategy

In the development of an integrated marketing communication plan, the strategic decision about the marketing communication mix should ideally precede any decisions about what kind of media to use. However, advertising usually will be the dominant form of marketing communication.

For this reason, media strategy will be covered in depth in Chapter 7. Related types of marketing communication, such as sales promotion, public relations, and direct marketing, which typically supplement traditional media such as radio, television, magazines, and newspapers, are discussed in Chapter 8.

Campaign Progress Checklist

At this point in the campaign you should be generally aware of the following points:

1. Campaign strategies should be based on a strategic foundation consisting of four elements: the management of brand equity, the positioning of messages, the funding of the marketing communication program, and the targeting and delivery of messages.

2. The long-term success of a brand requires that the intangible value, or equity, associated with the brand name be managed to avoid competing on the basis of price or product distinctions (which it may not have).

3. Cultivating brand loyalty is the most important aspect of managing brand equity.

4. For many brands, simple awareness is less important than top-of-mind awareness.

5. Perceptions of a brand's quality can be more important than its actual quality.

6. The associations consumers make with a brand influence how they think and feel about a product.

7. A company's proprietary assets, such as patents, characters, and channel relationships are an important part of the product itself and should be carefully evaluated and promoted or the brand may lose part of its value.

8. Positioning the product is an important strategic decision because it provides direction for the writers and art directors to follow helping to ensure that the ads will be on target and on strategy.

9. Understanding how the marketing communication appropriation was determined is important because it can have a profound influence on the way a company can compete.

10. There are at least three important targeting decisions: who to target, how to reach them efficiently, and how to use media and related communication tools effectively to get the message across.

Notes and References

[1] Aaker, D. A. (1991). *Managing brand equity.* New York: Free Press, p. 16.

[2] Munk, N. (1998, May 25). Why women find Lauder mesmerizing. *Fortune*, pp. 96–106.

[3] Serafin, R., & Johnson, B. (1993, October 18) Saturn-alia in Spring Hill next summer. *Advertising Age, 64,* pp. 1, 55.

[4] This article is an excerpt from *After-Marketing* by Terry G. Vavra. "After-marketing: How to keep customers for life through relationship marketing," *Brandweek,* December 7, 1992, volume 33, p. 20.

[5] Vavra, T. G. (1992, December 7). Learning from your losses. *Brandweek,* p. 21.

[6] Vavra, Learning from your losses, p. 20.

[7] Parente, D. E. (1995). A look at the way advertisers write objectives. Unpublished working paper, p. 9.

[8] Aaker, *Managing brand equity,* p. 63.

[9] Ries, A., & Jack Trout, J. (1993). *The 22 immutable laws of marketing: Violate them at your own risk.* New York: HarperBusiness, p. 18.

[10] Ries & Trout, *The 22 immutable laws,* p. 3.

[11] Popolillo, M. C. (1998, June 15). Private label strong, as branded items extend. *SUPERBRANDS,* p. S54.

[12] Elkin, T. (1998, June 15). Forecast more fluries. *SUPERBRANDS,* p. S58.

[13] Aaker, *Managing brand equity,* p. 1.

[14] Beer, Wine, Liquor, *Brandweek,* Oct. 9, 1995, p. 120.

[15] Khermouch, G. (1998, June 15). Pockets of success tempered by concern. *SUPERBRANDS,* p. S28.

[16] Popolillo, Private label strong, as branded items extend, p. S58.

[17] The information on the Green Giant character is abstracted from unpublished, undated, and un-numbered material on "Enduring Campaigns" from the Leo Burnett Company, Inc.

[18] Davis, S. (1998, May 25). Knowing when to do a brand do-over. *Brandweek,* p.17.

[19] Author. (1990, December 24). News makers 1990. *Advertising Age, 61,* p. 5.

[20] Crumley, B., & Bowes, E. (1992, November 30). Perrier moves to publicis. *Advertising Age, 63,* p. 53.

[21] *SUPERBRANDS* (1989–1994).

[22] Benezra, K., & Khermouch, G. (1998, June 15). Enough niche product, the cola giants strike back. *SUPERBRANDS,* p. S32.

[23] Magiera, M. (1993, June 21). Pepsi weathers tampering hoaxes. *Advertising Age, 64,* p. 46.

[24] Pollack, J., & Neff, J. (1997, September 15). Marketer decree: Be a top brand or be gone. *Brandweek,* p.2.

[25] Mehegan, S. (1998, August 4). P&G makes Tide more efficient. p. 9

[26] Underwood, E. (1995) Weathering the storm. *Superbrands,* p. 123.

[27] Aaker, D. A., Batra, R., & Myers, G. (1995). *Advertising management* (5th ed.). Englewood Cliffs, NJ: Prentice-Hall, pp. 190–201.

[28] For more information on marginal analysis, see Aaker et al. *Advertising management,* pp. 548–551

[29] Sissors, J. Z., & Bumba, L. (1995). *Advertising media planning* (5th ed.). Lincolnwood, IL: NTC Business Books, p. 407.

[30] San Augustine, A. J., & Foley, W. F. (1975, October). How large advertisers set budgets. *Journal of Advertising Research, 15,* pp. 11–16.

[31] Patti, C. H., & Vincent Blasko, V. (1981, December). Budgeting practices of big advertisers. *Journal of Advertising Research, 21,* pp. 23–29.

[32] Patti & Blasko, Budgeting practices, pp. 23–29.

[33] San Augustine & Foley, How large advertisers, pp. 11–16.

[34] Patti & Blasko, Budgetary practices, pp. 23–29.

[35] Lancaster, K. M., & Stern, J. (1983). Computer based advertising budgeting practices of leading U.S. advertisers. *Journal of Advertising, 12,* p. 6.

[36] Garfield, B. (1993, February 15). Coke ads great, but not always. *Advertising Age,* p. 60.

[37] Adapted from Ron Kaatz, An integrated media planning system, in Dean M. Krugman, Leonard N. Reid, Watson Dunn, & Arnold M. Barban, *Advertising: Its role in modern marketing* (8th ed.). (1994). Fort Worth: The Dryden Press, p. 327.

Chapter 6

Developing a Creative Strategy that Moves People

At BBDO ad agency, they used to say there were two big sins associated with the creative process: no creativity, and creativity for technique's sake. Today, the first sin is more serious than ever before. No matter where consumers go, some advertising message is likely to greet them: "Hi! (they seem to say) I'd like to tell you something about – – –" (fill in the blank). Or worse, a telemarketer on the other end of a phone says: "Hello. Are you interested in saving some money on your – – –" (fill in the blank). It's no wonder that consumers are not only jaded and cynical; they're downright annoyed! To get through a cluttered media landscape, an ad has to have stopping power—something in the ad that makes people pause and pay attention. That "something" must also trigger enough brand associations for consumers to remember the special feeling or information conveyed to them by the brand. It's easy to talk about "something" in the abstract but putting it into practice takes imagination and creativity.

Today, advertising can make you laugh and make you sigh. Whether or not these ads are persuasive generates a lot of debate. An ad that is creative but doesn't sell is what might be called "creativity for technique's sake." These are ads that appear to have been created to showcase some creative effect, even if the effect is simply to make people laugh. An ad might be a good piece of film (or tape), but not a good commercial. While it is probably true that some of these ads are created for the wrong reasons, many are the results of well-intentioned efforts to do something special for the brand. Naturally, executives would like to present ads that are both "creative" *and* persuasive. Although the creative and persuasive qualities of an ad are not necessarily inversely related, sometimes to achieve both creative and persuasive ads you might have to take a little away from one or the other. For example, one of the criticisms of the Nissan "Life is a journey, enjoy the ride" campaign was that the product wasn't shown enough. But if it had, it might have detracted from the entertainment value of the ads.

A copywriter's challenge is to balance an ad's need to be persuasive with a similar need to be creative. It's still very much an art. Our challenge in this chapter is to help the reader make these decisions based on something other than intuition. We divide this chapter into several sections as follows:

- The essential and optional elements found in a creative plan

- An analysis of the opportunity to develop a message strategy

- An examination of the strategic approaches to developing a message strategy

- A modest proposal on how to be creative

- Traditional approaches to creating advertising

- New rules for talking to today's consumer

We are mindful that trying to break down the creative process into discrete components is not without risks. There is a lot about why something is persuasive that defies analysis. Furthermore, we understand many advertising minds feel you can't really teach someone to be creative. Still, to repeat something we said earlier, we do have some suggestions.

ELEMENTS ESSENTIAL TO A CREATIVE PLAN

Following the situation analysis, the campaign should begin to take on a strategic focus. The creative, or message strategy, is often the most important part of this focus. Basically, there are four typical elements found in this section: target audience, objectives, strategy, and tactics.

The Creative Target Audience

This target audience is essentially the same as the campaign target audience, only it may be described somewhat differently. The target audience for a brand of hair shampoo may be females between age of 16 and 22. However, agency creatives may try to get a better feel for this consumer by describing them as "the hair involved." Naturally, in this situation, profiling the target with demographic characteristics is not enough. The target audience is often delineated more subjectively in the creative area because the writers have to create ads that are interpretational and this generally requires that they address the target in more personal terms. In fact, when account planners and creatives get together to write an informal creative brief they sometimes refer to the target using the name of someone they know (say, Sally, the switchboard lady). Although this information doesn't get put into the campaign report, it is useful in generating ideas. Profiling the target as "hair involved," however, will most likely make it into the campaign document.

Creative Objectives

An advertising objective consists of a message element and a media element. Creative objectives are the message part of the advertising objective. Note in the following advertising objective, the first part of the statement refers to a mental effect the ad is supposed to have (that is, the message), and the second part focuses on the delivery of the message (that is, the media).

- To establish top-of-mind awareness (the message part) in 60% of the target audience by the end of the first quarter (the media part).

There are a number of ways to take the above advertising objective and use it to write a creative objective. To do this, focus on the message part of the advertising objective, perhaps as follows:

- To get the target audience to associate the brand name with the product category before any other brands.

The objective of the creative strategy is to get across a message that affects the way the target audience thinks or feels about the brand. If planners understand correctly how consumers make decisions, then these thoughts and feelings should transfer to what the advertiser would like the consumer to do—that usually means buy the product. The mental effect that the writer or artist is trying to achieve with the ad is the core element in a creative objective. This effect is often some variation of the communication criteria we discussed in Chapter 4, such as awareness, comprehension, attitude, or image.

During the first few years after Bud Light was introduced in the early 1980s, it significantly lagged behind Miller Lite, the leader in sales, despite the superior brand equity it enjoyed because of the Budweiser name. Even though most beer-drinkers preferred Budweiser over Miller, many of these same people were ordering a beer by asking for a "light." Because Miller had pioneered the light concept, these consumers were receiving a Miller Lite even though, if they had thought more about it and had been specific, they might have preferred and received the Budweiser Light version.

The challenge to the Budweiser agency was to remind the target that if he or she simply asked for a "light" all sorts of strange things could happen, thus providing the brand with a strategic focal point around which they could develop interesting and creative executions. In the campaign "Give me a light," when customers ordered a light, instead of a beer they got all sorts of lights, including floodlights, spotlights, headlights, flashlights, even a blow torch—lit up. The customer in the ad would then say, "No, I mean a Bud Light." A voiceover reminded the audience, "If you want a Bud Light, you'll just have to say Bud Light."

Consider what the creative objective might have been for this campaign. In the beginning, it may very well have been *to leave a memorable impression of the difference between saying light and Bud Light.* Over the life of the campaign, the creative objective most probably changed from simply "leaving an impression" to "intensifying an impression." Since Bud Light is slightly easier to say (fewer syllables) than Miller Lite, and since consumers have generally preferred the Budweiser brand to any brand from Miller, it's not surprising that Bud Light would eventually pass Miller Lite in sales.

Creative Strategy
Creative strategy consists of the guidelines for the thoughts, feelings, and impressions that are communicated with advertising and other marketing communications. These guidelines provide direction for the copywriters and artists to develop ads that are on

target and within the message strategy. A creative plan is an articulation of the strategy. You might think of it as a map. This map outlines or profiles the important strategic considerations for the campaign's creative thrust, which ultimately drives the message.

There are many formats and structures available for creative plans, and each agency tends to use a different one. In the first edition of this book, we presented eight different versions.[1] In this edition, we decided to present elements that can go into a creative plan and let the account team custom tailor the elements that it feels are appropriate for the particular campaign. We call the more-important elements the **critical elements** of a creative plan.

Critical Elements of the Creative Strategy

There are at least three elements that ought to be part of every creative strategy:

- A strategic focal point

- A positioning statement

- A big unifying idea

Strategic Focal Points. To be sure all creatives concentrate on strategy it is helpful to state the creative focus clearly. You can also think of this focus as a statement of the creative strategy. The focal point is that particular aspect of the company's problem or opportunity the campaign is intended to address. We assume you realize that this focus doesn't materialize out of thin air, but evolves out of research. Exhibit 6–1 presents a list of creative strategy statements that appear to have been the focal points of some very memorable campaigns.

Positioning. Once you determine the focus of the creative plan, your next step is to provide the context, or the background, for the advertising messages. Positioning, as suggested earlier, refers to the way one generally gets consumers to think or feel about the product, especially with respect to the competition. Although the focal point of the Coca-Cola strategy in Exhibit 6–1 is to emphasize that Coke is the real thing, these messages are delivered amidst a wholesome background where consumers satisfy their taste for something refreshing with a Coke. On the other hand, Pepsi Cola uses a narrower type of positioning called **competitive positioning** by suggesting that consumers drink Pepsi—not Coke. Coke positions itself (as category leaders often do) against a broad range of competitors, whereas Pepsi often specifically mentions Coke. Pepsi extends the comparison by stating (in varying ways) that Pepsi is for young people and that Coke is for the older crowd.

Big Unifying Idea. It can be helpful to use an attention-getting device to make ads memorable and to tie together the various elements in a creative plan. Many agencies simply call this device a *big idea*. We call it a *big **unifying** idea* to signify that the idea should be a vehicle that provides a common bond to all the elements contained within an ad. Exhibit 6–2 presents our nomination of some of the more famous big unifying ideas in recent years.

Note the similarity between a creative strategy statement and a big unifying idea. For Energizer batteries, the strategic focus is placed on the idea that their batteries last longer.

Exhibit 6–1   Famous Strategic Focal Points

Brand	Creative Strategy Statement
Energizer	Energizer batteries keep things going (longer) than the other guys.
Marlboro	Masculine men, like cowboys, smoke Marlboro filter-tip cigarettes.
Lee Jeans	Lee makes jeans for women who have trouble finding pants to fit their body.
Wendy's	There's more beef in our burgers. "Where's the beef" in the other guy's?
Coca-Cola	Coca-Cola is the real cola (thing).
Charmin	Charmin is so squeezably soft you won't be able to resist squeezing it.
Miller Lite	Lite beer is a beer that masculine men like to drink because it tastes great and won't fill you up.
Nike	Nike has athletic footwear for people who know what it takes to win and *just do it.*
Gatorade	Gatorade is a drink that quenches the thirst of hardworking athletes.
Wheaties	Wheaties is a cereal eaten by famous athletes.

Exhibit 6–2   Memorable Big Unifying Ideas

Energizer	Toy bunny keeps going and going because Energizer batteries last longer.
Maytag	Maytag repairman is bored since he has nothing to repair because Maytag washers don't break down.
Big Red Gum	Makes your breath so fresh you'll want to kiss a little longer.
Michelin Tire	Baby/tire image evokes benefits of using safer tires on your family car.
Marlboro	Cowboy shows that masculine men smoke filter-tip Marlboro cigarette.
Secret Deodorant	Is strong enough for a man, but pH balanced for a woman.
Frosted Mini Wheats	Has good taste and nutrition for the adult and the kid in you.

The pink bunny gives them a vehicle to say it in many different ways and still stay true to the strategy. The three elements we've discussed so far (a strategic focal point, a positioning statement, and a big unifying idea) provide the bare outline of a creative strategy. To provide depth to a creative plan, other elements can be added to the plan to supply nuances and richness to the strategy. By using some of these optional elements, you can wind up with a more complex strategy that works on differing levels. The desired result is a total effect that is both synergistic and ultimately more persuasive.

OPTIONAL ELEMENTS OF THE CREATIVE STRATEGY

It's the interaction among the various elements in a strategic plan that give a campaign more persuasive power than merely using a series of unrelated ads. The idea is to integrate the elements into a cohesive selling message so that one aspect of the campaign reinforces another. These elements can be something observable (or physical) or simply something one thinks about (psychological). These elements weave a thread of continuity throughout the campaign and give it lasting power.

Physical Continuity

In a campaign, the general plan is to put something in each ad that leaves a similar impression with consumers so that they feel one ad is a continuation of the others. What separates a campaign from a collection of ads is the degree to which each execution is connected. Advertisements that look and sound alike help keep creative work on target. Roman and Maas, formerly of Ogilvy & Mather Worldwide, note that an "agency doesn't have to consider, and test, dozens of new ideas every time a new advertisement needs to be produced."[2] Consumers pick up on new ads and remember them longer when a common element (thread) ties together all the ads in a campaign.

Slogans, taglines, and **trade characters** are devices that add continuity to a company's advertising. For example, United Airlines introduced the tagline "Fly the Friendly Skies" in a 1965 ad. By 1966, the tagline was extended to subsequent ads as an umbrella theme to emphasize United's friendly service as well as an overall friendly flying experience. The tagline was originally inspired by a radar device installed in the nose of United airplanes to alert the pilot to the presence of "unfriendly skies."

A slogan or tagline may be used for a single campaign, or may endure for many years. In 1994, following the buyout of the airline by its employees, United edited the tagline to "Come Fly Our Friendly Skies." (In 1997, the skies were much less friendly to the people at Leo Burnett because United fired its long-time advertising agency.)

Like a good slogan or tagline, an effective trade character can last for years. The Leo Burnett Co. has been as successful as anyone in the business of developing trade characters. Some of the characters have been animated: Tony the Tiger, the Pillsbury Doughboy, and the Keebler Elves; and some have been live-action: Maytag's Lonely Repairman, Charmin's Mr. Whipple, and Morris the Cat. Exhibit 6–3 lists some of the trade characters developed by the Leo Burnett Co.[3]

The opening line in a commercial can also be used as a continuity device. For many years, the opening line "Do you know me?" clearly identified a commercial as one for American Express. Adding a distinctive sound is another way to add a unifying element to a campaign: The sound of a bass drum, followed by the gentle marching of a pink bunny, signals consumers of an arriving Energizer commercial.

Psychological Continuity

Advertisements may look and sound alike, but unless they are psychologically similar or consistent, they are not likely to function as a campaign. Advertisers strive to unify the way people think about their advertising by developing a consistent **theme, image, tone,** or **attitude** in their ads. Each of these constructs is similar to the other in that they affect the way people think or feel about an ad. Although a campaign may not have a consistent theme, image, attitude, or tone in every ad, the campaign will present a more cohesive message if they do.

Exhibit 6–3   Leo Burnett Trade Characters

Account or Product	Year of Arrival	Character
Green Giant	1935	Jolly Green Giant
	1973	Little Green Sprout
Pillsbury	1965	Pillsbury Doughboy
Frosted Flakes	1952	Tony the Tiger
Marlboro	1955	Marlboro Man
9-Lives	1969	Morris the Cat
Maytag	1967	Lonely Repairman
Starkist	1961	Charlie Tuna
Froot Loops	1963	Toucan Sam
Keebler	1968	Keebler Elves
U.S. Department of Transportation	1985	Vince and Larry (the crash test dummies)
7-UP	1988	Spot

The unifying element in most campaigns is the **theme**—the overall idea underlying the advertisement. The theme can be expressed in many different ways. It often is stated most clearly by a **slogan,** which is one reason why slogans are repeated so frequently. Slogans also add physical continuity because they invariably appear in print or as a graphic.

When Virginia Slims cigarettes were introduced in 1968, the women's movement was in its infancy. Philip Morris used the slogan "You've Come a Long Way Baby" to develop the theme that the modern female smoker should have a cigarette that recognized her unique style and attitude. The idea of being "liberated" was a popular one for women in the late '60s–early '70s (at least in the media), and the cigarette's slogan was a way for Virginia Slims to tie the product to an important part of many women's attitudes. By 1985, the brand's share of the cigarette market was about double that of all other women's cigarette brands combined. By the 1990s, the old appeals were losing their relevancy, and the theme in many ads for Virginia Slims stressed the importance of "being yourself"—because, for many women, there really is no other choice.

Knowledgeable advertisers recognize that a product's **image** can have a significant effect on sales. Campaigns can establish, reinforce, and intensify images or replace them with new ones. Perhaps the most successful image campaign of all time has been that of the Marlboro Man, which exemplifies each of these actions. Prior to 1955 (when the Marlboro Man was introduced), filter-tip cigarettes were largely smoked by women. Male smokers, however, far outnumbered female smokers. Recognizing the greater market potential in appealing to men, Leo Burnett, president of the company that bears his name, decided to replace the earlier, more feminine image, with one that would appeal to men by introducing what he called "The Marlboro Man," a rugged, self-assured individual. This mental picture established the brand as one with which men could feel comfortable.

In 1955, the Leo Burnett Co. reinforced this image by giving the Marlboro Man a tattoo, thereby distinguishing him from any male images used by competitors. In 1967, the company intensified this image by introducing in its television commercials music from

The Magnificent Seven, a movie about gunslingers that was very popular with men at that time. From this point on, the music influenced the character and quality—or tone—of all subsequent commercials. By 1975, Marlboro had become the number-one cigarette brand in the United States, and the Marlboro Man living in Marlboro Country set the tone and direction for all subsequent advertising. At the turn of the century, Marlboro is easily the best-selling cigarette in the world. For many people, especially those living in emerging nations, the Marlboro brand is a symbol of Western or American culture.

Campaigns with **attitude** tend to be judgmental, whereas image campaigns usually focus on an idea or concept of a product, person, or institution. People from certain schools, some companies, even various parts of the country often have similar attitudes. We frequently notice that some people simply have an *attitude*. Campaigns, too, can sometimes be described as having an attitude. The question for the marketing strategist becomes: Does the consumer agree/disagree or identify with the situation? The number-one animal in the world with an attitude is the common cat. Unlike dogs, cats assume no guilt for house-training mistakes, they won't try to make you feel better when you're down, and they don't get excited if you throw them a crumb. In fact, if you throw cats good food, they are just as likely to turn up their noses and walk away as they would with garbage. They're fussy, finicky eaters. Many cat owners both admire and love their cats for their independent ways.

In 1969, 9-Lives, a division of Starkist Foods, adopted a strategy using a trade character named Morris to show that 9-Lives has the cat food even finicky cats can't resist. Morris quickly became famous—costarring with Burt Reynolds in the movie *Shamus*, appearing on numerous TV shows such as "Lifestyles of the Rich and Famous" and "Good Morning America," and even visiting backstage with the Chicago and Boston casts of the show *Cats*. In the 1980s, *Young Miss* magazine readers regularly put Morris on their list of Most Admired Celebrities, finishing ahead of Bill Cosby, Ronald Reagan, Prince Charles, and Pope John Paul II. Eventually, 9-Lives got around to putting a picture of Morris on the product's packaging. Within four months of his appearance on the label, the company's share of market in two cat food categories doubled. Such can be the power of a trade character.[4]

Creative Tactics

Once the strategy has been developed, it must to be executed in a detailed way to get the most out of it. It's remarkable how writers and artists can take a simple strategy and turn it into something creative. The goal is not simply to create ads that entertain or appeal to one's aesthetic tastes; the goal is to create ads that help sell the product. Later in this chapter we'll cover some approaches to developing persuasive ads.

APPRAISING THE CREATIVE OPPORTUNITY

Once you understand what goes into a creative plan, the next task is to figure out how to do one. It's not enough to determine what you want to do, it's important to understand what you have a realistic opportunity to do—well. There are numerous approaches to figuring out how to proceed, everything from simple intuition to rigorous analysis. We'll explore only a few approaches. And keep in mind, these are only guidelines.

Probably the easiest and most direct approach is to analyze the product in order to determine what the product has that addresses what consumers want. If a product's want-satisfying qualities are significantly different than the competition, then the rest is easy. The most effective way to advertise, then, is to simply interpret the want-satisfying qualities of the product in terms of the needs or wants of the consumer.[5] Can there be a more effective way to advertise? To paraphrase Leo Burnett, if a product has something that meets the needs or wants of the consumer, that product is *inherently dramatic to them.* If you are working with a product that is not only significantly different from that of the competition, but better as well, the world will beat a path to your door. Maybe.

There are a few problems with this approach. Even if the product is significantly different than the competition, it can be a tough proposition to get the message through a cluttered media landscape and still have an impact with consumers who are often skeptical, indifferent, and perhaps even cynical. It's not enough to have the better product, consumers have to think or feel that it is better. A creative task that starts off sounding fairly simple and straightforward can quickly become complicated. As a result, many advertising people approach developing creative strategy largely on an intuitive basis. This approach may be appropriate if you are an experienced professional; if you are a student, we have some alternative suggestions.

The FCB Grid

Copywriters have several broad strategy options from which they can choose. The advertising can focus on product benefits, it can develop or reinforce brand personality, and/or it can evoke specific feelings and emotions. It can also develop group or brand associations.[6] At the Foote, Cone, & Belding (FCB) advertising agency, an analytical approach was developed to help their creative people understand how to focus message strategy. After conducting extensive research—in the United States and Europe—FCB concluded that it can classify products into four distinct categories. These categories are then assigned to one of four cells in a grid. The first classification includes products consumers primarily "think" about, as opposed to products they buy more on the basis of "feelings." The second classification depends on whether consumers feel high involvement with the product or low involvement. The classifications breakdown follows.

- Products consumers tend to **think** about and have **high involvement** (life insurance, car batteries, exterior house paint, and stereo components)

- Products consumers have **feelings** about and have **high involvement** (perfume, hair coloring, sports cars, wine for a dinner party)

- Products consumers tend to **think** about and have **low involvement** (liquid bleach, paper towels, insect repellent, regular shampoo)

- Products consumers have **feelings** about and have **low involvement** (peanut butter, barbecue sauce, diet soft drinks, fast-food restaurants)

These product categories are placed on a grid to illustrate the degree to which consumers have high or low "involvement," and the degree to which consumers relate to the product on the basis of "thinking" or "feeling." Exhibit 6–4 is an example of the FCB grid.

Using the FCB Grid. This grid is used to help guide both message strategy and executions. The FCB grid is based on Foote, Cone, & Belding's research. The location of a

Exhibit 6–4   FCB Grid

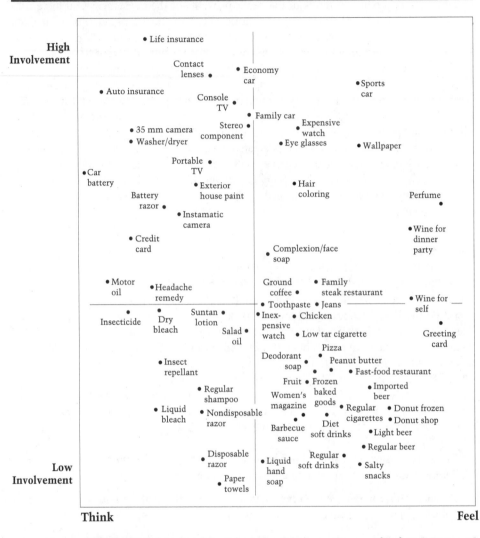

Source: Slightly altered version from John J. Rossiter, Larry Percy, and Robert J. Donovan.
"A better advertising planning grid." *Journal of Advertising Research* (October/
November, 1991), p.12.

brand or any number of products on a custom grid can be constructed using some of the
scales (or questions) we covered in Chapter 2 and Chapter 3. In fact, it should be understood that the grid location of the many brands *within a product category* will likely vary.
For example, Anheuser-Busch runs what they call "heritage" advertising on television. In
these spots, the commercials talk about the brewing traditions handed down from the
founder that make Budweiser the beer it is today. On the FCB grid, "regular beer" is placed

in the area of Low Involvement and Feel. Although a sense of tradition is something most people have feelings about, it is also clear that the heritage ads are designed to influence what people think about Budweiser.

The FCB grid is used to predict responses consumers make to advertising. There is another grid called the Rossiter–Percy model that offers an improvement over the FCB grid. The Rossiter–Percy model offers two additional classifications of motives consumers have for buying a product or brand. In addition to low/high involvement and think/feel motives, Rossiter–Percy suggest consumers have motives that derive from informational needs, such as the desire to solve or avoid problems; and transformational motives, which stem from the consumer's desire to find some meaning or satisfaction in the experience that surrounds the purchase of a brand. This model is divided into six cells and is an excellent model. We, however, use the FCB model because it keeps things fairly simple. Creatives, especially students, sometimes resist using complex analytical approaches to developing ads for fear of it inhibiting a process they regard as essentially intuitive and nonrational. Nonetheless, we recommend that the student/reader consult additional sources for more information.[7]

KNOWING YOUR CREATIVE APPROACH

Once you have a good grasp of your strategy and the creative opportunity, you need to decide on the best creative approach to meet your objective. Patti and Frazier cite seven creative approaches that can serve as a guideline for your crafting of ads (see Exhibit 6–5).

The **generic strategy,** which makes no competitive or superiority claims, is best used for products or brands that dominate a category. It is easily identifiable with a market leader and can rely on a combination of attributes and benefits, with little or no comparison to others made. The advertising for Campbell Soup has promoted the product as "Soup is good food." Since Campbell's sell well over 50% of all canned soup, the advertiser realizes that, if they can get people to eat more soup, the brand will reap most of the sales.

The **preemptive claim** predicts or upstages the competition by advertising a point of difference for the brand. Competing brands may provide similar benefits or have similar attributes, but not advertised those benefits or attributes. Thus, you can preempt them by being the first to lay claim to the key benefit or salient attributes. Coca-Cola has preempted the claim "It's the real thing." In its earlier days, getting this message out was important as other companies tried to trade on the value of Coca-Cola's name by selling brands, such as Cay-Ola, Candy Cola, Coca, Fig-Cola, Cola, Cold Cola, and Koca-Nola. These brands were outlawed by the courts in 1916.[8]

The **unique selling proposition** (USP) is used when a distinct competitive advantage exists; namely, a differentiating factor for your brand. Rosser Reeves made this technique famous with M&M candy's slogan, "Melts in your mouth, not in your hands." This strategy is difficult to employ in today's highly competitive environment, which is defined by explosive product and brand proliferation. Still, as you examine what your brand has or can do in relation to the competition, you should be watchful for positive and useful differentiating factors. Figure 6–1 for the Gillette Mach III is an example of an ad able to take advantage of a strong USP.

The **brand image strategy** relies on factors not inherent to a brand because specific product attributes are relatively meaningless. Rather, the advertising should build, reinforce, or change the target audience's attitude toward the brand, primarily by concentrating on psychological or emotional appeals. Figure 6–2 shows an ad for Tommy Hilfiger, a

Exhibit 6–5   Creative Strategy Alternatives: A Summary

Strategy	Description	Most Suitable Conditions	Competitive Implications
Generic	Straight product or benefit claim with no assertion of superiority	Monopoly or extreme dominance of product category	Serves to make brand synonymous with product category
Preemptive	Generic claim with assertion of superiority	Most useful in growing or awakening market where competitive advertising is generic or nonexistent	May be successful in convincing consumer of superiority of advertiser's product; serves to convince consumers of brand superiority
Unique Selling Proposition	Superiority claim based on unique physical feature or benefit	Most useful when point of difference cannot be matched readily by competitors	Advertiser obtains strong persuasive advantage; forces competitors to imitate or choose more aggressive strategy
Brand Image	Claim based on psychological differentiation; usually symbolic association	Best suited to homogeneous goods where physical differences are difficult to develop or may be quickly matched; requires sufficient understanding of consumers to develop meaningful symbols/ associations	Most often involves prestige claims that rarely challenge competitors directly
Positioning	Attempt to build or occupy mental niche in relation to identified competitor	Best strategy for attacking a market leader; requires relatively long-term commitment to aggressive advertising efforts and understanding consumers	Comparisons limit options for competition; counterattacks seem to offer little chance of success

Exhibit 6–5 *continued*

Strategy	Description	Most Suitable Conditions	Competitive Implications
Resonance	Attempt to evoke stored experiences of prospects to endow product with relevant meaning or significance	Best suited to socially visible goods; requires considerable consumer understanding to design message patterns	Few direct limitations on competitor's options; likely competitive response; imitation
Affective	Attempt to provoke involvement or emotion through ambiguity, humor, or the like, without strong-selling emphasis	Best suited to discretionary items; effective use depends on conventional approach by competitors to maximize difference; greatest commitment is to aesthetics or intuition rather than research	Competitors may imitate to undermine strategy of difference or pursue other alternatives

brand that sells largely on the basis of image. Note the multicultural diversity in the ad. Not only does this ad reflect the brand's popularity among African Americans, the designer also employs a distinct multicultural workforce. Thus, the advertising accurately reflects the company's corporate policy.

Product positioning is a strategy that calls for carving out a niche for your brand in consumers' minds relative to the competition. It's a means for differentiating your brand from that of the competition and is especially helpful for new brands or those wishing to gain on the competitive leaders in market share. Pepsi says they're hip and Coke is not.

The **resonance approach** relies on fond or positive memories or feelings the target audience associates with the brand. Obviously, the lack of differentiating characteristics for your brand would make this approach appropriate. The "Always Coca-Cola" campaign has been running for several years. When this campaign first began (1992), it had a minimal affect on the public (discussed in Chapter 1). The only copy in the early spots were the words "Always Coca-Cola." Over the years, those two words have come to mean something a lot richer than when the campaign first began. In fact, consumers will often attribute to Coca-Cola whatever positive feeling they have held about that brand over the years. So, to some people, Coca-Cola is a wholesome part of Americana. To others, the brand may simply be a dependable beverage to drink when he or she wants something

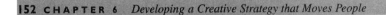

Figure 6–1 Ad for Gillette Mach 3 Razor

Figure 6–2   Ad for Tommy Hilfiger Tommy Fragrance

refreshing; to others, it may simply be a comforting image. The value of a resonance approach is the very general way images and brand associations bounce back and forth in the mind of the consumer.

An **affective strategy** seeks to form an emotional attachment between the brand and the consumers. Highly charged and symbolic images or words, often combined with music, evoke heightened emotional responses from consumers. Such a strategy is useful for brands with little to differentiate them in the marketplace or for those brands whose success depends on the emotional attachment of consumers. To convey the importance of buying a premium-priced product, the Michelin ad (see Figure 6–3) relies on the target audience's emotional attachment to babies.

Although we discuss these seven strategies or approaches as though they exist apart from other approaches, it is important to understand that they often overlap. For example, you may be inclined to use a *brand image strategy* in combination with a *resonance approach,* particularly if your brand lacks distinct differentiation based on attributes and seeks to create emotional ties with the consumer. In recent years, advertising campaigns for Ford Mustang often refer to the car nostalgically, affectionately, and simply as—"It's a Mustang." As you can imagine, the range of questions for your creative decisions is vast, especially when you begin to consider the relationship of various ads at different times or the dynamic interplay of graphics and copy in one ad or a combination of ads. Should you emphasize the product in use? use a strong, emotionally, charged symbol? show the

Figure 6–3   Ad for Michelin Tires

price/quality relationship? dwell on product characteristics or attributes? preempt your competition? acknowledge the competition in the hope of positioning yourself effectively against them? rely solely on a key benefit?

The list of questions could go on, but the key question for you to remember is this: What is there about your brand that satisfies a salient want or need of the target audience? The satisfaction consumers derive can be physical or psychological. If research tells you that something exists; if you're confident that it's critical to the selling of your product; if it fits with objectives in your strategy; and if you've found an original, creative idea or means to carry the message, then this is probably the most promising route for you to take. Note, though, how that decision greatly depends on a host of variables all of which demand careful consideration and thought.

On Being Creative

Describing creativity isn't very difficult. We can outline what we look for in a creative ad. We can even explain the stages the great ones go through to produce award-winning ads. But can we tell someone *how* to be creative? Not an easy question to answer. Keep this in mind as we try.

Creativity involves either generating completely new ideas or coming up with new takes on old ideas. Since we concede that we're unable to tell people how to think about things no one else has, our discussion focuses on how to turn common ideas into something different.

What Makes Strategy Creative Is that It Is Both Special and Different. Simply being *different* doesn't make something creative. Sometimes being different is, well . . . , maybe weird. As Leo Burnett was once reported to have said, "If all you want is to be different, you can come down in the morning with a sock in your mouth." To be creative, an ad has to be both different and in some way special. The consumer has to feel that the quality that makes something different is special in order to set a creative ad apart from an average one. Communicating a *special* feeling without that feeling being different won't necessarily make it creative either, especially if the feeling is something that has been expressed countless times, like saying . . . I love you.

The challenge for someone just starting out, like a student, is to figure out how to be special and different within the context of the strategy. It is, as they say, an art. But by paying attention to the research and by being attentive to details, an aspiring writer or art director can call upon the insights of others to be sure that his or her ideas are at least on target and on strategy.

One approach involves "shaking up" the way people think and overturning conventional wisdom, both in the way ads are used and in the way ads are created. This approach has been around for a long time and can be found in many creative ads. In recent years, the approach has received a lot of publicity because of the book, *Disruption,* by Jean-Marie Dru.[9]

Disrupting Expectations. As people go through life, their patterns of behavior are shaped by their experiences. They develop a complex bundle of expectations to help them navigate the world efficiently and effectively. We know that when we look both ways before crossing the street, we're likely to make it safely to the other side. When we extend our hand to someone that person is likely to shake it. We also have expectations about how that person will shake our hand. When the person is of slight stature—especially if that person is a female—and the grip is strong, it makes an impression on most people. It's something unexpected. Adolescent males often try to trick their friends by extending their hand only to withdraw it at the last moment, thumbing their buddy "outta here." (Lots of things are funny only to teenage boys.)

Catching people off guard can be funny and help people like the ad and, hopefully, the product. Perhaps its most important function, however, is to get people's attention. Jonathan Bond and Richard Kirschenbaum, founders of the award-winning agency, Kirshenbaum & Bond, suggest that today's consumers are cynical. Because of a massive overload of media messages, they've developed a filtering mechanism to screen out most of the messages aimed their way. They call this filter their personal "radar." To succeed in reaching today's consumer, Kirshenbaum and Bond suggest crafting ads in such a way as to get in "under the radar" (also the title of a popular book they've written for Adweek).[10]

Disrupting people's expectations is one way to make people pause and pay attention. If you can also get them to smile or laugh, so much the better. The key to disrupting consumers' expectations in an ad is contrast.[11] If consumers expect one thing, provide another. There's an old saying, "It's not whether you win or lose, but how you _____ the game" (most readers will add the word *play*). If you instead substituted place rather than play (that is, place the blame), you may get a few groans, but are likely to get people to pause and think, "Wait a second. What was that?" Of course, you have to use judgment, especially if you substitute a pun for the element people are expecting. As many people have said, puns are the lowest rung on the joke chain. They are nowhere near as funny as some people think.

The creative challenge is not only to attract people's attention, it is also to arrest their attention. While they are pausing, you want them to resolve their momentary confusion within the context of the strategy. Figure 6–4 shows an ad for General Foods International Coffees. Something seems not quite right with the headline, "Take the time to stop and smell the chocolate." Most people quickly make the adjustment substituting "smell the roses." But for chocolate lovers, smell the chocolate doesn't seem like such a bad idea either. If that momentary disruption gets people to pay just a little more attention—and perhaps, even read the label—then the ad is doing its job. The ad will work provided the product characteristics reflect the implied promise in the ad. In this ad, the implied message is "if you like chocolate and coffee, this brand is for you." Apparently, lots of people do.

An alternative to providing contrast is simply to shake up people by making them wonder what an ad means. The key to this kind of ad is to make the target *care*. In the second General Foods ad for coffee (see Figure 6–5), the headline reads, "Fat free? Very hip." This ad was placed in women's magazines, and targeted the millions of calorie-conscious women. It flags the target's attention with the words "fat free." Implied here is the promise that the brand is a smart, or hip, way to have hips like the model in the ad. Since this is only implied, it doesn't insult people by promising slim hips—something it can't deliver. But people do like to dream.

So far the disruption we've discussed has occurred mostly in the headline. Disruption through contrast can also take place within a picture. Figure 6–6 shows an ad for Home Depot. In this ad, the reader encounters the incongruous image of a miniature bride and groom placed on top of a wedding cake. The bride is holding a leaf blower, and the copy goes on to point out that a gift registry at Home Depot, while not as traditional as one for china and silver, is a lot more practical.

Figure 6–5 Ad for General Foods International Coffee French Vanilla - "Very Hip"

Figure 6–6   Home Depot Ad - Gift Registry

The Gift Registry

Okay, it's not as traditional as china or silver. But for practical gifts you'll actually use for years to come,
nothing beats Home Depot's Gift Registry. Tools, gas grills, lawn mowers. If you need it, your local Home Depot makes
it easy for friends and family across the entire country to purchase it for you. In fact, it's a piece of cake.

Contrast can also take place between or among the various elements in the ad. Contrast is possible with any of the elements in an ad; but it's far more dramatic if the contrast occurs in the major elements, like the headline and/or picture. Figure 6–7, an ad for Norelco razors, shakes up people—especially men—with the interplay between the headline and picture showing the anxiety-inducing look on the face of the man, and the action he appears ready to take.

Figure 6–7   Norelco Razor Ad

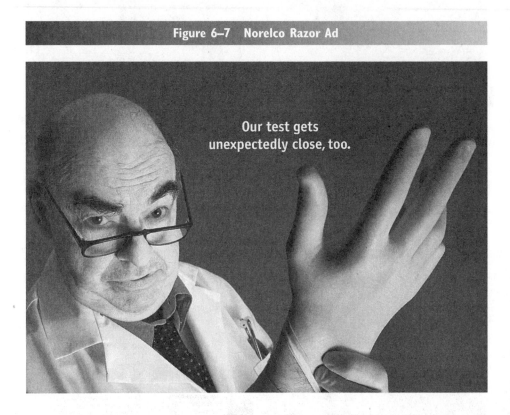

Our test gets
unexpectedly close, too.

Test the Norelco Reflex Action® Razor for 21 days. We think you'll like how it adjusts to the curves and contours of your face for an unexpectedly close shave without the nicks and cuts of a blade. But hey, if you're still unconvinced about our closeness after 21 days, we'll give your money back, guaranteed. For more information, call toll-free **1.877.NORELCO** 1.877.667.3526

Reflex Action system with adjustable floating heads.

*()***Norelco**®
PUT IT TO THE TEST

©1998 Philips Electronics North America Corporation www.norelco.com   **PHILIPS**

Exhibit 6–6   Creative Brief Format

1. What do we want this advertising to accomplish?
   It is important to keep the focus on the objectives.

2. Who are we talking to, and what insights do we have about them?
   In other words, keep the creative effort focused on the target audience. Use
   the insights found in research and intuition to guide the way you address the
   target.

3. How do we want consumers to describe the brand—its essence and personality?
   What do we want the brand to mean to the audience? Can we get them to
   think of the brand in the same way they think of a friend?

4. What's the single most important thing we want them to take out of this
   advertising? What's the most important idea, feeling, or memory we want our
   advertising to leave with the consumer?

5. How can we make our promise, claim, or even the ad, believable?
   Are we being honest with the consumer? Can we, and do we support the
   claims we are making in this advertising?

6. Is there anything worth thinking about that might help us achieve great
   advertising? Is there any current trend, fad, or news that we might in some way
   relate to our consumer insight?

7. Is there anything that we must get into our advertising?

IMPLEMENTING THE CREATIVE STRATEGY

Disrupting expectations may not be appropriate for all situations. Sometimes a simple direct approach focusing on the product makes more sense. However, taking a creative strategy and turning it into a creative execution does not lend itself to easy dissection. It takes lots of practice, and it helps to work alongside one who knows how. What often appears as discrete steps or concepts in a textbook, in practice may consist of concepts that overlap or steps that go in sequences other than what we recommend. It can inhibit the creative process to adhere to any formula or procedure rigidly.

So far we considered some ideas on getting creative. The next step is to take these ideas and translate them into **creative tactics.** When professionals get to the point where they're about ready to write ads, they often prepare what is called a *creative brief*—simply an outline to help them channel their thinking so that it is on target and within the strategy. Exhibit 6–6 is a copy of a creative brief, slightly modified from one used at the Foote, Cone & Belding advertising agency. Note how simple and straightforward the form is. Although we have been discussing quite a few concepts in this chapter, the idea is to keep these ideas in the back of your mind so as not to inhibit or impede the free flow of ideas. Later, when your ideas are in rough form, you can double back to see how you're doing conceptually.

Although there is value in keeping your mind open and receptive to all kinds of ideas, at some point you will have to focus your energy on creating ads that achieve creative and campaign objectives. We suggest you develop tactical focal points that you keep uppermost in your mind when storming for ideas to turn into ads. Next, we suggest you consider some of the tried and true principles creatives have used over the years, such as a product's attributes, features, or benefits. You should also consider a brand's image, personality, or position.

TRADITIONAL APPROACHES TO CREATING ADVERTISING

Although we tend to talk about these approaches conceptually, you will need to translate these ideas using specific details about the brand.

Attributes, Features, and Benefits

Whether it's a product, or a service that you're advertising, it has qualities, specific components, and/or characteristics that help the product perform in the marketplace. It helps to think of these qualities in terms of a triad of attributes, features, and benefits.

Think of **attributes** as what the product has (what it innately owns). Think of **features** as what the product does (how it performs, what it's used for). And think of **benefits** as what the product promises because of what it has or does. For example, Heinz ketchup has a combination of certain ingredients and a manufacturing process (attributes) that make it slower pouring out of the bottle (feature) than other brands of ketchup. The attributes and feature lead to the benefit, which may be described as richer taste. Ideally, the benefit should be competitive in that it solves consumers' problems better than the competition. A *benefit* may also be termed a consumer consequence because for the consumer it is a result.

Consider, for example, the laddering approach to attributes that was described in Chapter 2. Attributes lead to consumer consequences and ultimately to personal values. Even within the attributes and consequences you can subdivide categories so that some attributes become physical and some consequences become functional or self-involved. Of course, as you move up the ladder from attributes to personal values, you're moving away from the focus on the product to a tighter focus on consumers and how the product may affect them.

Important to your considerations of attributes and features that lead to benefits is the need to find the differentiating factor for your product. What is it that separates or differentiates your product from those of the competition? Again, in the case of Heinz ketchup, its slow-pouring feature differentiates Heinz from its competition. The idea of slowness and how that benefits the consumer is the tactical focal point in the ad you would be creating if you were creating an ad for Heinz.

Not all attributes, features, or the benefits leading from them, are equal. Some are more important than others. It all depends on which ones best address consumer needs, wants, and interests. Your research findings should help you identify areas of importance or unimportance. Meanwhile, as you dig and pick at the research, you should be sensitive to finding points of difference between your product and those of the competition. Eventually, this information will help you identify your brand's personality and position.

Branding

David Ogilvy has been a vigorous advocate for the importance of brand image over the past three decades. During this period the concept has evolved considerably. It has been dissected, analyzed, and reconstructed with varying definitions and parts. At its core, however, are brand image, brand personality, and brand positioning.

Brand Image and Brand Personality

A *brand's* **image** encompasses *all* the associations that consumers have for a brand: all the thoughts, feelings, and imagery that are linked to that brand in the consumer's memory, including colors, sounds, and smells. Within the overall brand image are associations with characters, symbols, endorsers, lifestyles, and types of users.[12]

From a creative standpoint, for your campaign, it is critical that your big unifying idea and its execution reflect the carefulness of a branding strategy, particularly in terms of your brand's image. For example, consumers perceive products and services (excluding, of course, new products), in meaningful ways. Depending on the past advertising and experiences consumers have with your brand and its competition, certain brand personalities emerge. These are based on the consumers' perceptions of the brands, which "typically capture a person's personality."

To understand brand personality as it leads to image, think of it on a personal level—your own. Your personality has no doubt led to the image you project within your circle of friends and associates. What is that image? Or, if you wish to construct an image over time, years from now how would you like to be known? You may want to answer that question by completing this statement: I would like to be known as a(n) _____.

How would you fill in that blank, either personally or professionally? Personally, would you fill it in with "good person," "loyal friend," "understanding partner," or any one of a number of other alternatives? Professionally, would you fill it in with "creative genius," "superb writer," "positive spirit among my colleagues," or again, with any one of a number of other alternatives?

Maybe you would like to fill in the blank with most, if not all, of those answers. But that's not what brand image is. With brand image, your answers are limited to other people's perceptions. These perceptions are based on your personality traits, which allow your friends and associates to create an overall meaning of you, your image.

Now, assume you fill in one answer. You would then consciously arrange your actions and behaviors to fit the brand image you want. So, if you wanted to be known as a positive spirit among your colleagues, you would behave in a positive way. You would, indeed, become a yay-sayer not a nay-sayer. You would applaud the achievements of others. In short, your actions would mirror the brand image you claimed as yours, in much the same way that advertising (the visible presentation of a product's personality) mirrors the brand image of that product. This is what David Ogilvy meant when he argued in favor of the long-term importance of brand image in advertising.

And if you expanded your self-description, how would you define the personality that led to the image? Friendly? Outgoing? Soothing? Adventurous? Exciting? Such descriptors also apply to products and contribute to the overall perception of a brand's image.

Typical in brand imaging is the association of feelings or emotions with the brand, sometimes termed **emotional bonding.** With this type of association, the consumers' perceptions play a leading role in aligning the brand with affective or emotional predispositions, usually based on past advertising, promotion, or experience.

Advertising that seeks this kind of bonding is often executionally based: How you say something (that is, execute it) is more important than what you say. But emotional bonding can evolve from several creative approaches. For example, your creative may use a functional, symbolic, or experiential approach depending on what your product has and does and what the consumer wants or needs from it. With a functional approach you concentrate on intrinsic product attributes, such as speed or performance. With a symbolic approach, you concentrate on extrinsic attributes, such as style or prestige. Fashion brands such as Polo or Tommy Hilfiger often use this approach. And with the experiential approach you concentrate on the pleasure consumers derive from the product, such as relaxation, excitement, or romance. Vacation cruises fit in well here.

You should strive to create this kind of consumer bonding with your brand. As we discussed with managing brand equity in Chapter 5, successful brands create emotional attachments with their consumers, whether through relationship marketing or positive and enduring brand associations. Important, too, is that the messages your creativity delivers tie in closely with your brand's core equities.

Brand imaging touches on all of these considerations and relies for the most part on the consumers' perceptions, which consumers develop from contact with the products' attributes, features, and benefits. In a sense, the consumer connects, often emotionally, with the brand, thus forming those perceptions. Through that connection, the brand gains equity in the competitive marketplace.

Brand Positioning

Advertising changes so quickly that yesterday's hot key concepts or terms have cooled off considerably today. Yet, some concepts are so solid at their base that they endure the test of time. Positioning is one of those concepts. **Positioning** describes advertisers' actions in trying to place their product in one place, or position, in relation to another according to their similarities or differences (see Chapter 5).

To understand positioning, think of it this way: You're in a crowded room, and attempting to find a place to stand and be comfortable. The room is analogous to a typical consumer's mind—crowded to the hilt with all sorts of competing products, brands, and messages. How do you find a place that's yours alone—where you feel comfortable? This search for a place is the essence of positioning.

Perhaps you'll have to elbow or wriggle your way to a good place, perhaps preempting someone else who also has an eye on that place (the "best" or leadership position, according to Bruce Bendinger in *The Copy Workshop Workbook*). Perhaps you'll have to wrestle head to head for the place you want (the **"against"** position). Perhaps you'll have to be content with a little room in the bigger space where others want to be simply because it is special or highly desirable (the **"niche"** position). Perhaps you'll have to move to a different place, one not so crowded (the **"new"** position).

Each positioning variation relates to which place you'll occupy in the consumer's mind—the position you'll own. Will you be faster? crunchier? shinier? more reliable? newer? newest? Of course, the list could go on. But the point is that positioning demands you find and occupy in the consumer's mind a certain place that is clear, unmistakable, valued, and yours alone. Positioning provides a direction or center point for your campaign around which your creative plan and the creative elements (such as graphics or copy) revolve.

You can't simply guess at the position you wish to occupy. Even traditional approaches may not work with consumers who have been exposed to countless ads. More than ever, writers and artists need to really understand consumers. Once again, this demands imaginative, insightful research. Bond and Kirshenbaum have 10 rules they follow to talk to today's cynical, busy, achieving, consumer.[13]

NEW RULES FOR TALKING TO TODAY'S CONSUMER

Don't Say It. Demonstrate It. Simply having a talking head tell why a product works isn't enough. Neither will dressing actors in white labcoats build credibility. Consumers literally will not buy it (that is, the product). If at all possible, show how the product works. Even with something seemingly as difficult to demonstrate as investing with a mutual funds company, an ad could demonstrate how employees rely on the company to invest their money. Fidelity Investments, the giant mutual funds company, was criticized for using a humorous approach in their commercials. The campaign used Lily Tomlin in various comedic situations to indicate the confusion many people face when trying to decide where to invest. In the ads, she encounters Peter Lynch, one of the most respected fund managers of all time. Lynch tells Tomlin to try Fidelity. The ads were criticized because of the association of slapstick humor with investing—a subject many people take very seriously. Instead, the ads could have talked about how Lynch relies on Fidelity to handle his money—which he does.

Don't Look or Sound Like an Ad. Consumers are immediately suspicious when they are being sold something—especially if there is something in the ad that strikes them as contrived. One of the regional phone companies ran a spot promoting their Internet-access service. In one of the television spots, a thirty-something man walks over to a open manhole where a worker is doing something underground. The man asks a series of questions related to Internet service. The worker responds with utterances that are difficult to understand. Near the end of the spot, the worker climbs out of the manhole and takes off her hardhat to reveal a luxurious head of hair. In real life, the probable response would have been—"how about that!" Viewing the ad, a typical consumer's response likely was—"I don't think so." In years past, when Oldsmobile told consumers, "This is not your father's Oldsmobile." The consumers liked the ads but recognized the line as a marketing ploy. Bond and Kirshenbaum emphasize, "Don't let your strategy show" if you want the ad to be accepted and believed.

Make the Ad the Logo. A certain "look" can be so intensely associated with a particular brand that the ad itself becomes an extension of the logo. Over the years, many people can immediately recognize a print ad for Volkswagen just by its use of a distinctive typeface and white space. Ads for Target have at times used the brand's distinctive bullseye logo as the main visual element in the ad. This helps make the ad seem less intrusive, something many consumers appreciate. Figure 6–8 shows what many people will immediately recogize as an ad for Volkswagen.

Treat Brands Like People. Develop the brand into *someone* consumers feel comfortable with. Comfort is often what motivates consumers to reach for a name brand, rather than a private label. During the 1997–1998 NBA basketball season, numerous games were

Figure 6–8   Ad for Volkswagen - "0 to 60?" "Yes"

0-60?

Figure 6–8 *continued*

Yes.

Drivers wanted.

cancelled due to an impasse between owners and players. Nike ran a series of humorous television ads that showed unskilled amateurs playing basketball—rather poorly. With tongue firmly in cheek, they implored both sides in the dispute to settle their differences and play the games. A cynic might note that Nike stood to lose a lot of sales if the season had been cancelled, but because of the low-keyed funny approach taken by Nike, fans could relate to the idea of "no games." In other words, the brand was acting like a fan.

Be Honest to a Fault. One small seed of doubt will send up consumers' red flags, so don't plant any. Many times ads are designed using models who represent what women would like to look like—great figure, stunning hair, or a super-smooth complexion. These ads are said to be aspirational, and generally connect with the target audience. But it is becoming increasingly more clear that many consumers do not relate to models in ads, especially with those models who are much thinner than the average woman. As a result, advertisers are beginning to use female models who are older and larger than those they used in the past. However, even when stores create a catalog featuring plus-size models, they usually do not go beyond using size-14 models. Since many women are a size 18 and larger, when they see nothing but 14s in the ads, seeds of distrust are planted.[14]

Involve the Consumer. Letting the consumer help or take part in the ad is one way to build a relationship between the brand and the consumer. Since 1981, the advertising for Absolut vodka has consisted of over 500 magazine ads, each of which invite the reader to solve the puzzle and figure out where the bottle is located in the ad. When the campaign began, the brand was selling 20,000 cases annually in the United States. Fifteen years later, the brand was selling over 3 million cases annually—an increase of almost 15,000%.[15] Can anybody tell the difference between one brand of vodka and another? (Note how we're trying to involve the reader in this paragraph.) Figure 6–9 is an example of involving the reader with the ad.

Use Humor to Create Camaraderie with Consumers. Using humor helps differentiate advertising from the bland competition. It can also help endear the brand to consumers who appreciate the value, however small, they get out of ads that make them laugh or smile. But the humor has to be a part of the selling message or consumers will merely laugh and ignore the point the ad needs to make. The ad for Armstrong laminate floors in Figure 6–10 shows how humor can be used to get across the selling message.

Sex Still Sells, But Be Careful. Sex remains one of the more powerful motives that influence behavior. However, sex has been so misused throughout the history of advertising that many consumers—especially women—are understandably sensitive. The use of sex appeal to sell products should be relevant to the product used. When in doubt, use sex appeal only to sell sexy products. Figure 6–11 shows an ad for Salvatore Ferragamo perfume. Since many people wear perfume to enhance a romantic moment, the use of sex appeal makes sense for perfume. This ad smartly gets across this idea in a elegant and understated way.

Don't Chestbeat. If consumers are already cynical about advertising, why would they believe a "We're Number 1" claim? Whether or not the claim is based on objective data, consumers often suspect the claim is subjective. However, when Hertz used to refer to itself as the "Super Star in Rent-A-Cars," it made sense because they were responding to

Figure 6–9   Absolut Vodka Ad - Absolut Peak

Figure 6–10 Armstrong Flooring Ad With Woodpecker

We set out to make the most incredibly durable, beautiful floor. We think we succeeded.

(knock on wood)

Experts on wood agree. Armstrong laminate floors are as beautiful as wood, but with unprecedented durability. And because they're Armstrong, the floors retain their shine, stay flat and look better than any other leading laminate floor. So come see the broadest range of wood, stone and marble designs available. They're beautiful, and they really take a pecking. For the nearest Armstrong flooring retailer, call 800-233-3823.

Armstrong
The beauty is, it stays that way.

Figure 6–11   Salvatore Ferragamo Perfume Ad

Avis, which was advertising "We're number two, so we try harder." In effect, Hertz was saying, "you're darn right we're the best, and here are some reasons why." Today, in a different advertising climate, they simply make the point, "There's Hertz and not exactly."

Now Break Rules. Consumers become immune to advertising approaches. As much as we hate to suggest this to beginners, consider breaking rules and exploring new approaches and techniques.

UNIFYING THE ADS

Because an advertising campaign contains various ads for diverse media, the tendency is to treat each ad independently, almost as if it exists in a vacuum. This is, of course, not the case. Rather, each ad builds on or complements the others regardless of the medium in which they're placed. As you create each ad, be sure to weave some thread of continuity through each of your executions so that when you are finished you have a campaign and not just a bunch of ads.

Campaign Progress Checklist

At this point in the campaign, you should generally be aware of the following points:

1. Creative ads should be designed to sell the product not to showcase some creative effect or technique.
2. There are four important parts to a creative plan: the target audience, objectives, strategy, and tactics.
3. Creative strategy should contain at least a strategic focal point, a positioning statement, and a big unifying idea.
4. To add depth and complexity to a creative plan, use slogans, taglines, and trade characters for physical continuity and a theme, image or certain tone or attitude for psychological continuity.
5. A grid like the one developed by FCB can help you evaluate your creative opportunity.
6. There are various strategic approaches around which you can build a message strategy, including a generic strategy, a preemptive claim, product positioning, brand image

strategy, a unique selling proposition (USP), a resonance approach, and an affective strategy.
7. To be creative, it's not enough to be different, it has to matter to consumers. One way to be different is to disrupt expectations. If consumers expect one thing, give them another.
8. When you get ready to do your executions, work up a copy brief to help keep the creative ideas on track.
9. For many brands, focusing on attributes, features, and benefits is the appropriate approach to promoting the product.
10. As you approach selling the product, remember the importance of building the brand in terms of an image or personality.
11. Even though there're rules one can follow to help develop persuasive ads, sometimes it's right to break the rules.

Notes and References

[1] Parente, D. E., Vanden Bergh, B., Barban, A., & Marra, J. (1996). *Advertising campaign strategy: A guide to marketing communication plans*. New York: Dryden Press, pp. 150–152.

[2] Liesse, J. (1994, February 7). Despite risks and little time, marketplace superstars emerge. *Advertising Age* (Special Report: Brands in Demand): p. S-1.

[3] Lawrence, J. (1994, February 7). P&G makes a new push with Tide. *Advertising*, p. 12.

[4] The information of the trade characters discussed in this section, as well as the information on United Airlines and Virgina Slims is abstacted from unpublished, undated, and unnumbered material on enduring campaigns from Leo Burnett Company, Inc.

[5] I first learned this concept in graduate school at the University of Illinois. It is hard to remember the source of this comment. My best guess is Charles H. Sandage.

[6] Batra, R., Myers, J. G., & Aaker, D. A. (1996). *Advertising management* (5th ed.). Upper Saddle River, NJ: Prentice-Hall, p. 275.

[7] For more information see John R. Rossiter, Larry Percy, & Robert J. Donovan, A better advertising planning grid. *Journal of Advertising Research* (October/November 1991), pp. 11–21. This topic is also discussed extensively in Batra, Myers, and Aaker, *Advertising Management*, pp. 281–285.

[8] Keller, K. L. (1998). *Strategic brand management*. Upper Sadle River, NJ: Prentice-Hall, 1998, p. 23.

[9] Dru, J-M. (1996). *Disruption overturning coventions and shaking up the marketplace*. New York: John Wiley & Sons.

[10] I am indebted to Tom Groth who helped me understand the concept of disrupting expectations. It's not surprising that his students have three times won the NSAC sponsored by the AAF.

[11] Batra, Myers, & Aaker, *Advertising Management*, p. 321.

[12] Adapted from Jonathan Bond and Richard Kirshenbaum, *Under the radar: Talking to today's cynical consumer*. New York: John Wiley & Sons, 1997, pp. 68–92.

[13] Bond & Kirshenbaum, *Under the radar*, pp. 80–81.

[14] Lewis, R. W. (1996). *Absolut book*. Boston, MA: Journey Editions, p. xi.

Chapter 7

Media Strategy and Tactics

Media decisions require much more than a calculator or a good computer software program. They require judgment. The basic purpose of media is to deliver messages efficiently and effectively. However, these two purposes can sometimes be at odds with each other. Efficient plans deliver messages to targets at a relatively low cost. They avoid wasting money on media that reach people who aren't likely prospects for the product or service. To deliver messages *effectively*, planners must select media that can both influence and enhance messages. Media can influence the impact of a message depending on the context in which the audience receives it. The context can vary from a medium's suitability to a creative approach, to the timing of ads, or to reaching targets in situations in which they normally don't expect to receive promotional messages. Smart planners sometimes ignore cost efficiency and select media on the basis of its ability to deliver messages effectively. Viewed this way, media are more than neutral or passive carriers of a message. They help the message achieve its communication objective.

This type of decision is often based on not much more than a gut reaction. The effectiveness of the decision is related to the decisionmaker's ability and experience. Beginners, especially students, may not have the ability, and certainly do not have the experience of a seasoned professional. In short, if you don't possess significant experience, it is best to base decisions on as rational a basis as you can. We usually advise beginners to make decisions based on both a careful analysis of quantitative factors (such as cost efficiency,) and on qualitative factors (such as the editorial or program content of a media vehicle). The purpose of this chapter is to examine some of the basic decisions that media people make and why they make them. Keep in mind: A creative media plan requires imagination and probably more information then we can provide in this book. Consider consulting a number of the very good texts on media planning.[1]

MEDIA DECISIONS AND THE CAMPAIGN PROCESS

Media decisions generally evolve out of the creative strategy. The basic idea is to figure out what you want to get across in a message and then decide the best way to deliver that message. The best approach, perhaps, is to make these decisions together. In many agencies, a brand team consists of both creative and media personnel. This way, when writers are storming for ideas, a media person can lend an in-depth understanding of the way potential messages are likely to be delivered and received.

However, with many established products, the basic media decisions do not vary much from one year to the next. In these situations, it is often wise to let media people go ahead and make decisions prior to creative decisions to allow them to capitalize on special media opportunities—or sometimes, simply to save time.

THE BASIC MEDIA DECISIONS: OBJECTIVES, STRATEGY, AND TACTICS

An important characteristic of an effective media plan is that it is comprehensive. The general objective is to deliver messages to as many prospects as is practical and cost effective—and to deliver these messages with sufficient frequency to achieve the desired effect. As a result, many if not most, media objectives are stated in terms of **reach** and **frequency.** To achieve these goals, planners carefully evaluate an ever-increasing number of media options. In the past decade, this number has increased at a remarkable pace. To be competitive these days, media plans need to be efficient, effective, and *creative*. Using new ways to deliver messages is one mark of creative media planning, but another may simply involve using delivery options that are already available. Keeping track of what's available can be a daunting task. We use the expression, **delivery option,** because there are literally uncountable ways to get a company's message across. We'll present a large number of these in this chapter, but Chapter 8 and Chapter 9 also include message delivery options. To help organize some of the details a planner has to consider, we've structured this chapter to focus on the basic decisions in a media plan: objectives, strategy, and tactics. Note that there is a strong linkage among the sections dealing with these three decisions. So if we discuss something that influences media objectives, say competitive activity, we are also likely to discuss this same influence in the sections on strategy and tactics. The linkage that connects together the elements within media is important, as is the linkage between the creative and the media sections. This linkage is what gives a campaign its synergy. Before we examine in some depth setting objectives, developing strategy, and executing tactics, let's take a brief look at the nature of the basic decisions in media: objectives, strategy, and tactics.

Understanding Media Objectives

At the root of a media objective is the principle: media deliver messages. How, where, when, and to whom the messages get delivered form the basis for setting media objectives.

The media you select influences the amount and type of exposure you get with a plan. Media can also have a significant effect on how the message is received. Consider the relative impact of two alternative ways to send the following message:

Jennifer,

I love you. Will you please marry me?

Archie

The first way is to e-mail the message. The other approach consists of hiring a company to post this message on a billboard across the street from where Jennifer works. Same message, but it will surely have a much different impact.

As a prelude to setting media objectives, planners need to have a clear understanding of the role media is to play in the advertising or marketing campaign. Is the role simply that of generating exposure, or is the role also associated with enhancing the message? Generally, planners focus on exposure. Typically, they set media objectives in terms of reach, frequency, gross rating points, and similar concepts. These are easy concepts to understand and set. They are quantitative in nature and relatively easy to measure.

Setting objectives that refer to the media's ability to enhance a message tends to be more subjective and less precise in nature. Qualitative objectives usually are more difficult to measure. Moreover, in setting qualitative media objectives, planners run the risk of a problem discussed in Chapter 4 (dealing with objectives) called **common effectiveness**. This problem refers to setting as a goal something that would normally be expected of all objectives. For example, if "using media that can enhance the message" is set as a media objective, it then becomes a matter of judgment of whether this goal is merely something expected of most plans, or whether this situation is really special. In the above example, it is clear that Archie expects the media placement of his message to have a significant impact on the message content.

Perhaps, because of the vagueness in setting qualitative objectives, many planners only set media objectives that are specific and measurable. We have no simple suggestions and will examine this subject in more detail on page 189.

Understanding Media Strategy

The strategic component of media planning essentially refers to the *general* plan involving the delivery of the advertising messages. The aim of a strategic plan is to give the company a competitive edge, although in some competitive situations a company has all it can do to hang in there and survive. Still, even small companies can often find creative ways to get their messages across that give them an edge in part of the market. Media strategy decisions usually focus on the following four elements, each of which we'll discuss later in the chapter:

1. Target audience (or market)

2. Media classes

3. Media mix

4. Media timing

Target Audience

Although this is an important decision, frequently the media target is exactly the same as the campaign target. If this is so, then the targeting decision is already predetermined for the media planner. However, in a marketing communication campaign, media (at least the major media) are merely one way to get out the message. For example, a company could use public relations activities to influence key decisionmakers and use traditional media to reach a more broadly based target. In this situation, there would be a target audience for the campaign, and a separate and at least slightly different target for the advertising media. One of the targets can be thought of as a primary target audience and the other a secondary target or they could both be deemed targets of equal importance.

Media Classes

Strategy decisions involve the selection of a media type, such as newspaper, television, or magazine. In contrast, media tactics usually consist of decisions to buy media vehicles, such as *USA Today,* "60 Minutes," and *Readers Digest*. However, for some national advertisers with large ad budgets, the selection of a media type, even television, is more of a tactical than a strategic decision, especially since they often allocate a considerable amount of money to other marketing communication options. It is also somewhat confusing to discuss media vehicle decisions with some media types, such as direct mail or outdoor advertising, since some would argue there are no vehicles within these media classes.[2] In short, the distinction between whether a media class decision is a tactic or part of the strategy is probably more important to academicians than advertising practitioners.

Media Mix

Decisions in this category refer to how much emphasis, sometimes called **advertising pressure,** to allocate to various categories, such as target audiences, geographical areas, time periods, brands, and most important, media types. In the campaign process, some of these decisions are often made before a media planner is involved. When this happens, these decisions are usually reflected in the media objectives. Keep in mind, although media objectives are considered before media strategy, it's usually wise to think of both types of decisions at the same time.

The most important weighting decision is the one involving the relative emphasis placed on different media types. Figure 7–1 shows a media mix in the form of a pie chart, a typical way to present this information in a plans book.

Media Timing/Scheduling

Timing is all about scheduling, and there are two basic decisions to consider. Decisions need to be made concerning when the ads appear, and the way these ads get scheduled over a period of time. Timing is an important component of media strategy because *when* someone is exposed can affect that person's receptivity to the advertising message. There are numerous reasons for scheduling advertising at various times. One of the more common reasons has to do with seasonal sales fluctuations. The sales of many products rise and fall with the seasons of the year. Scheduling media can be tailored to seasonal sales patterns and is referred to as **seasonality**.[3] Another phrase gaining increasing usage among media buyers is called **recency buying**. This idea involves reaching targets as close as possible to the point of sale. This aspect of strategy usually presumes building in a lot of frequency into the media schedule. Later in this chapter, we will examine other influences on media scheduling.

The second basic decision involving media timing focuses on the importance of providing *continuity* from one advertising message to another. For a plan to function effectively as a *campaign* there should be an interconnectedness among the ads in the campaign, each of them trying to achieve the same or interrelated objectives. The resulting effect is synergistic—where the whole is greater than the sum of its parts. Although it

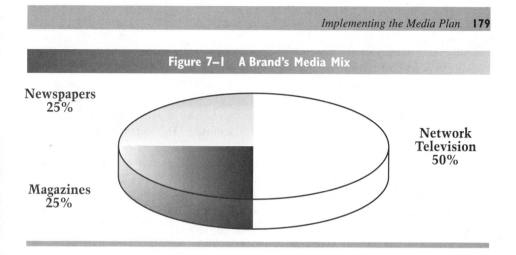

Figure 7–1 A Brand's Media Mix

Newspapers
25%

Network
Television
50%

Magazines
25%

might seem there are an infinite variety of patterns to follow in scheduling advertising, most are variations of three common types of continuity: flighting, pulsing, and continuous scheduling. We will discuss these on pages 203–205.

Understanding Media Tactics

Media tactics refer to the specific decisions that are made to implement the media strategy. Generally, these decisions involve buying specific advertising units (say, one-half page ad, or a 30-second spot), on specific media vehicles (say, *Sports Illustrated* or "60 Minutes"), and scheduling them within a specific period of time (say, once a month during the Christmas buying season). Within an agency, these tactical decisions are often referred to as the media schedule.[4]

Scheduling decisions are usually made by a media buyer, someone who selects the media vehicles and places the orders. Buyers need to be good at interpreting the media strategy to produce an effective plan. They also need to be especially good at producing a cost-efficient plan. This, in turn, requires the buyer to have a solid understanding of media audiences and cost analysis. The best buyers possess quantitative skills and an ability to negotiate with the media to secure low prices. The basic quantitative skills usually can be learned in a relatively short period of time. The ability to negotiate well takes experience. Buyers also negotiate with vehicles to obtain guarantees against audiences falling below expectations, to secure preferred positions within a vehicle, and to obtain merchandising support from the vehicle to support the sales effort.[5] In some agencies, the planners ARE the buyers. This is also true for many smaller and midsize agencies.

IMPLEMENTING THE MEDIA PLAN

So far, our discussion of media objectives, strategy, and tactics has been designed to give the reader a basic understanding of the kind of decisions that are made in a campaign with respect to media. Let's now examine how media objectives are set and media strategy and tactics are determined.

Setting Media Objectives

A planner's expectations for the media may include both delivering and enhancing messages. The basic unit of measurement used to determine whether a message is delivered is *exposure.* It's far more valuable to know whether an audience saw, heard, or read an ad, but these types of measurements are expensive and difficult to make. Audience measurements capture vehicle exposure and not actual ad exposure. The technical meaning of **exposure** is "open eyes (or listening ears) facing the medium."[6] Exposure indicates that an individual has the opportunity to see, hear, or read an ad. Exposure measurements differ for each medium. We'll examine five measures of exposure: reach, frequency, gross impressions, gross rating points, and targeted rating points. Because these measures can be stated precisely, we refer to measures of exposure as **quantitative** media objectives. The ability of the media to enhance a message is more subjective and does not lend itself to measurement, so we refer to these types of goals as **qualitative media objectives.**

Quantitative Media Objectives

Reach. Reach can be defined as the number of different people or households exposed to a media schedule within a given period of time. This number is usually expressed as a percentage of the target audience. The period of time can vary. It can refer to a four-week period, a four-month period, or the length of the campaign. Increasingly, time agencies are using time periods as short as one week. For example, media objectives can be written as follows:

- To reach 80% of women between age 18–24 each month of the year. OR . . .

- To reach 80% of women, age 18–24, by the end of the first quarter. OR . . .

- To reach 80% of men, age 18–24, by the end of the year (EOY).

We could also substitute for the above demos (short for demographic variables), the words *target audience* or even *primary* and *secondary target audiences.*

Frequency. Objectives also generally indicate the number of times the demo should be reached. The technical term for this number is frequency. **Frequency** can be defined as the number of times a person or household is exposed to a media schedule within a given period of time. This number is usually considered to be an average frequency. For example, an objective can be written as follows:

- To reach 80% of the primary target audience 3+ times each week during the first quarter.

Reach and frequency are companion statistics. It's hard to talk about one without considering the other; they are *inversely* related. The more frequency in a schedule, the fewer people it reaches. Planners have to balance the importance of reaching a lot of people a few times or a few people a lot of times. Maximizing both reach and frequency would require a budget of unlimited size.

Reach and frequency objectives need to be linked to campaign objectives. In order to get prospects to think, feel, or do something, you first have to reach them with a message.

If you wanted to establish brand awareness in 80% of the target audience, you would have to reach at least 80% of the target—in all likelihood, more. The number of times, or repetitions, needed to achieve the desired effect would depend on many things, including the effectiveness of the message.

The number of repetitions necessary to achieve a desired effect (for example, awareness, or sales) is called **effective frequency.** The number or percentage of people who are reached at the frequency level determined to be effective is called **effective reach.**

Planners consider effective reach and effective frequency when setting objectives to help them answer two important questions: (1) How *many* people or what percentage of the target audience should they reach? (2) How *often* should they reach them? Generally, advertisers want to reach as many prospects as they can. However, it may not be cost effective to do so. A media planner has to weigh the difficulty or expense in reaching each additional percentage of the target audience. At some point, the cost of reaching more prospects is not offset by sufficient sales increases. On a practical level, there are often budgetary constraints. Even though a planner may believe that reaching more prospects (and spending more money) makes sense, if the budget has already been set, a planner may have to work with the funds he or she has been allocated, depending on the flexibility constraints.

Determining effective frequency levels can be difficult to determine. All faculty struggle with questions about how many times they have to repeat themselves to get their messages across and understood. Telling a class it is dismissed usually has to be said only once. Explaining effective reach and effective frequency to a class usually requires more than one explanation. Similarly, effective frequency in advertising can vary depending on a number of variables, including the product, message, media clutter, competitive environment, and the target to whom the message is directed. Advertisers do research on this subject, but their conclusions are likely to be situation specific, applying only to their particular case. The most influential study on effective frequency was published in 1979 by the Association of National Advertisers, authored by Michael Naples. Some of its general conclusions are as follows:

1. One exposure of an advertisement to a target consumer group (within a purchase cycle) has little or no effect.

2. Because one exposure is usually ineffective, the main thrust of media planning should be on emphasizing frequency rather than reach.

3. Most research studies suggest that two exposures within a purchase cycle are an effective threshold level.

4. Three exposures within a purchase cycle, however, are felt to be optimal.

5. After three exposures within a purchasing cycle, advertising becomes more effective as frequency is increased, but at a decreasing rate. If this were drawn on a graph, it would appear as a convex curve rising from a zero point.

6. Wear-out of an advertising campaign is not caused by too much frequency per se. It is caused by copy and content problems.

7. Generally, smaller and lesser-known brands will benefit most by increased frequency. Larger, well-known brands might or might not be helped by increasing frequency, depending on how close they are to advertising saturation levels.

8. Different dayparts on television are affected by different frequency levels. A similar idea applies to thin versus thick magazines, with the thinner ones having better response effects than the thicker ones.

9. Frequency responses are affected by the amount of money an advertiser spends as a percentage of the product category total. Those brands with the greatest proportion of exposures within their category should also gain greater effects when frequency is increased. The responses due to increased frequency are not affected by different media. What is true for one medium is true for others. Each brand might require a different level of frequency of exposure. One cannot generalize from a given brand's experiences to some other brand. Specialized research is required to find the unique frequency level for a brand.

10. Two brands spending the same amount of money for advertising can have different responses to their frequencies.[7]

The Naples study remains influential, although not everyone agrees with some of its conclusions. One popular conclusion is that a frequency level of 3+ within a given week is the ideal level of exposure, but not everyone agrees. Recent thinking, based on John Phillip Jones's book, *When Ads Work: New Proof of How Advertising Triggers Sales*, suggests that one exposure is enough to be effective.[8] Some critics point out that the ideal level depends on the product category, something Naples did not find. Others have said that the ideal frequency depends upon the quality of the advertising message, something Naples did not consider.[9] Even though people disagree with parts of Naples study there does seem to be widespread agreement that frequent consumer exposures bring "positive results."[10]

A Time Frame Is an Important Part of the Objectives. Indicating a time frame in which the goals are expected to be met provides direction regarding when to advertise. It's not enough to say you want to reach 80% of the target audience a minimum of three times. You have to indicate when you want to achieve these goals. Achieving a frequency level of 3 during a 12-month period is significantly different than accomplishing these goals within a four-week period. In Chapter 4, we called including a date in the objective **time bounding** the objective. Objectives that are time bounded provide media buyers direction for scheduling the media.

Jack Z. Sissors and Lincoln Bumba in their book, *Advertising Media Planning*, suggest six points to consider in decisions about *when* to advertise:

- When sales are greatest or lowest

- According to budget constraints

- When competitors advertise

- According to the specific goals of the brand in question

- According to the availability of the product

- Depending on promotional requirements[11]

Using Sales to Guide Media Scheduling. An important principle in media scheduling is to advertise when consumers are inclined to buy. To help determine these inclinations, advertisers look at sales trend data. The sales of many products vary considerably over a period of a year, although these variations may be consistent from year-to-year. The Christmas selling season accounts for over 50% of the sales of many toy and game manufacturers. Linens, tablecloths, and towels sell best during the August and January "white sales." Later in this chapter will look at how buyers allocate media dollars on a seasonal basis.

Budget Constraints. Planners often have tough decisions to make because of budget limitations. On the one hand, they want to *effectively* reach their targets, but due to a limited budget may not be able to build sufficient frequency into their plan. To avoid "spreading themselves too thin," they often schedule periods of advertising followed by periods of no advertising (called **flighting**). This type of scheduling allows sufficient frequency to effectively reach the target at least in some of the time periods.

Scheduling When the Competition Advertises. Many people in business view marketing as a constant battle for the heart and mind of the consumer. Part of the battle involves maintaining a media presence when the competition advertises. Brand leaders often try to match up with the competition. The idea is not to give a rival a potential edge, especially if the leader has superior financial resources. To counter this strategy, a non-leader may advertise in different time periods to gain it an advantage, even though the time period may be less favorable. Sometimes it's hard to compete directly against the category leader.

Companies may also feel compelled to advertise during the same time periods as the competition. The reason is that consumers expect to see ads for some products during certain times and make a special point of looking for them. January and August is the expected time for "white sale" advertising. In many communities, Wednesday is considered the "best shopping day" in the newspaper and is the day most supermarkets take out major ads. However, in a smaller number of communities, Thursday is considered the "best shopping day" and supermarkets schedule most of their advertising on this day. They know shoppers tend to look for grocery ads when there are a lot of food ads in the paper.

Tailoring the Schedule to the Specific Goals of the Brand. The timing of the media schedule should always reflect advertising goals. But it is also worth mentioning that sometimes an unstated or implied objective of the campaign could also have an effect on scheduling. For example, if the company's marketing strategy suggests reacting aggressively to competitive initiatives, than this would suggest adding extra emphasis to counter some new activity, such as a new product introduction. To put extra emphasis and money one place might mean withdrawing media support from some other.

Product Availability. The availability of the product can result from numerous causes, including unexpected sales increases, labor problems, or material shortages. If the company cannot satisfy the current demand, it is often better to withdraw advertising exposure rather than risk alienating unsatisfied customers.

Promotional Requirements. Special promotions, especially price deals, require close attention to the timing of the advertising. Often sales promotion activities take place during the brand's regular advertising campaign, so that extra emphasis needs to be added to introduce the promotion.

Setting Objectives in Terms of Reach and Frequency

Reach, frequency, and continuity are core concepts in media planning. The basic purpose of the media is to deliver messages, and reach and frequency are measures that indicate what's expected in terms of message delivery. The timing or pattern of message deliveries is a result of the type of continuity used. A simple quantitative media objective has four parts:

1. A target audience or market

2. The desired amount of reach

3. The desired amount of frequency

4. The timing or pattern of the message deliveries

The following is an example of a quantitative media objective:

- To reach 60% of women ages 18–34, 3+ times each week during the first quarter of the campaign.

Problems with Using Reach and Frequency in Setting Objectives. At the conceptual level, it makes sense to set media objectives in terms of reach and frequency. Basically, this is what the media try to do—reach people. However, at the operational level, setting an objective in terms of reach presents problems both in estimating reach and monitoring whether the objective is accomplished. First, it can get complicated quickly when more than two or three vehicles are used with multiple insertions (frequency) scheduled in each vehicle. The problem becomes more complex when a schedule includes media that are very different from each other, such as newspapers and outdoor, or radio and magazines.

Second, there is mixed value in setting a numerical figure for reach (expressed usually as a percentage) unless you have a good way to measure whether the objective is accomplished. Notwithstanding, students are often advised to set objectives for reach in quantitative terms, even though they have no way of measuring them because it is a discipline they may use later. It is also a way to communicate more precisely what a planner has in mind when he or she talks about reaching an audience. Professionals, however, are more interested in setting objectives in terms they can monitor or measure, and for many professionals, it is too costly or complicated to measure reach—at least when more than several vehicles are used with numerous insertions. Agencies use numerous estimating formulas. These formulas are built into simulation models that use probabilities to estimate reach based on multiple exposures. Most major agencies have their own proprietary models and use them extensively to estimate reach. William J. Donelly, author of *Planning Media: Strategy and Development* reminds his readers that reach estimators produce radical estimates because they are estimates built upon estimates.[12] As a result, some professionals prefer to set objectives in other types of exposure measures that are easier to measure. The most common measures are **gross impressions, gross rating points (GRPS),** and **targeted rating points (TRPS).**

Setting Objectives in Terms of Gross Impressions, GRPs, and TRPs

Gross Impressions. An advertising impression (or simply an impression) occurs each time an individual (or household) is exposed to an ad. Gross impressions are the total number of impressions obtained from a media schedule within a given period of time. This term describes the sum of all vehicle exposures and counts every exposure in a schedule, even multiple exposures to the same person or household. To calculate gross impressions, multiply the reach of each media vehicle times the number of ads on that vehicle as follows:

Program A 1,000, 000 people reached $\times$ 4 Ads = 4,000, 000 impressions

Program B 2,000, 000 people reached $\times$ 2 Ads = 4,000, 000 impressions

Program C 3,000, 000 people reached $\times$ 4 Ads = 12,000, 000 impressions

Program D 5,000, 000 people reached $\times$ 1 Ad = 5,000, 000 impressions

Gross Impressions   25,000, 000

Note that the audience of Program A not only was exposed to an ad more than one time, but it is likely that at least some of them were part of the audiences of other programs. This kind of repetition is called **duplication.** Gross impressions are a way to look at the combined weight of a media schedule without regard to duplication of audiences in the schedule. In contrast, reach is expressed as an unduplicated number. In the media models used by some agencies, the weight of a media schedule is as important as the reach. In other words, you can reach a lot of people a few times or a few people a lot of times and the impact of the message may not be significantly different.

Gross Rating Points. Gross rating points (GRPs) are identical in concept to gross impressions and are another way to talk about exposure. Gross impressions indicate the amount of exposure in a schedule expressed in raw numbers; GRPs are expressed in terms of percentages, although the percent signs are not usually shown.

GRPs are a way to talk about the amount of exposure in a plan. A *rating point* indicates the percentage of a population that is tuned into a broadcast. (Or any medium for that matter. The actual operational definition depends on the medium measured and the company doing the measuring.) For example, a 20 rating in television indicates that 20% of the TV households (TVHH) were tuned into the telecast. This means that 20% of the approximately 98 million TVHH, or 19.6 million TVHH, were tuned in. To calculate the GRPs in a media schedule, first multiply reach times frequency to come up with the total rating points for each program. A program's rating is used as a measure of reach and the number of times a commercial appears on a program is used as a measure of frequency. Second, add the rating points for all programs together. An example follows:

Rating Points

Program A   20 rating $\times$ 3 ads = 60

Program B   15 rating $\times$ 3 ads = 45

Program C   10 rating $\times$ 2 ads = 20

Program D   13 rating $\times$ 3 ads = 39

Gross Rating Points   164

Exhibit 7–1 Media Flight Plan Software

Media Flight Plan Software . . .
Essential marketing/campaign planning tool

Media Flight Plan is a copyrighted text and software system with basic architecture designed by Professor Dennis G. Martin, Brigham Young University. Although it simulates "real world" industry software, *MFP* focuses on the basics and assumes users know little about media planning.

What does *Media Flight Plan* do?
MFP is a reach-frequency generator. Armed with a hand-held calculator and traditional "beta binomial distribution" models, it might take you several days of number crunching to achieve what *MFP* does in one hour. A sophisticated BBD model has been created especially for *MFP* by co-author Dale Coons, Vice President Media Research and Information Services, Campbell-Ewald. The good news is that *MFP* is completely transparent and does 100% of the math labor for you.

GRP Driven Simulation
Since the "real world" of media planning is Gross Rating Point (GRP) driven, *MFP* simulates this model. All planning and buying is based on GRPs, a relatively easy concept to learn.

Creativity & Experimentation
Media Flight Plan assumes marketers enjoy playing "what if?" Once you start buying "GRPs" in the media of your choice, *MFP* tells you the immediate effect it has on your reach/frequency. Since the combination of GRPs and media choices is infinite, experimentation and creativity is essential.

Basic Menus in *Media Flight Plan*
Users begin by pulling down a menu with six media planning "**Basics**."

- Target
- Scope
- Calendar
- Spot Markets
- Budget
- Ad Types

All six of these "**Basics**" are explained below.

1: Target
Defining target demographics is essential before estimating the amount of reach and frequency needed to sell your product or service. The Target Audience screen looks like this:

Select Target Audience			
Gender		**Age**	
• Men	☑ 18-24	☑ 50-54	
• Women	☑ 25-34	☑ 55-64	
• Adults	☑ 35-49	☑ 65+	

Exhibit 7–1 *continued*

2: Scope

What is the geographic strategy for your brand? Is it available nationally, or only in a few spot markets? *MFP* can estimate reach frequency for any of the three options shown below:

> Select one: ▣ **National Plan**
>   ▣ **Spot Only Plan**
>   ▣ **Both (National + Spot)**

3: Calendar (Select Launch Month)

Here's another strategic decision. Select the best month to launch your campaign and click on it.

4: Spot Markets

Want to estimate reach/frequency for one or more spot markets (up to 210)? Click on the markets below. *MFP's* database contains all costs for media choices, and you can modify costs if you want.

> **Select Markets below:**
>
>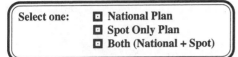
>
> | | MARKET NAME | RANK | %US POP |
> |---|---|---|---|
> | ▣ | **Abilene-Sweetwater TX** | 157 | 0.1 |
> | ▣ | **Albany, GA** | 153 | 0.1 |
> | ▣ | **Albany et al, NY** | 51 | 0.6 |
> | ▣ | **Albuquerque, NM** | 52 | 0.6 |
> | ▣ | **Alexandria, LA** | 173 | 0.1 |
> | ▣ | **Alpena, MI** | 210 | 0.1 |
> | ▣ | **Amarillo, TX** | 127 | 0.2 |
> | ▣ | **Anniston, AL** | 194 | 0.1 |
>
> **Scroll for more markets below (Up to 210 metros available)**

5: Budget

It's best to know your budget in advance, but sometimes that's impossible . After setting your Reach/ Frequency goals, type $1,000 and *MFP* will estimate the total budget needed beyond the $1,000.

6: Ad Types

Media come in all shapes and sizes. *MFP* lets you decide between 15 or 30 second TV spots and 60 or 30 second radio spots. You can also buy either full-page or half-page newspaper ads; same for magazines.

After you make decisions on the above six "**Basics**," you're ready to start buying with *Media Flight Plan*. This is when the simulation gets interesting, because nothing is linear. Every choice you make is interactive, and every buy you make affects the whole plan from top to bottom.

Media Flight Plan for Windows or Macintosh is published by **Deer Creek Publishing in Provo, Utah. Phone or fax: (801) 225-0702. Email: dmartin@cougar.netutah.net**

Like gross impressions, GRPs indicate the magnitude of a media schedule and can be used for various media forms. The amount of exposure a schedule delivers can be described for the population as a whole or for a particular population segment. To make clear the rating points refer to a specific demo, planners sometimes use the expression **targeted rating points.**

Targeted Rating Points (TRPs). TRPs mean the same thing as GRPs. It's generally a matter of personal preference as to which term to use. The following examples are basically the same:

- Achieve 50 GRPs per week against women 18–34 (W 18–34)

- Achieve 50 TRPs per week (W 18–34)

Which to Use: Reach? Frequency? Gross Impressions? GRPS? or TRPs?

The above five terms give planners a certain amount of flexibility in the way they can set media objectives. Reach and frequency tend to require more information both in estimating and tracking results. As mentioned, there are computer programs that provide planners with estimates of measures such as reach, frequency, and GRPs. Such computer software is used extensively in the advertising media industry. A software package that is especially useful for student advertising campaigns is "Media Flight Plan—IM" (3rd edition) by Dennis Martin of Brigham Young University, and Dale Coons, vice-president of media research for the Lintas: Campbell–Ewald advertising agency. This program is used to assist media planning as part of an advertising campaign. A brief overview of this software is given in Exhibit 7–1.

Setting objectives in terms of reach and frequency can be especially helpful for new product launches and for campaigns that undergo major strategic changes. For introductory campaigns, it's important to know what percentage of the target is getting the messages. If a product has an advantage, the window of opportunity to exploit that edge is often limited. It's an important strategic concern to know who is and who isn't getting the campaign messages. In addition, it's helpful to know how often they get a message.

Setting objectives in terms of gross impressions and GRPS or TRPS tends to be more relevant when a planner is interested in the weight of a plan, as they often are for products in the mature stage of their life cycle. As a brand matures, much of the advertising is of a reminding or reinforcing nature because the target audience is generally well aware of a brand. Therefore, planners accept more frequency in their schedules because it is more cost efficient rather than trying to maximize reach, which can be more costly. Generally, some people in any market segment are more difficult to reach than others—this translates as more expensive. In the introductory phase of a product life cycle, where a premium is placed on reaching targets at least once, planners are usually willing to tolerate less cost efficiency.

Planners tend to use rating points instead of impressions because they are easier to use. Since GRPs are based on percentages and impressions are based on actual head counts, the numbers for GRPs are usually reported in the hundreds and thousands, whereas the numbers for impressions are often stated in millions and billions. The smaller GRP numbers also make it easier to compare alternative media schedules. (For example, saying Schedule A delivers 90 GRPs a week and Schedule B delivers 120 GRPs is easier to grasp than saying Schedule A delivers 234 million gross impressions and Schedule B delivers 312 million gross impressions even though it's basically the same information.)

Expressing the size of the medium's audience in terms of impressions is used for various purposes. As Jim Surmanek has noted, advertisers like to impress retailers with the breadth and scope of the advertising that is planned to support a product line. Gross impression numbers in the millions sounds more impressive than a GRP number in the hundreds. In addition, impressions can be calculated for any media form (although that is also true of GRPs), and are a handy way to compare the audience delivery of different media plans.[13]

Qualitative Media Objectives

Setting objectives in terms of reach, impressions, and rating points gives some indication of the size of the audience a planner wants to expose to advertising. Of increasing interest to many planners is the ability of the media to enhance the messages that get delivered. Traditionally, academicians have shied away from recommending setting media objectives in terms of this ability because of the subjective nature of these kinds of objectives. Sissors and Bumba in their widely used textbook on advertising media note, "although messages seem to have more impact on consumers in one medium than they do in another, [impact is still a] hazy concept."[14] Hazy or not, it is clear that many agencies expect the media to do more than merely deliver the message.

The media, especially vehicles within a media class, can influence the impact a message is likely to have with the target. An ad for an investment broker in Forbes is likely to come off with more authority than one in *Playboy*. The advertising claims in an ad placed in *Parents* or *Good Housekeeping* are backed up by the magazines and are likely to be perceived with more credibility than an identical ad in *Modern Romance*. On page 191, we present a chart on qualitative media values. Consider the importance these values could have in affecting the way the target receives an advertising message for the brand you are working with. If it is especially important, then set the value up as a qualitative media objective. You might consider specifying that it is a *qualitative* media objective since people usually expect to see media objectives written in specific and measurable terms.

Determining the Media Strategy

The challenge to a media planner is to come up with a plan that gives the advertiser a competitive edge. A better plan can mean a more efficient one as well as a more effective one. Although it is easier said than done, it is important to have a competitive attitude. Let's look at the four major elements in a media strategy: target audience, media classes, media mix or weight, and media timing.

Identifying Target Audiences. Identifying the target audience is a critical decision that is at the very heart of an advertising campaign. The first step in identifying a target audience is to select prospect groups and target markets.[15] Prospect groups include individuals who have some likelihood of purchasing a particular product. Planners want to identify anyone who might be a prospect for purchasing a brand within a product category. Because this group is so diverse, nonspecific, and generally large, tighter criteria for targeting are often used.

Target markets is the term sometimes used to identify the geographic locations of customers and prospects (target audience is also acceptable). The geographic locations might include a region of the country (say, the Southeast), a specific state (Georgia), or city (Atlanta), or various other geographic boundaries (for example, a metropolitan area or a specific ZIP Code).

Variables for Profiling Target Audiences

Profiling target audiences within a media plan typically is done in terms of several types of variables: (1) demographic, (2) psychographic, (3) lifestyle, (4) product or brand usage, and (5) geodemographic. These variables can be used singly or in assorted combinations.

Demographics. Identifying a target audience by demography is one of the most common methods used in media planning, primarily because there is extensive information available on media audiences. The major syndicated media research firms, such as MRI and SMRB, provide a large number of demographic characteristics such as age, gender, income, education, and occupation. Thus, we might find a targeting strategy that states:

> *The primary targeted audience is women between the ages of 25 and 34. This primary target is weighted 75%* (so that this segment receives 75% of the budget allocation).
> *A secondary target is women between the ages of 18 and 24, which is weighted 25%* (and this segment receives 25% of the budget).

Such a targeting profile shows precisely to whom the planner wants the media effort directed. In this example, there are actually two targets—women ages 25–34, and women ages 18–24. Weights are assigned (75% and 25%) to each target. Such a targeting definition permits the media buyer to execute the plan as efficiently as possible. If the plan consisted solely of magazines, for example, the buyer would search mainly for magazines that deliver audiences of women in these age groups effectively. (Do keep in mind that most media vehicles cannot deliver an audience with absolutely no waste coverage—even direct mail—so the idea is to make buys that are as efficient as possible—given other constraints such as the creative strategy.) We have included a copy of a typical page from MRI in Figure 7–2, which reports on the readership of specific magazines by women according to four age groupings.

Psychographics. Another approach to targeting media audiences involves identification of prospects according to psychological characteristics, commonly called *psychographics*. In measuring the psychographic profile of consumer groups, the researcher attempts to classify people according to such things as their common beliefs, opinions, interests, personalities, and behaviors. For example, some people might be classified (in their shopping behavior) as "economy minded," others as "impulsive," and yet others as "experimenters."

The idea behind such groupings is that a person's shopping behavior is more influenced by sociopsychological factors than it is by their demographic characteristics. Some limitations, though, in using psychographics in media decisions are: (1) the research used to detect psychographic traits is questionable in terms of its reliability (psychological constructs are often difficult to measure), and (2) a lot of data about media usage is not currently available. Nevertheless, advertisers and advertising agencies today are experimenting with behavioral approaches to improve their media-planning processes.

Figure 7–2 MediaMark Research Inc. (MRI) Provides Magazine Readership According to Demographic Characteristics

BASE: WOMEN	TOTAL U.S. '000	18-24 A '000	B % DOWN	C % ACROSS	D INDEX	25-34 A '000	B % DOWN	C % ACROSS	D INDEX	35-44 A '000	B % DOWN	C % ACROSS	D INDEX	45-54 A '000	B % DOWN	C % ACROSS	D INDEX
All Women	96399	12883	100.0	13.4	100	22335	100.0	23.2	100	19151	100.0	19.9	100	12912	100.0	13.4	100
American Baby	2698	682	5.3	25.3	189	1399	6.3	51.9	224	438	2.3	16.2	82	*95	.7	3.5	26
American Health	2368	*135	1.0	5.7	43	*486	2.2	20.5	89	732	3.8	30.9	156	413	3.2	17.4	130
American Legion	1520	*21	.2	1.4	10	*110	.5	7.2	31	*267	1.4	17.6	88	*294	2.3	19.3	144
American Way	446	*72	.6	16.1	121	*77	.3	17.3	75	*98	.5	22.0	111	*101	.8	22.6	169
Architectural Digest	2123	*277	2.2	13.0	98	410	1.8	19.3	83	626	3.3	29.5	148	*369	2.9	17.4	130
Audubon	1182	*64	.5	5.4	41	*321	1.4	27.2	117	*302	1.6	25.5	129	*136	1.1	11.5	86
Baby Talk	2107	867	6.7	41.1	308	737	3.3	35.0	151	*216	1.1	10.3	52	*207	1.6	9.8	73
Barron's	*354	*104	.8	-	-	*33	.1	-	-	*36	.2	-	-	*89	.7	-	-
Bassmaster	577	*127	1.0	22.0	165	*224	1.0	38.8	168	*125	.7	21.7	109	*35	.3	6.1	45
Better Homes & Gardens	26515	2736	21.2	10.3	77	6010	26.9	22.7	98	6405	33.4	24.2	122	3736	28.9	14.1	105
BH&G(LHJ) Combo (Gr)	42754	4001	31.1	9.4	70	9264	41.5	21.7	94	10500	54.8	24.6	124	6291	48.7	14.7	110
Black Enterprise	957	*96	.7	10.0	75	*255	1.1	26.6	115	*323	1.7	33.8	170	*114	.9	11.9	89
Bon Appetit	3973	*334	2.6	8.4	63	758	3.4	19.1	82	993	5.2	25.0	126	677	5.2	17.0	127
Bride's and Your New Home	3867	1573	12.2	40.7	304	922	4.1	23.8	103	610	3.2	15.8	79	*464	3.6	12.0	90
Business Week	1836	*317	2.5	17.3	129	491	2.2	26.7	115	543	2.8	29.6	149	*153	1.2	8.3	62
Byte	*477	*114	.9	-	-	*104	.5	-	-	*144	.8	-	-	*60	.5	-	-
Cable Guide/TV Time (Gr)	9905	2100	16.3	21.2	159	2627	11.8	26.5	114	2237	11.7	22.6	114	1386	10.7	14.0	104
Car and Driver	732	*194	1.5	26.5	198	*296	1.3	40.4	175	*124	.6	16.9	85	*64	.5	8.7	65
Car Craft	*152	*20	.2	-	-	*37	.2	-	-	*44	.2	-	-	*12	.1	-	-
Colonial Homes	1906	*225	1.7	11.8	88	*384	1.7	20.1	87	513	2.7	26.9	135	*243	1.9	12.7	95
Conde Nast Limited (Gr)	21312	4689	36.4	22.0	165	5267	23.6	24.7	107	4652	24.3	21.8	110	2977	23.1	14.0	104
Conde Nast Traveler	883	*51	.4	5.8	43	*214	1.0	24.2	105	*234	1.2	26.5	133	*152	1.2	17.2	129
Conde Nast Women (Gr)	31339	11000	85.4	35.1	263	8189	36.7	26.1	113	5759	30.1	18.4	93	3638	28.2	11.6	87
Consumers Digest	2355	*244	1.9	10.4	78	*418	1.9	17.7	77	679	3.5	28.8	145	*393	3.0	16.7	125
Cooking Light	2516	*158	1.2	6.3	47	579	2.6	23.0	99	521	2.7	20.7	104	587	4.5	23.3	174
Cosmopolitan	11949	3483	27.0	29.1	218	3493	15.6	29.2	126	2495	13.0	20.9	105	1161	9.0	9.7	73
Country Home	5151	*569	4.4	11.0	83	1338	6.0	26.0	112	1392	7.3	27.0	136	781	6.0	15.2	113
Country Living	8018	*721	5.6	9.0	67	1823	8.2	22.7	98	2118	11.1	26.4	133	1524	11.8	19.0	142
Country Music	2529	*377	2.9	14.9	112	720	3.2	28.5	123	*490	2.6	19.4	98	*427	3.3	16.9	126
Delta's SKY Magazine	649	*169	1.3	26.0	195	*90	.4	13.9	60	*124	.6	19.1	96	*112	.9	17.3	129
Discover	2105	*437	3.4	20.8	155	541	2.4	25.7	111	*349	1.8	16.6	83	*237	1.8	11.3	84
Disney Channel Magazine	3977	*494	3.8	12.4	93	1419	6.4	35.7	154	1194	6.2	30.0	151	*470	3.6	11.8	88
Ebony	6374	1217	9.4	19.1	143	1841	8.2	28.9	125	1494	7.8	23.4	118	754	5.8	11.8	88
Elle	3595	1478	11.5	41.1	308	899	4.0	25.0	108	562	2.9	15.6	79	*425	3.3	11.8	88
Endless Vacation	908	*81	.6	8.9	67	*72	.3	7.9	34	*324	1.7	35.7	180	*181	1.4	19.9	149
Entertainment Weekly	2095	*626	4.9	29.9	224	581	2.6	27.7	120	*530	2.8	25.3	127	*97	.8	4.6	35
Esquire	1203	*168	1.3	14.0	104	*355	1.6	29.5	127	*300	1.6	24.9	126	*132	1.0	11.0	82
Essence	3710	811	6.3	21.9	164	975	4.4	26.3	113	994	5.2	26.8	135	*424	3.3	11.4	85
Family Circle	23529	2087	16.2	8.9	66	4823	21.6	20.5	88	5436	28.4	23.1	116	4203	32.6	17.9	133
Family Circle/McCall's (Gr)	39715	3979	30.9	10.0	75	8068	36.1	20.3	88	8926	46.6	22.5	113	6839	53.0	17.2	129
Family Handyman	1232	*80	.6	6.5	49	*267	1.2	21.7	94	*263	1.4	21.3	107	*290	2.2	23.5	176
Field & Stream	3318	*407	3.2	12.3	92	934	4.2	28.1	121	883	4.6	26.6	134	*437	3.4	13.2	98
First For Women	5362	1220	9.5	22.8	170	1803	8.1	33.6	145	1220	6.4	22.8	115	801	6.2	14.9	112
Flower & Garden	2890	*192	1.5	6.6	50	*579	2.6	20.0	86	625	3.3	21.6	109	*539	4.2	18.7	139
Flower & Grdn/Workbench (Gr)	3877	*216	1.7	5.6	42	793	3.6	20.5	88	951	5.0	24.5	123	716	5.5	18.5	138
Food & Wine	1968	*266	2.1	13.5	101	546	2.4	27.7	120	466	2.4	23.7	119	*361	2.8	18.3	137
Forbes	1378	*356	2.8	25.8	193	*203	.9	14.7	64	*325	1.7	23.6	119	*172	1.3	12.5	93
Fortune	1387	*230	1.8	16.6	124	*374	1.7	27.0	116	*300	1.6	21.6	109	*200	1.5	14.4	108
4 Wheel & Off Road	*384	*104	.8	-	-	*80	.4	-	-	*137	.7	-	-	*31	.2	-	-
Glamour	10108	3287	25.5	32.5	243	2881	12.9	28.5	123	1884	9.8	18.6	94	1125	8.7	11.1	83
Golf Digest	1392	*245	1.9	17.6	132	*388	1.7	27.9	120	*331	1.7	23.8	120	*109	.8	7.8	58
Golf Digest/Tennis (Gr)	2169	*458	3.6	21.1	158	582	2.6	26.8	116	535	2.8	24.7	124	*187	1.4	8.6	64
Golf Illustrated	750	*77	.6	10.3	77	*272	1.2	36.3	157	*196	1.0	26.1	132	*76	.6	10.1	76
Golf Magazine	1192	*99	.8	8.3	62	*316	1.4	26.5	114	*305	1.6	25.6	129	*123	1.0	10.3	77
Good Housekeeping	25099	2410	18.7	9.6	72	6051	27.1	24.1	104	5564	29.1	22.2	112	3868	30.0	15.4	115
Gourmet	3137	*281	2.2	9.0	67	592	2.7	18.9	81	753	3.9	24.0	121	562	4.4	17.9	134
GQ (Gentlemen's Quarterly)	1758	*808	6.3	46.0	344	*479	2.1	27.2	118	*295	1.5	16.8	84	*153	1.2	8.7	65
Guns & Ammo	801	*187	1.5	23.3	175	*371	1.7	46.3	200	*187	1.0	23.3	118	*11	.1	1.6	12
Hachette Magazine Ntwk (Gr)	32446	5258	40.8	16.2	121	7547	33.8	23.3	100	7102	37.1	21.9	110	4970	38.5	15.3	114
Hachette Men's Package (Gr)	4090	922	7.2	22.5	169	1265	5.7	30.9	133	859	4.5	21.0	106	635	4.9	15.5	116
Harper's Bazaar	2566	*586	4.5	22.8	171	*560	2.5	21.8	94	472	2.5	18.4	93	*401	3.1	15.6	117
Hearst Combo Power (Gr)	37734	3882	30.1	10.3	77	9089	40.7	24.1	104	8721	45.5	23.1	116	5642	43.7	15.0	112
Hearst Home Delivery (Gr)	17908	1549	12.0	8.6	65	3952	17.7	22.1	95	4620	24.1	25.8	130	3147	24.4	17.6	131
HG (House & Garden)	4633	*322	2.5	7.0	52	1132	5.1	24.4	105	1190	6.2	25.7	129	725	5.6	15.6	117
Home	3452	*489	3.8	14.2	106	830	3.7	24.0	104	906	4.7	26.2	132	513	4.0	14.9	111
Home Mechanix	636	*35	.3	5.5	41	*166	.7	26.1	113	*148	.8	23.3	117	*151	1.2	23.7	177
Hot Rod	1096	*557	4.3	50.8	380	*203	.9	18.5	80	*203	1.1	18.5	93	*87	.7	7.9	59
House Beautiful	5623	*334	2.6	5.9	44	1080	4.8	19.2	83	1420	7.4	25.3	127	978	7.6	17.4	130
Hunting	*504	*18	.1	-	-	*161	.7	-	-	*157	.8	-	-	*85	.7	-	-
Inc.	661	*193	1.5	29.2	218	*68	.3	10.3	44	*265	1.4	40.1	202	*88	.7	13.3	99
Inside Sports	555	*144	1.1	25.9	194	*119	.5	21.4	93	*118	.6	21.3	107	*69	.5	12.4	93
Jet	4912	1043	8.1	21.2	159	1170	5.2	23.8	103	1129	5.9	23.0	116	692	5.4	14.1	105
Kiplinger's Personal Finance	974	*42	.3	4.3	32	*128	.6	13.1	57	*134	.7	13.8	69	*256	2.0	26.3	196
Knapp Signature Coll. (Gr)	6096	*611	4.7	10.0	75	1188	5.2	19.2	83	1619	8.5	26.6	134	1046	8.1	17.2	128
Ladies' Home Journal	16239	1265	9.8	7.8	58	3254	14.6	20.0	86	4095	21.4	25.2	127	2555	19.8	15.7	117
Life	10363	2107	16.4	20.3	152	2718	12.2	26.2	113	2429	12.7	23.4	118	1237	9.6	11.9	89
Mademoiselle	6053	2613	20.3	43.2	323	1403	6.3	23.2	100	1035	5.4	17.1	86	*521	4.0	8.6	64
McCall's	16186	1892	14.7	11.7	87	3245	14.5	20.0	87	3490	18.2	21.6	109	2636	20.4	16.3	122
Men's Fitness	*149	*5	-	-	-	*38	.2	-	-	*59	.3	-	-	*34	.3	-	-
Metropolitan Home	2907	*147	1.1	9.4	70	*349	1.6	22.3	96	520	2.7	33.2	167	*274	2.1	14.3	107
Metro-Puck Comics Network	25853	3945	30.6	15.3	114	6084	27.2	23.5	102	4939	25.8	19.1	96	3584	27.8	13.9	103
Midwest Living	1349	*63	.5	4.7	35	*318	1.4	23.6	102	*273	1.4	20.2	102	*289	2.2	21.4	160
Mirabella	1618	*477	3.7	29.5	221	*351	1.6	21.7	94	*309	1.6	19.1	96	*288	2.2	17.7	132
Modern Bride	2880	1284	10.0	44.6	334	622	2.8	21.6	93	*467	2.4	16.2	82	*256	2.0	8.9	66

Lifestyles. According to Jugenheimer, Barban, and Turk, "Lifestyle profiles are intended to reflect the consumer's priorities—that is, they measure commitment of time, money, and energy to activities, interests, and viewpoints. To gain perspective, lifestyle surveys cover all sorts of things we do and care about."[16] Some examples of lifestyle profiling are:

- Activities (such as, sports, recreation, and entertainment)

- Preferences (such as, social causes and political perspective)

- Interests (such as, music, books, and hobbies)

Identifying target audiences according to lifestyle characteristics is similar to using psychographics, and the two approaches often are treated as one. By the same token, lifestyle research has the same limitations when used for media purposes.

Product or Brand Usage. Profiling target audiences according to the usage level of a product category or specific brand is widely used in developing media strategy. The method is as popular as defining by demography, and the two variables typically are used together. MRI usually reports product usage in three categories: "heavy," "medium," and "light."

In Figure 7–3 (on bottled water), note that some demographic characteristics, such as the education, age, and census region of bottled water users, are shown according to product usage levels (MRI also includes other demographic characteristics, but only a sample of these appear in the figure). We can use such data to provide an estimate of the size of a target audience and how its usage compares to average usage. MRI provides index numbers for population segments. Remember, an index number is a way of looking at the usage rate of a population segment compared to average usage. Think of the number 100 as indicating average usage and a number above or below 100 as above or below average usage. For example, an index number of 125 indicates a population segment has a usage rate of 25% above average usage.

Thus, referring to Figure 7–3, if we considered targeting our media to adults between the ages of 18 and 24, who are heavy users of bottled water and seltzer, MRI estimates that such a target consists of 2,037,000 adults (see column A under "heavy users"). These 2.037 million adults are 13.5% of all heavy users (that is, people who drink more than seven glasses per week). Note also that 8.3% of all adults ages 18–24 are heavy users (see column C). This figure is about 6% above average based on an index number of 106 (see column D).

Observing all of this information does not in itself tell us to whom to direct our media effort. Deciding the actual target audience is a decision the media planner must ultimately make. He or she will ask a host of questions about a possible target before making the final decision, including some of the following:

- Is the size of the target sufficient to meet marketing sales goals and advertising communication objectives?

- Can a large enough portion of the target audience be reached efficiently, with an adequate level of frequency?

- Does our media budget permit adequate delivery of messages to the possible target?

Geodemographics. With media vehicles becoming more and more localized according to geography, it is logical that planners would attempt to combine geographical patterns with demographic characteristics. For example, many consumer magazines today offer an advertiser wide choices for geographical pinpointing of target markets. You can buy an

Figure 7–3 Bottled Water & Seltzer

BASE: ADULTS	TOTAL U.S. '000	ALL A '000	ALL B % DOWN	ALL C % ACROSS	ALL D INDEX	HEAVY (MORE THAN 7) A '000	HEAVY B % DOWN	HEAVY C % ACROSS	HEAVY D INDEX	MEDIUM (2 - 7) A '000	MEDIUM B % DOWN	MEDIUM C % ACROSS	MEDIUM D INDEX	LIGHT (LESS THAN 2) A '000	LIGHT B % DOWN	LIGHT C % ACROSS	LIGHT D INDEX
						DRINKS OR GLASSES/LAST 7 DAYS											
All Adults	193462	55190	100.0	28.5	100	15069	100.0	7.8	100	20452	100.0	10.6	100	19668	100.0	10.2	100
Men	92674	21899	39.7	23.6	83	6076	40.3	6.6	84	8027	39.2	8.7	82	7796	39.6	8.4	83
Women	100788	33291	60.3	33.0	116	8994	59.7	8.9	115	12425	60.8	12.3	117	11872	60.4	11.8	116
Household Heads	117223	30364	55.0	25.9	91	8408	55.8	7.2	92	11314	55.3	9.7	91	10643	54.1	9.1	89
Homemakers	120984	36755	66.6	30.4	106	10247	68.0	8.5	109	13436	65.7	11.1	105	13072	66.5	10.8	106
Graduated College	41082	15205	27.5	37.0	130	4312	28.6	10.5	135	5466	26.7	13.3	126	5426	27.6	13.2	130
Attended College	51120	16649	30.2	32.6	114	4538	30.1	8.9	114	6482	31.7	12.7	120	5629	28.6	11.0	108
Graduated High School	65024	15724	28.5	24.2	85	4150	27.5	6.4	82	5653	27.6	8.7	82	5921	30.1	9.1	90
Did not Graduate High School	36235	7612	13.8	21.0	74	2069	13.7	5.7	73	2851	13.9	7.9	74	2692	13.7	7.4	73
18-24	24658	8158	14.8	33.1	116	2037	13.5	8.3	106	3220	15.7	13.1	124	2901	14.8	11.8	116
25-34	41962	14182	25.7	33.8	118	3746	24.9	8.9	115	5197	25.4	12.4	117	5239	26.6	12.5	123
35-44	42970	13572	24.6	31.6	111	3712	24.6	8.6	111	4857	23.7	11.3	107	5003	25.4	11.6	115
45-54	30865	9398	17.0	30.4	107	2610	17.3	8.5	109	3457	16.9	11.2	106	3331	16.9	10.8	106
55-64	21197	5071	9.2	23.9	84	1553	10.3	7.3	94	2011	9.8	9.5	90	1506	7.7	7.1	70
65 or over	31810	4810	8.7	15.1	53	1412	9.4	4.4	57	1710	8.4	5.4	51	1687	8.6	5.3	52
18-34	66619	22339	40.5	33.5	118	5782	38.4	8.7	111	8417	41.2	12.6	120	8140	41.4	12.2	120
18-49	127083	41352	74.9	32.5	114	11100	73.7	8.7	112	15158	74.1	11.9	113	15094	76.7	11.9	117
25-54	115796	37151	67.3	32.1	112	10067	66.8	8.7	112	13511	66.1	11.7	110	13573	69.0	11.7	115
Employed Full Time	107008	34391	62.3	32.1	113	9776	64.9	9.1	117	12415	60.7	11.6	110	12201	62.0	11.4	112
Part-time	17702	6245	11.3	35.3	124	1487	9.9	8.4	108	2263	11.1	12.8	121	2495	12.7	14.1	139
Sole Wage Earner	35152	10525	19.1	29.9	105	2816	18.7	8.0	103	3994	19.5	11.4	107	3716	18.9	10.6	104
Not Employed	68752	14553	26.4	21.2	74	3807	25.3	5.5	71	5774	28.2	8.4	79	4972	25.3	7.2	71
Professional	19050	7091	12.8	37.2	130	2069	13.7	10.9	139	2482	12.1	13.0	123	2540	12.9	13.3	131
Executive/Admin./Managerial	17654	6560	11.9	37.2	130	1821	12.1	10.3	132	2463	12.0	14.0	132	2275	11.6	12.9	127
Clerical/Sales/Technical	36512	13127	23.8	36.0	126	3436	22.8	9.4	121	5021	24.5	13.8	130	4670	23.7	12.8	126
Precision/Crafts/Repair	13368	3268	5.9	24.4	86	978	6.5	7.3	94	1256	6.1	9.4	89	1034	5.3	7.7	76
Other Employed	38125	10591	19.2	27.8	97	2959	19.6	7.8	100	3456	16.9	9.1	86	4176	21.2	11.0	108
H/D Income $75,000 or More	34245	12918	23.4	37.7	132	3890	25.8	11.4	146	4773	23.3	13.9	132	4255	21.6	12.4	122
$60,000 - 74,999	20204	6740	12.2	33.4	117	1764	11.7	8.7	112	2293	11.2	11.3	107	2683	13.6	13.3	131
$50,000 - 59,999	17746	5795	10.5	32.7	114	1635	10.9	9.2	118	2046	10.0	11.5	109	2114	10.7	11.9	117
$40,000 - 49,999	22067	6446	11.7	29.2	102	1615	10.7	7.3	94	2553	12.5	11.6	109	2277	11.6	10.3	102
$30,000 - 39,999	26072	7235	13.1	27.8	97	2096	13.9	8.0	103	2843	13.9	10.9	103	2297	11.7	8.8	87
$20,000 - 29,999	28213	6321	11.5	22.4	79	1770	11.7	6.3	81	2178	10.6	7.7	73	2373	12.1	8.4	83
$10,000 - 19,999	27851	6289	11.4	22.6	79	1396	9.3	5.0	64	2326	11.4	8.4	79	2566	13.0	9.2	91
Less than $10,000	17063	3447	6.2	20.2	71	904	6.0	5.3	68	1440	7.0	8.4	80	1103	5.6	6.5	64
Census Region: North East	39112	14146	25.6	36.2	127	4337	28.8	11.1	142	5645	27.6	14.4	137	4163	21.2	10.6	105
North Central	45331	10661	19.3	23.5	82	1951	12.9	4.3	55	3865	18.9	8.5	81	4845	24.6	10.7	105
South	67756	14467	26.2	21.4	75	3718	24.7	5.5	70	5337	26.1	7.9	75	5412	27.5	8.0	79
West	41262	15915	28.8	38.6	135	5063	33.6	12.3	158	5604	27.4	13.6	128	5248	26.7	12.7	125
Marketing Reg.: New England	10174	3659	6.6	36.0	126	1118	7.4	11.0	141	1465	7.2	14.4	136	1076	5.5	10.6	104
Middle Atlantic	32886	11379	20.6	34.6	121	3455	22.9	10.5	135	4456	21.8	13.5	128	3469	17.6	10.5	104
East Central	25885	5681	10.3	21.9	77	977	6.5	3.8	48	1944	9.5	7.5	71	2759	14.0	10.7	105
West Central	29342	7353	13.3	25.1	88	1475	9.8	5.0	65	2841	13.9	9.7	92	3037	15.4	10.4	102
South East	37012	6475	11.7	17.5	61	1798	11.9	4.9	62	2211	10.8	6.0	56	2466	12.5	6.7	66
South West	21905	6133	11.1	28.0	98	1495	9.9	6.8	88	2451	12.0	11.2	106	2188	11.1	10.0	98
Pacific	36256	14509	26.3	40.0	140	4751	31.5	13.1	168	5085	24.9	14.0	133	4673	23.8	12.9	127
County Size A	79362	30135	54.6	38.0	133	9138	60.6	11.5	148	11230	54.9	14.1	134	9767	49.7	12.3	121
County Size B	57583	14467	26.2	25.1	88	3711	24.6	6.4	83	5347	26.1	9.3	88	5409	27.5	9.4	92
County Size C	27751	5586	10.1	20.1	71	1187	7.9	4.3	55	2048	10.0	7.4	70	2351	12.0	8.5	83
County Size D	28765	5001	9.1	17.4	61	1033	6.9	3.6	46	1827	8.9	6.4	60	2141	10.9	7.4	73
MSA Central City	65429	19516	35.4	29.8	105	5207	34.6	8.0	102	6896	33.7	10.5	100	7414	37.7	11.3	111
MSA Suburban	89768	29103	52.7	32.4	114	8428	55.9	9.4	121	11191	54.7	12.5	118	9484	48.2	10.6	104
Non-MSA	38265	6570	11.9	17.2	60	1434	9.5	3.7	48	2365	11.6	6.2	58	2770	14.1	7.2	71
Single	44200	14892	27.0	33.7	118	4172	27.7	9.4	121	5605	27.4	12.7	120	5114	26.0	11.6	114
Married	112965	31764	57.6	28.1	99	8685	57.6	7.7	99	11512	56.3	10.2	96	11567	58.8	10.2	101
Other	36296	8533	15.5	23.5	82	2212	14.7	6.1	78	3334	16.3	9.2	87	2987	15.2	8.2	81
Parents	67742	21858	39.6	32.3	113	5469	36.3	8.1	104	7945	38.8	11.7	111	8444	42.9	12.5	123
Working Parents	52706	17457	31.6	33.1	116	4493	29.8	8.5	109	6175	30.2	11.7	111	6789	34.5	12.9	127
Household Size: 1 Person	24385	5826	10.6	23.9	84	1711	11.4	7.0	90	2311	11.3	9.5	90	1804	9.2	7.4	73
2 Persons	62064	16200	29.4	26.1	91	4438	29.5	7.2	92	5965	29.2	9.6	91	5797	29.5	9.3	92
3 or More	107013	33164	60.1	31.0	109	8920	59.2	8.3	107	12177	59.5	11.4	108	12068	61.4	11.3	111
Any Child in Household	81486	25818	46.8	31.7	111	6675	44.3	8.2	105	9523	46.6	11.7	111	9620	48.9	11.8	116
Under 2 Years	14735	5106	9.3	34.7	121	1303	8.6	8.8	114	1893	9.3	12.8	122	1909	9.7	13.0	127
2-5 Years	31551	10396	18.8	32.9	115	2546	16.9	8.1	104	3873	18.9	12.3	116	3976	20.2	12.6	124
6-11 Years	38084	11807	21.4	31.0	109	3084	20.5	8.1	104	4071	19.9	10.7	101	4652	23.7	12.2	120
12-17 Years	36369	11242	20.4	30.9	108	2766	18.4	7.6	98	4343	21.2	11.9	113	4134	21.0	11.4	112
White	163736	46476	84.2	28.4	99	12537	83.2	7.7	98	17487	85.5	10.7	101	16452	83.6	10.0	99
Black	22435	5791	10.5	25.8	90	1541	10.2	6.9	88	2024	9.9	9.0	85	2226	11.3	9.9	98
Spanish Speaking	17144	5884	10.7	34.3	120	1865	12.4	10.9	140	2232	10.9	13.0	123	1787	9.1	10.4	103
Home Owned	130597	35872	65.0	27.5	96	9515	63.1	7.3	94	13510	66.1	10.3	98	12847	65.3	9.8	97
Daily Newspapers: Read Any	106786	30170	54.7	28.3	99	8408	55.8	7.9	101	11372	55.6	10.6	101	10390	52.8	9.7	96
Read One Daily	86476	23808	43.1	27.5	97	6501	43.1	7.5	97	9130	44.6	10.6	100	8177	41.6	9.5	93
Read Two or More Dailies	20310	6362	11.5	31.3	110	1907	12.7	9.4	121	2242	11.0	11.0	104	2213	11.2	10.9	107
Sunday Newspapers: Read Any	122411	36100	65.4	29.5	103	9828	65.2	8.0	103	13570	66.4	11.1	105	12702	64.6	10.4	102
Read One Sunday	109654	31927	57.9	29.1	102	8551	56.7	7.8	100	12237	59.8	11.2	106	11139	56.6	10.2	100
Read Two or More Sundays	12757	4173	7.6	32.7	115	1277	8.5	10.0	129	1333	6.5	10.4	99	1563	7.9	12.3	121
Quintile I - Outdoor	38692	12213	22.1	31.6	111	3062	20.3	7.9	102	4399	21.5	11.4	108	4752	24.2	12.3	121
Quintile II	38692	11400	20.7	29.5	103	3017	20.0	7.8	100	4354	21.3	11.3	106	4029	20.5	10.4	102
Quintile III	38695	11179	20.3	28.9	101	3378	22.4	8.7	112	3965	19.4	10.2	97	3837	19.5	9.9	98
Quintile IV	38689	10346	18.7	26.7	94	2661	17.7	6.9	88	3936	19.2	10.2	96	3749	19.1	9.7	95
Quintile V	38694	10050	18.2	26.0	91	2951	19.6	7.6	98	3799	18.6	9.8	93	3301	16.8	8.5	84
Quintile I - Magazines	38688	13323	24.1	34.4	121	3769	25.0	9.7	125	5330	26.1	13.8	130	4225	21.5	10.9	107
Quintile II	38696	12453	22.6	32.2	113	3538	23.5	9.1	117	4805	23.5	12.4	117	4110	20.9	10.6	104
Quintile III	38693	11060	20.0	28.6	100	2748	18.2	7.1	91	3969	19.4	10.3	97	4343	22.1	11.2	110
Quintile IV	38693	9687	17.6	25.0	88	2799	18.6	7.2	93	3279	16.0	8.5	80	3609	18.3	9.3	92
Quintile V	38691	8666	15.7	22.4	79	2215	14.7	5.7	73	3070	15.0	7.9	75	3382	17.2	8.7	86
Quintile I - Newspapers	38695	12209	22.1	31.6	111	3420	22.7	8.8	113	4542	22.2	11.7	111	4247	21.6	11.0	108
Quintile II	38694	9870	17.9	25.5	89	2774	18.4	7.2	92	3792	18.5	9.8	93	3304	16.8	8.5	84
Quintile III	38680	11521	20.9	29.8	104	2959	19.6	7.6	98	4289	21.0	11.1	105	4273	21.7	11.0	109
Quintile IV	38701	11699	21.2	30.2	106	3288	21.8	8.5	109	4095	20.0	10.6	100	4316	21.9	11.2	110
Quintile V	38692	9891	17.9	25.6	90	2628	17.4	6.8	87	3733	18.3	9.6	91	3529	17.9	9.1	90
Quintile I - Radio	38694	11642	21.1	30.1	105	3014	20.0	7.8	100	4290	21.0	11.1	105	4338	22.1	11.2	110
Quintile II	38691	12446	22.6	32.2	113	3344	22.2	8.6	111	4472	21.9	11.6	109	4630	23.5	12.0	118
Quintile III	38692	11690	21.2	30.2	106	3286	21.8	8.5	109	4641	22.7	12.0	113	3763	19.1	9.7	96
Quintile IV	38693	10928	19.8	28.2	99	2907	19.3	7.5	96	3877	19.0	10.0	95	4144	21.1	10.7	105
Quintile V	38691	8483	15.4	21.9	77	2519	16.7	6.5	84	3172	15.5	8.2	78	2792	14.2	7.2	71

advertisement that will appear only in a particular region of the country (say, the Southwest), or a state (Texas). Some magazines even permit a metropolitan area split (Dallas). Other media types have long been structured to permit localized buys—spot television and cable, spot radio, newspapers, and out-of-home media, to name a few.

As we pointed out in Chapter 3, a number of research services such as PRIZM and Acorn have been developed to meet the desire of planners to use geodemographics in profiling target audiences. Such services report a variety of profile characteristics, such as income, education, occupation, ethnic affiliation, population density, and type of housing. Information for such characteristics can be presented for every ZIP Code in the United States.

Matching Target Audiences with Media Choices

Regardless of the variable or variables used to profile target audiences, the media planner ultimately must choose the target audience and then match it with available media. The difficulty in doing this is that information that permits a direct match often is not available. For example, if you target "economy-minded women between ages 20–55 and decide to use outdoor posters in the 50 largest cities of the United States, you likely will not have much usable information on how well that target is delivered by outdoor advertising. Your rationale for such a strategy may have to be based on intuition and creative logic or through using informal surveys of possible prospects.

Planners use syndicated research services, such as MRI and SMRB, to match up demographic and product-usage data with target audiences. Figure 7–4 shows graphically how the matching process might proceed. Thus, if you use a syndicated source to define your target in demographic terms, you will select media vehicles that show heavy usage of the vehicles in the demos in which you are interested. This matching process is shown on the left side of the figure.

When a target audience is defined in product-usage terms, two options for matching are available (see right side of the figure). The direct approach is to match the target audience with media vehicles according to the exposure level of users. If data exist for such a match, the planner will likely use this option. Another less direct approach involves a two-step process: (1) Determine the demographic profiles of the various levels of product or brand users, and (2) Look at the demographic profiles of a wide range of media vehicle audiences and match them to the user profiles.

According to Barban, Cristol, and Kopec, the less direct approach is desirable if the following conditions prevail:

1. Information on product users' media exposure is not available;

2. creative strategy relies heavily on a knowledge of the target market's demographic characteristics;

3. demographics significantly influence other marketing elements, such as distribution;

4. frequency of use is unknown as in the introduction of a new product, in which case the planner would focus on total usage in the product category as a basis for media-market matching.[17]

Choosing Media Classes

The second component of media strategy involves the selection of the media classes. This is a planning function. After the media classes are decided, and an appropriate mix of

Figure 7–4 Approaches to Matching Target Audiences with Media Choices

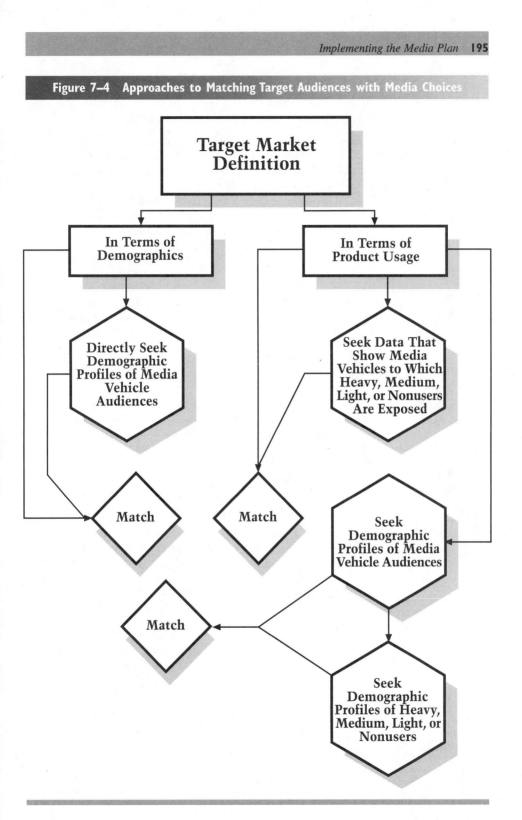

Figure 7–5 Media Characteristics and Recommendations

Major Media	Attributes	When to Use
Newspaper	• Mass audience • Excellent at reaching local market • Short lead time • Very current • Short life span • Poor reproduction quality • Allows comparison shopping • Provide "extra" services (such as ad designing) • Segmented sections used for consultation (travel, business)	• Local retailer • Targeting specific geographic market • Temporary offering (such as a sale) • Specific/special interest offering (such as current air fares) • Brand appearance not important • Need information to be distributed quickly (such as response to negative publicity)
Magazines	• Segmented audience • Long life span • Pass-along readership • Excellent reproduction • Not frequent • Long lead times • Not immediate	• Information intensive product • Rely on a "look" to create an image • Want long lasting image • Want image of editorial content to transfer to product
Television	• Combination of sight and sound allows for more complex messages to be delivered and remembered • Short-lived duration of messages (5-30 seconds) • High reach in general segments • High frequency in specific audiences • Accessible to everyone • Ads seen as intrusive and often ignored • Most cost efficient to reach large audience, although high absolute cost	• Want to build awareness for product (such as product introduction) • Require product demonstration • Want to use peripheral cues for low-involvement product (using popular music or celebrity to attract attention to brand) • Have financial resources to trade high absolute cost for more cost efficient medium • National brand

Figure 7–5 *continued*

Major Media	Attributes	When to Use
	• Market coverage flexibility (local or national buys)	
Radio	• Immediate delivery • Fleeting duration of message • Good for reaching local market • Low absolute cost • Stimulates imagination • No visuals eliminate using complicated messages or demonstrations • Mobile—able to reach consumers nearly anywhere, including when they are already out and about	• Want to stimulate impulse buying • Reminder advertising • Local retailer • Want to advertise offerings that change frequently (such as weekly grocery specials) • Consumer behavior motivated by time of day (such as eating out) • Product is simple to understand • Low advertising budget
Outdoor	• Excellent reach potential • Offers exposure near/ at point of purchase • Geographically selective • Fleeting message delivery • Limited reproduction quality	• Local business • Want to create traffic for local business • Segmenting audience according to geography • Want to build awareness within community • Want to reach mass community audience

media types is determined, typically this information is turned over to media buyers to execute, or implement, the plan.

One of the difficulties in making such decisions is the differential cost associated with each medium. A $1 million schedule of television and newspaper ads is different from a $1 million schedule of, say, radio and newspaper ads. Although the same amount of money in each mix is allocated to newspapers, newspapers are more important in the mix with television than with radio—$1 million of radio commercials will provide a much greater level of message repetition than $1 million invested in television. Thus, by comparison, newspapers will appear to have more impact in the television–newspaper mix than in the radio–newspaper mix. In the final analysis, however, these decisions are subjective, but with a goal of effectively matching the vehicles of each media type to the target audiences.

The rationale for choosing media classes is widely available in advertising media textbooks. We suggest you consult one to get an in-depth discussion of the advantages and disadvantages of choosing the various media. Figure 7–5 presents a simple listing of the characteristics of the major media and some suggestions as to when it might be appropriate to use them. A more comprehensive listing of minor media, including nontraditional media is available in Chapter 9. At DDB Needham Worldwide, they have expanded on some of the more traditional reasons for choosing media and have developed a grid to show how various message delivery options can enhance the advertising message. Figure 7–6 suggests "which media do it best."

Establishing the Media Mix

The third component or aspect of media strategy involves the amount of emphasis, or weight, put on the various media types and their relative importance.

The balance of the media types for a plan logically flows from the situation analysis, the target audiences to whom the plan is directed, and the media goals. Even if only a single media class is chosen—say, network television—there will typically be a mix. The mix might consist of a balance among television dayparts—that is, available segments in a 24-hour schedule. For example, a planner may spend 35% of the budget on daytime programs, 50% on evening programs, and 15% for late evening television. Or, even if the planner chooses only one daypart (say, evening programs), there might be a mix among different programming formats: situation comedies, action drama, and news magazines.

Factors to Consider for Media Weighting

There are several factors a planner likely will consider in determining the weighting of a particular set of media.

Target Audience. A media planner typically will have to decide on different media based on the size and composition of the target audience or audiences to whom the media effort is directed. A narrow target might be reached effectively by a single media type, but an assortment of different media may be required to reach a diverse population. The planner and media buyer will usually look to audience data to see how different media vehicles deliver specific targeted audiences. For example, *Redbook* magazine may be quite efficient in reaching your target and thus would be a part of your mix. Yet, the number *Redbook* delivers may be only a small proportion of the total audience sought, and you will have to bring in several other magazine vehicles, say, *Ladies Home Journal* and *McCall's.*

Target Market/Geographic Region. As mentioned earlier, a target market relates to the geographic location of customers and prospects. In developing a media mix, with appropriate weights among media types, the planner must look to the size and potential product or brand use of differing geographic areas. Some media types deliver audiences directly on a national scale, for example, network broadcast media (television, cable, and radio) and many magazines. However, other media types can be bought in a variety of geographical ways. Thus, daily newspapers are available in more than 1,500 local cities;

WHICH MEDIA DO IT BEST
Media Personalities

	Television	Magazines	Newspaper	Radio	Outdoor	Place Based	Direct Mail	Public Relations	Point of Sale	Event Marketing	Packaging
Authority	S	S	S	G	G	G	A	G	A	G	A
Beauty	S	S	A	A	S	A	A	A	A	G	G
Bigger-than-life	G	G	G	A	S	G	A	G	A	S	A
Credibility	G	S	G	G	G	A	A	S	A	G	S
Demonstration	S	G	A	A	A	A	G	S	S	S	A
Drama	S	G	A	G	S	A	S	S	A	S	A
Education	S	S	G	G	A	A	S	S	A	G	G
Elegance	G	S	A	A	G	A	G	G	A	G	G
Emotion	S	G	A	G	S	G	G	G	A	A	A
Entertainment	S	G	A	S	S	G	G	G	A	A	A
Excitement	S	G	G	G	G	G	G	S	A	S	A
Flexibility	G	G	A	S	A	S	A	G	A	G	A
Humor	S	G	G	S	S	A	G	A	G	A	A
Imagination	S	G	A	S	S	G	A	A	A	G	A
Immediacy	G	A	S	S	G	S	S	S	S	G	A
Information	G	S	S	G	A	G	S	S	A	G	S
Influence	S	G	G	A	A	A	G	S	A	G	A
Innovation	G	G	A	G	G	S	G	G	G	S	A
Intimacy	G	G	G	S	A	A	S	G	A	A	A
Intrusiveness	S	A	S	S	G	G	S	S	S	G	A
News	S	G	S	G	A	A	S	S	A	A	G
Quality	S	S	G	A	A	A	S	S	A	A	A
Permanence	A	S	A	A	G	G	A	G	A	A	A
Price	G	A	S	G	G	A	G	A	S	A	G
Recipe	G	S	G	A	A	G	S	A	S	S	S
Sensuality	S	G	A	S	G	G	G	G	A	S	G
Spectacle	G	G	A	A	S	G	A	A	S	S	G
Style	G	S	G	A	G	A	A	G	A	G	G
Unconventional	G	S	A	S	S	G	G	A	A	S	G

KEY: S Superior G Good A Acceptable

television can be purchased on more than 1,300 individual stations in around 230 markets in the United States.

A planner must take into account the various potentials of certain geographic areas in arriving at media weights. Consider the following hypothetical example about product usage arranged by major marketing regions:

Region	Number of Users of the Product Category (in millions)	Index of Product Users
Northeast	22	89
East Central	13	83
West Central	22	119
South	37	111
Pacific	17	89

The South is the largest region in terms of product users, 37 million. Note that the relative use of this product in the South is above average (the index of 111 indicates an 11% above-average use). This information might suggest to a planner to add some extra media effort to Southern markets. However, all five regions have sizable numbers of users (the East Central is the lowest but has 13 million product users), and none are dramatically above or below average (index ranges from 83 to 119). So a planner has to be careful not to spread the advertising effort "too thin" across these other markets. In the final analysis, interpreting such data is subjective, and a planner's decision must be justified on the basis of the analysis and intrinsic logic.

Linking the Media Mix with Other Strategies

Although there are countless ways to compose a media mix, two quite varied approaches delineate the situation. Media mix strategies can be viewed as being either concentrated or assorted.

A concentrated mix is one in which you typically use a single media type, say, network television. You can also think of a concentrated mix as including one or a very limited number of vehicles within a media type (say, only *Sports Illustrated* as your magazine choice).

Concentration provides some of the following benefits:

- **Effect on Competitors**—by focusing your media effort in a very limited way, there is a strong chance of dominating that medium relative to competition. Thus, your advertising likely will have greater impact in the minds of consumers exposed to that medium or vehicle.

- **Effect on Dealers**—by limiting media buys, dealers may readily note your advertising and be impressed by its concentrated effort. Perhaps you have chosen to put most of your money into a single vehicle (say, an important miniseries on television or a blockbuster event such as a Super Bowl game). This may have a desirable effect on the retailers and wholesalers in the channel of distribution.

- **Effect on Media**—by concentrating your media money in a single type, and a few vehicles, you will often gain a negotiating advantage with the media. They may be more inclined to offer better prices or merchandising help because you are spending the bulk of your media dollars with them.

- **Effect on Production Costs**—there will likely be certain economies of scale associated with a concentrated media buy. If you use both television and magazines, for example, the cost to produce commercials and advertisements will be greater than if you used a single media type. The same may be true if you spread your vehicle buys over a large base.

An assorted mix uses several media types in the mix by spreading dollars across a large base of media opportunities. Certain situations may more logically warrant this approach over a concentrated one. For example, if a target audience is subdivided into several components, you will be more likely to use an assortment of media. A primary target of "working mothers" and a secondary target of "working mothers' children," for example, may logically break down into magazines for the primary target and Saturday morning television for the secondary target.

Assorted mixes can result in some of the following advantages:

- **Effect on Target Audiences**—An assortment of media facilitates delivering different messages to different people. Today planners use many media types, especially some of the nontraditional media, to reach increasingly smaller audience segments. The more targeted audiences are split, the more likely an assortment of media will be used.

- **Effect on Message Content**—if you would like to communicate with the same prospects but in different psychological contexts, assortment makes sense. This approach might be used where there is a lengthy period through which messages take a prospect through the communication cycle, from initial awareness of a brand to getting a prospect to intend to make a brand purchase. Each of these stages may best be presented in different media.

- **Effect on Reach and Frequency Goals**—whereas a concentrated mix often results in frequency being more easily attainable than reach, an assorted approach can affect both. Most typically, however, assortment translates into reach being extended beyond that which a concentrated mix provides. Because there are heavy and light users for each medium, adding a second (or third or fourth) medium will usually extend the reach of a single medium. For example, you may get a reach of 75% against the target with a network television buy. By shifting some of the money spent in television to magazines, the television reach may go down somewhat, but the combined television–magazine delivery may increase to, say, 80%.

The effect of an assortment on frequency comes about through a balancing of exposure opportunities. In some concentrated media schedules, frequency exposures are particularly high at the low and high ends of the distribution. In other words, the number of target audiences exposed is relatively large for those who receive only one and two exposures, as well as by those receiving the largest possible number of exposures. If additional media are included into the assortment, the extremes of the exposure distribution usually are reduced, with a corresponding increase in the midrange exposures. This process smooths out the overall frequency distribution and may result in a more effective achievement of media objectives.

Media Timing

When to Advertise. The last component of the media strategy involves the timing, or scheduling of the advertising. As we discussed earlier in the chapter, there are two basic decisions related to timing: when to advertise and what kind of continuity, or pattern, to use. (see page 178–179) The timing of the advertising can be based on many factors including a number of considerations internal to a firm. For example, a company may schedule advertising depending on product availability or when new products are introduced. The following are some of the more common considerations planners address:[18]

1. **Budget Constraints**—This factor influences scheduling in many ways. Is there sufficient money available to initiate a campaign at reach and frequency levels the planner deems necessary and still have enough left to sustain the campaign over an extended period of time? If not, an all too common reality, a planner will have to make some tough decisions about when to advertise, and the type of continuity used when the brand is advertised. Budget constraints influence each of the following considerations.

2. **Seasonality**—The sales of many products vary with the time of year. Mens' casual slacks sell best during spring and fall, as do many types of clothing. A media schedule will need to support sales efforts during these time periods.

3. **Purchase–Repurchase Cycle**—Ideally, advertisers want to advertise before consumers make each purchase decision. "Recency buying" underscores this desire by striving to schedule advertising as close as possible to the time the consumer makes a purchase. Depending on the length of the purchase–repurchase cycle, it can get expensive—especially when you realize that it is generally not enough to simply reach consumers during this cycle, they also need to be reached with sufficient frequency to achieve the desired effect, usually sales.

4. **Stage of the Product Life Cycle**—Products in the introductory phase of the product life cycle generally require more advertising—more defined both in terms of exposure and dollars expended. New brands generally require more exposure than mature ones to get a message across and accepted. Moreover, during an introductory period, it's important to reach prospects quickly. If a brand has a differentiating feature, it may only have a small window of opportunity to capitalize on its advantage before the competition catches up and copies its edge. Some prospects are expensive to reach, but in an introductory period it's important to reach them. As a product matures, you can often reach them in different ways that are frequently more cost efficient.

5. **Competitive Advertising Patterns**—Since strategy is competitive in nature, it's important to know when the competition is advertising in order to plan how to match their promotional efforts. There really are no simple, safe generalizations about whether it is better to confront or avoid the competition. For example, the media expenditures for Burger King and the Miller brands are proportionately higher than those for McDonald's and Budweiser respectively. In the case of Burger King, the

higher expenditures may be because the company feels it can increase its share of the fast-food business at the expense of McDonald's—which it has done in recent years. In the case of the top two Miller brands, the company is actually outspending the amount spent by the Budweiser brands even though it has been generally losing share of market. Although there are similarities between the two brands, there are enough differences to underscore the importance for media planners to have a firm grasp of the company's marketing strategy and corporate culture—how ambitious is the company? How much risk is it willing to tolerate?[19]

6. **Media Dominance**—This consideration is related to the previous one on competitive activity not only in its concern about whether to confront or avoid the competition, but also how to match them. Many companies, especially category leaders, want to dominate a medium or a vehicle to demonstrate to consumers that they are the brand leaders.

Continuity. Media practitioners use the term **continuity** in a variety of ways. We refer to continuity as the way media messages are scheduled over a period of time. Although we present three specific types, or patterns, of continuity—continuous, flighting, and pulsing—planners commonly use variations of these types adapting them to meet the requirements of the situation. The continuity used for a particular media plan depends on many of the same factors that influence media timing. Figures 7–7A, 7B, and 7C show graphs (media schedule) of the three patterns.

A **continuous** continuity pattern (Figure 7–7A) is one in which approximately the same amount of money is spent in each period of the campaign. Such a strategy might be related to a brand with a relatively fixed share of market, with sales fairly equal across each month or period. This pattern is sometimes called straight-through advertising.

In a **flighting** strategy (Figure 7–7B), advertising varies from period to period. During certain times of the campaign, there is no advertising at all. This approach is often considered for a brand with a limited budget relative to competitors and a varying sales pattern throughout the year. A brand like FTD Florists schedules their advertising in flights to time their advertising before major flower-giving holidays such as Valentine's Day, Easter, Mother's Day, and Secretary's Day.

A **pulsed** schedule (Figure 7–7C), or pulsing, is similar to flighting—advertising varies from period to period—but there is at least some advertising media scheduled in each period. For example, a heavy media effort may be placed just before a peak sales periods yet at other times media messages would continue in order to maintain top-of-mind brand awareness.

It is important to realize that continuity means more than simply scheduling impressions over a period of time. The impressions contain information, ideas, or images designed to achieve communication goals. In the end, it is the messages that should have the strongest influence on the particular continuity schedule selected. An example of campaign continuity follows:

Example
The brand's new advertising theme will be introduced to the target audience during the first two months of the campaign (January and February), followed by a three-month period of focusing on brand attributes (March, April, May). There will be no advertising scheduled

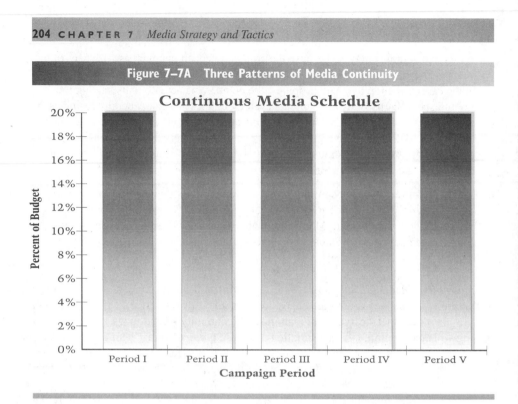

Figure 7–7A   Three Patterns of Media Continuity

Continuous Media Schedule

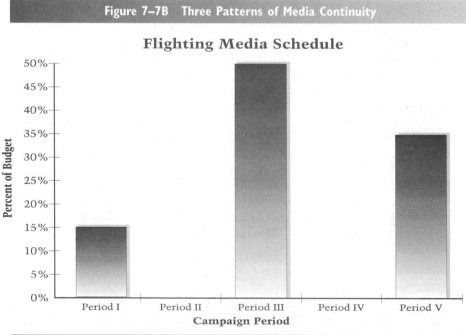

Figure 7–7B   Three Patterns of Media Continuity

Flighting Media Schedule

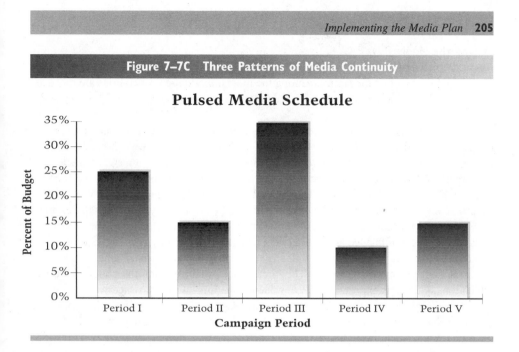

Figure 7–7C   Three Patterns of Media Continuity

Pulsed Media Schedule

during the low sales months of summer (June, July, August), followed by a big back-to-school push in September because of peak sales. The campaign will finish the year using a message strategy designed to build the brand during the last three-month period (October, November, and December).

Determining the Media Tactics

Once the strategy is determined, the next step is to implement the plan by making the media buys. In the business world, the actual buys will depend on a number of factors that are difficult to fully consider in a textbook, including the availability of advertising space or time, the negotiating skill of the buyers, and special media opportunities, some of which present themselves on a nonrecurring basis. For example, there is a finite amount of broadcast time and billboard space available to purchase. Unlike newspapers and magazines that can add pages to an issue, a TV station can't schedule additional time, and an outdoor advertising company can't add additional billboards (at least not in the short run) to meet new demand.

Historically, the rates media set for advertising space or time have been subject to varying amounts of negotiation. Broadcast media rates have been heavily negotiated, print media much less so. In the nineties, virtually all media rates are subject to negotiation to some extent. Basically, the rates that can be charged for a media vehicle are a function of supply and demand.

Buyers also consider **special opportunities** on both a regular and a nonrecurring basis. Magazines offer special demographic breakouts from their regular editions geared toward special segments, such as a students' edition. Newspapers periodically offer special features centered around a theme such as "Gardening" or "Automobiles." The 1996 Olympics in Atlanta offered a special opportunity for Coca-Cola inasmuch as its world headquarters is located in Atlanta.

Making the Media Buys

Since the media buy is an execution of the media strategy, all the factors that influence the strategy will also affect the tactics. Among the most important considerations are those associated with the target audience, costs, seasonality, and geography.

Target Audience. Selecting media vehicles that reach the target audience makes obvious sense. It is also important to reach targets with a minimum of *waste*—media talk for reaching nonprospects. Another relevant consideration in matching the right vehicle with the target audience involves the circumstances surrounding the conditions under which the target will be exposed to the vehicle. At DDB Needham Worldwide they've developed a proprietary system called Aperture to evaluate people's receptivity to an advertising message. This system looks at when and where the target is exposed to an ad because these considerations can influence how the audience feels about the messages in the advertising. A radio spot on Saturday night will typically reach people in a different frame of mind than the same spot on Sunday morning. The circumstances surrounding the conditions under which the audience is exposed to an ad influence the impact of a message.[20]

Considering how a vehicle will impact a message is always important when matching specific vehicles with a target audience. Yet all too frequently, media buyers purchase a vehicle on no more than its ability to deliver reach at a cost-efficient price. We hope this discussion emphasizes the importance of using judgment in making media purchases. It also underscores the importance of understanding the target beyond demographic considerations.

Costs. Purchasing media at cost-efficient prices is a critical part of media buying. The greater the savings, the more money that can be committed to increasing the advertising weight of the media plan. To help evaluate the relative cost efficiency of various media vehicles, a planner can use three related measures: cost-per-thousand (CPM), cost-per-thousand prospects (CPMP), and cost-per-point (CPP).

CPM. This is the basic measure used to compare media vehicles and/or media schedules. It can be used for intermedia comparisons (between media) or intramedia comparisons (within a media class). It refers to the cost of reaching every 1,000 individuals or homes with a particular media vehicle or schedule, and can be calculated as follows:

$$\frac{\text{Cost of the unit} \times 1,000}{\text{audience base}} = \text{CPM (audience base)}$$

The unit can refer to a unit of time or space, such as 30-second spots, full-page ads, or column inches. The audience base can be households, circulation, demographic or product usage segments.

Consider the following example from *Ladies Home Journal*:

$$\frac{\$127,000 \text{ (4-C Page)} \times 1,000}{4,915,000 \text{ circulation}} = \$25.84 \text{ CPM circulated copies}$$

Analyzing media vehicles on the basis of circulation or total audience provides a media buyer with the relative value a vehicle has in delivering all the people that are exposed to the vehicle. However, the real value of a vehicle is in delivering prospects (that is, people who may be predisposed to buy the product). In the above example, a buyer will want to know how efficiently *Ladies Home Journal* delivers people who are in the target audience. So instead of calculating the CPM for circulated copies, or the total audience in the case of television, a CPM is calculated for the target audience. To find information on the exposure of various demographic segments to media vehicles look in *MRI* or *SMRB* (the demographic volumes—not the product usage ones).

Cost-per-Thousand Prospects (CPMP). CPMP is a measure that is sometimes used to focus on the efficiency with which a vehicle delivers the target audience. Let's say in the above example, the target audience is women between ages 25 and 54. To calculate a CPMP, first determine the number of women ages 25–54, who are in the audience of *Ladies Home Journal*. This figure can be obtained from *MRI* or *SMRB*. Next, calculate the CPMP as follows:

$$\frac{\$127,000 \times 1,000}{9,560,000 \text{ (W 25–54)}} = \$13.29 \text{ CPMP (or CPM W25–54)}$$

Note that in the above two examples, the denominator for cost-per-thousand prospects (9,560,000) is larger than the denominator for CPM circulation (4,915,000). This is because the audience figure, women between ages 25–54, is arrived at by multiplying the audience figure by the readers per copy (RPC).

Comparing the cost efficiency of vehicles on the basis of circulation or total audience rather than on the basis of prospects can obviously lead to differing conclusions. For example, comparing *Ladies Home Journal* to a similar magazine such as *Good Housekeeping* led to the following comparison (the calculations are derived from Optimum Media Research based on data obtained from *SRDS* and *MRI*):

	CPM Circulation	CPMP (W 25–54)
Ladies Home Journal	$25.84	$12.29
Good Housekeeping	$33.14	$11.59

In the above example, *Ladies Home Journal* is the more cost-efficient purchase based on circulation, but *Good Housekeeping* is more efficient based on cost-per-thousand prospects. Media buyers nearly always want to know the cost efficiency of a vehicle in delivering the target audience, but this information isn't always available (especially to students). Sometimes the relevant information is contained in psychographic data and is not easily (or inexpensively) obtainable. Sometimes you end up comparing what you can, especially if you are with a small organization.

Cost per point (CPP). Cost per point, also called cost per rating point, is another measure used to compare media alternatives. It is used mostly for broadcast media and is arrived at by dividing the cost of the commercial by a program's rating as follows (although this example uses TV, CPPs can be calculated for other media as well):

$$\frac{\text{Cost of a commercial}}{\text{Program rating}} = \text{Cost per point}$$

Example

The first dollar amount ($595,000) is the cost of a hypothetical top-rated situation comedy.

$$\frac{\$595,000}{20 \text{ rating}} = \$29,750 \text{ CPP}$$

CPPs can be used to compare alternative broadcast vehicles or they can be used to compare alternative media schedules. They are also often used to indicate the amount of exposure that can be obtained from a defined budget in a local market. For example, if you have a budget of $1,000 and an estimated CPP of $10, you can purchase 100 rating points of exposure.[21] Although CPPs are used primarily with television and radio, they can also be used with print media. Analysts use the concept of coverage as a substitute for a rating since coverage can be expressed as a percentage of a demographic or product usage segment.[22]

Note of Caution. Cost efficiency analysis is an important part of media buying. Nonetheless, it is important to remember that these analyses are based on exposure, they really tell nothing about the likely effectiveness of the media selected. In other words, buying the most efficient media won't necessarily give you the most effective plan.

Seasonality. The seasonal allocation of media dollars is one way media buyers schedule advertising over the campaign period. The idea here is to coordinate media expenditures with the varying sales pattern of the brand.

By scheduling advertising in line with existing sales trends, the advertising attempts to channel the needs or wants of the consumer into demand for the brand. Naturally, there may be some corporate strategic reasons to even out sales patterns related, for example, to managing the labor force. Usually, however, it's a lot easier to "go with the flow" than to try to change existing patterns of consumer behavior.

Exhibit 7–2 is a simplistic example of how a packaged goods advertiser allocates its media budget on the basis of bimonthly sales.

Usually advertising is scheduled during a period prior to when sales are anticipated. Jim Avery, in his book *Advertising Campaign Planning*, points out that to do otherwise assumes "that the advertising works instantly." He uses a statistical approach called "smoothing" to allocate media dollars over a period of a couple of months so that there is an advertising "lead-in" to when sales are expected to take place.[23]

The timing of the advertising schedule is also often influenced by the purchase–repurchase cycle (discussed on page 202). A buyer needs to know the strategic importance of scheduling advertising as close to the time consumers make a purchase, or whether he or she should give substantial lead time preceding when the consumer is likely to make a purchase.

Geography. The geographical allocation of media dollars is based on the same idea we considered with seasonality—advertise where (or when) there is a history of sales doing well. Naturally, there may be strategic reasons why you may want to put extra emphasis in areas where sales are low, but the general rule is to advertise in line with existing trends of consumer behavior.

There are two basic geographical considerations: (1) Advertise only in those areas where there is sufficient market opportunity, and (2) Advertise everywhere (that is, nationally) and add extra emphasis, or weight, in selected areas where the brand sells

Exhibit 7–2   Seasonal Allocation of Media Dollars

Months	Sales	Percent of Total Sales	Index	Media Budget*	Budget Allocation**
Jan./Feb.	$54,233,600	9.7%	57	$57,088,000	$5,420,336
March/April	$97,620,480	17.1	106	$57,088,000	$9,762,048
May/June	$117,601,280	20.6	124	$57,088,000	$11,760,128
July/Aug.	$128,448,000	22.5	136	$57,088,000	$12,844,800
Sept./Oct.	$105,041,900	18.4	111	$57,088,000	$10,504,192
Nov./Dec.	$67,934,700	11.9	72	$57,088,000	$6,793,472
Total	$570,879,960	100		$57,088,000	$57,088,000

*Media budget is approximately 10% of sales
** Budget allocation is determined by multiplying percent of total sales by the Media Budget ($57,088,000)

especially well. For example, in Exhibit 7–3 half of the brand's budget of $57 million is allocated to national advertising (say, network television), and half of the budget is earmarked toward adding extra advertising pressure (say, spot television) in the four geographic regions where sales are proportionally higher.

Contingencies and Alternative Plans
As you develop the strategy and tactics, it is wise to consider alternative courses of action should unexpected conditions occur during the life of the campaign. This is called **contingency planning.** Some of the problems that can influence a decision to move the campaign in a different direction include the following.

- **Changing Economic Conditions**—For certain products, the general economic condition affects sales. If we based our media plan on a particular forecast, what changes should we make if the economy turns downward (or upward)? Also to be considered is that economic changes usually affect different parts of the country and different cities in varying ways. A national plan may have to switch to a more localized plan under unanticipated changes.

- **Changing Sales Results**—Regardless of how general economic conditions affect a product class, individual brands can go through sales changes that were not expected when the media plan was finalized. Sales expectations could decrease or increase. The key is to know how best to change a media plan if this occurs.

- **Changing Competitive Activity**—It usually is difficult to predict how competitors will behave in the future. Thus, the media activity of competitors may be a contingency

Exhibit 7-3 Budget Allocation of Select Geographic Markets

Marketing Region	Users (000)	Percent of Users	Index Number	Adjusted Percentage**	Budget Allocation***
		Geographical Distribution of Brand X Users			
New England	3,659	6.6%	126*	10%	$2,854,440
Middle Atlantic	11,379	20.6	121*	32	$9,134,080
East Central	5,681	10.3	77		
West Central	7,353	13.3	88		
South East	6,475	11.7	61		
South West	6,133	11.1	98*	17	$4,852,480
Pacific	14,509	26.3	140*	41	$11,703,040
Total	35,680	100		100%	$28,544,040

*Markets selected for heavy-up emphasis for highest index numbers
**Adjusted Percent determined by dividing 64.6 (that is, the sum of the top four market's Percent of Users) by each market's percent of users
***Budget Allocation is determined by multiplying the Adjusted Percent of the top four markets by $28,545,040 (the budget)

area. For example, you might have planned a four-month introduction of Milky Way II on the premise that major competitors do not have similar brands. But, if Hershey Foods introduced a similar brand a month before your introduction, your timing pattern, among other things, would likely be affected. In turn, media objectives would probably need revision.

The logical follow-through to the consideration of contingencies is to formulate alternative plans. If a particular contingency occurs, there will be a specific alternative plan ready to go on short notice. The whole process of formulating contingencies and alternative plans is like a "what if" game. What if predicted economic conditions—estimated at a modest 2% growth next year—turn downward? What would our alternative plan be under these circumstances?"

Taking into account contingencies and alternatives, of course, complicates the entire planning process. If it is difficult to develop a single plan—and it usually is—what about having three or four alternatives? Yet, many media people believe that having other options available if something unforeseen occurs is worth the added effort. Companies often build into their budget a dedicated amount to handle contingencies. This part of the budget is sometimes called a **contingency fund,** or simply a **reserve.**

Finishing the Media Effort
At this point in the campaign, the media section is unlikely to be finished. Still ahead is the task of determining media prices and putting together a budget. In addition, a **media**

calendar (also called a **continuity schedule**), needs to be prepared. These documents provide a sense of what is being planned for the media so that planners and buyers can reevaluate the situation should conditions change. We'll cover these documents in Chapter 11 on putting the plans book together.

A modern marketing communication campaign consists of more than advertising media. It includes other tools such as sales promotion and direct marketing. Increasingly, the distinction between one of these tools and the media is blurred. We cover these tools in Chapter 8.

Finally, agencies increasingly are marketing their media services apart from the rest of what they offer a client. Creative media planning is a label they often attach to their ability to do more than just the quantitative or negotiating aspects of planning and buying. In short, creative media plans should be different or unusual. Part of what makes a plan different is its use of nontraditional media outlets. In Chapter 9, we'll take a look at some of the extra things creative media planners can do to enhance the marketing communication effort.

Campaign Progress Checklist

At this point in the campaign you should generally be aware of the following points:

1. The best media plans evolve from a creative effort and enhance the way the message is received.
2. Media objectives are generally set in terms of exposure (reach, frequency, gross impressions, GRPs, and TRPS), but also consider setting qualitative objectives that are designed to enhance the creative strategy.
3. Media strategy generally includes decisions about target audience, media classes, media mix, and media timing.
4. Each quantitative objective should normally include the desired target, the desired amount of reach and frequency, and the timing or pattern with which the messages are expected to be delivered.
5. In defining the target audience, it is often helpful to go beyond demographic and product usage variables and delineate the target in terms of psychographic, lifestyle, and geodemographic variables.
6. In selecting media classes it is often a good idea to look at more than the traditional characteristics of the media and look at how media add something to the message.
7. The strategic decision about when to advertise not only influences the cost effectiveness of a plan, but can also influence the target's receptivity to a message.
8. The cost efficiency of a plan is best measured by the cost of reaching prospects who are most likely to buy a product.
9. The seasonal and geographical allocation of media dollars is a way to efficiently get the messages to the target audience where and when they are most likely to buy the product.
10. Contingency planning and the dedication of a portion of the budget as a contingency fund is one way to plan for unexpected changing conditions in the marketplace.

Notes and References

[1] For more information, see Helen Katz, *The media handbook* (Lincolnwood, IL: NTC Business Books, 1995); Donald W. Jugenheimer, Arnold M. Barban, & Peter B. Turk, Advertising media: *Strategy and tactics* (Dubuque, IA: WCB Brown & Benchmark, 1992); Jack Z. Sissors & Lincoln Bumba, *Advertising media planning* (5th ed), (Lincolnwood,IL: NTC Business Books, 1996); Jim Surmanek, *Introduction to advertising media: Research, planning, and buying* (Lincolnwood,IL: NTC Business Books, 1993); Arnold M. Barban, Steven M. Cristol, & Frank J. Kopec, *Essentials of media planning* (3rd ed.), (Lincolnwood, IL: NTC Business Books, 1993); William J. Donnelly, *Planning media: Strategy and imagination* (Upper Saddle River, NJ: Prentice-Hall, 1996).

[2] Jugenheimer et al., *Advertising media*, p. 12.

[3] Avery, J. (1993). *Advertising campaign planning: Developing an advertising-based marketing plan.* Chicago: The Copy Workshop, pp. 143–144.

[4] For an expanded discussion on media tactics, see Jugenheimer et al., *Advertising media*, pp. 264–283.

[5] Wells, W., Burnett, J., & Moriarty, S. (1998). *Advertising principles & practice* (4th ed.). Upper Saddle River, NJ: Prentice-Hall, pp. 361–363.

[6] Sissors & Bumba, *Advertising media planning*, p. 69.

[7] Naples, M. (1979). *Effective frequency.* New York: Association of National Advertisers Inc., pp. 63–82.

[8] Jones, J. P. (1995). *When ads work: New proof that advertising triggers sales.* New York: Lexington Books.

[9] Sissors & Bumba, *Advertising media planning*, pp. 141–145.

[10] Donnelly, *Planning media*, p. 151.

[11] Sissors & Bumba, *Advertising media planning*, pp. 222–225.

[12] Donnelly, *Planning media*, p. 157.

[13] Surmanek, *Introduction to advertising media*, p. 82.

[14] Sissors & Bumba, *Advertising media planning*, p. 159.

[15] The discussion of these terms is based on Jugenheimer et al., *Advertising media*, pp. 186–187.

[16] Jungenheimer et al., *Advertising media*, p. 193.

[17] Barban et al., *Essentials of media planning*, p. 49.

[18] Barban et al., *Essentials of media planning*, p. 72.

[19] According to Competitive Media Reporting data, the top two Budweiser brands had media expenditures of $154.1 million and top two Miller brands spent $170.5 million. Reported in Gerry Khermouch, Pockets of success tempered by concern, *SuperBrands* (June 15, 1998) p. S28.

[20] For more information, see Bruce G. Vanden Bergh & Helen Katz, *Advertising principles: Choice, challenge, change* (Lincolnwood, IL: 1999), p. 286.

[21] For an expanded discussion on cost per rating points, see Surmanek, *Introduction to advertising media*, pp. 95–104.

[22] For an expanded discussion of coverage in print media, see Sissors & Bumba, *Advertising media planning*, pp. 88–91.

[23] For an expanded discussion of "smoothing," see Avery, *Advertising campaign planning*, p. 167.

Chapter 8

Related Marketing Communications

To this point in the campaign planning process you have been building your campaign by carefully researching your target market and competition, setting marketing and advertising objectives, and developing creative and media plans that will accomplish those objectives for your client. Now we turn to those related marketing communication elements that will help you to integrate and extend your strategy. These marketing communication elements are sales promotion, public relations, and direct marketing.

DEVELOPING RELATED MARKETING COMMUNICATIONS

Your approach at this stage of campaign development should be to continue to think strategically. The success of your related marketing communications recommendations will depend on the degree to which you are able to integrate them with your advertising plan so that your target audience gets a consistent message and "feel" from every contact it has with your promotional activities. Consistency does not necessarily mean that all campaign materials must look alike. It does mean that the target audience members should receive messages and promotions that are consistent and carefully developed to reflect their past and present experiences with your client's product or service.

How much emphasis to put on each element in the marketing communication mix will be one of your key decisions. Although this is to a large degree a budget allocation and payout problem, there should be good strategic rationale behind your spending decision. A place to start is to analyze your consumers in terms of where they are in the sales process or purchase cycle, what types of responses you are looking for from them, and how selective (that is, targeted) you want your strategy to be in light of the relative costs of your media and promotion alternatives.

Your analysis should begin with where your consumers are in the sales process. If they are prospects who have yet to purchase the product, then you may have to improve their product knowledge through awareness-building communication such as advertising and public relations. You might also consider using sales promotion to induce consumers to try your product. People who have purchased your product in the past can be further analyzed according to how much and how often they buy. Past purchasers may also be good prospects for a sales promotion to stimulate more frequent or larger purchases. Direct marketing and personal selling are other options, but can be more costly. Nonetheless, they might be cost efficient in terms of the likely sales response of your prospects. For your loyal customers you might consider reinforcing types of promotion, such as public relations, to maintain your ongoing relationship with them. Figure 8–1 provides a three-axis matrix against which you can compare your marketing situation to determine the relative strategic weight to give to your marketing communication elements.

As a general rule, the more targeted your media and closer to actual sales you want the customers' responses to be, the more costly your per-customer marketing communications plan will be. The less targeted and further from sales (awareness, for example) you want the responses to be, the less expensive per customer your plan will be. However, the more expensive plan on a per-prospect basis could be more cost efficient overall if the targeted consumers are better prospects than those targeted by the other plan. Awareness is easier to achieve than sales, and exposing a large, undifferentiated audience to a message is less expensive per audience member than a more targeted effort to reach high-potential prospects. Your ability to develop an integrated marketing communications campaign depends on the quantity and quality of information you have about your target consumers.

Let's assume for the sake of an example that you have been able to build a database of information from primary and secondary research sources, such as those covered in chapters 2, 3, and 7. This database might include demographic, psychographic, geographic, and geodemographic characteristics about your target. Additionally, you should have information on purchase behavior and media usage. With this basic information you should be able to subdivide your market into consumer segments. Basically, you should be able to determine who are your best customers, who buys your product less frequently, who buys your competitors' brands, and who are the people who do not at all purchase the product.

Next, your task is to determine how to employ available marketing communications elements to meet your objectives against the various identified consumer segments. Suppose you decide that to increase sales and gain market share you will have to retain current customers while influencing the less-frequent purchasers and competitors' customers to buy your brand. This strategic decision confronts you with three consumer segments, each with a different profile and purchase behavior pattern. Your potential target groups might be labeled and described as follows:

- **Your Brand Loyals**—These are your best customers who purchase large quantities of your brand on a fairly regular basis. When your brand is not available, they will wait until it becomes available or go to another store to find it.

- **Brand Switchers**—This is a group of less frequent purchasers of your brand who also buy your competitors' brands. They might switch brands for a change of pace or because of a promotional incentive, such as a price reduction, sweepstakes, or premium. They move from brand to brand and are not loyal to any particular brand in the product category.

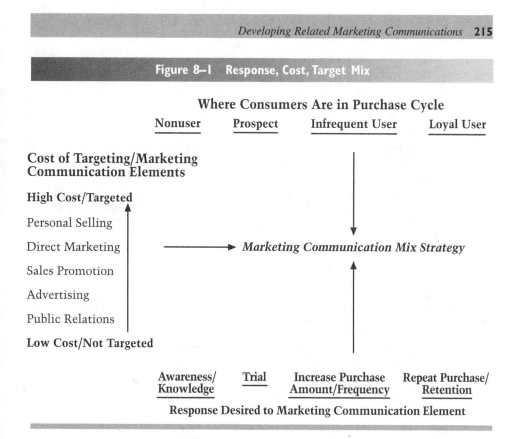

Figure 8–1   Response, Cost, Target Mix

Where Consumers Are in Purchase Cycle

Nonuser   Prospect   Infrequent User   Loyal User

Cost of Targeting/Marketing Communication Elements

High Cost/Targeted

Personal Selling

Direct Marketing   ⟶   *Marketing Communication Mix Strategy*

Sales Promotion

Advertising

Public Relations

Low Cost/Not Targeted

Awareness/   Trial   Increase Purchase   Repeat Purchase/
Knowledge   Amount/Frequency   Retention

Response Desired to Marketing Communication Element

- **Competitors' Brand Loyals**—These brand-loyal consumers are loyal to your competitors' brands. They purchase a lot of your competitors' brands on a fairly regular basis, and will shop around for those brands when they are not available in the stores where they typically shop.

This market situation can be reduced to one of retention of your brand loyals, building volume for your brand among switchers, and initiating trial and gaining some conversion among your competitors' loyals. This is a difficult marketing task that requires strategic differences in how you approach each consumer segment.

What might you do? As we look across your marketing communications options, we have to ask ourselves which combination of elements is best suited to meet the objectives for each segment. Also, we have to consider how to allocate the budget and activities against these segments. Sales-promotion incentives delivered through direct-marketing channels, might be a consideration for building volume among switchers and initiating trials among their loyals. These same incentives, supported by image-oriented advertising, could also increase volume among loyals while rewarding them for being your best customers. Special events and carefully placed public relations items might also impress your loyals and convey the message that you really value their business.

This marketing situation is probably unrealistic for most marketers because it is difficult and expensive to dislodge your competitors' customers. However, the example demonstrates how marketing communications should be approached from a strategic perspective

Exhibit 8–1   Promotional Options for Extending Your Campaign

Sales Promotion

Consumer Promotions
Sampling, couponing, premiums, rebates and refunds, contests and sweepstakes, bonus packs, price-offs, and event sponsorships

Trade Promotions
Slotting allowances, off-invoice allowances, dating, free goods, price reductions, display and merchandising allowances, advertising allowances, count/recount allowances, point-of-purchase displays, cooperative advertising, sales contests, trade shows, and sales meetings

Public Relations

Product Publicity
News stories (new product introductions, dispelling misinformation, and the like), press kits, newsletters, pamphlets, brochures, press conferences, staged events such as celebrity appearances, event sponsorship and trade show support, annual reports, and information hotlines

Direct/Database Marketing
Direct mail, direct response advertising (delivered through all traditional advertising media), catalogs, infomercials, TV home shopping, telemarketing, and interactive computer services

---

by considering your client's relationship with potential consumer segments as the starting point and then determining which mix of elements is most appropriate to stimulating the consumer responses desired. Tactical considerations concerning what the messages and activities follow after the strategic integration of the marketing communications elements has been thought through.

The goal of integrating your marketing communications elements is summarized in the following American Association of Advertising Agencies' definition:

> Integrated Marketing Communications: A concept of marketing communications that recognizes the added value in a program that integrates a variety of strategic disciplines, e.g., general advertising, direct response, sales promotion and public relations—and combines these disciplines to provide clarity, consistency and maximum communications impact.[1]

The true integration of marketing communications can be compared to the work at an air traffic control tower. The elements of marketing communications are flights landing and taking off from an airport. Some jets have just completed their tasks, some need repair, and others are just starting out. Integrated marketing is accomplished by managing all of the elements so that they complement each other while allowing each to achieve its separate objectives.

Your integrated marketing communications program should be based on a clear-cut strategy for each of your target consumer segments. To help you build an integrated marketing communications campaign, we will discuss the major promotional elements advertisers and marketers consider when deciding how to approach their target audiences. The following sections focus on the use of sales promotions, public relations, and direct marketing to achieve your marketing and advertising campaign objectives. Exhibit 8–1 will give you some feel for the scope of the promotional activities available to you as you plan to extend the impact of your campaign by integrating them into your plan.

SALES PROMOTIONS

The rise in importance of sales promotions to marketing programs over the past 20 years highlights significant changes in the marketplace and the way marketers allocate their promotional dollars. Two decades ago it was not unusual for the typical consumer products advertiser to spend almost 70% of its promotion budget on advertising. By 1981, the percentage of the promotion budget spent on advertising was down to 43%, and by 1992 it was down to 27%. In the same period of time, various types of sales promotions had grown from less than 30% to more than 70% of most consumer marketers' promotion budgets.[2] As an example, Leo Burnett USA and H. J. Heinz ended a 36-year relationship in 1994 because of Heinz's decision to reduce its advertising spending from more than $130 million to close to $40 million and putting more of its marketing budget into couponing, trade promotions, and price deals.[3] By 1998, Heinz and Leo Burnett were again working together as Heinz felt they needed to put more of its promotional effort into consumer advertising.

Advertising started to regain some of its lost ground in 1995 due to an improving economy and the industry began to place increased faith in advertising. However, it is still too early to know if confidence in advertising can be restored to previous levels—the lessons learned from the period between the late 1970s to the 1990s will not soon be forgotten. The 1980s will always be the decade that saw a complete turnaround in emphasis away from advertising and toward sales promotions. What happened?

There are many possible explanations for how and why advertising gave way to sales promotions as the marketing communications element of choice. The late 1970s and early 1980s saw a tremendous increase in advertising clutter, making each ad or commercial less effective. At the same time, new technology in the form of the videocassette recorder (VCR) allowed consumers to tape their favorite shows and edit out the commercials. Television remote control devices added to the technological onslaught that gave consumers more control over TV viewing. Zapping, zipping, and channel surfing became the TV-viewing terminology to describe how viewers skipped around the TV channel landscape often avoiding TV commercials.

Inflation during the 1970s made consumers more price sensitive. Marketers were also caught in a battle between keeping up with the inflationary rises in prices (to make a profit) while trying to offer consumers and retailers incentives for buying their products. During this decade marketers started to use trade promotions, which often came in the form of discounts to retailers, in return for extra or better shelf space or promotion support in the store's weekly advertising flyers and newspaper inserts. These promotional allowances and discounts became addicting and more entrenched as retailers gained power through size and increased technological sophistication. This newly acquired power allowed retailers to demand discounts and incentives from manufacturers who found themselves in an increasingly competitive marketplace.

Other marketplace forces were also at work during this period of time:

1. More parity among brands in the same product category making sales promotions a point of differentiation.

2. A short-term managerial orientation that led to reliance on sales promotions to achieve short-run sales and profit objectives. Fierce competition among brand managers to get ahead created pressure to emphasize immediate rather than long-term results.

3. Consumers became more accepting of sales promotions incentives and perhaps had been taught to expect them.

4. To some extent, manufacturers became caught in a competitive situation where they were afraid to reduce their reliance on sales promotions while competitors continued to reap the short-term sales benefits of its use.[4]

5. The soft economic conditions of the early 1990s further reinforced a short-term outlook among manufacturers too uncertain about the future to return to a heavy reliance on advertising alone.

The main controversy surrounding the use of sales promotions has been the question of its long-term impact on brand equity. Marketers who would like to see a return to the day when advertising was king argue that promotions are simply a bribe to steal sales and market share at the expense of brand equity. The more you induce purchase through "deals," the argument goes, the less likely consumers can be persuaded of a preference for one brand over another based on tangible or intangible qualities promoted through advertising. Sales promotions' experts counter with the fact that in a cluttered marketplace other aspects of the marketing program, such as shelf placement and in-store display, are important contributors to a brand's image, an important part of brand equity. Busy consumers, they add, have less time than ever to ponder and absorb the clutter of messages from typical national brand advertising.

The key argument for a primary role for sales promotions in marketing programs is that sales promotions provide companies the ability to combine short-term sales results with long-term equity building. Manufacturers are no longer in a situation where they can make a choice between the long-term equity-building strengths of advertising and the short-term sales-generating advantage of sales promotions. They simply have to be able to achieve both. Think of McDonald's as a prime example of this tug of war where hamburgers have to be sold system-wide day in and day out. And at the same time, McDonald's has to maintain its wholesome all-American family image so that the decision to eat there becomes routine for its target audience (mostly parents and their kids). One executive at McDonald's put it succinctly when he said that the company has to think like a retailer and act like a brand. The message here is: So does everybody else who wants to be successful in the changing marketplace. And the way to do this is through the successful integration of all aspects of your marketing and advertising programs.

Sales Promotions Defined

Sales promotions offer an incentive to buy a product that takes the form of either a price reduction or value-added offer.[5] Sales promotions' activities can be divided into consumer-oriented and trade-oriented promotions.

Consumer-oriented promotions are targeted to the final consumers in the channel of distribution to induce them to buy your brand. Consumer-oriented promotions include product samples, coupons, premiums, rebates, contests and sweepstakes, bonus packs, price-offs, and event sponsorship. The goal of these promotions is to stimulate demand, usually at the retail level.[6]

Trade-oriented promotions (usually shortened to trade promotions) are aimed at distributors and retailers to influence them to carry a product and give it added emphasis in their effort to sell it to their customers. Trade promotions account for over two-thirds of all sales promotions and half the dollars spent on promotions and advertising combined.[7] The dollars taken away from advertising over the past 20 years have gone primarily into trade promotions. There is some evidence that trade promotions' share of marketing budgets is declining slightly in favor of consumer promotions and advertising. However, it is not clear if this is a trend or a temporary blip in the cycle.

Manufacturers can choose from a number of trade promotion alternatives to try to induce distributors and retailers to push their products. Typically, they employ some combination of trade allowances, dealer contests, point-of-purchase displays, cooperative advertising, trade shows, and other incentive programs. A **trade allowance** is a reduced wholesale price charged to distributors and retailers in return for preferential treatment. It has been the most widely used promotion and the most controversial. It is perceived by some as a payoff or bribe to the distributor for special consideration. And because the allowance is often subtracted from the advertising budget, this special treatment is sometimes used at the expense of equity-building consumer messages. The goal of a balanced campaign should be to incorporate the advantages of both trade promotions and advertising in gaining trade acceptance and stimulating consumer purchases. Exhibit 8–2 presents some of the more common types of trade spending.

To successfully incorporate promotions into a marketing communications campaign plan, it is important to know which type of objectives can reasonably be set for the sales promotion component of your marketing and advertising program.

Sales Promotions' Objectives

Sales promotions' objectives are always set with the bigger picture of the marketing plan in mind. Like all promotional elements of the marketing plan, the objectives for sales promotions are more specific and focused than are the marketing objectives. Good sales promotions' objectives are targeted and measurable. However, sales promotions' objectives have the added characteristic of being directed specifically toward increasing the speed or frequency (sometimes referred to as **sales velocity**) with which consumers buy your brand. They are, among all of the marketing and promotion objectives that you set, the most focused on achieving a sales response.

As you think about where sales promotions fit into your campaign plan, some of the general types of goals you might use follow.

- Induce new customers to try your brand. Samples, coupons, or refund offers can help move consumers toward consideration and eventual trial of your brand.

- Retain your current loyal customers and perhaps influence them to buy more of your brand. Premiums such as recipes and calendars that provide ideas for new product uses can help to reinforce and increase usage of your brand.

Exhibit 8–2   A Glossary of Widely Used Trade Promotion Terms

A trade-speak-to-English glossary of some of the most common types of trade spending, translated by A.T. Kearney consultant Burt Flickinger III.

Off-invoice allowance: A per-case rebate paid to retailers when order is placed.

Billback: Additional money paid for retailers' display, ad or price cut.

Market development funds (MDFs): Money spent via a retailer to expand category sales; used to develop share in markets where category growth is high and a brand's share is embarrassingly low.

Brand development funds (BDFs): Similar to MDFs, this money pinpoints problems by brand rather than geography.

Category development funds (CDFs): Specifically drives a given category, supporting all brands at once.

Street money: Cash spent in the field, i.e., "at street level," to get more display.

Spiff money: Rewards brokers and buyers with everything from thermoses to TVs to Hawaiian vacations for "assist" in hitting case sales objectives.

Cooperative merchandising agreement (CMA): Annual incentive contract to get retailer to commit to ad, display or price feature for a brand for a time period.

Corporate sales program (CSP): An umbrella promotion across a marketer's total brand portfolio. Products often are shipped directly from the factory in ready-to-display pallets.

Producing plant allowance (PPAs): An incentive to retailers to buy full or half-truckloads direct from the factory. Saves manufacturers distribution costs.

Back haul allowances (BHAs): Money manufacturers pay retailers who'll send trucks to pick up shipments at manufacturer's own plant or distribution center.

Drop ship allowances (DSAs): Money to retailers who bypass the grocer's distribution center for preplanned orders or customized pallets.

Cross-dock or pedal runs: Cash incentives for placing full-pallet orders for four or five stores, distributed by a single truck. Marketer saves distribution costs.

Display-ready cases and pallets: Marketers pay retailers for using these cost-efficient shipments ready for immediate display.

Source: *Brandweek* (March 13, 1995): 32.

- Increase the overall sales of your brand. Special sizes, multiunit packaging, and premiums can be used as incentives to induce consumers to buy and use more of your product.

- Reinforce your advertising efforts by incorporating sales promotion into your campaign. Contests and sweepstakes, for example, can generate consumer and trade involvement and excitement in a campaign.

- Sales promotions activities can help to build trade support for a campaign. The goal is to demonstrate to the trade your effort to stimulate sales, which is the retailers' primary motivation for considering carrying your brand.

- Sales promotions' support for a campaign can breathe excitement into the salesforce for the brand at all levels of the distribution channel. Contests, special displays, premiums, and price-off incentives can all provide a salesperson with an extra edge.

From this general sense of what sales promotions can accomplish, you can start to think about the specific sales promotions' objectives of your campaign. Sales promotions should be integrated into your campaign so that they reinforce and extend your advertising and other promotional efforts. As such, sales promotions not only add an action-oriented component to your consumer campaign, but also provide a vehicle for reaching the trade and salesforce. Trade objectives for sales promotions often include obtaining or improving shelf space and position, building inventories for your brand, gaining trade support in terms of display and advertising help, and generating enthusiasm for a new product introduction. A distributor's salespeople can be influenced to give your brand a higher selling priority and put more effort and enthusiasm behind selling it when they know that it is supported by a good promotional program.

Sales promotions' objectives should be stated in the same concise terms as all the objectives that you write for your marketing communications plan (see Chapter 4 for more on writing objectives). The results you expect in terms of sales, product trial, multiple purchases, or improving product display should be stated clearly and specifically. Sales promotions' results, like all marketing communications elements, are expected to occur within a specific time frame that should be included in the objective. Your promotional programs and objectives should be single-minded and targeted to one market segment at a time. Do not expect too much from your sales promotions' effort. It is unusual for one program to accomplish multiple objectives against differing target audiences.

Sales Promotions' Techniques

After you have set your objectives for sales promotions, you can start to think about specific techniques to use in implementing your plan. The simplest way to think of the options available is to divide them into consumer and trade promotions. Consumer promotions can then be grouped into the major types used by marketers, including:

sampling
couponing
premiums
contests and sweepstakes
refunds
bonus packs
price-off deals
event sponsorship

Trade promotions take the form of different purchase and performance incentives and allowances that encourage the members of the distribution channel to carry, store, and promote your brand. Together, trade and consumer promotions become part of a **push–pull strategy** to move your brand through its channel of distribution to the final consumer. Consumer promotions pull the ultimate consumer into the store to buy your brand, and trade promotions push your product through the distribution channel to the retail outlet.

Consumer Promotions

Sampling is a highly effective but relatively expensive way to achieve a trial of a product. The expense comes from having to manufacture, inventory, and distribute special trial sizes of your product. However, it is a sound way to get your product into the consumers' hands at no charge or risk to them. Sampling has gained favor with marketers because the amount of time in which a product has to succeed has dwindled, in some instances, from a year down to three months. Product trial, therefore, has become a more urgent objective to new product introductions than ever before. If you cannot get people to try your product, you can never achieve repeat purchase behavior, which is the lifeblood of business success.

Sampling can be accomplished through a number of different delivery systems. The most common distribution systems are placement in the store, delivery by mail or door-to-door placement, and inclusion with the package. In-store sampling can be done by placing the trial-size products in special point-of-purchase bins or displays. Sometimes a demonstrator is hired who can help customers sample products such as new food items, cosmetics, or home appliances. This demonstrator can also provide additional product information and help deliver other promotional items, such as coupons.

Samples can be delivered to customers' homes by mail or through the use of delivery companies. Mail delivery can be an effective way to combine sampling with direct marketing to target consumers who are most likely to use your product.

Samples may be attached to or included along with another of a company's products. This is a good method when the market for original purchase is also the market for the new product being sampled. Other distribution possibilities include magazine and newspaper distribution for small products and sample packs, such as those given out to college students at the beginning of a new school year. Organizations such as Welcome Wagon that greet newcomers to a neighborhood, town, or city are also potential distributors for your sampling program.

Sampling is not without its disadvantages. Remember that the same device that can speed the acceptance of a new product can also spell quick demise for an inferior product. In addition, in-store sampling (which is usually the most desired form of sampling because it is so close to the point of purchase) requires the support of the trade that can result in additional fees and allowances to keep them happy and behind your program. The method you select to deliver the sample has to be measured against the expense of doing so. Be sure that the payoff is worth the expense.

Couponing is a promotional practice dating from the late 1800s. A coupon is a certificate of specific value, such as a cents-off or free product offer, that the consumer presents to a retailer along with an appropriate purchase for its stated redemption value. Coupons have a number of advantages that make them worth considering as part of a sales promotions' strategy. Taken as a group, these advantages might be labeled *flexibility*. Coupons can be used in many different ways. First, coupons allow you to offer a reduced price on a product to those in your market who are price-sensitive without having to offer the discount to everybody. Second, unlike trade allowances that a retailer does not have to pass along to customers, a coupon assures the manufacturer that the savings are going to consumers. Third, coupons offer a temporary price reduction that is seen as a special offer and not perceived as a permanent reduction in price. When the offer is over, the return of the product's price to normal should meet little resistance from your customers. Fourth, retailers can use coupons for their own promotional programs, by offering double or triple the face value of the coupon to consumers. This way, retailers can use the coupons as a traffic-building promotional device.[8]

Couponing is not without its problems. Due to the popularity of couponing, increased clutter has led to a decline in redemption rates. Redemption rates themselves are difficult to predict and vary by product type and distribution method. It is also hard to target consumers (the right people) to use your coupons. Often, it is the already established consumer who uses coupons, whereas the marketer had issued the coupons to tempt new users to try the product with the incentive of a price-off or free-product deal. *Coupon fraud* can also be a problem and should be taken into consideration. The ease of implementing a coupon program can be counterbalanced by very low redemption rates among your target consumers. Successful coupon programs are a good example of the adage that things are seldom as easy as they seem.

Couponing, when carefully planned, can be used effectively to accomplish a number of different objectives for your sales promotion program:

1. Coupons can be an enticement to gain initial trial and awareness for a new product introduction. The coupon can either be in the form of savings on the first purchase, or can be part of a free-sample-offer program. Both techniques reduce the risk of the trial purchase for your target market.

2. Couponing can be used to encourage repeat purchase by including it in or on the package as a reward for a purchase. This method lets you reward both new and loyal customers.

3. Coupons can be a method for enticing consumers to trade up to larger sizes or multiple units of a product. This type of couponing is often done as a short-term competitive strategy to take customers out of the market for a period of time (especially when you know that competitive promotional activity is going on) by getting them to load up on a product.

4. Couponing can be an effective strategy for enlisting trade support. You can gain retailers' support in a number of ways, including having the manufacturer distribute its own coupons free of charge to the retailers or by working out a cooperative arrangement so that a retailer can build its store promotions around the coupons.

5. Coupons can be used selectively to target different markets. You can offer competitors' customers and nonusers a different coupon deal than the one for current users to get them to try your brand. This works best when there is little media overlap across these groups.

6. Coupons can be used to cushion a price increase by offering temporary relief from that increase.

7. Coupons can be a delivery system for more than just price-off deals. They can be integrated with other promotional elements to collect consumer information for databases, used as entry forms for contests and sweepstakes, and used to add excitement to a typical advertising or marketing campaign. Exhibit 8–3 presents some of the basic types of coupon deals upon which other variations can be built.

Exhibit 8–3 Basic Types of Coupon Deals

Coupon Deal	Description
Cents-off	Most common form of couponing. Deal is a certain amount off the regular price for a specified period of time.
Free	Free product offered to those redeeming coupon. Efficient method of sampling because you only give a free sample to consumers who are interested in it.
Buy one, get one free (BOGO)	Get a free product with purchase of product at regular price. Stimulates multiple purchases. Can be used to reward regular customers. Can require customers to buy more than one unit to get the free one.
Time release	Several cents-off coupons are offered at same time but with different expiration dates to encourage repeat purchase.
Multiple purchase	Coupon offer only good when more than one unit of product is bought. Can be used to increase sales and consumption in short term or to take consumers out of the market by loading them up with the product.
Self-destruct	Two or more coupons are printed to overlap each other so that when one is redeemed the other is destroyed. Can be used to create different deals for different consumers without having to print multiple coupons. Can also be used with the time-release deal to encourage customer to redeem earlier to get a better deal.
Personalized	Coupon is personalized by location or store so that it can only be redeemed at that location. Can be used to get trade support from retail outlets.
Cross-ruff	Purchaser gets a coupon for another unrelated product with the purchase of a product. Can work when users of one product overlap with those of another.
Related sale	Coupon received from the purchase of one product is for a related product. Food manufacturers that sell related products, such as condiments that might go with cold cuts or hot dogs, could place coupons for one of their related products in the package of the other product.
Sweepstakes entry	The coupon also becomes the entry form for a sweepstakes promotion. Consumer information for databases can be collected this way.

Source: Tamara Brezen Block, "Couponing," in *Sales Promotion Handbook*, 8th ed., ed. Tamara Brezen Block and William A. Robinson (Chicago, Ill.: Dartnell Press, 1994), 103–104.

Most coupons (upwards of 80%) are delivered to consumers in *freestanding inserts* (FSI) in their newspapers. This type of distribution system takes advantage of consumers' newspaper reading habits, which include searching for coupons in the inserts that typically arrive with the Sunday paper or on its featured food day. However, the clutter of the FSIs has cut into the redemption rates for coupons.

Coupons can also be delivered through the mail, in stores, on and in product packaging, in newspapers as part of the *run-of-the-paper* (ROP) *advertising*, and through other media such as magazines. Manufacturers and retailers are constantly searching for new ways to deliver coupons. Stores have experimented with coupon dispensers attached to shelves near products, coupons on the back of receipts, and coupons handed out by product demonstrators. Many marketers predict eventual widespread use of systems that deliver coupons to customers at home via e-mail or fax machines connected to home computers and entertainment systems.

Stimulating consumers to redeem coupons is the objective of any couponing program. By following these simple design guidelines when you create your coupon, you can help achieve that goal:

1. Make the coupon instantly recognizable as a coupon.

2. Be sure that the face value and expiration date are easy to see and read on the coupon.

3. Include the UPC and manufacturer's coupon code.

4. Put a picture of the package on the coupon to help the consumer redeem the coupon for the right product.

5. Do not bury the coupon in complicated graphics in an ad or wherever it is being displayed.[9]

Figure 8–2 is an example of an ad with coupons from an FSI for Yoplait yogurt. Note the content of the two coupons. They include the standard and necessary coupon information: savings amount, expiration date, bar code, manufacturer's code, and pictures of Yoplait products.

Sampling and couponing are among the most frequently used forms of consumer promotions. Premiums, rebates, contests and sweepstakes, bonus packs, price-offs, and event sponsorship tend to be more problematic but can also be effective devices.

Premiums, or merchandise incentives, are offers of merchandise or services (such as travel) for free or at a reduced price as tangible rewards or incentives for the purchase of a product. Consumer premiums can be offered free of charge, or they can be self-liquidating. Free premiums are often small items included in, on, or near the product in the store. Cracker Jacks is one of the most recognizable brands that uses in-pack premiums in the form of small toys. Cereal companies make similar use of in-pack incentives. Consumers like in-pack or on-pack premiums because they get an immediate reward for buying the product. Mail-in premiums, on the other hand, require that consumers respond to an offer by mailing in their request. A typical premium tries to stimulate repeat purchases by having consumers mail in proof of having made more than one purchase of a product. Response to mail-in premiums is much lower than to in- or on-pack premiums.

Figure 8–2 Yoplait Ad with Coupons from FSI

Figure 8–2 Yoplait Ad with Coupons from FSI

A self-liquidating premium is an offer for which the consumer pays all or part of the cost of the premium (including mailing costs) before receiving it. Self-liquidating premiums are often merchandise of some value to the consumer that the manufacturer can offer at greatly reduced prices. The goal is to offer something of real value that enhances the brand's image and creates goodwill among consumers and the trade. The manufacturer's goal is only to recoup the costs of offering the premium and not to make a profit off the promotion itself. Marlboro cigarettes, for example, offers a western apparel catalog that contains clothing and outdoor items that reinforce its brand image. These items were selected to be consistent with and extend Marlboro's image and reinforce its advertising efforts.

Premiums can also be used as part of *continuity* plans to encourage consumers to use the brand on a continuous basis by saving coupons, proof of purchase, stamps, or some item that is then turned in for the premium. The purpose of a continuity plan is to bring your customers back time and time again or to establish purchase continuity for your brand. Airline frequent-flyer programs are among the most popular continuity programs. These programs encourage travelers to fly one airline in order to accumulate enough miles to earn free tickets and other perks. Retailers employ this type of premium-driven program when they ask customers to save their receipts (usually requiring that a minimum amount be spent over time) for a period of time and then turn them in for cash or premiums. The key to a successful continuity program is a premium or reward of enough value to keep the customer interested and involved in the program.

Rebates and **refunds** are offers by product manufacturers to reimburse some portion of the purchase price of a product upon receipt of consumer proof of purchase. To obtain a refund or rebate, consumers are typically required to send in proof of purchase to the manufacturer. The refund-and-rebate program has the advantage to the marketer of being easy to set up on short notice to combat competitive activity. The program requires no merchandise inventories or elaborate coupon-redemption procedures. Computer technology allows companies to keep track of who has already received a refund so as not to get caught by consumers trying to take advantage of the offer.

Rebates and refunds are used by a wide variety of companies from marketers of packaged goods to automobiles to computers. Refunds are used to stimulate product trial, move large inventories, and boost sluggish sales of durables. The delay between purchasing and receiving a refund is the main deterrent to consumers' responses to the offer. Automotive manufacturers overcame this problem by allowing consumers to use the rebate as part of their down payment on a car, which gave them an immediate reward for their purchase. Marketers have to be careful not to rely too heavily on refunds and rebates because consumers will become sensitive to the practice and only buy during the refund-and-rebate program.

Contests and **sweepstakes** have become popular with consumers and marketers, growing by 74% in the 1980s to a level where more than a billion dollars is spent on this form of promotion every year. A contest is a promotion that awards prizes based on a test of skill or talent. It can require the submission of recipes, photographs, slogans, an essay, or other evidence of an ability. Judges select winners among the entrants based on their skills or talents. A sweepstakes is a promotion in which prizes are awarded based on chance. Sweepstakes are closely regulated by federal and state lottery laws, which should be researched prior to embarking on this type of promotional activity. One common lottery law requirement is that consumers not be obligated to purchase a product to enter a sweepstakes. Most sweepstakes do not require a purchase but do ask that an entrant to do something such as write the brand name on a card.[10] A game is a type of sweepstakes where winning is based on chance but involves collecting game pieces or removing ink from a scratch-off card to win. A game can be extended over a period of time to encourage repeat purchases.

Consumers prefer sweepstakes and games to contests because they are easier to enter or participate in. There are some basic types of sweepstakes, games, and contests. Sweepstakes can take the form of a simple entry blank mailed to the target audience, included in an ad, or made available at the point of purchase. Consumers enter by mailing a form or dropping it into a box at the point of purchase. The drawing takes place at a specified date. Another version of the sweepstakes requires consumers to submit multiple entries to become eligible for winning different prizes. Each prize then becomes equivalent to a separate sweepstakes, which can increase consumer involvement in the game. In yet another form of sweepstakes, entrants read an ad and write down the key copy points to be eligible to enter. A similar sweepstakes mechanism asks entrants to qualify by solving a puzzle or guessing an answer to something based on clues provided. Finally, some marketers have been using coupons as entry forms. This sweepstakes requires entrants to fill out their name and address on the redeemed coupon.

Games are typically used to build store traffic. They come in three varieties. The matching-instant-winner game requires customers to match something from an ad to something at the store to win. There are games in which the consumer has to collect parts to a puzzle or game pieces to be able to win. And then there are the instant-winner games often requiring consumers to peel off or scratch off the surface of a card to see if they have won.

Contests have not changed much over time.[11] However, if you stretch your imagination, you can create unique ways to use this old promotion standard. Rolling Rock beer turned a company mystery into a contest by asking customers for their theories on what the number "33" on their bottles means. There is no answer, so the prize goes to the best theory. The prizes are running the theory as a caption with a cartoon on the subject of the mysterious 33 and payment of $3,300, to tie in with the number.[12]

Contests and sweepstakes can add obvious excitement to an advertising campaign, but should be planned very carefully. When you consider using these forms of promotion, you should think about the potential for these activities to detract from the brand image of your product and become the entire focus of your campaign.

Bonus packs add value to a purchase by giving customers an added quantity of the product for the regular price. Compared to coupons, refunds, and rebates, bonus packs provide consumers with more immediate value. However, if the bonus pack increases the size of the product, shelf space could become a problem with the trade because retailers will have to provide this extra space. Bonus packs can also be a good competitive maneuver to counter promotional activity by other brands because they load up consumers with your product.

Price-off promotions are reduced-price deals that are indicated on the package. The consumer knows immediately that this is a deal and may use the price reduction to save money or buy more of the product. The price-off promotion can be popular with both consumers and the trade when the manufacturer allows the retailer to maintain margins. The marketer incurs the reduction as a promotional cost and passes along the savings directly to the customer.

Event sponsorship has become one of the more popular types of promotions over the past several years. Some estimates put event-marketing expenditures above the $5 billion mark. The idea behind event sponsorship is that a marketer associates its product or company with entertainers, athletic events, or other notable people or occasions for the purpose of trading off on their popularity to achieve its marketing objectives. Sponsorship of an event can be an important focal point to an integrated marketing communications' campaign. First, the event can support and be supported by advertising and public relations. Second, the event can involve all important targets of a campaign from consumers to the trade to the salesforce. The event not only builds enthusiasm, it also invites participation by members of the trade and salesforce.

Marketers' logic behind event sponsorship is that some of the enthusiasm the highly involved and loyal audience members or fans feel for the event will rub off on the brand. Also, the assumption is that fans of an entertainer or sporting event have something in common that has brought them to the event. The event transcends differences and allows the sponsor to associate its brand with this commonality. Most important is that event sponsors believe that the association with the event translates into sales for their brands.[13]

Note in Figure 8–3 how Champion sportswear ties in its advertising with its participation in the sponsorship of the 1994 Winter Olympics. The statistics on the value of the Olympics are staggering and reinforce its value as an event to sponsor. More than 60% of all American families watch the Olympics, and 94% of these families see sponsors as successful companies. Just over 80% believe that Olympic sponsors are dedicated to excellence, are vital and energetic, and are industry leaders.[14]

Sporting events receive most of the event sponsorship money (more than two-thirds). Golf, tennis, auto racing, volleyball, college basketball and football, and skiing are among the events marketers like to sponsor. Although beer, cigarette, and car companies have been the big sponsors in the past, the appeal of these events is broadening to other marketers.

Figure 8–3 Champion Sportswear Promotes its Sponsorship of the Winter Olympics

Trade Promotions

One of the important goals of any sales promotions' program is to gain the support of the retail trade and distributors as well as to elicit a consumer response. Certain techniques are geared specifically toward the trade.[15]

We described earlier in the chapter the reasons for the rather massive shift in marketing dollars from consumer advertising to trade promotions. Almost 45% of all marketing expenditures go toward trade promotions. You will recall that the purpose of trade promotions is to obtain distribution and support for new products, maintain support for established products, and gain a priority for certain brands in terms of display support, shelf position, and advertising and other promotional support. (Note that different industries use different trade promotions. You should research the industry you are working in for the acceptability of these practices.) Trade promotions can be divided into those that are primarily purchase incentives and those that are performance allowances. Additional trade support is often provided through sales contests, point-of-purchase display items provided by the manufacturer, cooperative advertising money to support local promotion of the brand, and participation in industry trade shows and sales meetings to get distributors and retailers behind an advertising campaign.

Purchase incentives are payments made primarily in the packaged goods business to distributors and retailers to encourage them to purchase your product if they have not done so before, restock it if they do carry it, and increase their inventory of the product. Purchase incentives can be offered in four basic ways: (1) as a slotting allowance, (2) as an off-invoice purchase allowance, (3) as dating, or the extension of payment terms, and (4) in the form of free goods.

A *slotting allowance* is a payment to distributors and retailers to gain distribution, warehouse space, computer space, and shelf space. It is typically 5% to 15% of the non-promotional cost of the product being sold and comes directly out of the marketing budget. Although slotting fees help to gain distribution, they are problematic for new products because they take away significant amounts of money from introductory advertising efforts.

Off-invoice purchase allowances are reductions in the price of your product to the trade, usually in the range of 5% to 25% of the regular invoice price. These allowances are limited to a certain period of time and number of orders. The objective of using this type of trade promotion is to obtain higher-than-normal inventories.

Dating, or the *extension of payment terms*, is a trade promotion that gives the distributor a discount if payment is made within a specific period of time, such as 10 days, but allows a longer period of time, such as 60 days, before full payment is required. This incentive lets the trade buy inventory early or use the savings to purchase more of your product, or both.

Marketers can also use purchase incentives to offer *free goods*. Free goods are provided to the distributor at no cost based on a predetermined ratio to cases or amount of product purchased (for example, 10% to be added to amount purchased). Free goods are an effective way to build inventories of your product and tend to be more effective than invoice allowances.

Marketers offer performance allowances to distributors and retailers as incentives to get them to increase their products' rate of sale to the consumer. The marketers' aim is for distributors and retailers to push the product through the channel of distribution by (1) price reductions to consumers, (2) advertising your product in store advertising, (3) point-of-purchase and other display support, (4) expanded shelf space, and (5) in-store demonstrations.

Distributors and retailers are not going to participate in these activities of their own volition. Performance allowances in the form of price reductions to the trade, display allowances, advertising allowances, and count/recount allowances can be effective in obtaining trade support for your product.

Price reductions to retailers so that they can then reduce the price of a brand to the consumer have become the largest category of marketing and promotional spending for many brands. It is an effective technique for gaining retailer support for your brand because it has a direct effect on sales. However, price reductions have also become the primary reason for declining support for brand advertising.

Display and *merchandising allowances* are paid to retailers to obtain extra in-store effort to make a product more visible to consumers. Allowances may also be used to encourage other forms of merchandising, such as product sampling, in-store demonstrations, and support for special celebrity appearances. The difficulty for marketers is in monitoring retailer compliance with this type of deal, but in-store support from the retailer can have a significant effect on the sale of your product.

Price reductions and in-store merchandising support work best when backed up by store advertising that includes the brand. Thus, *advertising allowances* are normally part of a marketer's performance-based trade promotions' package. This allowance is paid to the retailer in return for advertising the product in the retailer's store ads. Normally, the marketer provides an illustration of the product for the retailer to use in the ad. Some allowances carry stricter creative requirements, but most give the retailer a fair amount of leeway in developing the advertising.

Point-of-purchase display items that manufacturers provide to retailers can add to brands' visibility in stores. These items can vary from something as simple as a shelf-talker (a small sign on the front edge of the shelf) or poster to elaborate bins that add shelf space to a retailer's store. The primary disadvantage of point-of-purchase materials is that retailers do not use a lot of the items manufacturers provide. To prevent this type of waste and ensure retailer support, it is important for manufacturers to support these activities with other forms of trade promotion.

Cooperative advertising is an agreement between the manufacturer and retailer to share the cost of promoting the brand at the local level. The agreements can vary, but a 50–50 split of the cost is common. Most cooperative advertising is placed in newspapers but radio, television, and other media can also be used. Although advertising allowances can be provided for the inclusion of a brand in a store's advertising, most cooperative advertising is designed to feature the manufacturer's brand and provide a smaller space for listing a retailer's name and location.

Trade shows and *sales meetings* are two promotional channels that should be considered in the marketing communications' campaign for a brand. Trade shows exist in almost any industry and provide an important opportunity to showcase and demonstrate new products to members of the trade. Distributors as well as retailers attend their industry's key trade shows to identify new products to stock and sell. The trade show is also an important social occasion for manufacturers to meet with and entertain their best trade customers.

Sales meetings are promotional opportunities for kicking off an advertising campaign or introducing a new product to distributors' salesforces. Automotive manufacturers, for example, conduct annual sales meetings for dealers to introduce new models of their cars. Special meetings are held when an entirely new nameplate is being introduced to build enthusiasm for its launch. Sales meetings can be very simple or very elaborate. A big sales meeting in an enticing travel destination can be an added incentive to the trade to get behind a manufacturer's brand.

Trade promotion has become an important part of the promotional program for the typical consumer-goods marketer. However, marketers should make a careful assessment of trade receptivity and competitive activity within a given industry before blindly recommending trade promotions as part of an integrated marketing communications campaign.

PUBLIC RELATIONS

The strategic use of public relations to achieve the objectives of a marketing communications campaign requires the understanding of public relations at two levels. First, we will have to distinguish between corporate public relations and marketing public relations. And second, we must have a clear sense of public relations and its relationship to the other primary marketing communications elements: advertising, sales promotion, and direct marketing.

The role of public relations in a corporation also defines its place among advertising, sales promotion, and direct marketing in the marketing communications plan. The role for public relations varies by industry and company. But in a more general sense, regardless of the emphasis given to public relations, its role is to bring about public understanding and acceptance of an organization's relevant policies and procedures.[16] In some businesses, such as health-care providers (HMOs), companies often have to deal with negative publicity about their businesses. As a result, public relations takes on a dominant role in the achievement of their marketing communication objectives. Smaller firms in the industrial and business-to-business arena might see the potential for public relations in a less integrated fashion and as separate but equal in value to that of marketing. The approach in this book is to view public relations from the perspective of the large consumer-goods firm, where it has taken on a new role as marketing public relations.

Marketing public relations is differentiated from corporate public relations in terms of the scope of planning and activities that are involved as well as its function in a firm. *Corporate public relations* activities are focused on the nonmarketing communication goals of a company, which might fall broadly under the corporate umbrella image. This is a long-term mission of any company to maintain open lines of communication with its various constituencies or publics to ensure that they understand and accept its policies, procedures, and activities. It is easy to see that some relationships a firm might have with its publics are nonmarketing, but the selling function can fall under the broad mission of public relations. Public relations can be employed to support the purchase process and maintain long-term consumer satisfaction with your company. This is the role for marketing public relations in the marketing communications campaign.

Marketing Public Relations

Marketing public relations brings some advantages to the marketing communications' program that are distinct disadvantages of advertising, sales promotion, and direct marketing. Consumers understand that the intent of advertising, sales promotions, and direct marketing is to sell them something. Thus they approach these types of promotion with a fair degree of skepticism. Public relations in the form of news stories prepared by a company can be more credible to your customers because it is not overtly identified with your company but with the medium (such as a newspaper, magazine, or TV station) that carries it. Because the media tend to have more credibility with your customers, awards and recommendations from them (such as *Good Housekeeping*'s seal of approval or *Motor Trend*'s car of the year) can be used to add believability and trust to your campaign. The downside of this advantage is that you forego control over message content and timing, and that control is the main advantage of advertising.

Public relations activities in general are less expensive than other kinds of promotion. Refer to Figure 8–1 to see that cost is a major consideration in deciding how to integrate the marketing communication elements of your campaign. Public relations efforts often require more sweat and tears than money. One public relations' professional advised students interested in a career in PR not to be afraid of staplers, scissors, tape, and rubber cement. The tradeoff, once again, is that the precision and control you pay for in advertising, sales promotions, and direct marketing has to be achieved through hard work and the powers of personal persuasion with the media (contacts) when you add public relations to your plan.

Public relations can easily be integrated into a campaign to support other marketing efforts. For example, event sponsorships and trade shows certainly suggest a primary role for public relations. News stories in key media vehicles can provide information about the events or shows to gain initial awareness and interest among consumers and the trade. Interviews, press conferences, social events, and press releases can all be used to achieve this type of exposure. Likewise, new product introductions can be supported with public relations activities that will extend the exposure offered by advertising. PR's use with new product introduction is unusually effective when the product is a technological advance that creates natural interest in the media.

Hard-to-reach audiences can make public relations a welcome option for your campaign. Some audiences might be too hard or expensive to reach using traditional promotional devices. Suppose your campaign requires the support of your employees, government officials, stockholders, or the local community. Public relations' professionals call these people *publics* or *stakeholders* in your business. Activities such as meetings, workshops, annual reports, company newsletters, executive speeches, and information hot lines can reach these groups when advertising cannot.

Marketing public relations offers a great deal of flexibility that can help you to fill in the communication gaps in your marketing plan. This advantage should be counterbalanced against the reality that public relations' activities take more coordination ability than most other forms of promotion. One of the most important marketing publications relations' activities in this regard is the generation of positive publicity for your brand and company.

Product Publicity

The effective use of public relations in marketing often comes down to getting good publicity for a brand. To get positive publicity, it is necessary to provide interesting and newsworthy information to the media. Positive publicity can contribute to your ability to achieve your marketing objectives by . . .

- . . . informing your customers how to select, buy, and use your product. Informational brochures and product literature can be useful in helping consumers learn to use complex or risky products. News stories and pamphlets might inform people about the broader issue of knowing how to select a car, computer, insurance carrier, or legal service, for example.

- . . . persuading your target audience to purchase your brand. Well-placed and well-timed stories can carry more persuasive power than advertising and might be the extra nudge consumers need to buy your brand.

- . . . dispelling negative opinions or information about your brand. Consider what you might do if someone found a syringe in a can of your product, or you had to recall several hundred thousand cars or trucks. Publicity can help to counteract misunderstandings that people have formed about your brand. The next time you watch the evening news, consider how much of a story about a company might have been generated by well-placed publicity.

- . . . building store traffic. The appearance of celebrities in a store, for example, can get customers to come out when they otherwise would not. These types of events are more successful when supported by publicity.

- . . . supporting event sponsorships, trade shows, and other promotional activities. Good publicity can persuade your key publics or audiences to turn out for company-sponsored activities. Advertising can only go so far in building awareness. Sometimes good publicity and associated word-of-mouth communication can be the missing ingredient to the achievement of your objectives. Something as simple as a news story on the business page of a local newspaper can result in hundreds of people attending the opening of a new McDonald's restaurant or Barnes & Noble bookstore.[17]

Publicity and public relations can play supportive roles for a large marketer with the resources to spend on advertising, sales promotion, and direct marketing. However, public relations can be an important promotional element for the small regional or local company. With small clients, public relations are an important strategic and practical consideration.

DIRECT MARKETING

When you integrate direct marketing into an advertising campaign, you combine the typical image-oriented qualities of advertising with the opportunity for the consumer to respond directly to your offer. This type of strategy could be used to maintain the image and equity in the brand while also achieving short-term sales goals.

The simplest definition of direct marketing is attributed to direct-marketing pioneer and expert Drayton Bird. Direct marketing is "any activity whereby you communicate directly with your prospect or customer and he or she responds directly to you."[18] This definition takes into account the tremendous changes in direct-marketing technology to include the growing importance of **database marketing.** Database marketing has made any channel of communication a potential vehicle for direct marketing. One only has to watch the infomercials, television commercials with 800 telephone numbers, and home-shopping channels to see that direct marketing has grown beyond the U.S. mail as its only distribution channel.

Direct marketing has grown in importance for a number of reasons, which together have changed the marketplace and influenced campaign planning immeasurably. Those changes most closely associated with the new and growing importance of direct marketing to the campaign planner are as follows:

- **The Credit Card**—The convenience and widespread use of credit cards have made it easy for consumers to purchase products through direct response channels. Credit cards have also reduced the financial risk for the direct marketer because payment is immediate and automatic.

- **The 800 Telephone Number**—The 800 telephone number has added to credit cards' practicality and convenience. Purchase and payment are easy, quick, and practical. Together with credit cards, the 800 number has allowed direct marketers to sell both low-cost and high-cost merchandise to consumers who purchase easily by picking up the telephone.

- **Computer Technology**—Advances in computer technology have made it possible for direct marketers to gather, store, and analyze enormous amounts of consumer information. This information is used to segment and target consumer audiences and to customize offerings. Marketers and advertisers can develop their own computer databases, or buy them from direct-marketing and other commercial cluster-segmentation firms that have built large databases of consumer information.

- **Accountability**—Advertising has one major weakness that also happens to be the key strength of direct marketing—accountability. When you use direct marketing, you know right away whether or not it is working. You can gauge the response and tell how effective your offer has been.

These reasons for the growth of direct marketing highlight an ever-increasing sophistication by advertisers and marketers to identify and reach their target audiences with as little waste in coverage as possible. This ability has been enhanced because direct marketing has become database-driven to the point that some marketers have suggested changing the name direct marketing to database marketing.

Database Marketing

Database marketing starts with either the existence or development of a database of customers' and prospective customers' information stored in a computer electronically. Most databases are built around the names, addresses, and purchase histories of customers. The more purchase-relevant information that can be added to this basic data, the better an advertiser or marketer will be able to establish an ongoing relationship with his or her customers.

Databases vary widely by product categories and company needs. However, the following basic customer information is a typical starting place for company-created databases:

1. Accurate names and addresses of individuals or organizations, including ZIP Codes

2. Telephone number

3. Source of inquiry or order

4. Date and purchase details of first inquiry or order

5. Recency/frequency/monetary purchase history by date, dollar amounts of purchases, and product or product lines purchased

6. Credit history and rating

7. Demographic data for individual consumers, such as age, gender, marital status, family data, education, income, and occupation

8. Organizational data for industrial buyers, such as Standard Industrial Classification (SIC) code, size of firm, revenue, and number of employees[19]

The effectiveness of database marketing depends on keeping the database up to date, qualifying customers, segmenting the market, and being able to predict who your best prospects are. Database information can quickly become dated (no longer useful). Because most of your strategic and tactical decision-making will utilize database information, the currency and accuracy of the data are crucial. Keeping the database current should become part of a firm's normal direct-marketing activities. Exhibit 8–4 illustrates how some companies have collected their data as part of promotional programs.

Various strategic and tactical programs can be tested using a database because you will know exactly how your customers are responding to different approaches and appeals. The measure of the effectiveness of your direct-marketing efforts is built into your direct-marketing items because you are always asking for some type of response. The response to different creative executions, for example, can be tracked using database marketing.

Example

An advertiser of many years' standing told the copywriter he did not know whether his advertising was worth anything or not. Sometimes he thought that his business would be just as large without it.

The writer replied, "I do know your advertising is utterly unprofitable, and I could prove it to you in one week. End an ad with an offer to pay five dollars to anyone who writes to you that he or she read the ad through. The scarcity of replies will amaze you."[20]

A database is a powerful tool for profiling your customers and organizing them into meaningful consumer segments from which you can select your target markets and audiences. After your target prospects are identified, you can turn to strategic decisions involving the positioning of your product or service offering. Databases can help you to combine demographic, geographic, lifestyle, purchase, and ZIP Code information to locate your most appropriate target customer. Most advertisers and marketers do not have access to this much information on their customers, but syndicated cluster-segmentation services based on geodemographic data exist for the marketer who can afford them. The better-known segmentation systems have been described in Chapter 3. Lifestyle, socioeconomic status, demographics, ZIP Code location, purchase data, media usage, census data, and other data collected via questionnaires are combined to create meaningful consumer segments that can be located by the use of ZIP Code maps (see Chapter 3 for a detailed description of the PRIZM system).

Database marketing offers marketers the potential to more precisely identify their target prospect and that prospect's likely response to the message—but this should, of course, be the goal of *all* your advertising and marketing planning. Database marketing provides the technology to achieve optimum results. However, even if you find yourself in a position where database marketing is not affordable, you can use its strategic principles to improve the sophistication of your campaign planning.

Direct Marketing Objectives and Strategy

Your direct-marketing objectives and strategy should be developed with the overall advertising and marketing communications' campaign objectives and strategies in mind. Your direct-marketing plan should evolve from your total plan and identify those direct-marketing actions and activities that must be accomplished for the overall plan to be successful. To

Exhibit 8–4   Database Users and How They Collect Their Data

Company	Brands	Data-Collection Program
Procter & Gamble	Cheer Free, Cascade Liqui-Gel, NyQuil LiquiCaps	Collects data through reply cards in freestanding inserts offering free product samples by mail. P&G can recontact consumers about future line extensions or related new products.
MCI Communications	Long-distance service	Friends & Family program offers 20 percent discount to customers who identify people called regularly. MCI then targets those names with mail and phone solicitations.
AT&T/Walt Disney World		Callers enter joint sweepstakes using interactive phone program and are asked about Disney product and resort usage for future contacts by company.
Kimberly-Clark	Huggies diapers	Buys lists of new mothers and sends coupons, brochures, and new-product information during babies' diaper-wearing stage.
Pepsi-Cola	Pepsi	"Summer Chill Out" promotion developed mailing list with discount offer to kids.
Hallmark Cards	Greeting cards	Envelope glued to magazine so when filled out with buyer demographics and where buyer shops can be redeemed for free greeting card.
Coca-Cola	Coke Classic	"Pop Music" promotion provides CD buyers' names to partner, SONY.
Philip Morris	Merit cigarettes	"Blind" freestanding insert mail-in coupon offered unidentified product sample as part of contest promotion.

Source: "Data Collection Activity by Major Marketers," *Advertising Age* (October 21, 1991): 22.

be a vital component of the overall marketing communications effort, the direct-marketing portion of the plan should have its own objectives and strategies.

Your direct-marketing objectives are statements that accurately describe what is to be accomplished over a specified period of time. The objectives are the results that must be achieved for the direct-marketing effort to be successful. Direct-marketing strategies are the methods, activities, and events that will be employed to reach the objectives. The list of strategies should include who in the organization is responsible for what and when.

The objectives for direct marketing will flow from the problems and opportunities that have been identified during the early stages of campaign planning. Some of the problems and opportunities will suggest the use of direct marketing if it is to become part of the overall campaign. For example, IBM recently decided to enter the direct-marketing business by publishing its own personal and small-business computer catalogs. Dell, Gateway 2000, and others were pioneers in this kind of direct marketing. However, IBM (as well as Apple and Compaq) believed that it was time to use the advantages of direct-response technology, such as 800 numbers, together with the ability to build relationships (and gather database information) with its smaller customers. IBM's direct-marketing effort was launched around a 38-page catalog listing 400 products including some non-IBM brands. In the first two waves of this effort, 1.3 million catalogs were sent to prospective customers. IBM's decision to compete in this marketing communications' channel resulted from the lesson it learned and the market it lost when it had not been competitive in the personal-computer market, which allowed PC clones to monopolize this end of the computer business.[21]

Direct-marketing objectives (along with sales promotions) are among the most action-oriented of the marketing communications objectives you will be setting for your campaign. Typical objectives will include consumer responses such as:

> generating inquiries about a product or service
> purchasing the product or service
> gaining trial
> increasing usage
> enhancing a product's image among a well-defined target audience
> gathering information
> building an ongoing relationship with your customers

The ultimate reason for including direct marketing in your plan is to stimulate action on the part of the consumer and build a relationship that leads to repeat purchases. Direct marketing is a long-term commitment to information-gathering, storage, organization, management, and its effective use. It is not a one-shot tactic in one campaign.

Your direct-marketing strategies will be influenced by your ability to develop a well-defined target audience who can be reached with direct-marketing channels. Also, your strategy must be built around a well-conceived offer that will encourage consumers to respond. Ten factors to consider when in creating your offer are as follows.

1. Price. The product's offering price should be both competitive and enticing and allow you to make a profit. Over time, you should test this element of your direct-marketing strategy.

2. Shipping and handling. The cost of shipping and handling might have to be incorporated in the price. Most direct marketers do not charge more than 10% of the base price for shipping and handling.

3. Unit of sale. Your direct-marketing objectives will help guide you in the selection of how to offer your product. If you want to gather information, you will get more responses by offering smaller units (one or two). If you want to increase the number of units sold, then multiple units such as sets might make better sense.

4. Optional features. Some products lend themselves to the addition of optional features. Colors, sizes, personalization, and unusual options that cannot be found in stores can add value to the offer. You will have to charge extra for the option, but good options pull in more sales revenue.

5. Future obligation. One common way of keeping a customer over the long term is to make the initial offer unbelievably good (10 records for $5) in return for membership that requires buying future products at higher prices. Record and book clubs offer these "continuity" programs. However, both the initial and future offer must be of value to the customer.

6. Credit options. Credit cards have been a primary reason for the growth in direct marketing. When customers can charge their purchases, sales increase. Other possible credit options are paying on installment and/or delaying the first payment for a specified period of time. Recently, many companies are offering customers credit cards with their own imprimatur; for example, MCI, AT&T, and GM. The credit-card purchases made by the consumer earn credits toward lower down payments on the next purchase of a car (GM), or free calling time (AT&T).

7. Incentives. Including incentives in direct-marketing offerings carries the same risks as integrating sales promotion into the overall campaign. You want your customers to buy your product for its value and not because of the incentive. Therefore, incentives should be tested when and where possible. Free gifts, coupons, and sweepstakes are among the more common incentives. Incentives such as toll-free ordering can add to the ease of purchasing a product and do increase sales.

8. Time limits. All direct-marketing programs should prod the customer to take action as soon as possible. One way to create this sense of urgency is to add a time limit to the offer.

9. Quantity limits. A limited supply of an item can add value to the product in the customers' minds. Watch the home-shopping channels on cable TV, and note that quantity limits are displayed on the screen for some items, especially for collectibles. The notion of a limited supply makes the item more enticing.

10. Guarantees. Guarantees are essential to direct marketing because consumers' risks associated with buying items that cannot be inspected firsthand are reduced. You must guarantee customers' satisfaction up front by allowing them to cancel and receive a refund or a replacement. This assurance gives customers confidence in what they are going to buy.[22]

After you have considered these factors in building your direct-marketing offer, you can then engage the creative process to make the offer as enticing as possible. Additionally, the offer must fit (be integrated) with the rest of your marketing communications' plan. If you do not think creativity, style, and humor are as important to direct marketing as they are to general advertising, look at the Kenneth Cole shoe catalog pages reproduced in Figure 8–4. Also, note the toll-free 800 number at the lower left of the second page in the example.

The creative principles covered in Chapter 6 apply to direct marketing as well as to general advertising—only more so. Because the main task of direct marketing is to elicit

Figure 8–4 2-Page Ad for Kenneth Cole Shoes

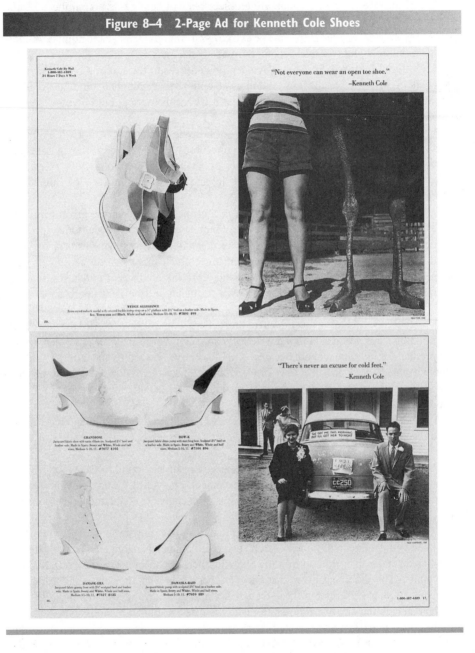

an immediate response, all copy and design work must work together toward that end. The wide range of media channels available will alter the actual execution of a direct-marketing item. To illustrate this, we'll use the classic direct-mail piece, and outline the use of copy and design that come into play when creating effective direct-marketing programs.

Copy Guidelines

The first and perhaps most important thing a copywriter can bring to a direct-marketing task is the attitude that the job at hand is to sell the product or service, and not to write prose. Direct-marketing expert Don Kanter says that writing is to copywriting what talking is to a salesperson. In both cases, the job is not to write or talk but to sell persuasively.[23]

Direct marketing differs from other forms of selling in that consumers cannot inspect the product—he or she does not get to handle the item physically. Therefore, the customer must rely on the content of your copy. The most important things to sell are (1) the value of the benefit to be derived from the product or service, and (2) confidence in the company. All advertising and marketing communications should be benefit-oriented. The value of a product to a consumer is the perceived benefit divided by the price. Confidence in the company can be enhanced through the use of testimonials from satisfied customers, experts, or celebrities. Guarantees, free-trial offers, right of cancellation, and the company's reputation can all help to reduce the risk of purchasing through direct marketing.[24]

All effective advertising and marketing communications' writing relies on appealing to basic human nature in a way that is relevant to the product or service benefit being offered. Products or services can either help one gain something or do it better, or avoid some pain or loss. Most people like to make money, save time, avoid extra effort, and be praised and popular. Likewise, they would like to avoid the opposite of these situations. In copywriting, the link between the product benefit and the human want or desire is called the "big idea" or "position." Figure 8–5 provides an example of direct-marketing writing that achieves this link between the product's benefit and the human desire it fulfills. Note the simple appeal to owning something that reflects the readers' desires for harmony, simplicity, and beauty (also a hallmark of the Lenox line). The copy follows through on the headline and illustration with warm, folksy copy that brings the scenes depicted on the china to life. Also note that this series of plates is not available in stores, which makes the offering exclusive. The last line of the copy builds up the readers' confidence by allowing cancellation at any time.

Chapter 6 has covered the key principles of good copy. Here, we provide only a checklist of pitfalls for the copywriter to avoid when creating good direct-marketing items—from ads to brochures and beyond. The following advice has been suggested by Carol Nelson in her book, *The New Road to Successful Advertising: How to Integrate Image and Response:*[25]

On Headlines

1. Avoid headlines that fail to involve your readers (appeal to their basic human nature and self-interest).

2. Never assume your reader knows as much as you do (provide information).

3. Stifle the urge to be subtle or obscure (the appeal and offer should be obvious).

On Visuals

1. Get rid of visuals that do not reinforce the written message.

2. Eliminate visuals that overpower the message and therefore create confusion.

3. Do not use clever visuals as an excuse for not being able to create a genuine message.

Figure 8–5 Lenox Direct-Response Ad

On Consumer Motivation

1. Do not confuse your enthusiasm and knowledge of your product with the fact that others will not know how good it is unless you tell and show them.

2. Do not assume that simply showing your product will make people run out to buy it or order it from you. Sometimes they need an extra incentive, time limit, or promise of exclusivity to get them moving.

On the Offer

1. Fine print, tiny type, asterisks in your copy, and mini-supers on TV put your customers on guard and work against their confidence in your offer.

2. Offers with strings attached or hidden disclaimers will hurt your image and future sales.

On Your Ego

1. The reader does not care about you but about what you can do for him or her. This is a business transaction.

2. Make your reader feel special even when you are claiming that he or she is one of a large group of people who have bought your product or service.

Media Alternatives

One of direct marketing's main advantages is in the flexibility it offers because of the variety of media, both conventional and unconventional, that can be used to deliver a message and product or service offering. This versatility translates into more room for creativity and more strategic alternatives to be considered as you integrate direct marketing into your overall campaign strategy.

Direct-marketing media are used to achieve better selectivity and segmentation of the target audience than we usually strive for with our general advertising buys. In addition, the goal of most direct-marketing campaigns is to emphasize frequency of exposure over reach. Because we are using direct marketing to narrow in on people who have potential to buy our product, we would like to establish an ongoing relationship with them. This type of strategy requires frequent contacts with our target audience. As we shall see in our discussion of individual direct-marketing media vehicles, some of these media also offer flexibility in terms of timing and ability to personalize the message.

For years, most consumers thought of direct marketing as "junk mail" that accumulated in their mailboxes. Although direct marketing has grown beyond its emphasis on the mail, direct mail is still among the top advertising media categories in terms of advertising expenditures. Only newspapers garner a larger share of the total advertising expenditure pie. Figure 8–6 illustrates a direct-mail piece that appeals to an upscale audience demonstrating that the old image of direct mail has given way to more targeted efforts that include consumer groups with higher income levels.

The **mailing list** is the most important element in a direct-marketing effort that uses the U.S. Postal Service. Keeping the list up to date is important, but acquiring and building a good list are the foundation for a successful direct-mail program. There are two basic types of mailing lists: internal and external. The internal list of past customers that many companies maintain is a place to start. This internal database can save you a lot of money because external lists purchased from a list service or another company (compiled from its own customer base) can be expensive. Typically, you will want to start with the company's internal customer list, assess its value as a mailing list, and then decide what type of external list to buy.[26]

If you are building a mailing list for the first time, you have to consider its cost in relation to your long-term commitment to direct marketing and the value of your customers as repeat purchasers. Seldom is the commitment to direct mail a one-shot proposition. Direct mail, as we will now see, has been the primary medium of the catalog business.

Catalogs have become the primary medium used to sell merchandise to highly segmented and target audiences on a national scale. Major reasons for the growth and success of the catalog business include the decline in the quality of service at the retail level, and

Figure 8–6 Bloomingdale's Direct Mailer

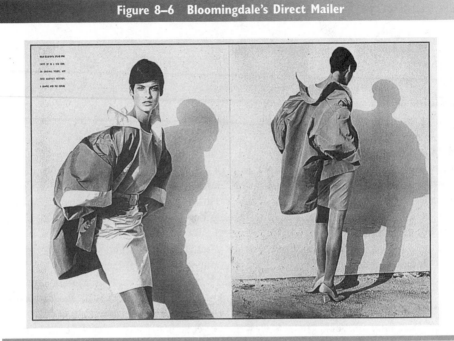

the shrinking leisure time for most consumers. The catalog business has expanded at the same time other time-saving devices have appeared, including automatic teller machines, toll-free numbers, credit cards, overnight mail delivery, computer online inventory confirmation, and improved service from the catalog companies themselves. All these developments allow us to control "when we do things, where we do things, how fast we do things, and how much hassle we're willing to put up with."[27]

There may come a time in the not-to-distant future when the telephone wire connected to a personal computer with a fax/modem will become the primary device for delivering (downloading) catalogs to our homes. This eventuality will also make purchasing and data collection more convenient. Every consumer purchase will represent an opportunity to improve a company's database and relationship with that customer. In a sense, the catalog business will merge with the new interactive computer technology and become part of the information and shopping superhighway.

In fact, a company known as 2Market is already offering catalogs through America Online and on CD-ROM. Among the catalogers participating are Lands' End, Spiegel, and Sony Music. The service is supported by advertisers such as Visa USA, whose business is highly interrelated to the catalog business.[28]

Some companies (such as Sears) have decided to exit the catalog business in favor of focusing on in-store retail business. Successful catalogers have done just the opposite—they have expanded into the retail store business. Eddie Bauer, Banana Republic, and Lands' End are among the catalog business group that now have stores in many shopping malls nationwide. Figure 8–7 demonstrates L.L. Bean's use of direct-response advertising

Figure 8–7 L.L. Bean's Ad for its Catalogs

to promote its catalog business. Also, note that the company offers a toll-free number, coupon, and overnight delivery. Figure 8–8 illustrates how targeting a special consumer group can be combined with the power of a relevant celebrity personality to sell collectibles through a catalog.

Direct marketing has made some of its most dramatic inroads into the electronic media, where the applications run from direct-response TV spots to infomercials and from home-shopping networks to direct marketing on computer online services. Once the domain of companies selling books, audiotapes, CDs, and magazines, direct-response advertisers on TV have expanded to include American Express, Time-Life, Soloflex, and other formidable marketers.

Part of the attraction of direct-response TV advertising has come from the growth of cable TV. Viewers/subscribers of cable TV are more clearly defined, so advertisers and marketers can reach audiences with specialized interests such as sports, news, business and finance, movies, music, and even legal cases.

Figure 8–8   Upper Deck Sports Collectors' Catalog

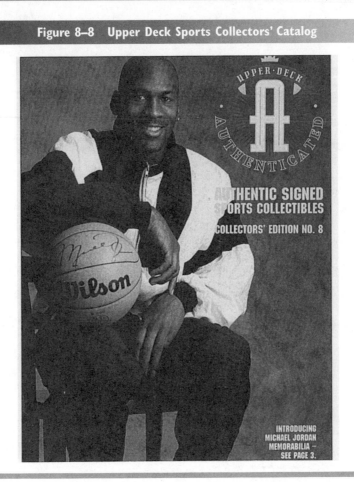

The relatively low cost of buying time on **cable TV** and the availability of nonprogrammed time has spawned a long-form direct-response spot called the **infomercial.** The decision whether or not to use infomercials is no different than buying traditional TV advertising time. Infomercials are judged by the amount of business or sales they generate, not by the TV rating for the time purchased. Thus, infomercials are created, used, and evaluated in the same manner as any other direct-marketing effort.

An interesting phenomenon of the past decade or so has been the success of **home-shopping networks** on TV. Home-shopping shows such as QVC broadcast 24 hours a day, seven days a week. They provide prescheduled programs often based around specific product categories, such as jewelry, clothing, or electronics. QVC takes viewers' phone calls on the air to increase their involvement with the programming. It also uses traditional direct-marketing techniques, such as limiting quantities and time to order. The toll-free phone number flashing on the screen and credit-card payment options make shopping on QVC easy.

Computer **online services** are clearly the wave of the future for direct marketing. These interactive services are already attracting the first round of marketers who see early entry into this medium as an opportunity to learn and grow in the new interactive environment. Catalogs are becoming available on CD-ROM, as previously mentioned. Consumers use computer technology to shop the catalogs by specifying price ranges, subject interests, age groups, and gift occasions, for example. The interactive nature of the experience and power to use computer technology to make shopping easy and efficient are likely to make shopping in cyberspace a major competitor in the media landscape.[29] Already an increasing number of companies each week are advertising their products on the Internet. As part of a $300 million campaign to launch the Mach 3 razor, Gillette dedicated a budget for online marketing which includes site construction and Web buys. It purchased banner ads on sites such as Lycos, MTV Online, ESPN SportZone, and Happy Puppy. Its strategy was to steer traffic to its own site to get consumers to interact and learn more about the product.[30]

Print media provide traditional delivery systems for direct marketing in the form of direct-response advertising. Magazines provide both mass audience and highly selective vehicles to choose from. The added high production quality can help to increase response rates to an offer. Newspapers have the value of natural timeliness and immediacy, so important to achieving consumer response. Direct marketers can consider as possible outlets run-of-the-paper placement, freestanding inserts, or the magazine sections that come with the Sunday paper. Because many of these media are also used for advertising and sales promotions' delivery, they can be combined in these vehicles.

Radio is a little more difficult than other media to use in a direct-marketing program because of its lack of a visual component and the fleeting nature of radio spots. This difficulty can be offset by high levels of repetition of product information and telephone numbers announced during the spot. The use of radio also requires that you run your spot frequently to get listeners to remember it. Local radio is very selective, which increases its ability to reach narrowly targeted audiences and is relatively inexpensive compared to other media.

Telemarketing (selling via the telephone) is a rapidly growing form of direct marketing. There is considerable consumer resistance to telemarketing as an intrusion on privacy resulting in rather low response rates. Yet, the use of 900 and 800 numbers has created the voice information-service phenomenon through which a company can provide information, entertain, and market its products. These services have a somewhat sleazy image because many consumers associate them with "sex talk" promotions. Also, consumer advocates have managed to accomplish the enactment of laws, which limit the time of day when telemarketers can call.

The future for direct marketing looks bright because it relies heavily on the improving media and computer technology. The options for its use appear to be limited only by marketers' imaginations. It is likely that many student projects will involve small companies without the resources and knowledge to become serious users of direct marketing. However, the targeting-and-response emphasis of direct marketing should be carried forth into your campaign in principle as you develop your other promotional areas.

FINISHING THE RELATED MARKETING COMMUNICATION PLAN

The integration of the marketing communications' elements of advertising, sales promotions, public relations, and direct marketing is a process of evaluating each element's strengths and weaknesses in being able to (1) reach your target audience with a minimum of waste, and (2) elicit the responses that will result in the accomplishment of your marketing objectives. You will not always have the luxury of unlimited resources with which to make these decisions. Therefore, you have to learn to live with trade-offs and still meet the requirements of your marketing communications' program.

As this chapter has illustrated, the four major marketing communication elements have tremendous complementary value. Sales promotions and direct marketing push the hardest for an immediate response, often in terms of product sales. Advertising and public relations are aimed more at communications' objectives, such as awareness and acceptance. However, it is when you bring the four qualities together that you realize a strong campaign can strive for both communication and sales objectives.

You should always be aware of where your target consumers are in the purchase-and-response cycle in relation to your brand. You want to reach your customers with the right combination of promotional messages that will take them to the next desired step in the purchase process. This level can be awareness and trial for an introductory campaign or a higher velocity of purchase for established products.

Stay on top of the emerging new technology. An interest in sales promotion and direct marketing will assure that you will be where the latest technology is being applied to marketing. Computer technology will soon change the way we deliver messages and offers to consumers in their homes. The technological advances in interactive media will demand

Campaign Progress Checklist

At this point in the campaign, you should be generally aware of the following points:

1. Related marketing tools such as sales promotion, public relations, and direct marketing are a way to extend and integrate the marketing communication strategy.

2. The related marketing communication tools each have their own objectives, strategy, and tactics and, in return, should be linked to the creative and media plans so that they put forward an interrelated complementary message.

3. The use of sales promotions' tools to supplement advertising can be a point of differentiation between brands.

4. Care needs to be excercised in using sales promotions to avoid training consumers to respond to inducements rather than other intangible aspects associated with the brand.

5. Public relation can include corporate public relations designed to help consumers understand the company's policies and activities

6. Marketing public relations, another form of PR, can be thought of as working similar to advertising, especially product publicity.

7. Direct marketing is increasing in importance to advertisers because of companies' increased ability to reach highly selective groups of consumers through database marketing.

8. Some marketing communication activities such as sales promotion and direct marketing can be an effective way to stimulate sales in the short run. Companies, however, should continue to employ strategies to build over a long term.

full integration of image-oriented promotions with response-based promotions. They will become one and the same, which will improve accountability for all forms of promotion.

Remember, you have to strive for both short- and long-term results in today's marketplace. You have to be able to think like the trade and push for sales results while striving to maintain the valuable equity in your brand. Marketing and advertising have become more competitive and more results-oriented. The campaign that wins the day is the one that reflects this reality and takes advantage of the new opportunities to create the many brand contacts that form the consumers' reality of your integrated marketing communications campaign.

Notes and References

[1] Stone, B. (1994). *Successful direct marketing methods* (5th ed.). Lincolnwood, IL: NTC Business Books, p. 7.

[2] Author. (1994). *Media trends 1994*. New York: DDB Needham Worldwide, p. 9.

[3] Burnett, Heinz split up, *Advertising Age* (daily fax) (November 23, 1994), p. 1.

[4] Blattberg, R. C., & Nelson, S. A. (1990). *Sales promotion: Concepts, methods, and strategies*. Englewood Cliffs, NJ: Prentice-Hall, pp. 15–16.

[5] Smith, K. (1994). Introduction and overview, in *Sales promotion handbook* (8th ed.) Tamara Brezen Block & William A. Robinson, Eds. (Chicago, IL: Dartnell Press), p. 5.

[6] Belch, G. E., & Belch, M. A. (1995). *Introduction to advertising and promotion: An integrated marketing communications perspective* (4th ed.). Chicago, IL: Irwin, pp. 470–471.

[7] Belch & Belch, *Introduction to advertising and promotion*, p. 472.

[8] Block, T. B. (1994). Couponing, in *Sales promotion handbook*, pp. 99–100.

[9] Block, Couponing, in *Sales promotion handbook*, p. 111.

[10] Jagoda, D. (1994). Sweepstakes, games, contests, in *Sales promotion handbook*, p. 129.

[11] Jagoda, Sweepstakes, games, contests, in *Sales promotion handbook*, pp. 133–143.

[12] Rolling Rock asks what "33" means. Promo (1994, September), p. 22.

[13] Wulff, K. (1992, Spring). How to compete at sports marketing, *The Advertiser*, pp. 73–76.

[14] D'Alessandro, D. (1993, July). Event marketing winners: Olympics, local, causes. *Brandweek*, p. 16.

[15] This section is based in part on James Kunz, Trade promotion, in *Sales promotion handbook*, pp. 320–334.

[16] Belch & Belch, *Introduction to advertising and promotion, p. 514*.

[17] Yale, D. R. (1995). *The publicity handbook*. Lincolnwood, IL: NTC Business Books, p. 3.

[18] Roman, K., & Maas, J. (1992). *The new how to advertise*. New York: St. Martin's Press, p. 59.

[19] Stone, *Successful direct marketing methods*, p. 38.

[20] Hopkins, C. C. (1987). *Scientific advertising*. Lincolnwood, IL: NTC Business Books, p. 316.

[21] Khermouch, G. (1993, July 12). Lands' End does it. Dell does it. Why not Big Blue? *BrandWeek*, pp. 22–24.

[22] Stone, *Successful direct marketing methods*, pp. 79–81.

[23] Stone, *Successful direct marketing methods*, pp. 376–377.

[24] Stone, *Successful direct marketing methods*, p. 377.

[25] Nelson, C. (1991). *The new road to successful advertising: How to integrate image and response*. Chicago, IL: Bonus Books, p. 195.

[26] Stone, *Successful direct marketing methods*, pp. 212–215.

[27] Walker, J. (1990, December 31). Catalogers, there may be a fax in your future, DM News, p. 23.

[28] Goldman, K. (1994, November 18). Holiday shopping comes to cyberspace, Wall Street Journal, sec. B, p. 5.

[29] Levin, G. (1994, November 21). Catalogers take Wares 2 market. *Advertising Age*, p. 15.

[30] Warner, B. (1998, August 24). Gillette's Mach 3 media heft hits Web: European sites next? *Mediaweek*, p. 34.

Chapter 9

Enhancing the Marketing Communication Mix

Competition can be brutal. Often times it's not enough to be satisfied with the status quo. Things can change dramatically overnight. In the age of information, consumers know more and change faster than ever before. Consider what has happened to Michelob. How did such a popular beer lose favor to where today the brand is a faint image of what it once was? Times, styles, and tastes change. Companies need to make the most out of their opportunities. If they don't, a rival will. Allow a company a small part of your market share, and you run the risk of the competitor using its new position as leverage to acquire an even greater share of the market. Agencies also hate losing even a small part of an account to another agency.

Consider McDonald's. In 1977, DDB Needham was named Agency of the Year by *Advertising Age*. Two years later the agency was fired and replaced by Leo Burnett. After several years, McDonald's gave DDB Needham some assignments and gradually it got back a small part of the business. In 1998, McDonald's gave DDB Needham the lead role for its account. Leo Burnett? It got to keep a smaller part of the account (the advertising to kids and "tweens.") Why didn't McDonald's give all its business to one agency and "integrate" its marketing communication effort by consolidating it in one source? The answer may be complex, but one bet is that it keeps both agencies hustling.

Although this chapter sounds like it consists of the extra things companies do to maximize their opportunities, many of the things we will talk about in this chapter are today considered *essential*. We've roughly divided this chapter conceptually into thirds. In the first section, we discuss the special audience segments advertisers target in addition to the

251

target audience they set for the campaign. The second section examines some of the less common strategies advertisers employ that are not typically associated with traditional message strategy. The last section focuses on special media strategies, including the use of nontraditional media.

SPECIAL MARKETS

To fully exploit a company's sales potential, marketers increasingly look both beyond and within their traditional markets for additional sources of opportunities. Within an overall market, there are other and usually smaller markets that don't quite identify with advertising that is more mainstream in nature. We've identified some of the more important markets: (1) global, (2) African American, (3) Hispanic, (4) Asian, and (5) gay/lesbian.

Globalization

It's only because we're sensitive about the length of this book that we don't devote a entire chapter or more to this very important market. For many advertisers, sales outside the United States are higher than their sales within the United States. There are numerous reasons why firms must consider the entire world when considering their opportunities, and include some of the following.

- There are obviously more consumers outside than inside the United States. According to the *Statistical Abstract of the United States*,[1] in 1995, the gross domestic product (GDP) of the European Union alone was $6.925 million.The GDP of the United States was $6.955 million.

- Many overseas markets are less developed than those in the United States. Competing in some markets can be easier than competing at home.

- Brands from Western countries in general and those from the United States in particular are in high demand in many parts of the world.

- The information age is here. Marketing to locations around the world are only a click away in cyberspace.

- Multinational companies headquartered overseas are continuing to come to the United States in increasing numbers. Allowing them to come here without our going there could mean that these firms eventually would get bigger in size than your company. Sometimes size matters.

- The United States does not have a monopoly on ideas. There is much we can learn from other countries. London, in particular, has been a vibrant source of many advertising ideas. The account planning revolution began there.

- Selling overseas helps ease the trade deficit.

Understanding Global Marketing Communications. Most people realize intuitively that advertising is different in other parts of the world. Because the United States has been such a dominant economic and military power, there may be a tendency on the part of some to assume that we understand how advertising works better than "they" do. That is a mistake. Advertising is different in other parts of the world often because it needs to be

Exhibit 9–1	International Advertising Mistakes

When Vicks first introduced its cough drops on the German market, they were chagrined to learn that the German pronunciation of "v" is f which in German is the guttural equivalent of "sexual penetration."

Not to be outdone, Puffs tissues tried later to introduce its product, only to learn that "Puff" in German is a colloquial term for a whorehouse. The English weren't too fond of the name either, as it's a highly derogatory term for a non heterosexual.

When Pepsi started marketing its products in China a few years back, they translated their slogan, "Pepsi Brings You Back to Life" pretty literally. The slogan in Chinese really meant, "Pepsi Brings Your Ancestors Back from the Grave."

When Coca Cola first shipped to China, they named the product something that when pronounced sounded like "Coca Cola." The only problem was that the characters used meant, "Bite the wax tadpole." They later changed to a set of characters that mean "Happiness in the mouth."

A hair products company, Clairol, introduced the "Mist Stick", a curling iron, into Germany only to find out that mist is slang for manure. Not too many people had use for the manure stick.

When Gerber first started selling baby food in Africa, they used the same packaging as here in the USA with the cute baby on the label. Later they found out that in Africa companies routinely put pictures on the label of what's inside since most people can't read.[2]

When Nokia adapted its "freedom of expression" slogan promoting its differently colored mobile phones for the German market they inadvertently substituted the German equivalent of the Latin saying "to each his own" which had been posted above the entrance to the notorious Buchanwald concentration camp during World War II. Around 3,000 billboards were quickly covered over when Jewish groups voiced their outrage.[3]

different. It would be the height of American arrogance to assume that what works here ought to work in other places that have older and probably much richer cultures than ours.

There are numerous ways in which other countries differ from the United States—far too numerous to categorize and adequately explain here. The more obvious differences which, unfortunately, are not always so obvious to American tourists, involve language and culture.

Understanding Language Problems. It's not enough to study language out of a book. It helps to have lived in the country to understand the subtleties that words can convey in any language. Even within a country, not everyone understands the connotative meaning that words pick up through usage. A simple word like *bad* clearly is perceived as something negative among most Americans. But it can also mean that the word is referencing something cool. It may also mean you are using a word that is "so like 1980s." Every country has language peculiarities (semantics) that are not so easy for foreigners to pick up. Some words have neither literal translations nor pronunciations. Take the pronunciation of the author's name, Parente. Americans tend to pronounce it Parent $\overline{\text{ee}}$ or Parent ay. The actual pronunciation in the Italian language is somewhere in between. Exhibit 9–1 shows what can happen if the translator does not have a good grasp of the local language.

Understanding the Importance of Cultural Differences. Difficulties with language problems often exist on the surface. Once they are pointed out, it's easy to see them and make the appropriate modifications to a campaign. However, cultural differences are not always so easy for outsiders to see or understand. For example, it's easy for Americans to see that European advertising differs from their own. The advertising is usually more entertaining, contains less hard sell, and takes a more liberal approach to the use of nudity. What we often see are the differences in the way advertising is executed. We may not fully appreciate that the differences are more strategic and stem from the differing cultural values in various countries.

It's been observed that in France, less than 10% of the commercials feature someone who addresses the camera; whereas in the United States, better than 70% of the commercials have this feature. In the United States, salespeople are often advised to look the customer in the eyes. It can be a mark of sincerity. In contrast, the French are more reserved and consider it a lack of modesty to be so straightforward with a sales pitch.[4] Similarly, Japanese place a high premium on social harmony. The Burger King campaign that suggests, "Sometimes you just gotta break the rules" goes against Japanese values. The campaign works just fine in the United States or Australia where individualism is valued.

Coordinating Global Marketing Communications. Increasingly, companies are restructuring, reengineering, and refining their operations to compete in the global marketplace. Companies plan ahead comprehensively, controlling an array of functions in every detail. They analyze situations, specify policies and procedures in meticulous detail, then spell out for their workers what can and cannot be done in particular circumstances.[5] They analyze risks, set objectives, establish strategy, and anticipate contingencies. Like a socialist or communist economy, this type of centralized control has limitations.

Its major limitation is that it inhibits initiative. If managers at the local level do not have the opportunity to experiment or adapt their ideas to the local market, the company may not be taking advantage of the people who best know the consumer. Not surprisingly, companies have come to understand the merits of the saying, "Think globally, but act like a retailer." Yet, there can be advantages to making decisions centrally. Companies with strong brands have considerable equity tied up in specific brand associations. Companies such as Coca-Cola are reluctant to let local offices tinker with their core equities. Coca-Cola has literally spent billions of dollars getting the world to think of Coke in a certain way. The world is figuratively getting smaller every day. They do not want to compete with themselves to maintain their image.

There are at least three models a company can use to coordinate its global marketing communications:

1. A centrally directed campaign with minimal local options. We hesitate to mention this one because we don't think very highly of it. It works fairly well for brands like Coca-Cola and Marlboro cigarettes where the companies largely use appeals and imagery much like they do in the United States. Except for India, Coca-Cola makes very few changes to its advertising worldwide. It works for Marlboro in many places precisely because the local population does identify it as an American brand. In many countries, especially in Asia, people identify Western culture as modern, hip, and ambitious. Unfortunately, smoking Western cigarettes is a relatively inexpensive way many consumers "improve" their self-image by adopting Western products and habits. The primary limitation of this approach is that other countries differ from the United States—in major and minor ways.

2. A regionally directed campaign with local flexibility. This approach is used by companies for a variety of reasons. It permits a company, such as Procter & Gamble, to exercise some control over the way their products are marketed, yet still allows a local office the flexibility to adapt a local campaign to what is likely to work in its area. It works for Procter & Gamble because they promote their products on the basis of the functional value of the products. Telling consumers that Tide gets clothes clean is basically similar in all countries.

3. A locally directed campaign with regional direction. This approach works far better for companies that operate in countries at different stages of development. What works in Germany may not have the same effect in India. Moreover, McDonald's sells its products on the basis of an emotional reward. They not only sell hamburgers, they also sell the experience it's wrapped in. McDonald's does give its local operators direction, but it's more along the lines of telling them how to start up the business and then telling them how to anticipate where the business is going to be in 10 years. McDonald's allows its stores outside the United States far more latitude than they allow domestic stores because of the considerable differences in cultures. As a result, McDonald's restaurants can look considerably different, even in the same country. Switzerland is a small country, but it has three very different cultures that tend to cluster in different regions: Italian, German, and French. The stores in each of these countries are often very different in terms of style and appearance.

African Americans

It has only been since the mid-1960s that African Americans have been represented in advertising appearing in the mass media. Before this period, advertisers used specialized media such as *Ebony, Jet*, and "ethnic" radio stations to reach this segment of the population. Despite the widespread use of African-American models in mass media advertising, companies still understand the value of developing advertising with this specific segment in mind. African Americans are not simply consumers with dark skin. They have different values, lifestyles, interests, and tastes. In short, they are different and special.

African Americans tend to be identified by skin color or genetic heritage, no matter their religion or nationality.[6] African Americans don't mind being referred to as black, although African American seems to be the preferred term to use in more formal situations.

Demographic Information
Information on African Americans can be found in many sources, *including Simmons Market Research Bureau* (SMRB) and Mediamark Research Inc. (MRI). The most comprehensive data comes from the U.S. Census:

Population: 34,525,000
Percentage of Population: 12.7%
Average Income: $12,351
Education: 70% are high school graduates or more; 11.9% have a bachelor's degree or more[7]

Many U.S. metropolitan areas such as Memphis, New York, Atlanta, and Washington, DC have populations with over one-quarter African Americans. Census projections indicate a faster than average population growth rate into the next century.[8]

Values. As a result of their historical experiences, African Americans value together-ness and take pride in their heritage. African Americans like to define their own style rather than follow what the establishment dictates.[9] Family, religion, and church are very impor-tant to African Americans. Since 1986, 6 million people have attended black weekend "fes-tivals," a celebration consisting primarily of family reunions.[10]

To understand what distinguishes African Americans from other market segments, you have to remember that, unlike other immigrants, they were brought to this country against their will. As a result, African Americans often seek products that give them a sense of empowerment and that show that they are important members of society, according to Ken Smikle, publisher of Target Market News.[11]

Consumption Habits. This quest for empowerment may also explain why many low-income African Americans buy expensive liquor. Eugene Morris, president of E. Morris Ltd., suggests it's a way to make a statement about themselves at an affordable price. By-ron Lewis, chairman of UniWorld Group, reports that African Americans tend to spend their money on status symbols such as cars, electronics, and jewelry because they can't acquire the house they want.[12] Marlene L. Rossman, author of *Multicultural Marketing*, suggests this desire for status helps explain why upscale African Americans tend to buy generic equivalents and private label goods while less affluent African Americans buy na-tional brands.[13] Data from the Yankelovich Partners and Consumer Expenditure Survey, reported in *American Demographics*, shows the following:

- Blacks spend significantly more than average on personal-care services for both women and men, such as hair styling, massage, and manicures.

- Black households spend more than average on hosiery, women's accessories, jewelry, and home electronic equipment.

- Blacks are willing to pay more to get "the best."

- Blacks spend less than average on housing, appliances, furnishings, home mainte-nance, repairs, and insurance.

- Blacks prefer to shop at department and specialty stores.[14]

Best Way to Reach This Segment

In the late 1960s, advertisers struggled with how best to reach this market. They questioned whether it would be best to use specialized media or to simply use black models in their advertising and appeal to African Americans at the same time they appealed to the rest of the market. Today, advertisers do both. In fact, a long list of advertisers such as Kmart Corp., L'eggs Corporation, Kraft General Foods, Quaker Oats Co., and Polaroid Corp. have all hired agencies that specialize in advertising to the African-American market, such as Burrell Communications Group Inc.

An influential study done by the Yankelovich Partners for the Burrell Group found that 60% of black consumers feel that the majority of television and print ads "are designed only for white people." Reflecting this point, there are approximately 800 media outlets catering to the African-American market. The Black Entertainment Television Network (BET) reaches 55% of black households. Essence magazine reaches 4 million readers, approximately 25% of black women. More than 70% of African Americans read community-based publications.[15] Network television also does a good job of reaching crossover audiences of black and white viewers age 12–17 and age 50 and over.[16]

When developing a campaign or part of a campaign to reach the African American market, consider the following points:

- Think of the African-American market as a subculture of the overall market with values, lifestyles, consumption, and media habits that differ from the overall population.

- Use people or agencies who are familiar with this subculture. (Procter & Gamble Co. makes hiring minorities to work in its marketing area a high priority.[17])

- Design a campaign apart from the mainstream strategy that reflects what is special about this market.

- Be sensitive to appealing to African Americans on the basis of what makes them special without using negative stereotypes.

- Recognize that African Americans have many things in common with each other, but diversity exists in this segment just as it does in the overall population.

- Consider cause-related marketing to show this segment the company thinks of them as more than merely consumers.

- Use media that specifically target African Americans.

Hispanics

Increasingly, advertisers are aware of the growing importance of the Hispanic market. Currently, it is the second largest minority group. By 2010, it is projected to be the largest minority group in the United States. Due to both a high birthrate and immigration, its percentage of the U.S. population is projected to increase from a current 11% to 14% by 2010. During this period, Hispanic buying power is expected to triple from $350 billion to $940 billion.[18] There are more Hispanics living in the United States than there are people living in Canada.

Demographic Information
Population: 30,769,000 (Hispanic origin, of any race)
Percentage of Population: 11.4%
Average Income: $10,773
Education: 51.5% are high school graduates or more; 8.7% have bachelor's degree or more[19]

Hispanics have a higher birthrate and larger families than the American average. Although household income is less than average for Hispanics as a whole, the growth of this market makes them attractive to companies.[20]

Identifying Who Is Hispanic. There is no consensus on the identifying characteristics of exactly what makes someone Hispanic. In the 1970 U.S. Census, the choices included "Mexican," "Mexican-American," "Chicano," "Puerto Rican," "Cuban," and "other." Advertisers sometimes use the terms "Latino" or "Latin," as in the "Latin market" to refer to

Hispanics in Los Angeles, New York, and Miami. Presumably, however, *Latin* does not refer to someone of Italian, French, or Romanian heritage, other cultures that also have Latin roots. In the 1980 and 1990 U.S. Census, respondents were simply asked if they were "Spanish/Hispanic" or "non-Hispanic." The identity issue is an important one because the cultural value orientations of the different subcultures within the "Hispanic" market can have a fundamental role in consumer behavior.[21] In other words, one has to be careful not to assume all Hispanic subgroups are the same. A 1991 *Forbes* article even questioned whether the Spanish media weren't overselling the importance of using specialized media to reach the Hispanic market.[22] The argument was based on the idea that many Hispanics had integrated into the overall culture to the point that a specialized approach wasn't necessary. Still, it is clear advertisers such as J.C. Penney, Procter & Gamble, Kraft Foods, Avon, Nike, Allstate, and all the major brewers have made strong efforts to target the Hispanic market. Rossman suggests that *Hispanic* refers to an origin or ethnicity, not a race. Hispanics can be a mixture of several races, white, brown, or black. The major unifying factors are the Spanish language and Catholicism.[23]

Values. Hispanics care greatly about preserving their culture, traditions, and language; they have persistently resisted assimilation into the American mainstream. The majority of Spanish-speaking Americans continue to use their native tongue at home and socially. They appreciate music and the arts and are enthusiastic fans of sports such as soccer, baseball, and boxing.[24] They place a great deal of importance on family and children They take a strong interest in personal appearance and aesthetics. The quality of their lives is very important. As a group, they can be outgoing, and their emotions are often visible.[25]

Consumption Habits. Hispanics can be very conscious of brand names, and loyally reward companies that advertise in Spanish. Although the average household income is less than that for the general public, it can vary significantly even within the same Hispanic subgroups. For example, Cubans who have lived in Miami since the 1960s are often wealthy landowners; whereas Cubans who have recently emigrated to the United States in boat crossings are often of a much lower socioeconomic status. Proportionally, Hispanics spend the same amount of money as the general public on cameras and other goods geared toward family occasions.[26] In fact, they are willing to pay extra for quality goods that are family related.[27]

According to Standard Rate and Data Service (SRDS), there are 42 major Spanish-language magazines, 31 English or bilingual Hispanic-oriented magazines, 103 Spanish-language newspapers, and more than 300 radio stations with Spanish programming. Television choices include Univision and Telemundo broadcast networks and the Galavision cable network.[28]

Best Way to Reach This Group

A 1992 joint survey conducted by Yankelovich Partners and Market Development indicates that large numbers of Hispanics (86%) watch Spanish TV during the week and appreciate Spanish-language advertising.[29] Stuart Livingston of Galavision recommends reaching this group through grassroots community efforts such as funding literacy and scholarship programs, sponsoring athletic teams, and promoting special events such as festivals and fairs. Regional companies also enjoy an advantage by targeting only one specific group.[30]

Exhibit 9–2	Spanish Translation Mistakes[32]	
Company	**English Slogan/Product**	**Spanish Translation**
General Motors	Chevrolet Nova	Chevrolet doesn't Go
Braniff	Fly in Leather	Fly Naked
Eastern Airlines	We Earn Our Wings Daily	Final Destination Heaven
Coors	Turn It Loose	Suffer from Diarrhea
Budweiser	King of Beers	Queen of Beers

It's also important to understand that Hispanics tend to congregate in major cities. Los Angeles, San Francisco, and Chicago are primarily Mexican; New York City has a large Puerto Rican population; and Miami has large numbers of Cubans.

What Not to Do. It's important to tap into the characteristics that make Hispanics special without fostering negative stereotypes. If at all possible, use someone who is familiar with the specific subculture. If advertising in Spanish, keep in mind that approximately 20 Spanish-speaking nationalities reside in the United States and that individual words can vary in meaning from group to group.[31] Do not assume that English-language campaigns can translate literally into Spanish. Exhibit 9–2 is an example of what can happen when you do.

Asian Americans

Asian Americans belong to the fastest-growing, most affluent, and most highly educated ethnic group.[33] The Asian American market is an important one, but unlike the Hispanic market they do not share a common language or culture. There are six distinct Asian markets and at least several smaller ones such as Thais, Laotians, and Malays (Indonesians). The six major Asian markets are as follows.

1. **Fillipinos.** This is the largest and most "assimilated" group of Asian Americans. Most Fillipinos still speak Tagalog, the native language of the Philipines. However, many also speak Spanish and/or English.

2. **Chinese.** This group usually speaks Mandarin or Cantonese and identify themselves as American-born Chinese (ABC) or fresh-off-boats (FOB). Not surprisingly, the Chinese who have been here the longest are more upscale, and the more newly arrived Chinese tend to be more blue-collar, conservative, and patriarchal.

3. **Japanese.** This group often speaks English very well, are upscale, and tend to live in the California or the New York City region.

4. **Koreans**. This group tends to cluster in large metropolitan areas. Many Koreans are small business owners.

5. **Vietnamese.** This is the fastest-growing Asian group. They tend to be lower on the socioeconomic scale than other Asian American groups, given their relatively recent

arrival in the United States. Approximately one-third of all Vietnamese living in the United States reside in California.

6. **Asian Indians.** This group is not as geographically clustered as other groups. There are many highly educated professionals in this group.[34]

Demographic Information

Population: 10,504,000 (The fastest-growing minority group)
Percentage of Population: 3.9 %
Average Income: $18,226
Education: 38% hold bachelor's degrees or more.[35]

Values. Asians place a very high priority on group harmony and family togetherness. They are much more likely to use the pronoun *we* than *I*. Asians identify with other Asians, if only because non-Asians are unaware of the often significant differences among Asian subgroups. Even the geographic region Asians come from is much more spread out than non-Asians generally realize. The Asian region is approximately twice as wide east to west and twice as long north to south as the United States. Asians tend to place a high value on education, often sacrificing household extras to educate the children.

Historically, Chinese, Japanese, Korean, and Vietnamese families differ somewhat from one another, but many derive their basic norms and values from Confucianism. These include obedience to and responsibility for parents, patrilinearity, patriarchy, a preference for sons, respect for education, the use of shame and guilt to control behavior, and considerable personal interdependence. Much of the same has been true for Asian Indians.[36]

Consumption Habits. Although Asian Americans have a lower average income than whites, their median household income is significantly higher due to having more people in the household and workforce. As a result, some Asian subgroups, such as the Japanese, Chinese, and Indians, have significantly more disposable income than whites. Jessie Fan's extensive study of the U.S. Consumer Expenditure Survey discovered the following facts about Asian American spending:

- Asians spend more of their budget on shelter.

- Asian households are motivated to save and invest.

- Asians spend more of their budget on education and significantly more of their budget on health care.

- Asian American households spend significantly less on food at home than Hispanics and whites and more on food away from home than black households.

- Asian Americans spend less of their budget on fuel and utilities.

- Asian Americans spend significantly less on household equipment and operation, entertainment, alcohol, and tobacco than white households.

- Asian Americans spend less on apparel than both black and Hispanic households.[37]

A study conducted by Market Segment Research also discovered that when compared to other ethnic minorities, Asians are reluctant to flaunt their wealth, are less spontaneous shoppers for small-ticket items, but are less likely to bargain hunt and budget for grocery shopping.[38] Although status conscious, Asian Americans are not particularly brand loyal.[39]

Best Way to Reach This Segment
Advertisements targeting Asian Americans should contain messages promoting the family and traditional values. Advertisements currently in use highlight cooperation, support traditional sex roles, portray actors or models as successful professionals, and frequently feature elderly family members who are highly esteemed in Asian society.[40] Advertisers can effectively target the six main subgroups using native-language media in their tightly concentrated communities located in major metropolitan areas in California, New York, Hawaii, and Texas.[41] It is important to recognize differences as well as similarities in the Asian market and to portray Asians in a positive way.[42]

What Not to Do. Do not try to challenge the status quo in advertisements targeting Asian Americans. Advertisements with sexual themes or stressing individualism are not well received.[43]

Gay/Lesbian
This market received increasing emphasis in the 1990s. Today, society is somewhat more accepting of gays and lesbians, and marketers have become increasingly aware of this group's considerable disposable income. The market is comprised mainly of white males. Subgroups include black homosexuals, older white homosexuals, and lesbians.[44]

Demographic Information
Obtaining accurate information for this population segment is difficult. Some gays and lesbians are reluctant to identify themselves or respond to a survey. The estimated information that follows is based on several sources that are likely not as accurate or objective as the U.S. Census:

Percentage of Population: 6%–16%
Average Income: $36,800
Education: over 59% have a college degree[45]

Values. The gay and lesbian community places a high priority on the value of friendships. Among heterosexuals, the patterns of social behavior often take place with members of one's family or coworkers. Contrastingly, the gay community interacts more with friends, usually those who share the same sexual orientation. Delozier and Rodriguez found that gays and lesbians are very aware of current social issues and are often politically active. Gays and lesbians most often reside within a city in major metropolitan areas and are highly interested in career building. Homosexuals living in suburban areas tend to be interested in traditional focuses such as home ownership, gardening, and community activities.[46]

Consumption Habits. There is widespread consensus that gays spend freely on a wide variety of goods and services.[47] Reports suggest that gays' spending at least equals and probably exceeds that which heterosexuals spend, especially on entertainment, dining out, travel, exercising at private clubs; and material goods such as liquor, clothing, fragrances, books, greeting cards, and compact discs. Gays are thought to be very brand loyal.[48]

Best Way to Reach This Group

Gays appear to be especially receptive to companies that are accepting of their lifestyle even if they aren't totally satisfied with their goods and services, according to Steven M. Kates, author of *Twenty Million New Customers*. On the other hand, they will avoid and even boycott companies they feel are "homophobic." [49] In the late 1970s, Coors allegedly performed polygraph tests on employees. Among the questions they asked were ones about sexual orientation. Even though Coors now includes sexual orientation in its antidiscrimination policy, many gays harbor negative feelings about the brand.[50] To convince this segment that a company is at least tolerant of their lifestyle, some experts suggest a company needs to be proactive and do something significant, such as sponsor socially responsible events. This involvement can range from supporting the arts or AIDS research to sponsoring community specific events, such as the Gay Games and Gay/Lesbian Parades.[51]

There are a growing number of media vehicles to reach this group, including the following:

- Local and regional gay/lesbian newspapers

- Cable and public broadcasting service television programs

- Radio shows

- National magazines, such as *The Advocate, Out, Deneuve, Genre, 10 Percent, QW, On Our Backs, Outweek,* and *50/50.*

There are also a small number of firms that specialize in offering advertising and marketing services to companies interested in reaching the gay and lesbian market.[52]

Special Message Strategies

The first section of this chapter described how advertisers target special population segments to get the most out of their market opportunities. Here, we examine some of the special strategies companies use to influence the way consumers think or feel about the brand and/or the company. These special strategies can be part of the mainstream campaign, but are usually in addition to what the company might do normally.

Multitiered Advertising

Companies have long used a multitiered approach to pricing their products. Anheuser-Busch Inc., for example, sells a popular-priced beer, Busch; a premium-priced beer, Budweiser; and a super-premium beer, Michelob (although in some markets, Michelob is barely priced higher than Budweiser). Similarly, Gap Inc. sells upscale clothes at Banana Republic, moderately priced clothes at its Gap stores, and uses its Old Navy division to sell budget-priced clothing.

Companies, however, do not generally like to run more than one message strategy at a time. The feeling is the messages diffuse the effectiveness of the strategy by competing with each other, even if only slightly. Advertisers do, however, occasionally use differing message strategies. Although advertisers seldom use more than two strategies, theoretically, the number used could be unlimited. The idea behind the multitiered approach is to communicate different layers of meaning to the audience. This is not unlike the approach used to promote Saturn automobiles. The national campaign has been heavily image-oriented, promoting the idea that Saturn is a different kind of a car made by a different kind of company. In a separate campaign funded by the Saturn dealer associations, the emphasis is on product advertising, which is a trade expression meaning they promote the car, not the image. Similarly, advertising by the big tire brands, such as Michelin and Goodyear, often feature image advertising on the national level to "build the brand." On the local level, the ads are more product-oriented. To extend the reach of local advertising, companies provide substantial co-op funds to dealers for advertising placed locally.

The above examples are typical of an advertiser that wants to build the brand and at the same time push product sales. What's more unusual is for an advertiser to run separate image campaigns that all target basically the same audience. There is substantial risk involved in this approach. The more firmly you establish one image with the audience, the more difficult it is too establish another. But this is exactly what Anheuser-Busch has tried to do with its Budweiser brand.

For the past decade, sales have been somewhat flat for Budweiser. To be sure, Budweiser is still the top-selling beer in the United States. However, worried executives were concerned that stagnant sales could be a portent of future problems. Every one in the beer industry is mindful that in the 1970s, Schlitz was the number two brand of beer in the United States. Part of Budweiser's problem can be traced to the increased popularity of imported and craft-brewed beers, such as Samuel Adams. Another part of the problem, however, could be traced to the brand's weakness in attracting young consumers, many of whom have been attracted to beer brands that have been in existence less than 10 years.

To counter this problem, Anheuser-Busch has employed a variety of youthful images, namely ants, frogs, and lizards. This campaign has freshened up what had previously been a fairly conservative image. The danger in this approach is that it can erode the substantial brand equity that built up in the Budweiser name over the years. Aware of this potential problem, the company launched its Budweiser heritage campaign. In this campaign, August Busch III, a descendant of the founder, talks about Budweiser's adherence to traditional standards, thus assuring confirmed Budweiser consumers that the brand is still the same. This two-tiered approach works for Budweiser because it has the financial muscle to run two separate campaigns essentially at the same time. In 1997, the company's estimated media expenditures were over $150 million for Budweiser and Bud Light.[53]

Not many companies can afford to run separate campaigns. McDonald's, however, in effect runs at least four major campaigns and likely several minor campaigns simultaneously. McDonald's, however, is not targeting the same audience. Instead, one agency handles their national campaign ("Did somebody say McDonald's?"), another agency develops the marketing communication program aimed at "kids and tweens," and separate agencies are used to advertise to the African American and Hispanic markets.

Cause-Related Marketing

Companies understand that in the new marketing environment, it is not enough to gain sales, a company also has to capture customers. Companies are now rethinking how they address consumers' needs and wants. They are shifting away from transaction-based marketing designed primarily to stimulate sales to relationship-based marketing designed to build the brand over the long haul. However, it's not enough to tell consumers that the company understands them. A company needs to prove it. Convincing skeptical consumers that the company understands them better than the other firms can be difficult. Today, consumers buy products for psychological as well as physical reasons. **Cause-related marketing** refers to the activities a company undertakes to support causes that are in the public's interest, such as AIDs awareness and research, environmental concerns, animal rights programs, homeless shelters, and diseases, such as sickle-cell anemia, cystic fibrosis, and muscular dystrophy.

In **transaction-based marketing,** the relationship between a seller and a buyer is of short duration. Once a sale takes place, the buyer and the seller may not connect again until the next buying opportunity presents itself. In the meantime, another company may win the attention if not the heart of the consumer. The idea behind relationship marketing is to let customers know that the company thinks consumers are important before, during, and after the sale. Cause-related marketing is a way for the company to demonstrate to skeptical consumers that the company shares some of the same core values as the customer.

An important dimension to a relationship-marketing program is the bond that ties together the seller and the buyer. The minorities profiled above tend to be strongly brand loyal. Perhaps because they are not part of the majority, they appreciate the recognition companies pay to their core values and interests. A company that sponsors or contributes money to a cause helps reaffirm to people that their values and interests are important. Tanqueray vodka raised more than $5.5 million to benefit AIDS research by sponsoring a California AIDS Ride (for bicyclists). On the retail level, they sponsored 180 AIDS awareness' nights at bars and restaurants throughout San Francisco and Los Angeles. The company also provided samples at both bars and fund-raising home parties melding business with corporate philanthropy.[54]

Ben & Jerry's Homemade Inc. contributes a percentage of all profits to help social and environmental concerns. The founders, Ben Cohen and Jerry Greenfield, espouse a corporate philosophy of "caring capitalism." Consumers generally like the quirky names the company gives to its flavors like Cherry Garcia and Rainforest Crunch. The company is perceived by consumers as different, both in the way it names its products and in its corporate philosophy. At least in part because of their cause-related marketing philosophy, consumers of the brand are said to be "extraordinarily brand loyal."[55]

Cause-related marketing does not produce positive results automatically. The Council on Foundations in Washington and Walker Research conducted a poll to learn how consumers value good corporate citizens. In their 1997 study, 90% of polled households couldn't link specific philanthropic efforts with specific companies. But 40% indicated that they would choose the "altruistic" company if two products were equal. This study suggests that a firm can improve its image by participating in cause-related activities that are in some way related to the company's image. Arizona, the iced tea and juice brand, played on its so-called western heritage to fund a campaign to save mustangs and burros (the company was founded in Brooklyn, NY). It offered consumers signed lithographs and museum-quality posters of "western impressionist" art. All proceeds were to go to the International Society for the Protection of Mustangs and Burros.[56]

Cause-related marketing works best when both the community and the company benefit. Calphalon, a maker of gourmet cookware, has aligned with the antihunger organization, Share Our Strength (SOS). Twice a year the company sells a cooking pan with the

SOS logo on the packaging, promising that the company will donate $5 for every pan sold. Sales of the pan with the special label were said to have increased tenfold over what they were without the special designation.[57]

Consumers can suspect the motives of a company's charitable activities, particularly if the recipient is a member of the fine arts. If the charity is not something an average consumer can identify with, he or she may feel that the top executives are merely supporting activities that they attend personally—selfish rather than altruistic motives. While conventional wisdom suggests that consumer skepticism can be reduced if a company's altruistic activities are related to what the company sells, a recent study published in the *Journal of Public Policy and Marketing* suggests it may not matter. Consumer responses to a cause-related marketing campaign were found to be more strongly affected by the amount of money or the help they expect the cause to receive than by the motives attributed to the firm for participating.[58]

Target Stores has a policy of giving back to the community and contributes 5% of its federal pretax profit to charitable programs. Target, through all its charitable endeavors, hopes to raise several million dollars.[59] Along similar lines, Tom's of Maine, a company specializing in all-natural products, contributes 10% of all profits to charity. Both companies are said to enjoy strong brand loyalty to their products.

Green Marketing

Green marketing is a variation of cause-related marketing. It refers to the activities a company takes to protect and enhance the environment and make this information known to the public. Increasingly, companies are aware of the public's concern about environmental problems. A 1995 Gallup poll reported that 75% of Americans consider themselves to be environmentalists.[60] Companies' activities can range from producing toxic-waste-free products to recycling waste material and using recycled materials. Companies understand that they have a social responsibility to be good corporate citizens, but they also know that it can be good for business. However, when a company makes green claims it needs to be cautious because there is considerable consumer skepticism about environmental claims. Consumers are generally confused over what claims really mean. The Federal Trade Commission, for its part, has tried to reduce confusion by issuing guidelines to prevent the misleading use of environmental terms in both advertising and packaging.[61] One expert advises that it is not enough to talk green, a company must *be* green. If the company doesn't have a solid record of environmental accomplishments, consumers will be skeptical at best or resentful at worst.[62]

Cross Promotions

Increasingly, companies are teaming up with each other to get more mileage out of their promotional campaigns. Cross promotion is a strategy whereby marketing partners share the cost of a promotion that meets mutual needs.[63] These cooperative arrangements can be fairly simple, such as when Oscar Mayer hot dogs and French's mustard are included in the same ad. This arrangement makes sense since the demand for each product is somewhat derived from the use of the other. The brand equity in each brand can help leverage the demand for both products, and the cost of the advertising is shared—it can be shared equally, or can vary depending on how much focus is on each product.

Arrangements can be informal and consist of no more than a brand like Nabisco advertising that its cookies contain Hershey chocolate chips. Or the partnership can be more complex, such as the 10-year deal McDonald's and Disney have formed whereby each company agrees to promote the other company's products. Basically, McDonald's agrees to spend millions of dollars promoting Disney movies and, in return, McDonald's gets to use Disney movie characters, such as Mulan and Flubber, to attract consumers to stores where they can buy toy replicas. Disney will also promote McDonald's at its Epcot Center theme park.[64] There are several different forms of cross promotions, including co-branding, co-marketing, and coalition marketing. There are at least two benefits common to each of these substrategies.

First, there is a potential synergistic effect whereby each brand gains some increment of value in associating with the other. If this does not occur, then the partnership is destined to fail. Many credit card companies have teamed up with national advertisers to jointly offer a credit card. However, some companies, like Ford, have learned that consumers do not always have pleasant thoughts about their credit cards. As a result, Ford dropped its association with Citibank, concerned that those negative feelings might rub off on their products

The second benefit from cross promotions occurs through the potential for increasing the number of brand contacts by being included in another brand's marketing communication. Sun Maid is featured on the boxes of all Post Raisin Bran cereal thus giving it far more exposure than it could get on its own promotional budget. The Taco Bell logo appears on the package of Doritos tortilla chips. Both Doritos and Taco Bell are divisions of Pepsico.

Co-branding. This type of strategy exists when two or more companies closely link their brand names together for a single product.[65] This approach has been very popular in the credit card field as numerous companies, such as State Farm, Met Life, Hartford, General Motors, Ford, and True Value Hardware Stores have all sought to extend their equity by combining forces with a financial institution. There are also several types of co-branding, including **ingredient branding** as with a microprocessor (such as Intel) included in a personal computer (such as Compaq). There's also **cooperative branding** where two brands receive equal promotion borrowing on each other's equity, such as with credit card partners American Airlines and Citibank or American Express and Sheraton Hotels. A third type of co-branding is called **complementary branding** where products are advertised together to suggest joint usage, such as when Seagram's whiskey is paired up with a mixer like 7-Up.[66] Part of the value of co-branding is that it gives a company an opportunity to move into a new area to sell its products. When Fannie May Candies paired up with Hallmark Stores and placed the Hallmark's Gold Crown Logo on its Celebrated Collection chocolates, part of the benefit was that, it gained entry into over 1,000 Hallmark stores.

Co-marketing. This strategy involves a partnership between two or more companies to jointly market each other's products.[67] The emphasis with this strategy is on marketing. Brands such as Frito Lay and Pepsi-Cola can combine promotions and together approach a retail chain, such as Wal-Mart to secure in-store deals on pricing, end-aisle displays, and chainwide ads.[68] As big as each brand is, the combined marketing muscle of both is considerably larger.

Manufacturers often contact retailers with suggested promotions built around a theme. For example, Procter & Gamble might develop a special spring cleaning promotion for retailers like Wal-Mart centered on the use of its cleaning products. Procter & Gamble provides marketing expertise and the retailer furnishes in-store resources in the form of personnel, additional space, and promotional funds.[69]

Coalition Marketing. This strategy resembles but differs from the frequent-flyer programs offered by many airlines. In coalition marketing, a third party coordinates the awards that consumers earn by trading at a wide variety of places including airlines, hotels, rental companies, and even purveyors of packaged goods. A company such as Loyalty Management Group's Air Miles allows members to redeem their points for many of the same kind of purchases for which they received points. This includes airlines such as United, American, and Northwest; and companies such as Hertz, Hyatt, Citibank, and Lenscrafters. The idea behind this approach is that it gives consumers flexibility where and when they make their selection. Businesses can benefit because much of the administrative arrangements are handled by a third party. However, much of the success of these programs depends on participating businesses to keep restrictions to a minimum.

Special Media Strategies

All of the following strategies fall into the category of what might be called non-traditional media. While we have relegated these strategies to a place in the book following other marketing communication tools, we recognize that in the twenty-first century many of these strategies will occupy a position of importance comparable to the "major" media.

Advertising and the Internet

The Internet is no longer simply an option in a company's communication strategy. It is an essential element. The Internet, and especially the World Wide Web, is relatively new to consumers. Millions of consumers are now regularly logging in online. They are still, however, in the process of forming what they want to do when they get there. Like someone moving to a new city, consumers will be reevaluating with whom they will do business.

In 1997, advertising expenditures on the Internet nearly reached $1 billion, a sevenfold increase in less than two years. By the end of 1998, Internet advertising had more than doubled and was projected to reach $2 billion.[70] By the year 2000, advertising expenditures are expected to top $4 billion.[71] Companies that ignore the Internet, or ones that wait to see how it develops, run the risk of giving rival firms an advantage that they might not overcome. Barnes & Noble, refers to itself as the world's largest bookseller, yet its market value is considerably below that of Amazon.com, a company that only sells books online. Amazon.com saw an opportunity early and moved fast, Barnes & Noble waited and now is struggling to catch up; and they're still having problems with their Website.

In her book, *The Internet Strategy Handbook,* Mary Cronin suggests that it's not enough for companies to get involved with the Internet, they have to do it right. If it's not working for them, then they need to figure out what's missing. Planners need to link any Internet strategy to corporate and marketing goals. Selling, and even advertising on the Web can have a profound effect on the way the company does business. What they sell online can affect the way people do their jobs. Price sales, inventory control, customer service all need to be coordinated with the information going out on the Web.[72]

There are at least three ways in which the Internet can be of value to a company.

1. Internet as a Direct Marketing Tool. There is enormous potential to sell directly to consumers. But companies may not have much choice to sell this way if their competitors are already actively doing so. In many product categories, this is exactly what the competition is doing or will be doing in the near future. And there are advantages to getting there first, as Barnes & Noble discovered.

2. Internet as a Medium. Advertising expenditures on the Internet are still less than 1% of what businesses spend on advertising.[73] But it would be a mistake to think of the Internet as simply another medium. Consumers interact with this medium unlike other media. Moreover, the Internet of today will be profoundly different tomorrow.

3. Internet as a Tool for Various Communication Purposes. Companies can establish Websites to connect with consumers in a variety of ways. Websites can deepen a relationship between a company and the consumer on a one-to-one basis. The Website can also be a source of public relations-oriented information, it can provide electronic coupons, shopping opportunities, and/or simply entertainment.

Shopping Online. E-commerce has become a reality. Within a period of less than five years, shopping online has grown from next to nothing in sales to where Forrester Research projects that it will reach $17 billion by 2001. Dell Computers sells $5 million per day, an annual rate of $1.8 billion, from its Website.[74] Stock market investors were so bullish on Amazon.com, the online bookseller, that at one point, they bid up the market value of the company to $29.2 billion. In contrast, Sears Roebuck has been in business over a century and is only worth $16.5 billion. What makes Amazon.com's story so remarkable is that the company has never made a profit in a single year. Clearly, investors see great potential. What they see is that consumers want to shop online.[75] However, in early 1999, a dose of reality hit the stock market and the market value of the company dropped dramatically to $14 billion—still impressive for a company that has only been in business since 1985.

In late 1998, Levi Strauss & Co. finally got around to selling online after resisting the opportunity for more than three years. The company had a Website as early as 1995. It was a hip site with lots of things to look at including graffiti "art." It had lots of interesting stuff except what consumers most wanted—a way to purchase jeans online. The company was wary about incurring resentment from its big retail customers, which generate nearly all of $7 billion in sales. However, the company has been steadily losing market share since 1990 and competitors, such as Eddie Bauer and the Gap, that do sell online, were gaining share-of-market. In the end, the company may have felt it had no other choice.[76]

For companies that understand online shopping, the rewards seem considerable. The key to successful online marketing is to understand why consumers shop and what they are looking for when they get online. Gary Hamel, chairman of Strategos, an international firm specializing in strategy, believes online shoppers want freedom, choice, and control. Shopping online lets consumers avoid pesky salespeople and allows them to shop at their own pace. They buy what they want, when they want, without any distracting interruptions from salespeople anxious to earn a commission.[77]

Online marketers are likely to find the competition in cyberspace even more competitive than at the local mall. Companies have to provide real value to customers. Online shoppers generally want what all shoppers want, but their priorities may differ. The following points are worth considering in evaluating what consumers want when they shop online:

- **Convenience**—The hectic lives of many consumers make it difficult to find the time to travel to stores. This is undoubtedly the reason why catalog sales are so popular.

Companies need to reinforce the convenience of shopping online by making sure consumers have easy access to whatever information they desire.

- **Variety**—It is difficult for many stores to stock the many sizes wanted by consumers. With an online operation there are economies in distribution and a company should be able to stock unusual sizes.

- **Information**—For a variety of reasons, consumers sometimes do not get the information they need. Consumers may be in a hurry, or the salespeople aren't knowledgeable. Consumers also simply may not feel they can trust the salespeople to tell them what they want to know. Fully 16% of car buyers shop online for information before they go to a dealership. They learn about a car's options, but mostly they find out information about dealer costs.[78]

- **Service**—Consumers do want service, but they want it on their terms—they want to be in control. Without adequate arrangements to service inquiries, an operation can get into trouble quickly. Charles Schwab is the No.1 Internet brokerage firm. Its share of the daily trading of stocks and bonds is roughly equal to the next three online competitors combined. Schwab's online commissions are considerably higher than other discount brokers like E*Trade and Ameritrade. What Schwab offers its customers, according to co-CEO David Pottruck, "is the ability to deliver personalized information to the customer in real time, at virtually no cost."[79] Schwab, the discount broker, may compete on the basis of price, but service is the key to its success.

- **Price**—Yes, consumers want low prices, but it may not be the overriding factor in influencing buyer behavior. Even if it were, companies need to be as wary of competing on the basis of price online as they do off line. Unless companies provide additional value to consumers, their attraction to consumers can be tenuous at best.

- **Security**—Consumers don't quite trust giving credit card information online. They are nervous about credit card fraud. Even though consumers would lose no more than $50 under the terms of their card, they still feel uneasy. The best thing a company can do is to invest in the hardware and software to provide secure socket communication to ensure that all credit transactions are secure. The next thing is to educate consumers about its value. In the meantime, company's can provide an 800 number for those people who are still concerned about security.

Companies also need to understand there are risks involved when selling online. If the company isn't offering consumers real value, it's much easier for consumers to comparison shop. But there are also risks in *not* selling online. Consumers are increasingly aware that they do not have to accept high-priced inferior quality merchandise simply because there aren't any nearby alternatives. Today, consumers can shop all over the world in minutes.

Advertising on the Internet

With all of the hype associated with the Internet, advertisers are bound to become disappointed with lackluster results. The information highway is not paved with gold. Companies cannot simply transfer their experience with traditional media to advertising on the Internet. There are profound differences both in the way consumers are exposed to the media and in the Internet's potential to involve the consumer in a selling message.

On the World Wide Web, there are over 1,300 sites that sell ads, everything from banner ads, interstitials, popups, and site sponsorships. It's estimated that 80% of the inventory is unsold. Despite the steady increase in advertising on the Web, there is the nagging feeling that it does not work very well. Part of the problem is due to the increasing plethora of ads on the Net. Clutter now unofficially exists on the Web in much the same way it exists elsewhere. According to Net Ratings, an Internet measurement company, fewer than 1% of all ads get a follow-up log-on click for more information. In the last six months of 1998, the rate fell from 1.4% in May to less than .5% by the end of the year.[80] Let's look at some of the more popular types of advertising on the Web and evaluate why they may or may not work:

Banner Ads. By far the most popular ads on the Web, these are strip ads placed within or near the edge of pages on advertising-supported sites. Banners can be nonenhanced or enhanced. With nonenhanced banners, when the user clicks on a banner, another screen appears. With enhanced banners, all of the information appears on the banner and the user never leaves it. Enhanced banners promote consumer involvement by allowing them to type in information. On some sites they can e-mail a friend.

First generation banners were static—nothing moved. Today's banners can be animated with GIFs to increase the likelihood of attracting the consumer's attention. Most of these ads are fairly easy to construct and are relatively inexpensive. There is also some question regarding their effectiveness.

Interstitials. These are flashes of images or information that appear between the pages of a site and within a site. Usually, they are the first images to appear as a page loads. For example, if you are at the Yahoo site and click on Business and the Economy you might get an interstitial near the top of the page promoting Visa's e card. If you then click on the interstitial, you wind up at a Visa site informing you how you can sign up for this special platinum credit card. Although conventional wisdom suggests these ads can be irritating, an industry-sponsored study found that only 15% of respondents found the ads to be "irritating" compared to 11% for split-screen ads, and 9% for banner ads.

Pop-Up Windows. These ads are separate windows, which appear at the top of a page while it loads. The idea behind a pop-up is that they don't get in the way of the content on the page. Double exposure pop-ups are another kind of pop-up that reappear after 5 seconds. The disadvantage to an advertiser is that site visitors can close the pop-up—which they often do. The disadvantage of pop-ups and double exposure pop-ups is that they can be irritating to have to close if you don't want to see or use it.

Split-Screen. These ads appear on a portion of a site's page. The advantage and disadvantage are related to the same point. A split-screen ad takes up space that would otherwise go to content. According to one study, split-screen ads achieve recall rates of 71% compared to 51% for banner ads.[81]

Content or Site Sponsorships. This arrangement exists usually when an advertiser is identified as the sponsor of some content on a site. For example, Kraft's Maxwell House sponsors an online "coffee break" that utilizes the *New York Times*' crossword puzzles and book reviews.[82] This approach has the advantage of taking on the credibility of the site.

Detractors say it blurs the lines between advertising and editorial matter, something they find undesirable.

The Future of Advertising on the Internet

It is difficult to predict what advertising will be like even in the near future. What is clear is that it will be different. Already the industry and the federal government are planning the next generation Internet. The basic change involves switching language formats from Hyper Text Transfer Language (HTML) to Standard General Markup Language (SGML). The resulting switch should make it easier to manipulate and share documents across the Web. Along with this development should come the widespread availability of greater bandwidth via either television cables or phone lines. This increased bandwidth should allow access across the Web to be up to 100 times faster than the standard 28.5 dial-up modem, and faster than even the new 56 k modems. In addition, new technological breakthroughs promise to deliver even more technical surprises.

In the future, the distinction between a television set and a computer screen will get somewhat blurred. At some point in the future, the images on the respective screens will begin to resemble each other. Although cable providers are now offering an Internet connection service, until television goes interactive universally, there will remain some profound differences. Unless, of course, you happen to be one of 10,000 people who sign up to receive a fully loaded Compaq computer with guaranteed access to the Internet—all free. In 1999, a new company, Free-PC, is planning to make this offer. The catch is that you have to fill out a form and include your social security number, the number of kids in your house, your exact street address as well as other information. The computer will come with an "unturnoffable" strip down the right-hand side which will continually show advertising. The company hopes to cover its costs and make a profit selling advertising.[83]

Early promoters of Internet advertising talked about the ability of the Internet to deliver thousands of eyes. But people who use the Internet are not passive viewers and will actively tune out content that does not interest them. Unlike television, where you must sit through a commercial (unless you use a remote to switch channels), on the Internet consumers can control exposure by clicking past an ad—especially as more bandwidth delivers faster speeds.

What is also clear is that, in the future, advertising on the Internet will be every bit as important to an advertiser as television. However, the distinction between television and the Internet will not be that clear to the typical consumer, especially as television too becomes an interactive medium on a widespread basis. This scenario is still off in the future, but the future may not be as distant as most people believe. Part of the motivation for advertising on the Internet is to get in on the "ground floor" so that when the medium really takes off a company isn't left behind.

The key to advertising effectiveness on the Internet is to involve consumers so that they interact with the advertising. The best way to do that is to offer consumers value, either in the form of entertainment, more information, or the opportunity to make a satisfying purchase.

Website Communication

A Website offers a company numerous opportunities to enhance its marketing communication program. Website communication combines the ability to drive awareness, develop interest, and move consumers to action, including getting people to buy products. Many companies understand what a Website can do, if only intuitively. An important key is to figure out how to do it better.

Websites must be even more consumer-centered than traditional media. To visit a site, Web surfers must go out of their way. To attract them, a site must be sufficiently entertaining and interesting. But interesting can be interpreted in different ways. A site can look interesting because of "cool" graphics or it can be interesting because consumers perceive they will receive something of value from the site. Companies that had sites in the early days of the Web had an advantage over a company that waited. Something is usually better than nothing. In the new marketing environment, having a Website is no longer distinctive, it is the norm. Therefore, companies must strive to construct superior sites for the same reasons they try to make better television commercials or new product innovations. The Web is another channel to deliver a company's message. But unlike most media advertising, the messages can be multiple, and are delivered in a low-keyed style over an extended length of time.

To understand how to build better sites, consider the basic building blocks of a Website. First, there is the Website's infrastructure. This refers to the wire or fiber optics that connect a site to the switchers and routers that connect the Web surfer to the site somewhere in cyberspace. Since companies all get their service from the same providers, such as MCI World Com, and Sprint, there isn't any point of differentiation here.

Second, sites consist of content. To provide information, the full range of marketing communication tools can be employed. In the advertising area, companies provide all kinds of promotional information in depth. Search virtually any automobile Website, and you'll find more information than you probably want to know. Companies also use their Websites to communicate their public relations efforts. Most sites have news releases to read and, if not, they are likely to describe in detail their community-oriented activities. If they are involved in cause-related marketing, you're also likely to read about that in their site. In the sales promotions' area, many companies give away free samples, provide coupons, and invite visitors to enter contests or sweepstakes. (If you haven't received a free sample of jelly beans from Mr. Jelly Belly, be sure to go to the site early in the morning because the company only gives away 500 samples a day, and they go fast.) In the direct marketing area, companies not only sell products, but numerous product paraphernalia as well, such as hats, tee-shirts, jackets, umbrellas, and tote bags all imprinted with the company or brand logo.

If the above sounds typical, that's because content is not really a point of differentiation for most sites. Sites have many of the same kind of problems that parity products face. It's not easy to differentiate themselves from the competition. Neither is spending large sums of money any more likely to produce effective sites than it is to produce strategic advertising that works. For most Websites, the critical task is to build a better site.

Context is the third building block of a Website. It is this element that offers the best opportunity to exploit.[84] Context refers to the environment or distinctive atmosphere that exists within a site. For example, if you enter some sites, say the Nike site, there are vivid colors and interesting graphics. It is as some might say, a cool site. Whether this is important or merely nice depends on how the site's context meets consumer expectations. Levi & Strauss had a "cool" site for three years before they conceded that what their visitors really wanted was to buy jeans. Can you have both? Perhaps, but there are trade-offs site builders need to consider. The more graphic details you put into a site, the longer it takes to load. The site planner needs to understand what consumers want and expect when they visit a site.

Understanding Website Visitors. Earlier in this book, we emphasized the importance of understanding how and why consumers buy certain products or brands. It is equally important to understand why someone might visit a Website. Are they curious? Do they want to be entertained or play games? Do they want information? Are they simply interested in making a transaction quickly and easily? For many, online shopping will never replace shopping in a mall or in a brick-and-mortar store because they enjoy the whole experience surrounding a shopping expedition—getting out, meeting and seeing new people, window shopping, trying things on,—all can add value to what a consumer actually buys.

Consider why Web surfers visit Yahoo, a popular search engine. It's not because the site is interesting. The dull gray background and minimal use of graphics does not make for a very interesting site. Web surfers who use Yahoo want information, they want it quickly, and then they want to leave. Site interest is not a priority. In this case, less can be more. In contrast, when you visit the Nike site the appearance of the site is visually stunning. Inside the site, there is a lot of information on training for various sports. It appears to be a site that people want to visit and stay a while. But the site can take a long time to load during times of heavy Web traffic, particularly if the visitor is accessing the site from a home computer with a relatively slow modem. But because visitors plan to stay awhile on the site, the wait is apparently acceptable. Visitors to the Charles Schwab discount broker site want information and the ability to execute trades quickly and easily. The investors who trade at the E* Trade and Ameritrade brokerages are there because they charge the lowest commission fees. These visitors expect less advice and are primarily interested in making trades quickly. Waits are unacceptable.

There are companies that specifically research Web consumers, such as Forrester Research and Jupiter Communications. SRI International, the company that produces the Values and Lifestyles typology is redoing a study they call iVALS which focuses on Internet users. Although some companies will get information from a syndicated research service, many of the techniques we discussed in Chapter 2 and Chapter 3 can easily be adapted to learn about the target audience's Web usage and their expectations.

Building the Brand and Websites

Along with many people in advertisers, we stress the importance of building the brand. A Website provides a company a unique opportunity to reinforce and expand upon the brand associations and other intangible qualities consumers attach to both the company and its brands. A Website can help build the brand because visitors are usually willing to spend time when visiting a site. Although visitors may be at a site merely out of curiosity, once they are there, a company has an opportunity to build a relationship between the visitor and the company and its brands. The key is to give the visitor value. But it has to be value on the consumer's terms, not the company's. The persuasive appeals that work on television have the luxury of at least a semicaptive audience. Site visitors will quickly click through the site unless interest is developed quickly. The Internet is a content-oriented medium driven by consumer interest.[85]

A Website is not just a marketing communications' medium, it is a *communications'* medium capable of delivering what consumers get from the media in general: news, entertainment, information, education, shopping opportunities, and more. A Website can provide the above delivered with a full multimedia experience: sight, sound, motion, and interactivity. Some of the media experiences, such as motion, are not as good as they can get elsewhere, but they will be tomorrow.

Using a Website to sell to consumers on the basis of convenience or price can move a lot of products, but the bigger opportunity is to get consumers to connect with the brand and deepen the relationship between the company and consumers. At the Robert Mondavi Winery Website, you cannot buy any wine. Mondavi wines sell in the premium, super premium, and ultra premium price categories. The Mondavi Winery has long been a producer of high-quality wines. The prime prospect for Mondavi wines has an above average income, and generally knows more about quality wine than the average consumer. The Website is filled with information on wine, gourmet recipes, and the winery. The winery is a tourist destination and visiting this site is designed to increase interest in the winery. Like many companies, Robert Mondavi participates in numerous charitable activities. Many of their cause-related activities involve contributions of special wines to raise funds for charitable organizations. To a wine aficionado, this information can be interesting because even if they do not attend these functions, they often imagine what it might be like to be a purchaser of special wines. There are no coupons, rebates, or sales offers on this site, and that helps reinforce the image that Mondavi wines are special.

It's no mystery that Websites offer great potential. By the year 2002, Website spending is estimated to reach $12.7 billion.[86] Three things will increasingly become apparent: First, companies that do not have a Website will be operating at a competitive disadvantage. Second, companies that do have sites will face increasing competition for a decreasing amount of time consumers can spend at their sites. And third, companies need to do a better job with their sites than they are now doing.

Nontraditional and Traditional Media Options*

When people think of advertising, they usually think of traditional media, such as newspapers, magazines, television, radio, billboards, yellow pages, and perhaps direct mail. As consumers grow numb (and eventually immune) to the ads that inundate them through traditional media channels, advertisers seek new formats to distribute their messages. Increasingly, marketers are looking for new, unexplored ways to reach their target audience. Sometimes it also makes sense to capitalize on existing nontraditional approaches that they may not have previously considered. Below is a list of media options that have found some acceptance as advertisers continue their never-ending search to reach elusive consumers.

Transit

car cards	ads on outside of public transportation
train/subway station posters	commuter station posters
clocks	air terminal posters
signage	framed displays

*These media options were obtained from a variety of sources including: George E. Belch and Michael Belch, *Introduction to advertising and promotion: An integrated marketing communications perspective* (Chicago: Richard D. Irwin, 1995). Donald W. Jugenheimer, Arnold M. Barban, and Peter B. Turk, *Advertising media: Strategy and tactics* (Dubuque, IA: William C. Brown,1992). Optimum Media, *Media 98: Upping the ante to stay in the game* (Chicago: DDB Needham, 1998).

In-Store Media
Point-of-Purchase

banners	racks
cash-register units	wall units
clocks	testers/sampling
counter units	window/door units
floor stands	on-product units
aisle displays	signs
overheads and mobiles	shelf units/extenders
pole displays	interactive units
electronic displays	shopping carts
bags	in-store television and radio

Sports and Theatrical Events

programs	stadium scoreboards
poster type ads	stadium signs
revolving banners	

Nontraditional Out of Home

audience segment "hangouts"	health clubs
truck stops	ski resorts
golf course signage	displays on military bases
college campuses	concert halls
painted walls	trucks/vans/cars
kiosks (malls, airports, outdoor)	station clocks
"metrovision" (TV color monitors in high traffic areas)	sailboats (sail canvas)
restroom advertising	shopping mall displays
bus shelter displays	bus stop benches
inside taxicabs	public telephones
skywriting	banner pulling
blimps	hot air balloons
freestanding inflatables	moving billboards
in-flight advertising (airlines)	

Directories

Yellow pages	universities
churches	professional associations

Display Advertisements
trademark headings

Electronic Advertising

online/Internet	pop-up windows
video graphics	banners
interstitials	newspapers/magazines

Motion Picture Advertising

product placement videocassette
"Channel One"

Miscellaneous

audiotext	videotext
guest placement	game show sponsorship
hotel movie channel preview	infomercials
Fax services	CD-ROM

Specialty Advertising

calendars	business gifts
writing instruments	desk accessories
wearable items	trade shows
airline ticket envelopes	

Imprinted Specialties

money clips	thermometers
golf ball markers/tees	drinking glasses
calculator cases	tape measures
clocks	balloons
flashlights	stadium seats
cork removers	tote bags
paper hand fans	beverage coasters
key rings	mug insulators
bumper stickers	card cases
shoehorns	bookends
pocket planners	maps/travel guides
nail files	coffee mugs
tire gauges	shoelaces
vinyl cushions	trash bags
eyewear retainers	auto sun protectors
candle holders	luggage tags
knives (pocket)	calculators
magnets	trivets
matchbooks	ashtrays
buttons	rulers
notepads	coin holders
litter bags	letter openers
mousepads	combs
ice scrapers	hats

Major Media

Newspapers

dailies	weeklies
Sunday	tabloids

audience targeted sections
(businesspeople, Hispanics)

special sections (Sunday supplement)

preprinted inserts

free standing inserts (FSIs)

controlled circulation ("shoppers")

Magazines

consumer (geographical breakouts)

consumer (demographic breakouts)

business

farm

"Fan zines"

ethnic

women's

men's

Television

network

national cable

syndication

national spot

local spot

non-network cable

ethnic cable

special features

event advertising

infomercials

public service announcements (sponsored)

educational

political campaign

election specials

Radio

spot

network

national

regional

state

program

flash sponsorship

news announcement sponsorship

time segment

feature sponsorship

Direct Mail

sales letters

leaflets

booklets

brochures

folders

circulars

flyers

postcards

catalogs

wraparounds

Outdoor

billboards

poster panels

storefronts

signs

displays

spectaculars

marquees

shelter advertising

wall paintings

mosaics

blimps

park bench backs

lightpost flyers

airplane trailers

Telemarketing

The most important other media strategy is not in this paragraph, but in the readers' imaginations. In a dynamic and competitive media environment, it's hard to stay ahead of the competition. It takes imagination, but it also takes initiative and courage to do something unique. As examples, we'll examine two strategies that have been used occasionally: ambush marketing and fresh TV.

Ambush Marketing. Ambush marketing is a promotional strategy aimed at creating the false impression that a company is an official sponsor of an event when it is not. The best examples occur around major events such as the Olympics. The worldwide sponsorship market has grown from $2 billion in 1984 to $16.57 billion in 1996.[87] Event managers offer varying degrees of corporate sponsorship. Companies sign on for the prestige of associating the brand with the event. There are numerous ways to give what many people call a misleading impression. One way is to buy commercial time on the broadcast rather than pay the event committee a sponsorship fee. One celebrated example involving Fuji Film and its chief competitor, Eastman Kodak, occurred in the 1984 Olympic games. Fuji was a worldwide sponsor of the Olympics. Kodak was not an Olympics sponsor, but instead became a heavy sponsor of the ABC broadcasts at a price considerably less than what Fuji was paying. Fuji resented Kodak's perfectly legal strategy. In 1988, Fuji countered Kodak's official

Campaign Progress Checklist

At this point in the campaign you should be generally aware of the following points:

1. The extra things that companies do to enhance their campaigns are increasingly likely to be essential in the new marketing environment.

2. Companies can no longer ignore global markets. To compete overseas, companies need to tailor their campaigns to local markets, being sensitive to language and culture differences.

3. Specialized markets such as the African American, Hispanic, Asian American, and gay/lesbian respond favorably to targeted appeals. However, companies need to understand how these markets differ from mainstream markets in terms of values, consumption habits, and the way these markets respond to promotions.

4. Occasionally, it can make sense to use more than one message strategy in the same campaign. This, however, should be an exception rather than the rule.

5. Companies that are involved in charitable and other altruistic activities often find that communicating their efforts to the public in a sensitive and appropriate way makes good business sense.

6. Cross promotions are an effective way to leverage the equity in another brand and synergistically improve the image and the sales of all parties involved.

7. The Internet is no longer an optional element in a company's communication program. Involvement is essential.

8. Although online shopping seems to offer a company the quickest return, it is likely that advertising will begin to catch up and eventually pass e-commerce in importance.

9. Website communication is an excellent tool to deepen the relationship between a company and the consumer on a one-to-one basis.

10. Creative media planning often consists of using nontraditional media options, but can also include many of the special options associated with traditional media that have been underutilized.

sponsorship with a minor sponsorship of the U.S. swim team. Fuji aggressively promoted the connection giving the impression it was an Olympic sponsor, which it no longer was.[88]

In the 1996 Olympics held in Atlanta, Visa paid $40 million to be an exclusive sponsor in the credit card category. Yet, when a survey conducted a month after the Olympics asked consumers to name official sponsors of the Olympic games, 72% named Visa, but 54% also named American Express, which was not a sponsor. Significantly, American Express was referred to as an "ambush marketer."[89]

Depending on one's perspective, ambush marketing can be referred to as "parasitic" marketing, "stealth" advertising, "guerrilla" marketing, or simply clever marketing. Our point in discussing this strategy is to use it as an example of a creative approach to getting a message across not to pass judgment on whether or not it is ethical.

Fresh TV. This strategy is an example of how the creative use of media can enhance a message. Fresh TV is really more of a technique than a strategy. It refers to producing and airing a commercial within a matter of a few days, if not hours. As an example, the day after the Super Bowl, viewers often see the game's top performer's promoting some product or their impending trip to DisneyWorld.

In actuality, the term "Fresh TV" dates back at least to 1992. To illustrate that Chevy's Mexican Restaurants was dedicated to serving fresh food, the advertising agency Goodby, Berlin and Silverstein filmed a series of commercials very early in the morning and aired them later that night. The spots utilized a man-in-the-street interview format to help establish credibility. In one spot, the day's newspaper was shown to prove the spot had been shot that day. As a result of its innovative approach, the company got significant publicity in the media and sales were said to have increased significantly. The timing of the commercials helped reinforce the company's "fresh" positioning in consumer's minds.[90]

Notes and References

[1]U.S. Bureau of the Census. (1997). Gross domestic product by country: 1980–1996. *Statistical Abstract of the United States* (117th edition). Washington, DC, p. 839.

[2]Excerpted from Louisa Ha. (1999, January 28). Home page. Classical examples of international advertising mistakes," from *American Demographics.* International Advertising Resource Center (http://www.getbiz.com/~louisaha/home.htm)

[3]Author. (1998, June). Nokia hastily pulls ad using Nazi slogan. *Advertising Age International,* p. 5.

[4]Dru, J-M. (1996). *Disruption: Overturning conventions and shaking up the marketplace.* New York: John Wiley & Sons, p. 3.

[5]Ohmae, K. (1982). *The mind of the strategist: The art of Japanese business.* New York: McGraw-Hill, p. 3.

[6]Costa, J. A., & Bamossy, G. J. (Eds.). (1995). *Marketing in a multicultural world: Ethnicity, nationalism, and cultural identity.* Thousand Oaks, California: Sage Publications, p. 32.

[7]U.S. Bureau of the Census. *Resident population of the United States: Estimates by sex, race, and Hispanic origin, with median age* (1998); and U.S. Bureau of the Census. *Money income in the United States: 1997.*

[8]Fisher, C. (1996, September). Black, hip, and primed (to shop). *American Demographics,* p. 53.

[9]Keller, K. L. (1998). *Strategic brand management: Building, measuring, and managing brand equity.* Upper Saddle River, NJ: Prentice-Hall, Inc., p. 585.

[10]Rossman, M. L. (1994). *Multicultural marketing: Selling to a diverse America.* New York: AMACOM, pp. 142–143.

[11]Jewler, A. J., & Drewniany, B. L. (1998). *Creative strategy in advertising* (6th ed.). Belmont, CA: Wadsworth Publishing, p. 48.

[12]Ibid.

[13]Rossman, p. 126.

[14]Fisher, pp. 53–55.
[15]Rossman, pp. 129–130.
[16]Fisher, p. 56.
[17]Neff, Jack. (1998, February 16). Diversity. *Advertising Age*, p. s1.
[18]Davids, Meryl. (1998, June 1). Spanish steps. *Adweek*, p. 24.
[19]U.S. Bureau of the Census, *Resident population*, and *Money income*.
[20]Livingston, Stuart. (1992, March/April). Marketing to the Hispanic-American community. *Journal of Business Strategy*, p. 54.
[21]Kara, A., & Kara, N. R. (1996, Spring). Ethnicity and consumer choice: A study of Hispanic decision processes across different acculturation levels. *Journal of Applied Business Research, 12,* pp. 22–35.
[22]Author. (1992, December 23). No habla espanõl. *Forbes*, p. 140.
[23]Rossman, pp. 46–47.
[24]Livingston, p. 55.
[25]Rossman, p. 48.
[26]Rossman, pp. 48–55.
[27]Livingston, p. 57.
[28]Rossman, p. 52.
[29]Van Hoof, K. (1994, July 18). Surveys point to group differences (ethnic differences). *Brandweek, 35,* p. 32.
[30]Livingston, pp. 56–57.
[31]Ibid., p. 55.
[32]White, D. When slogans go wrong. *American Demographics,14*, p. 14.
[33]Gitlin, S. (1998, January 5). Cars: Dealing with Asians. *Brandweek*, pp. 15–16.
[34]Rossman, pp. 86–87.
[35]U.S. Bureau of the Census. *Resident population and money income.*
[36]Fan, J. X. (1997, June). Expenditure patterns of Asian Americans: Evidence from the U.S. consmer expenditure survey, 1980–1992. *Family and Consumer Sciences Research Journal*, 25, p. 341.
[37]Ibid., pp. 359–361.
[38]Crispell, D. (1993, August). Materialism among minorities. *American Demographics,15*, p. 15.
[39]Burton, J. (1993, January 21). *Advertising: Targeting Asians. Far Eastern Economic Review, 156*, p. 41.
[40]Ibid., pp. 42–43.
[41]Gitlin, p. 16.
[42]Seitz, V. (1998, Winter). Acculturation and direct purchasing behavior among ethnic groups in the U.S.: Implications for business practitioners. *Journal of Consumer Marketing*, 15, p. 27.
[43]Burton, p. 43.
[44]Delozier, M. W., & Rodriquez, J. (1996). Marketing to the homosexual (gay) market: A profile and strategy implication. In Daniel L. Wardrop (Ed.), *Gays, lesbians, and consumer behavior: Theory, practice, and research issues in marketing.* New York: Haworth Press, pp. 203–204.
[45]Delozier & Rodriguez, pp. 203–204; and L. Penaloza, "We're here, we're queer and we're going shopping!: A critical perspective on the accommodation of gays and lesbians in the U.S. marketplace. In *Gays, lesbians, and consumer behavior*, p. 25.
[46]Delozier & Rodriguez, p. 205.
[47]See B. Johnson, The gay quandary: Advertising's most elusive, yet lucrative target market proved difficult to measure, *Advertising Age, 64* (January 18, 1993), pp. 29, 35; P. Schwartz, Gay consumers come out spending, *American Demographics, 14* (1992), pp. 10–11; G. Levin, Mainstream's domino effect: Liquor, fragrance, clothing, advertising ease into gay magazines, *Advertising Age, 64* (January 18, 1993), pp. 30, 32; and C. Miller, Gays are affluent but often overlooked market, *Marketing News, 24* (December 24, 1990), p. 2.
[48]Nancy A. Rudd, Appearance and self-presentation research in gay consumer cultures: Issues and impact. In *Gays, lesbians, and consumer behavior*, pp. 111-112, and C. Miller, Two new firms market exclusively to gays, *Marketing News, 26* (July 10, 1992), p. 8.
[49]Kates, S. M. (1998*). Twenty million new consumers!: Understanding gay men's consumer behavior.* New York: Harrington Park Press, p. 125.

[50]Baker, Daniel B., O'Brien, S. et al. (1995). *Cracking the corporate closet*. New York: Harper Business.

[51]Delozier & Rodriguez, p. 210; and Penaloza, p. 27

[52]Penaloza, p. 27.

[53]Khermouch, G. (1998, June 15). Pockets of success tempered by concern. *Brandweek/Superbrands*, p. s28.

[54]Author. (1996, February 20). Sports & event marketing awards: Gold winners. *Brandweek*, p. 44.

[55]Author. (1992, July 15). Life's just a bowl of cherry garcia for Ben & Jerry's. *Wall Street Journal*, p. B2.

[56]Khermouch, G. (1996, October 21). Arizona gets on high horse with first cause-marketing program. *Brandweek*, p. 16.

[57]Lodge, S. (1982, June). Is cause-related marketing worth it? *Sales and Marketing Management*, p. 72.

[58]Webb, D. J., & Mohr, L. A. (1998, Fall). A typology of consumer responses to cause-related marketing from skeptics to socially concerned. *Journal of Public Policy and Marketing*, p. 234.

[59]Heller, L. (1998, April 6). Cause still prominent in marketing mission. *Discount Store News*, p. 85.

[60]Mackoy, R. D., Calantone, R., & Droge, C. (1995). Environmental marketing: Bridging the divide between consumption culture and environmentalism. In M. J. Polonsky & A. T. Wimsatt (Eds.), *Environmental marketing*. Binghampton, NY: Haworth Press (pp. 37–54).

[61]Author. (1992, July 28). *FTC News*. Washington, DC: Federal Trade Commission.

[62]Ottman, J. A. (1998, October 26). Back up green program with corporate credibility. *Marketing News Chicago*, p. 9.

[63]Adapted from Louis E. Boone & David L. Kurtz, *Contemporary marketing*. Fort Worth: Dryden Press, 1999, p. 633.

[64]Kramer, L. (1998, May 11). McD's Disney: Year-old pact is a happy deal. *Advertising Age*, p. 24.

[65]Boone & Kurtz, p. 351.

[66]Thompson, Stephanie, "Co-Branding," *Brandweek*, February 23, 1998, p. 26.

[67]Boone & Kurtz, p. 351.

[68]Benezra, K (1998, June 1). Pepsi's supermarket squeeze. *Brandweek*, pp. 1, 6.

[69]Burnett, J., & Moriarity, S. (1998). *Introduction to marketing communications*. Upper Saddle River, NJ: Prentice-Hall, p. 325.

[70]Maddox, K. (1998, November 2). IAB: Ad revenue online projected to hit $bil in '98. *Advertising Age*, p. 38.

[71]Maddox, K (1998, April 6). Internet ad sales approach $1 billion. *Advertising Age*, p. 32.

[72]Excerpted from Mary Cronin (Interview), Getting your company's Internet strategy right. *Fortune* (March 18, 1996), pp. 72–78.

[73]Kroll, L., Pitta, J., & Lyons, D. (1998, December 28). World weary web. *Forbes*, p. 28.

[74]Maddox, K. (1998, October). E-commerce becoming reality. *Advertising Age*, p. s12.

[75]Smith, E. B. (1999, January 12). They're going to the moon now, but are they worth it. *USA Today*, p. 1B.

[76]Kroll, L. (1998, December 28). Digital denim. *Forbes*, p. 102.

[77]Hamel, G. (1998, December 7). The E-Corporation. *Fortune*, p. 82.

[78]Ibid.

[79]Schonfeld, E. (1998, December 7). Schwab puts it all online. *Fortune*, pp. 92–100.

[80]Kroll, Pita, & Lyons, pp. 98–100.

[81]Innerfield, A. (1998, February 2). Building a better ad. *Advertising Age* (Supplement), pp. 30a–32a.

[82]Cleland, K. (1996, November 4). Web narrows gab between ads and editorial. *Advertising Age*, pp. 3, 6.

[83]Kirkpatrick, D. (1999, March 1). The $0.00 PC. *Fortune*, p. 36.

[84]Gehman, J. (1999, February 1). E-Commerce: Size doesn't matter, context is everything, *Marketing News*, p. 2.

[85]Uppgren, J. (1996, February). Time for next stage in the Internet pageant. *Brandweek*, p. 16.

[86]Author. (1998, November). Small businesses to spend $4B on websites. *Direct Marketing*, p. 1.

[87]Meenaghan, T. (1998, July). Ambush marketing: Examining the perspectives. *Psychology and Marketing, 15:4*, p. 301.

[88]Meenaghan, T. (1998, July). Ambush marketing: Corporate strategy and consumer reaction. *Psychology and Marketing, 15:4*, p. 311.

[89]Shani, D., & Sandler, D. (1999, January 18). Counter attack: Heading off ambush marketers. *Marketing News*, p. 10.

[90]B. Carlino, Creative marketing fuels customer recognition, *Nations Restaurant News* (1992, October 12) p. 52; and Gold, fast food & family restaurants: Chevys, *Brandweek* (1992, June 15), p. S 12.

Chapter 10

Evaluating the Effectiveness of the Campaign*

Searching for a good way to measure the effectiveness of advertising is like searching for the Holy Grail—it goes on and on and on—for two basic reasons. First, the evaluation of advertising is often a critical factor in marketing success. A slight change in an advertising campaign brought about through some form of evaluation can lead to significant increases in sales and profits. In an aggressively competitive market, an insightful evaluation can provide a company with an edge over its rivals. When other types of marketing communications' tools (such as sales promotions and public relations) are included in the promotional mix, it further underscores the importance of a good measure of effectiveness.

Evaluation also gives businesses some means of control over the tremendous sums of money spent on marketing communications. Increasingly, many companies, including RJR Nabisco, Campbell Soup Company, Hershey Foods, and Nestlé Enterprises, tie their advertising agency compensation to performance evaluations.[1] Thorough and accurate evaluations not only enhance the success of the marketing communications' program, they also strengthen the morale of the internal and external people working on the campaign.

Second, the search continues because it remains difficult to isolate the effects of a marketing communications' campaign on sales. The measurement task is not impossible, but the large number of controllable and uncontrollable factors can turn even a simple

---

*This chapter has been developed and written in part by Michael P. Kalasunas, senior vice-president and director of Planning at J. Walter Thompson in Chicago. Mike has been at JWT for more than 20 years and directs all advertising research for the agency. Increasingly, he spends a good measure of his time on strategic planning.

market test into a meaningless exercise producing useless data. A simple market test can easily become complicated. In the pizza delivery business, companies often use a direct-mail firm like Advo Inc., the largest direct mail services company in the United States, to deliver coupons to households in their market areas.

Normally, the effects are fairly easy to measure. Sales typically rise dramatically the day coupons are delivered, and continue to be high for the remainder of the week. If it rains, sales spike upward even higher. But if the competition is also running coupons the same day—a common situation—it is nearly impossible to determine the effect of each variable on sales. The situation is complicated even further if you consider that there are variations in the intensity of rain and differences in the degree to which a rival company is a direct competitor of the product being evaluated. Traditional researchers might describe this situation as confounding the effects of the variable you are interested in (that is, direct-mail-delivered coupons) with extraneous variables (i.e., rain and competitive promotions) so that their effect on the variable you are measuring is all mixed up. A typical manager is likely to ponder these questions and simply conclude that measuring these relationships is scarcely better than using personal judgment.

EVALUATION AS A STRATEGIC CONCERN

Managers, of course, realize that evaluation is vital to all aspects of the campaign. In today's intensely competitive marketplace, enlightened management understands that the older style of marketing practices that were often based on experience and even hunches are not likely to be as effective in the future as they were in the past. As Phillip Kotler of Northwestern University observed, "Companies find themselves competing in a race where the road signs and rules keep changing, where there is no finish line, no permanent 'win.'"[2] Smart companies integrate evaluative procedures into all areas of their decision-making, including marketing communications. These procedures are often part of a system rather than project- or task-oriented.

Evaluation has been an important part of each chapter in this book. Chapters 2 and 3 examined many of the tests, techniques, procedures, and sources of information that are part of the research used to develop the strategic foundation of the campaign. This aspect of research is sometimes referred to as **developmental research**. Chapters 4 through 8 integrated the concept of evaluation as part of the method to develop the objectives, strategy, and tactics of the campaign.

The focus of this chapter is primarily on measuring the effectiveness of advertising and secondarily on evaluating related marketing communications. This focus is less a comment on the relative importance of advertising and more a function of the scantiness of methodologies known for measuring the effectiveness of other types of marketing communications. The measurement for advertising and related marketing communications is sometimes referred to as **evaluative research.**

Planners tend to ask three basic questions before measuring the effectiveness of a campaign:

1. Whether or not to measure?

2. When to measure?

3. What to measure?

Each of these questions is fundamentally connected to the other, so much so that a reasonable argument could be made that each of the above questions should be considered first. The second question, when to measure, is probably the most logical place to start, but usually the decision to use or not use measurement is decided first. The first two questions—whether to measure and when to measure—have an obvious effect on what to measure, but, in many ways, the last question is the most important of the three. Because of the problems associated with measurement, what to measure frequently gets translated to what you *can* measure, either because of the cost of a measurement or because planners do not feel they can measure what they would really like to evaluate, as we will later discuss. These feelings no doubt cause some planners to question whether it is worth measuring anything.

WHETHER OR NOT TO MEASURE EFFECTIVENESS

In their book *Advertising and Promotion*, George and Michael Belch point out that to ensure success in a marketing communications' program, it is important to determine how well the program is working by measuring its performance against some predetermined standards. They offer the following reasons why companies do or do not use measurement:[3]

Reasons for Measuring Effectiveness

1. Avoiding Costly Mistakes. In 1997, according *to Competitive Media Reporting*, more than $73 billion was spent on advertising in measured media in the United States. This amount probably constitutes less than half of all the money spent on marketing communications. If measurement could potentially increase a campaign's efficiency or effectiveness as little as 1%, then it would amount to savings of more than $5.6 million for Kellogg Co. (based on total advertising expenditures of $558.2 million), and more than $5.8 million for Gillette Co. (based on total advertising expenditures of $578.4 million).[4]

2. Evaluating Alternative Strategies. Human behavior can rarely be predicted to any degree of certainty. Advertising is still very much an art. Companies often have more than one strategy under consideration, each of which seems promising and each of which may have its own supporters within a company. The right kind of test can reduce the uncertainty in decision-making. For example, Coors is a heavy buyer of spot television. Frequently, Coors tests alternate versions of its advertising to determine which strategy or execution is the most effective.[5]

3. Increasing the Efficiency of Advertising in General. The advertising business is replete with many highly competent and creative individuals. These people often have so much of their spirit and individuality invested in an assignment that it is difficult for them to be completely objective when evaluating their own work. The instincts of even the most successful and talented people can sometimes be wrong. When millions or tens of millions of dollars are on the line, measuring effectiveness as an aid to judgment often helps decisionmakers discern a near miss from a big success.

Not Measuring Effectiveness

1. Cost. Research can be expensive. As companies strive to keep costs down, research is one of the first expenses cut or significantly decreased. Measures to evaluate advertising after it is run are particularly vulnerable. In the 1970s, when many agencies were able to retain a full 15% commission on advertising they placed for their clients, advertisers often requested their agencies to conduct special studies as part of the compensation agreement. In the 1980s, when companies began to negotiate reductions in the commissions agencies were allowed to keep, agencies increasingly returned the task of measuring the effectiveness of advertising back to the companies. Many companies found it difficult to fit the cost of testing into their budgets. Companies, and especially advertising agencies, often rationalize that if they put more effort and expense into the developmental phase of the campaign, it will be less important to measure its effectiveness later.

2. Research Problems. Advertising people are uncertain about the methodologies that research organizations use and the criteria they test for. For example, many researchers agree that a good test for copy should measure multiple criteria.However, they are still not satisfied with the ones that do. There is frequent disappointment with the limitations of research. Planners are often disenchanted with tests that only measure communications' effects, such as awareness and recall. They want tests that isolate and reveal a direct causal relationship between advertising and sales. Few tests achieve these ends.

3. Disagreement Over What to Test. Along with the debate over the value of measuring communications' effects, may be a disagreement over which aspect of the campaign to test. A sales manager may want to assess the impact of promotions on sales, whereas the corporate hierarchy may be more concerned about the company's image. Disputes over what to test can sometimes lead to no testing.

4. Creativity Objections. Many creative people do not like copy testing. They say it inhibits their creativity. Because many tests are inexact and measure only one aspect of communication, such as awareness, copywriters sometimes protest that they do not measure the full impact of an ad, especially television commercials. Moreover, pretesting finished advertising limits creativity. Television commercials, in particular, are expensive to produce. If they do not score well on a test, a lot of money has been wasted. Wasting money is especially irksome if there has been no general agreement about the value of the test in the first place. Advertising can be tested in rough form with storyboards, "animatics," or "photomatics," but since these are not the actual commercial, some may argue that it limits the ability of the researcher to generalize the results from the test situation to the real world.

5. Time. Copy testing and other effectiveness measures take time; executive judgment and creative decisions must sometimes be made quickly. Many planners are concerned that with the passage of time they may lose a window of opportunity.

RESOLVING THE DEBATE OVER MEASUREMENT

Measurement is used to add greater precision to marketing decisions. Despite the problems associated with measurement and the need to make decisions in the face of insufficient information, it does not mean there is a good argument for intuitive decision making. Rather, as Kotler says, "it is an argument for improved marketing theory and tools of analysis."[6] Progressive companies should strive to be on the cutting edge of how they evaluate campaigns in the same way that they compete to produce better products.

DEVELOPING A RESEARCH SYSTEM

To foster a corporate environment that encourages innovation, it is important to view evaluative measures as part of a system. This approach tends to offer a firm some of the following advantages over evaluating a campaign on an ad hoc basis.[7]

Systems Tend to Evolve. Once a system is built, it can be fine-tuned and refined to improve its efficiency and effectiveness. Ad hoc studies tend to be viewed as more discrete projects. They start, are executed, and end.

Systems Provide Benchmarks for Learning Over Time. After a system is established, it is easier to measure performance against results because the data tend to be collected and analyzed using common terms, standards, and databases. In a world where we rarely measure absolutes, measuring relative change is important.

Systems Promote a Holistic Approach Rather than a Functional Approach to Solving Marketing Communications' Problems. Ad hoc studies often begin with a single aspect, or part, of the campaign (such as specific ads), which an analyst then strives to understand by piecing together all the parts in an attempt to understand the complete impact of a campaign. In contrast, systems foster a mindset that encourages planners to begin with a concept (such as integrated marketing communications), and follow through with measures or procedures that are designed to evaluate both the effects of various aspects of the campaign and the way in which they interact. In other words, systems help predispose the planner to evaluate the impact of the entire campaign.

Research Systems Reside in the Company (or Its Agency). Many ad hoc studies are produced by outside suppliers. Often data that are used to create a report exist outside the company in the supplier's database. Storing data with the supplier makes it difficult for companies to access the data should a need arise. Having a system does not preclude the use of outside suppliers, but a company with a system usually integrates data collected by others into its own database—or at least makes provisions to access the information online.

EVALUATION IS NOT GETTING EASIER

Even as the systems and techniques to evaluate campaigns get more sophisticated, and presumably better, the task itself appears to get more difficult. The very companies that are likely to use the most advanced systems—the large consumer-goods companies—are the same companies that often employ the strategy of surrounding the consumer with myriad points of brand contact. Not surprisingly, many of these points of contact include nontraditional media that often do not lend themselves to measurement. Advertising, along with other communications' tools (such as sales promotions and public relations), is only one of a number of factors that can influence sales.

Companies such as Procter & Gamble, Quaker Oats, and Kraft General Foods have fairly sophisticated and proprietary systems to evaluate their campaigns. However, it is doubtful that even these companies have obtained the Holy Grail of campaign measurement—a true measure tracing a direct causal relationship between the campaign and sales.

TOWARD A SYSTEM FOR EVALUATING A CAMPAIGN'S EFFECTIVENESS

A comprehensive, detailed system to evaluate the effectiveness of a campaign is beyond the scope of this book, but we can outline some of the fundamental elements involved. Assuming a decision is made to proceed with the development of a system, one can be organized along the lines of the questions when and what to measure. We suspect many, if not most, companies organize their systems on the basis of what they want to measure. These systems focus directly on what the research is supposed to accomplish and are objective-oriented. Although this is a sensible approach, many companies, and especially students working on class projects, may find a task-oriented approach to be more practical. *This approach organizes evaluative measures chronologically, according to when the need typically arises to evaluate some aspect of the campaign.* We will now look at the various stages in a marketing communications' campaign and examine some of the more common evaluative measures companies use, including what typically gets measured.

When and What to Measure

There are at least four stages of a campaign during which it is common to use some type of evaluative testing:

- At the beginning of the creative process-concept testing

- In the middle and at the end of the creative process-copy testing

- While the advertising is appearing in the media-concurrent testing

- After the advertising has appeared in the media-posttesting

Concept Testing

Following the situation analysis and until just before the actual ads are completed, planners often use some type of evaluative testing to get a feel for whether their ideas and strategies are likely to be on target and on strategy. The purpose of this type of testing is to get feedback from the consumers before a lot of time, money, and effort are spent on producing expensive ads.

What to Test. Concept testing is as much a check on the strategic development of the campaign as it is on specific executions. The testing tends to be somewhat exploratory in nature, although tentative ideas and concepts have been developed. Among the concepts typically evaluated are product names, slogans, campaign themes, advertising claims or promises, and the basic product positioning (sometimes referred to as the product concept definition). Later, during the copy-testing phase, specific variables that affect the execution of an ad can be tested (such as the selection of music, choice of words, use of art or humor, and the arrangement of these elements). This is also a good stage to evaluate campaign spokespeople. Celebrity endorsers usually command substantial fees; it is imperative to get some feedback on them before contracts are signed.

How to Test. Because concept testing tends to be exploratory in nature, the research techniques tend to be more qualitative than other types of testing. Among the more common ways of gathering information are the following:

- Focus groups

- Mall intercepts

- One-on-one interviews

One of the keys to obtaining information that is meaningful is be sure that the subjects in the test groups are representative of the target audience. Although widely used, focus groups are not generally satisfactory for checking communications or getting evaluative feedback. The interaction that takes place among respondents in developmental research (see chapters 2 and 3) is desirable. In evaluative research, it is better to measure the effects of an ad on an individual consumer without the potential biases that sometimes result from one member of a group influencing another. Because of potential problems with interaction effects, mall intercepts and one-on-one interviews are generally more appropriate for concept testing.

Within the various testing situations there are a wide variety of techniques and tests to elicit information. Some tests and techniques, such as projective tests and laddering techniques, are more commonly used in developmental research, although they are occasionally used for concept testing. Some of the more common tests and techniques are:

- Projective tests

- Laddering techniques

- Structured and semistructured questionnaires

- Attitude and opinion scales

- Paired comparison tests

The information obtained from concept testing is generally used to firm up message strategy as well as to evaluate key elements within the strategy. The next step in the campaign is to execute the strategy by developing individual ads or promotional pieces.

Copy Testing

Most of the evaluative testing conducted by companies and their agencies falls into the category of copy testing. It can range from consumer feedback to rough ads obtained from informal interviews to the quantitative measurement of consumer responses to finished commercials. Because the testing takes place before the ads are run in the media, it is often referred to as **pretesting**.

Purpose. Copy testing is used primarily to predict the effectiveness of an ad or a campaign. A secondary objective is to help understand the ad so it can be developed further. Over the years, many people have questioned the efficacy of copy testing, challenging either specific tests or the concept in general. To assess the value of these tests, the American Research Foundation sponsored a massive project in which it conducted between 12,000 and 15,000 interviews. Called the ARF Copy Research Validity Project, it was completed in 1990, after nearly eight years of struggling with the formidable problems associated with such an ambitious project. Although the project limited itself to television commercials, the general conclusion was that copy testing works. The study confirmed what many copy researchers had theorized: Copy testing is efficacious in identifying television commercials that generate sales.[8] Although this is helpful information to know, the typical copy test is not able to establish a causal link between an ad and sales.

Value. The value of most copy tests is derived from the ability of the test to evaluate the effectiveness of an ad defined in terms of some criterion such as awareness, persuasion, or likability (also referred to as liking). After a system is used repeatedly, average scores, or norms, are quickly developed by product type. Frequently, the research company supplying the service provides these norms. Each ad is tested against a norm to assess its effectiveness. As planners become familiar and comfortable with a technique, the results may be used to help make decisions. However, smart managers know that a copy test should only be used as a guide to decision-making and not as a substitute for executive and creative judgment.

What to Test. There are two types of copy tests: diagnostics, to help planners understand the strengths and weaknesses of an ad; and evaluative tests, which commonly focus on one of three criteria: communication playback, likability, and persuasion.

Although many copy tests have diagnostic value, there is a particular type of copy test that is referred to as diagnostics. We'll look at an example of a general diagnostic test and then consider two more specialized tests: frame-by-frame diagnostics and picture sort techniques.

Diagnostics is a type of testing designed to improve ads. It is rare, however, that a diagnostic test tells a creative person how to improve a commercial. Diagnostics may suggest what is wrong with an ad, but it is highly unlikely to suggest what to do to correct it. These tests are frequently used to pretest television commercials at the rough stage. In a typical 30-second commercial there are numerous scenes, and within each scene there is a variety of elements that can be manipulated. Tests that are designed to improve specific elements within a commercial are sometimes referred to as **executional diagnostics**. In a general diagnostics test, viewers are exposed to a television commercial and then given a series of open-ended questions about reactions to specific elements as well as structural statements to which they indicate their agreement or disagreement.

Example
Please answer the following questions.

1. What were your overall feelings as you were watching the commercial?

2. Can you describe what happened in the commercial from beginning to end?

3. What things did you learn or find out?

4. What did you like or dislike about the commercial?

5. How do you feel about specific elements in the commercial?

Using the following scale Agree Completely (1), Agree Somewhat (2), Disagree Somewhat (3), Disagree Completely (4), please indicate how each statement describes the way you feel.[9]

1. This ad told me something new about the product that I didn't know before. _____

2. This ad helps me find the product that I want. _____

3. This ad is funny or clever. _____

4. I learned a lot from this advertising. _____

5. I find this advertising artistic. _____

Although companies generally use diagnostics to help them understand and improve ads, the ARF Copy Research Validity Project found that the responses to some of the statements in a diagnostics test helped companies to predict fairly well which commercials would be most successful in generating sales. The most useful questions were those that dealt with the information content of the ads, such as questions 1, 2, and 4.

Frame-by-frame diagnostics are frequently used to help marketers understand why a television commercial has not tested very well on some other type of test, such as one dealing with recall or persuasion. Even simple commercials are often compilations of separate elements. These tests can provide clues as to which parts of a commercial are connecting with viewers and which parts of a commercial have "dead spots." Before rejecting a commercial, managers will sometimes see if there are any parts of the commercial worth salvaging. Frame-by-frame tests evaluate consumers' reactions to the individual scenes in a television commercial. In a typical test, a copy-testing organization, such as VIEW-FACTS, invites consumers to a minitheater to view a series of commercials. The respondents are instructed to depress buttons indicating how much they like or dislike what they are seeing. Later, an interviewer queries audience members about the reasons for their reactions to specific scenes. Frame-by-frame tests provide the researcher with clues as to the parts within a commercial that work well and those that do not. These clues can be used to provide guidance to creative personnel for further copy development.[10]

Picture sort techniques is another diagnostic tool that can be used to understand the inner workings of a television commercial. One of the most widely known techniques (developed by Euro RSCG Tatham) uses a deck of still photographs taken from the television commercial being tested. Respondents are recruited and screened for target audience membership at mall intercept locations. Respondents are given a randomized deck of photographs and are asked to sort them into two piles—the pictures they remember seeing and the pictures they do not. Researchers then assign a value to each scene in the commercial according to the extent to which respondents indicate they saw it in the ad. A high score indicates that a high percentage of respondents remember seeing the particular scene. An analyst can then plot these scores from the beginning of a commercial to its end to provide insight about the attention value of each scene as the commercial unfolds.[11]

An effective commercial is one in which each scene has a consistently high level of recognition. It yields a line on a graph that is smooth rather than choppy or disjointed. The researchers at Euro RSCG Tatham call this smooth transition from one image to another "visual connectedness," and supported the validity of this approach by establishing a positive relationship between visually connected ads and ads that were independently judged to be persuasive by American Research System (ARS), one of the most respected copy testing services in the United States.[12]

Communication playback is a type of test that can be used for both diagnostic and evaluative purposes. The intent of this test is to evaluate whether or not the essential points within an ad have been communicated. The ability of respondents to recall specific information about an ad is an important measure of effectiveness. Communication playback tests can also be used as a diagnostic tool. Viewers are often asked to re-create visual and verbal elements of an ad in their own words.[13] Researchers usually pay special attention to the consumers' recall of the brand name, specific attributes or qualities of the product, the main selling message, and reactions to music, special effects, main characters, key phrases, and story lines. In the ARF Copy Research Validity Project, the researchers used the following on a paper-and-pencil test: "Of course, the purpose of the commercial was to get you to buy the product. Other than that, what was the main selling point of the commercial?"[14]

Communication playback information can be obtained using a variety of methods, including focus group discussion (although, as previously stated, it is a misuse of focus groups), one-on-one interviews, mall intercepts, and dummy advertising vehicles. In the latter method, a dummy vehicle can be made to look like an actual magazine, complete with editorial matter and advertisements. Subjects are asked to read the vehicle as they would normally read a magazine. The interviewer then questions the respondent on a number of criteria, including recall, main selling message, and general opinions and attitudes. Dummy vehicles are used widely because they present a fairly realistic situation to subjects.

A related type of measure can also be obtained via physiological methods. A mechanical device known as a tachistoscope, or *t*-scope, measures respondents' perceptions of various elements in print ads. This instrument is like a slide projector with a shutter attached to it that is able to vary the amount of time a picture is shown on a screen. In the beginning of the test, the image of the ad will flash on the screen so briefly that it will be below a respondent's threshold of awareness (that is, subliminal). Gradually, as the researcher lengthens the amount of time the image is on the screen, viewers are increasingly able to perceive various elements or messages in the ad, including the brand name, product attributes, and the main selling message. Interviewers then question respondents, as they do with dummy vehicles. The *t*-scope does not appear to be used as much today as it had been in the past.

An eye-movement camera is another mechanical device that can provide an analyst with some insight into how consumers perceive elements within a print ad. There are a couple of variations on the basic methodology. Usually, viewers are seated in front of a desk with a large mechanical device placed on top. While they are viewing test ads, a sensor directs an almost invisible beam of infrared light at one of the viewer's eyes. The beam then follows the viewer's eye and superimposes the path the eyes follow onto a layout of the ad. An analyst is then able to determine which element in the ad first received the viewer's attention (that is, the dominant point of entry), which path the viewer followed next within the ad and, finally, how much time each element was viewed.

If an analyst wanted to know whether a sexy-looking model attracted attention to the product (rather than detracted from it), an eye-movement camera could provide an objective measurement that might differ from a viewer's verbal reconstruction of viewing patterns. The chief objection to the use of the camera is that viewers are tested under highly artificial conditions rather than as they would normally react. Recent technological developments enable the camera to be concealed within a reading lamp so that unobtrusive measurements can be taken. It remains to be seen if this technological development will overcome researchers' resistance to its use.

Likability measures appear to be increasing in usage. If this is really occurring, it is unclear whether it is because of a trend in some areas toward more entertainment-oriented ads or because of evidence that suggests that likability measures do a good job of measuring advertising effectiveness. In the ARF Copy Research Validity Project, "the most surprising finding in the study was the strong relationship found to exist between the likability of the copy and its effects on sales." As the researchers pointed out, it was generally believed that the function of copy was to sell, and whether the copy was likable was unimportant. The "ARF study strongly suggests that ads that are liked outsell those that are not."[15]

Likability measures are very similar to attitudinal measures in that both types of measurement probe the evaluative dimension of what an ad means to a consumer. There are many direct and indirect questions that can be asked to probe likability. In the ARF study, the question that was successful at predicting sales was fairly straightforward and is as follows:[16]

Thinking about the commercial you just saw, please tell me which of the statements on this card best describes your feelings about the commercial.

I liked it very much. _____

I liked it. _____

I neither liked it nor disliked it. _____

I disliked it _____

I disliked it very much. _____

Of all the pretest measures, **persuasion measures** are probably the ones most respected by people in the advertising business. To be persuaded is to be won over to another point of view. The viewpoint of interest to people in advertising is consumers' interest in obtaining or purchasing a particular brand. Although there are numerous variations of a persuasion test, the basic design is used typically to evaluate television commercials and is fairly simple.

Subjects are asked to indicate their brand preference or usage prior to exposure to a series of television commercials. After exposure, they are retested and asked to indicate their brand preferences should they win a drawing giving them a market basket full of various products, including brands appearing in the tested commercials. Any shift in brand preference is assumed to be a function of exposure to the viewed ads. There are at least several companies that offer this service: Mapes and Ross, which offers a parallel system for evaluating magazine ads; ASI Market Research Inc., which conducts tests with viewers in their own homes via cable channels; McCollum/Spielman, which also offers a parallel system for testing magazines; and American Research Systems (ARS), the successor to Schwerin Research, the company that pioneered the basic system now widely in use.

Television Tests

Testing television commercials can be very expensive, so researchers test them in a wide range of forms. The closer a commercial looks to its finished form, the more realistic the test is likely to be. However, relatively unfinished commercials do a surprisingly good job of serving as a surrogate for the final ad, especially in view of the amount of money spent in producing them. The following are among the most common stages of unfinished television commercials used in tests:[17]

- **Story Boards**—a series of visual frames and script of key audio used to represent a proposed commercial

- **Animatic**—film or videotape of a series of drawings with audio used to represent a proposed commercial

- **Photomatic**—film or videotape of a series of photographs with audio used to represent a proposed commercial

- **Ripamatic**—footage taken from other existing commercials and spliced together (also called stealamatics)

- **Liveamatic**—rough film or videotape of live talent photographed for a proposed commercial; can be close to a finished commercial but does not necessarily use actual sets or talent who will be used in the finished commercial

METHODOLOGY AND PRACTICES

Providing copy-testing services to advertisers and their agencies has become a highly competitive business. Not surprisingly, there are disputes and controversy over techniques, methodology, and standards-in effect, over which supplier has the better service. In an effort to resolve some common concerns about copy testing, a coalition of 21 major advertising agencies got together and reached "a high degree of consensus" on nine fundamental principles underlying a good copy-testing system. The coalition was called PACT, an acronym for Positioning Advertising Copy Testing.[18] The PACT principles appear in boldface:

1. **A good copy-testing system provides measurements that are relevant to the objectives of the advertising**. This principle underscores the importance of evaluating a test on the basis of its ability to assess an ad's potential to achieve stated objectives.

2. **A good copy-testing system is one that requires agreement about how the results will be used in advance of each specific test**. This principle emphasizes the importance of specifying how the test will be used in advance of the results.

3. **A good copy-testing system provides multiple measurements because single measurements are generally inadequate to assess the performance of an ad**. This principle calls attention to the difficulty of separating out the effects of advertising from the many other factors influencing sales. Because there is no universally accepted single measurement that can serve as a surrogate for sales, multiple measures are necessary.

4. **A good copy-testing system is based on a model of human response to communication—the reception of a stimulus, the comprehension of a stimulus, and the response to the stimulus**. This principle recognizes that ads usually function on several levels:
   - On the "eyes" and "ears"—it must be received (reception)
   - On the "mind"—it must be understood (comprehension)
   - On the "heart"—it must make an impression (response)
   Therefore, a testing system should strive to answer questions on more than one level.

5. **A good copy-testing system allows for consideration of whether the advertising stimulus should be exposed more than once**. This principle endorses the idea that in some test situations the learning of test material is much higher after two exposures than it is for one, indicating that there are situations where a single exposure test could be inadequate.

6. **A good copy-testing system recognizes that the more finished a piece of copy is, the more soundly it can be evaluated and requires, as a minimum, that alternative executions be tested in the same degree of finish**. This principle is concerned with the biases that can creep into a test when alternative executions are tested in different stages of finish.

7. **A good copy-testing system provides controls to avoid the biasing effects of the exposure context**. This principle points out the potential biasing effects of the context in which a program is viewed, such as an off-air test versus an on-air test, a clutter reel of commercials versus a program context, and one specific program context versus another specific program context.

8. **A good copy-testing system is one that takes into account basic considerations of sample definition**. This principle emphasizes the importance of proper sampling procedures, especially ones dealing with the size and representativeness of the sample.

9. **A good copy-testing system demonstrates reliability and validity empirically**. This principle underscores the importance of testing systems that yield the same results each time the advertising is tested (that is, reliability). For validity, this principle encourages users to provide results or evidence about validity "which are relevant to marketplace performance." The PACT agencies were concerned that there were many systems in use for which no evidence of validity was provided.

Concurrent Testing

This type of testing refers to research that takes place while the campaign is running in the marketplace. There are two basic types: tracking studies, and coincidental studies. Of the two, tracking studies are far more important.

Tracking studies are often a major part of the management of a marketing communication campaign. According to a 1988 study by the Association of National Advertisers, more than 85% of the respondents to its survey indicated that they track advertising results.[19] Although the most important tracking a company can do is to monitor sales, a tracking study usually refers to some type of consumer survey. Tracking studies are a way to monitor the pulse of a campaign. If there is some aspect of the plan or some area within the marketplace that is doing particularly well, an alert, well-informed company can often increase its marketing advantage. On the other hand, the marketplace can be brutal to companies that fail to respond quickly to their problems.

Tracking studies work best when they are part of an ongoing information-gathering system. The basic idea behind tracking is to keep in close contact with what consumers are thinking, feeling, and doing. Companies are interested in information like the following.

Awareness. Companies want to know about brand awareness and top-of-mind awareness as well as consumers' awareness of new information on the product, such as new features or a change in the positioning of a brand.

Attitude. Companies like to know a consumer's attitude toward the product because of the widespread belief that attitudes strongly affect the consumer's predisposition to buy a product. The nature of the relationship between an attitude and purchase behavior can vary considerably.

Communication Playback. Basically, companies want to know if they are getting the right message across. As companies employ new and different strategies, tracking studies enable them to closely monitor whether or not they are achieving their objectives. Traditionally, very simple recall measures were used, but in recent years there has been diminished interest in recall.

Reported Product Usage. Companies regularly monitor sales on a daily, weekly, monthly, and yearly basis. Some of this information comes from within the organization. Large consumer-goods companies also supplement their databases with information from syndicated research services. Tracking studies are used to understand the nature of the sales taking place. For new products, consumers are asked whether their purchases are new (or trial) or repeat. For existing products, consumers are asked about their frequency of use.

Product Satisfaction. With the increased emphasis on relationship marketing, many companies are sensitive about satisfying consumers and want to know if consumers like their products and their advertising. Among the important measures of consumer satisfactions are questions focusing on consumers' intentions to repurchase a product.

To obtain the above information, companies either conduct in-house testing or use outside suppliers. Agencies do not typically provide this type of research. A company usually sets up a system to gather information on a regular and periodic basis. The system can function on an ongoing basis (weekly, even daily), or it can gather data in large blocs of interviews at a time, called **waves**.

Companies either set up their own panels or use ones set up by research firms. A problem with panels occurs when consumers become overly sensitized to participating in the study, or have reactive effects, and respond in ways that differ from the consumers they are supposed to represent. Some of the more popular tracking methods companies use to gather the information include:

- **Telephone Interviews**—This method is probably the most popular because it is quick, easy, and inexpensive. Consumers can be asked a full range of questions, from those dealing with awareness to questions on product satisfaction.

- **Diaries**—Consumers are asked to keep a record of various activities such as brands purchased, brand switches, use of coupons, and exposure to competitive promotions.

- **Pantry Checks**—This method provides much the same kind of brand usage information as diaries. Although this method is more expensive to use, the information obtained is more reliable.

- **Mall Intercepts**—Although this method is used widely for other types of consumer research, it is used only occasionally for tracking studies. Its chief advantage is that it is one of the easiest and quickest ways to obtain large quantities of information.

- **Product Audits and Scanner Data**—Traditionally, companies had supplemented internally generated sales data with marketplace product-movement data from research firms such as AC Nielsen. These firms were able to estimate product movement by monitoring the flow of goods in and out of retail locations and area warehouses. Estimates were based on location visits as well as store and warehouse records. Today, the information is based largely on scanner data.

The two dominant firms in the business of gathering product and scanner data are AC Nielsen and Information Resources Inc. (IRI). Both firms offer much of the same type of information. In the interest of brevity, we will look at Nielsen, the larger of the two companies.

AC Nielsen is the world's largest marketing research company. Although most people are familiar with the Nielsen name from its media research unit, it earns most of its revenue from marketing research services. Nielsen is a true information conglomerate in that it offers services too numerous to explain in one chapter (let alone in a small section). The major users of its syndicated measurements are large companies (such as food manufacturers and those producing health and beauty aids). By the early 1990s, approximately three-fourths of all the companies purchasing scanner data accounted for nearly $300 million in business annually, with the average firm spending more than $1 million.[20]

Nielsen monitors retail activity at the store level through the electronic capture of all UPC bar-coded transactions recorded via scanning technology. Some stores are also measured with physical audits. The basic system is called SCANTRACK, and a related system is called PROCISION. Generally speaking, SCANTRACK is the service that provides information for food, grocery, and general-merchandise manufacturers; and PROCISION is the service for health- and beauty-aids manufacturers. Companies buy information on the United States as a whole or any of 50 major markets. The heart of the SCANTRACK system is a sample of 3,000 supermarkets with more than $2 million in all-commodity volume (ACV, or the total amount of sales in a given category).[21]

Nielsen strives to be a full-service market research company providing information on all the major elements in the marketing mix. Some of the information Nielsen provides can be summarized as follows:

- **Product**—Provides sales figures for specific categories for the total U.S. market, each of the 50 major markets, and customized geographic trading areas. Sales figures include those for all significant brands in the ACV.

- **Pricing**—Provides information on the prices retailers charge for the brands in an ACV. This information can be broken down into types of retailers, such as supermarkets, mass merchandisers, drugstores, warehouse clubs, convenience stores, and independent drug or grocery stores.

- **Distribution**—Provides information on how a category is performing within a specific retail account or type of store versus the market. Also provides information on which key items are handled in the market but not in certain retail accounts. ACV is generally expressed as a percentage of the sales volume in a product category that can be accounted for by stores that distribute the product. If a particular store or chain has an ACV of 50% in a market, that means it sells 50% of all the products in its category in that particular market. ACV indicates the extent to which one's product is available to consumers.

- **Promotion**—Provides information on the amount of merchandising support (for example, features and displays) to brands and categories. The media research unit provides information on ratings, and Nielsen Monitor Plus provides information on media occurrence (also called incidence), expenditures, and ad descriptions for network television. Nielsen Monitor Plus also provides occurrence data for national and local newspapers (top 50), outdoor, freestanding inserts, and magazines (national, Sunday, and top 50 local).

Coincidental studies, another form of concurrent testing, are designed primarily to evaluate or measure advertising and media usage while consumers are exposed to the media. The telephone interview is the principal means by which information is obtained. This method used to be called the telephone coincidental method. Interviewers usually ask respondents questions pertaining to what they were doing just before they answered the phone. Its chief advantage is the reduction in measurement error due to memory loss. The use of this technique in recent years has diminished considerably.

Posttesting

The distinction between posttesting and concurrent testing is mostly semantic, but it is also traditional. Essentially, both types refer to testing for the effects of an ad after it has appeared in the media. Posttesting usually refers to testing at the end of a campaign, whereas concurrent testing generally refers to testing that takes place in an ongoing campaign. Posttesting is done for two basic reasons: (1) measuring the effects of a campaign provides a rigorous, objective way to assess the performance of the individuals, including agencies, who have worked on the campaign; and (2) a well-conceived testing program can provide benchmarks against which future campaigns can be developed.

From an operational point of view, it is important for management to have a thorough understanding of which aspects of the campaign have gone well, which should be replaced or improved, and which should be avoided in the future. This understanding extends to the people working on the campaign, including those at the advertising agency. By establishing benchmarks based on past performances, management can use the information to fine-tune day-to-day operations as well as to integrate the information into the strategic foundation for the planning of the next campaign.

Posttesting can be divided into two types: tests measuring communication effects, and those measuring behavioral effects. The following criteria are among the most popular used for posttesting:

- **Recognition** (a communication effect)
- **Recall** (a communication effect)
- **Attitudes, awareness,** and **likability** (communications' effects)
- **Sales** (behavioral effects)
- **Inquiries** (behavioral effects)

Recognition tests are some of the most widely used forms of posttesting, especially for print ads. The *Starch Readership Report*, offered by Starch INRA Hooper, is a popular test of this type. The basic technique involves sending out a battery of interviewers the day after an issue of a magazine has hit the newsstands. A minimum of 100 readers of each sex, who indicated that they have read the publication, are interviewed. The interviewer goes through the issue page by page and asks the interviewee to respond to certain questions about each ad as a whole and various elements within the ad such as the headline, illustration, copy blocks, and logo. The test produces the following scores for each ad in the issue:

- **Noted**—the percentage of issue readers who remembered having seen the ad previously.

- **Seen Associated**—the percentage of readers who remembered seeing some part of the ad that clearly indicated the brand name or advertiser.

- **Read Most**—The percentage who read 50% or more of the copy in the ad.

- **Signature**—the percentage or readers who remembered seeing the brand name or logo.

A recognition test is a memory test. As we previously pointed out, it is based on the assumption that an ad cannot affect a purchase decision if consumers cannot remember the advertising. However, even though consumers may not remember a specific ad, they may have internalized its message. So an ad with a low recognition score does not necessarily mean the ad failed. Another limitation of the Starch service is that their study is not conducted on targeted consumers; companies generally want information on their target audience. Unless the readership of the magazine closely approximates the company's target audience, the information may not be usable.

For all its limitations, the Starch service is still used, partly because it is relatively inexpensive and partly because Starch is the grandfather of all advertising research companies and many people are familiar with it.

Recall tests are a form of posttesting that appears to be on the decline. There are two basic types: unaided recall, which is similar to fill-in-the-blank tests; and aided recall, in which a respondent is asked to recall an ad as an interviewer provides subtle cues to aid the respondent's memory.

Gallup and Robinson is a company that offers posttesting services for both magazines and television. Its InTeleTest service is a test based in part on recall that is designed to provide at least four measures of the impact of a television commercial:

- **Intrusiveness**—This measure is an indicator of the commercial's ability to get the viewer's attention. It is defined as the percent of respondents who can describe the commercial accurately the day after exposure.

- **Idea Communication**—This measure is defined as the percent of respondents who can recall the commercial, including specific sales points.

- **Persuasion**—This is determined by a pretest and posttest measurement of respondents' "favorable buying attitude." The pretest questions about attitude and awareness are administered to respondents during a telephone call inviting them to be in the test. The following day, each respondent is given the same set of questions, and any change in attitude represents a measure of persuasion.

- **Commercial Reaction**—This measure looks at the degree to which consumers like a commercial (as measured on a 5-point scale) and the degreee to which cosumers agree or disagree on the excellence of a commercial (also measured on a 5-point scale).[22]

The Gallup and Robinson Rapid Ad Measurement (RAM) is one of the best known of the magazine-aided recall tests. The test produces measurement scores similar to those obtained for the company's InTeleTest television service: proven name registration, idea communication, favorable buying attitude, and Net Effectiveness.[23]

Over the years, recall tests have been one of the most widely used forms of posttesting. There are indications that recall will not be as popular in the future. One of the more widely used recall measures of the 1980s, the DAR (day after recall) measure, offered by Burke Marketing Research, is no longer in use. Burke sold its commercial evaluation business to ASI, which incorporated it into its Apex system, which measures persuasion. The separate services are now called Recall Plus and Persuasion Plus.

There have been numerous articles questioning the value of recall testing, especially as compared to persuasion measures. One of the strongest articles was by Gibson, who summed up his analysis and review of the literature on the recall/persuasion controversy as follows:

> Our summary can be brief because the record on recall is so clear. We know that recall data are inherently weak. We know that the theory on which recall data are based is empirically shaky. We know that the evidence for the validity of recall is—to be charitable—"checkered." This "checkered" validity of recall is in striking contrast to the evidence for the validity of persuasion.
>
> We may not know the answer to the longest playing controversy in all of marketing research, but we do know what the answer is not—and it's not recall.[24]

In 1990, King, Pehrson, and Reid surveyed research directors with the largest agencies and advertising executives with the largest 200 advertisers.[25] Their findings revealed that recall measures were still widely in use, although used less frequently than reported in a similar study in the late 1970s.[26] They hypothesize that this decline may in part be due to a shift in emphasis from quantitative techniques to more qualitative ones. Perhaps because some of the negative publicity directed at the measure focused on the word *recall*; some systems may use the words *communication playback* to refer to measures that have traditionally been called recall. Still, there is a long tradition of using recall measures. Researchers are familiar with its use and have developed norms for its usage. Although recall testing may not be as popular in the future as it has been in the past, it will likely remain in use for some time.

Attitude, awareness, and likebility tests appear to be used more at the pretesting and tracking stages than as posttest measurements. This timing is due—at least in part—to the widespread availability of syndicated services that measure other posttesting criteria, such as recall and persuasion. Syndicated studies are usually cheaper than customized testing, although the latter can be conducted with a minimum of ease and expense, depending on the extensiveness of the sample. Syndicated sources usually provide ad norms as part of the service so that advertisers can compare the relative effectiveness of their advertising against their competition's.

Attitude testing is conducted because many advertisers believe that favorable attitudes are a necessary precondition to purchasing. Although this point is widely questioned, many companies try to affect attitude change as part of their marketing communications' strategy, and testing for this effect can be viewed as part of their evaluative program. Companies can use a wide variety of tests to measure for attitudes, awareness, and likability, including the ones discussed earlier in this chapter and in Chapter 3.

Many advertisers believe that measuring communications' effects is not a valid indicator of advertising effectiveness. They may believe, as does Josh McQueen (director of research of Leo Burnett U.S.A.), that testing recall and persuasion is not relevant to what advertisers want to accomplish. McQueen argues for measuring clear behavioral objectives.[27] For most advertisers, this means drawing a causal relationship between advertising and sales or inquiries, the two most common behavioral measures. For many companies, the task is not as difficult to accomplish as one might assume, judging from what is written about this problem in textbooks and journals.

One reason so little is written about successful measurement systems is that they are proprietary, and are likely to work only in very specific situations. Thus, even if they were published, the applicability of the techniques employed would be limited. Moreover, a test's usefulness or value to a company may be more as a partial indicator of a campaign's success rather than as the one indicator of an ad's or a campaign's ability to stimulate sales. Commercial testing organizations face a near impossible task of developing systems that can be of value to a wide variety of companies and still be without some methodological flaw. Almost every technique or test that has been described in the literature about testing has some limitation.

Using sales as a criterion for the posttest measurement of an ad or a campaign's effectiveness is done widely. Most of this evaluation, however, is informal. For example, McDonald's is able to monitor the sales of its stores on a daily basis. The day after a new ad or campaign breaks in the media, the company can "feel" and measure the impact in the marketplace. From a methodological point of view, there could be all kinds of factors that could be responsible for the ad's success or lack thereof, but from McDonald's perspective, its experience enables the company to feel confident about separating the winning ads from the also-rans.

Companies do use more sophisticated techniques. Typically, these are quantitative models that include gross rating points and persuasion measures as key variables influencing sales. The companies may develop these advertising/sales models internally, or may rely on an outside supplier such as AC Nielsen, especially since Nielsen collects most of the data needed as input for these models. Nielsen has a special unit that offers customized models to clients. This unit largely replaced one of the most talked-about testing procedures in recent years: single-source data measurement.

Single-source measurement used scanner technology and media exposure data to monitor product movement (that is, sales), sales promotions, and advertising exposure from the same panel of respondents. Because all of the information was obtained from the same set of respondents, an analyst could evaluate which ads and promotions appeared to have the strongest effect on sales. In the late 1980s and early 1990s, single-source data analysis was widely lauded as the closest technique yet to a Holy Grail of advertising measurement. By 1993, interest had diminished considerably, and the largest of the systems, based on Nielsen's SCANTRACK data, was officially discontinued.

What happened? Within a span of about seven years, there were three systems from which companies could choose: InfoScan by Information Resources Inc., a variation of BehaviorScan, the first service offered by IRI or any company; SCANTRACK by AC Nielsen; and SAMSCAN, which was the last system in and the first system out of the marketplace, offered by an alliance between the SAMI Corporation and Arbitron.[28] These systems were able to do a sophisticated job of isolating the effects of advertising and other promotional tools on sales. Because of these systems, many large companies, such as Procter & Gamble, Helene Curtis, and Campbell Soup, were able to evaluate their promotional campaigns in terms of behavioral criteria, such as sales and market share. However, the single-source research systems that were able to produce these results did not offer bulletproof evaluations.

Although these systems did a fine job of tracing the short-term effect on sales of a particular ad, promotion, or campaign, they were unable to assess the longer-term effects on brand equity. Moreover, for many companies, the quality of the information was less important than the cost and time it took to complete a market test.

Along with a number of concerns about methodology, there were some practical concerns that probably led to the downfall of single-source systems. In the 1990s, companies were desperately trying to cut costs because of a sluggish economy. Nielsen's system was not only expensive to buy, it also was apparently prohibitive to maintain. The expense of installing and maintaining people meters in particular was too costly in view of declining sales. Moreover, some of the clients that were using the SCANTRACK system contracted with Nielsen for other services from their Advanced Analytics unit, such as customized modeling systems. Media buyers also failed to embrace Nielsen's system because the SCANTRACK system provided target audience information on a household level, and buyers preferred the information on a person or individual level. Finally, even though a company might receive usable information about what had occurred, there was no guarantee that what was successful in the past would operate the same way in the future. In the end, the Nielsen system that had shown so much promise ended without any fanfare.

Using inquiries as a behavioral measure is one of the oldest and easiest ways to evaluate advertising. Adding a coupon to an ad or using 800 phone numbers are two methods of inviting inquiries and providing an easy way of comparing one ad to another, especially through the use of split-run techniques. In a typical example, alternate copies of a single issue of a newspaper or magazine will carry one ad or another that is being tested. The ad that produces the most coupons returned or 800 calls is judged to be the most effective. Companies may also track which inquiries were later converted into sales.

The major disadvantage of inquiry testing is the difficulty in relating inquiries to sales or communications' objectives, particularly when it is uncertain if the coupon clipper or 800 caller is a typical consumer. Inquiry tests are a popular method with industrial advertisers who use the inquiries as a prospect list for their salesforces.

EVALUATING OTHER MARKETING COMMUNICATIONS' TOOLS

The evaluation of other promotional tools, such as sales promotions, public relations, and direct mail, is a complex but often neglected part of a marketing communications' campaign. Measuring the effects of sales promotions should be more than counting coupon redemptions, measuring the value of the public relations' program should be more than keeping track of exposures in the media, and evaluating direct mail should be more than checking sales figures. Many of the techniques discussed earlier in this chapter with sometimes only slight modification can be used to evaluate the complete marketing communications' plan. Indeed, many of the research companies mentioned in this chapter routinely test other elements of the promotional mix besides advertising. Readers are encouraged to consult publications in the marketing area for more details.

A FINAL NOTE ON EVALUATION

Throughout this book we have stressed the importance of looking ahead and thinking strategically. We recognize that most of the people who read this book will not be using the principles, procedures, and sources discussed in this chapter, at least not in the near future. This information will have applicability in the years ahead. We also believe that a sound system of evaluation should be built into all strategic plans. Such a system should improve efficiency and effectiveness so that a firm can take full advantage of its marketing opportunity in the short run and develop new, market-winning strategies for the future.

Campaign Progress Checklist

At this point in the campaign you should be generally aware of the following points:

1. Evaluation can be a critical factor in marketing success.

2. Evaluation remains an inexact science because of the difficulty in isolating the effects of a marketing communication campaign on sales.

3. Research activities tend to be divided into developmental research, which is used to develop a campaign; and evaluative research, which is used to evaluate the effectiveness of the marketing communications' campaign.

4. There are at least four stages during which evaluative testing commonly take place.

5. Concept testing is used at the beginning of the creative process.

6. Copy testing is used in the middle and at the end of the creative process.

7. Concurrent testing takes place during the campaign.

8. Posttesting takes place after advertising has appeared in the media.

9. Although the focus of many of the tests in this chapter has been on advertising, many of the tests and procedures work well with other marketing communications' tools.

10. A system of evaluation should be built into all strategic plans to improve the campaign's efficiency and effectiveness.

Notes and References

[1] Burnett, J. J. (1993). *Promotion management*. Boston: Houghton Mifflin, p. 603.

[2] Kotler, P. (1994). *Marketing management*. Englewood Cliffs, NJ: Prentice-Hall, p. xxiv.

[3] Belch, G. E., & Belch, M. A. (1997). *Advertising and promotion: An integrated marketing communications perspective*. Homewood, IL: Irwin, pp. 564–566.

[4] Author. (1998, September 28). 100 leaders by U.S. advertising spending. *Advertising Age*, p. s4.

[5] Belch & Belch, *Advertising and promotion,* p. 565.

[6] Kotler, *Marketing management,* p. xxvi.

[7] Some of this material has been adapted from D. J. Curry, *The new marketing research systems* (New York: John Wiley & Sons, 1993), p. 19.

[8] Haley, R. I., & Baldinger, A. L. (1991, April-May). The ARF Copy Research Validity Project. *Journal of Advertising Research*, pp. 27–28.

[9] The directions and the statements that follow were adapted slightly from the ones used in the ARF Copy Research Validity Project.

[10] For more information, see W. Wells, J. Burnett, & S. Moriarity, *Advertising: Principles and practice* (4th ed.), Upper Saddle River, NJ: Prentice-Hall, 1998, pp. 621–622.

[11] Young, C. E., & Robinson, M. (1987, June-July). Guidelines:Tracking the commercial viewer's wandering attention. *Journal of Advertising Research, 27,* pp. 15–16.

[12] Young, C. E., & Robinson, M. (1992, March-April). Visual connectedness and persuasion. *Journal of Advertising Research, 32,* pp. 51–59.

[13] Haskins, J., & Kendrick, A. (1993). *Successful advertising research methods*. Lincolnwood, IL: NTC Business Books, p. 313.

[14] Haley & Baldinger, ARF copy research, p. 18.

[15] Haley & Baldinger, ARF copy research, p. 29.

[16] Haley & Baldinger, ARF copy research, p. 18.

[17]These forms are adapted only slightly from the classification in the survey reported in K. W. King, J. D. Pehrson, & L. N. Reid, Pretesting TV commercials: Method, measures, and changing agency roles. *Journal of Advertising, 22* (September 1993), p. 91.

[18]PACT-Positioning Advertising Copy Testing (The PACT Agencies Report, 1982), pp. 10–27. Also reprinted in the *Journal of Advertising.*

[19]Haskins & Kendrick, *Successful advertising research methods,* p. 298.

[20]Blankenship, A. B., & Green, G. E. (1992). *State of the art marketing research.* Lincolnwood, IL: NTC Business Books, p. 301.

[21]Nielsen Select (Nielsen North America publication, 1994), p. 3.

[22]For more information, see J. J. Davis, *Advertising research theory and practice* (Upper Saddle River, NJ: Prentice-Hall, 1997), p. 564.

[23]Davis, *Advertising research theory and practice,* p. 574.

[24]L. D. Gibson, Not recall, *Journal of Advertising Research, 23* (February/March 1983): p. 45. For other criticism, see also, H. A. Zielske, Does day-after-recall penalize "feeling" ads? *Journal of Advertising Research, 22* (February/March 1982): pp. 19–22.

[25]King, Pehrson, & Reid, Pretesting TV commercials, pp. 85–97.

[26]See also L. E. Ostlund & K. J. Clancy, Copy testing methods and measures favored by top ad agency and advertising executives, *Journal of the Academy of Marketing Science, 10* (Winter 1982): pp. 72–89.

[27]McQueen, J. (1990, August-September). The different ways ads work. *Journal of Advertising Research, 30,* pp. 15–16.

[28]For more information on the early development of these systems, see Curry, *The new marketing research systems,* pp. 66–74.

Chapter 11

Preparing the Plans Book

APPROACHING THE PLANS BOOK

Putting a plans book together can be a daunting task. Some of you may wonder how you will ever be able to get one finished. Trust us . . . you will. Take our advice, but be sure to leave room for your own way of presenting the material. You want this to be your plan, not ours. When you finish, you'll not only feel a sense of relief, but it will also likely leave you feeling empowered. You will realize your next campaign is likely to be even *better.*

Approach this task systematically and carefully. Don't be meek about it. Throw yourself into this project with passion. These will be your ideas you're putting on paper. Let them reflect the full measure of you ability. However, profit from the accumulated wisdom of others. Even though this plan should consist of your ideas and work, consider letting it also reflect the procedures, ideas, and concepts we've presented in this book. It can work.

You should begin by thinking about just what it is your plans book is supposed to accomplish. First, think about its purpose. No two advertising situations are exactly alike and, therefore, no two plans books should be either. Your book should reflect who your client is, what the client's problem is, how you are going to solve these problems, and why your recommendations are superior to other possibilities. You want to demonstrate that you have a firm understanding of the client's current situation and the expertise and experience to achieve the objectives set forth in your recommendations.

Although plans books can differ, there is a general form beginners can follow. We provide a general outline in this chapter. Over the course of your career, some of your assignments might call for writing a full-blown plans book for a total marketing communications campaign while others might require that you write only a fragment of a plan for a special project. Clients and situations vary. The people you will be working with will also change over time. Knowing the general form of a plans book will allow you to make adjustments as situations differ. Following are some situations for which you could be asked to write marketing communication recommendations.

A Special Project Involving a Small Client with a Limited Budget. This could also be an issue advocacy campaign. Your plans book should be short, and focus on a smaller number of media and promotional opportunities. The budget will probably be limited, and even though you may not be able to afford a research or evaluation plan, follow the steps of the campaign process as best as you can.

The National Student Advertising Competition Sponsored by the American Advertising Federation (AAF's NSAC). The competitive factor and the AAF's guidelines will dictate a particular type of plans book. This is a textbook situation in which you are expected to demonstrate that you can develop a complete marketing communications' program. This competition provides a good opportunity to learn how to balance comprehensiveness with precision in writing a plans book.

A New Product Introduction. Most of the marketing and advertising information will be entirely new. Our book has been designed to handle these situations. You can follow our recommendations from the analysis of primary and secondary research through strategic planning and tactical executions. Your written recommendations are likely to be quite comprehensive for a new product introduction. Appendices or optional fact books can supplement your written plan.

A Small Campaign. Small campaigns are usually narrowly focused in terms of time, budget, and the target to whom the campaign will be directed. These kind of assignments are quite common in advertising. Advertising agencies often have preprinted covers ready to go for the plans that are written for clients as part of a longer-running business relationship (as opposed to a new business presentation).

A Marketing Communications' Campaign. This requires knowledge and use of sales promotion, public relations, or direct marketing, or a combination of these skills, in addition to advertising. This situation is an ideal application for this text because it requires the broadest set of planning abilities.

A Local or Regional Campaign or Test Market Effort. These situations have distinct limits, so be sure not to extend a test market or more limited campaign plan into a national campaign. Recognize the part of the total effort you are being asked to work on.

A Trade Campaign aimed at Building Support among Distributors and Retailers. This is another specialized situation. Know your client's needs. This is *not* a consumer situation. Chapter 8 on related marketing communications provides a discussion of trade considerations and how marketing communications are used to build trade support. Be sure your plans book reflects these differences.

These are but a few possibilities. There are many variations on the above. For example, if the client sells a service, the principles are likely to remain the same, but the terminology will probably differ. The bottom line is that your plans book is the product of your thinking. It is what you say and why you say it that will make the difference. In fact, that has been the point of all the chapters in this text to this point: To provide you with the tools for arriving at your recommendations and developing the reasoning behind them.

PERSPECTIVE ON THE PLANS BOOK

Before you begin, consider how a plans book functions, including its limitations. First, there is no sure-fire formula for writing the plans book. There are guidelines, but be sure you adapt and extend our guidelines to your particular situation.

Second, your plans book will recommend that the client spend a considerable sum of money. Your thinking and presentation must be well organized and flow logically from problem analysis through strategic and tactical recommendations. Your reasoning should be apparent and well supported. Remember, you are asking for business. You have to establish client confidence in your plan.

Third, if you are pitching an account, the plans book will become the key document through which you will manage the campaign should you win the account. Ultimately, you will be working with a team of people from many departments who have to understand the details of the campaign plan. The plans book will provide the appropriate direction and standards for what needs to be a collaborative effort. Otherwise, the client will take his or her business elsewhere.

Fourth, a plans book should tell the client what is right and wrong with the current market situation, and what should be done to resolve the problems. It should also include the strategies and tactics recommended to correct the situation. This approach is analogous to what you want from your doctor when you are ill. You want to know what's wrong and what to do about it. That's what your client wants too.[1]

WRITING THE PLANS BOOK

First, we recommend you defer preparing the cover, title page, table of contents, and executive summary until you have finished writing the body copy of your plan. Next, quickly get started.

The Introduction

This section is optional. If you include an executive summary in your report, you won't need an introduction. Otherwise, the purpose of the introduction is simply to give the reader an overview of what they will be reading explained in very general terms, usually no more than a paragraph. Consider including the nature of the assignment (say, a marketing communications' campaign for brand X), the campaign length, and the budgeted amount of money.

The Situation Analysis

Analyses of each of five subparts—company, consumer, market, product, and competition—are covered in the situation analysis. Each of these sections should interrelate with the others. In the event a different individual is assigned to each section, it is important to emphasize the importance of establishing who is covering each aspect of the various analyses. The idea is to avoid redundant information, an all-too-common problem in student group projects. A major question to consider is how to handle primary research.

Company Analysis

In many ways, the company analysis functions as the introduction to the campaign, but this should be kept relatively brief. You will have to gather more information, and understand more about your client than is necessary to include in the plans book. Never confuse what you need to know to produce a campaign with what you need to report to the client. The bottom line is that the client needs to know that you understand the company, its mindset, where they have been, and where they want to go. You don't want to write about these points extensively, but you do need to establish that you and the company are on the same wavelength. To convince the client that your team is the one they want to work with, it helps if you can show them how their problems are the same or differ from those incurred by similar companies in their field. You might also include in this information a special section called "Industry Analysis," or "Environmental Analysis." How important is it to set up a special section? It really depends on how much of the company's problems are a reflection of what is going on in the industry. At a minimum, you should refer to what's going on in the industry. In the company analysis, consider addressing the following points, not necessarily in the order listed below:

- The company culture and its mission

- A history of the company's problems

- Industry or generic demand trends

- Miscellaneous trends

- Company opportunities

Company Culture. It's important that you understand the kind of a company you are dealing with. If the company has a mission statement, you may get an idea what it stands for and what it wants to pursue in terms of opportunities. Often, however, this isn't going to help very much. Still, you need to understand the kind of business people you are working with. Are they conservative? ambitious? Do they have specific ideas about how they want to grow?

You probably won't put any of this information in your report, but you will want to keep this information in the back of your mind when you reach conclusions. For example, if you believe there is an opportunity for the company to venture out in a new direction, it's helpful to know how receptive the company is likely to be to new ideas. Keep in mind: Clients like to work with agencies they feel comfortable with, not necessarily the agency they feel will deliver the best work.

Company Problems. Executives lose sleep over problems, even small ones. Your plan is, in essence, recommending that the client spend a significant sum of money. Convince your clients that you are at least aware of the things that most concern them. Few things are more tiresome for a busy executive than to wade through page after page of material before he or she reaches the company's problems. If you don't convince your client from the get-go that you understand the company's problems, you run the risk that the executive will simply skim the pages until he or she finds the section on problems. Few problems are more serious than those associated with sales and/or profits. Arrange your plans book so that this material appears early on. It helps if you can show sales trends over a period of four or five years.

Industry or Generic Demand Trends. Company problems are often influenced by problems that are endemic to the industry. It's important to show whether the company's problems are better or worse than the industry norm. If you can include sales data for either the industry or the generic category, this should provide some perspective on whether the solution to the company's problems are related more to the industry's or whether the solution lies in what the company can do for itself. When you're reporting on generic trends, remember: it is related to, but not quite the same thing as what you might cover in the competitive analysis. To be sure the material is covered only once, discuss how the material will be covered with whomever will be doing the competitivie analysis (in the event more than one person works on this section).

Miscellaneous Trends. Numerous things can obviously have a strong effect on the company's problems, such the social, cultural, economic, political, and legal environment. This section takes the broadest view of the marketing environment for a brand by including sales trends, geographical patterns, technological trends, economic trends and influences, regulatory considerations, changes in competitive activity, and changes in consumer attitudes and lifestyles. The important point here is to relate how what's happening in the environment is influencing the company's problems and opportunities. The idea here is to focus on *trends*. Charts and graphs are often a good way to present this material.

New Opportunities. Change generally comes in increments—new customers, styles, colors, sizes, flavors, or line extensions. Chances are the client has already thought of most of these. It may not even be within your discretion to recommend something dramatically different. However, at this point in the plans book you want the reader to believe that your campaign is going to do significant things for the brand. Although we are firm believers in setting realistic goals, as opposed to stretch objectives, painting a rosy picture for the brand is desirable. If you can't demonstrate optimism, the client may feel you are not the right agency for the job. If the plans book is going to be read by a panel of judges, they are likely to think much like a client. If you want them to think your report is special then make sure you describe the opportunities for the brand to the best of your abilities. However, you want to be sure whatever you suggest in this section can be supported in later sections. This means you should avoid clichés, especially the word *great*, when describing the company's opportunities. The opportunities you describe, along with the problems you suggest the company needs to resolve will, in part, form the basis of the campaign objectives.

Primary Research

There is no set way on how to handle this topic. One suggestion is to hold off discussing primary research until you encounter a need to discuss your research findings. Typically, this point comes in the consumer analysis, but put your findings in the sections where they best belong. Include consumer research findings in the consumer analysis section and perhaps in the product analysis section. The description of the methods you used to gather your data should be placed immediately before the report of your findings regardless of where in the plans book you include your research results. If you choose to divide up your findings and place them in more than one section, be sure to describe your research methods before the first discussion of the primary research.

Don't elaborate on all your findings at this point, include a brief discussion of your methodology, and only those findings necessary to underline the point you are making. Additional information should be presented only as needed in subsequent analyses. A copy of the questionnaire and a summary of your findings should be included in an appendix at the back of the report. Another somewhat more formal approach is to present your research in a special section called "Primary Research" and place it before the consumer analysis. Describe your research plan as precisely as possible, and include its objectives and methodology. Tell the client what information you wanted to know but did not have. Describe the type of research you decided to conduct, the sampling scheme, the questions asked, and how the data were analyzed. Then provide a summary of your findings as a foundation for your analyses, objectives, and subsequent strategy recommendations.

Research should be performed with a purpose in mind. Do not get caught up in doing research just for the sake of presenting it. Be sure your research is well conceived and clearly presented. Interpret the results for the client. Do not merely present data without explaining to the client exactly what they represent.

Make judicious use of tables and graphs to present your research findings. Also, place your questionnaire and any detailed analysis of your data in an appendix. You do not want to interrupt the flow of your plans book with your research materials. However, you do want these items to be available in your plans book should someone want to refer to them.

Consumer Analysis

The consumer analysis is the most important section in the plans book. As a result, it is likely to be two or three times longer than any of the other sections. The important thing in this section is to both describe the consumers in some detail and provide some insight into how they think, feel, and behave. The key word here is *insight.* Can you suggest something about the consumer that will provide some key motive that relates to why they may or may not buy your brand? Keep in mind: This is not the section where you determine the target audience. At this point in the book, you're merely analyzing consumers. The targeting decisions should be presented following all the analyses (usually, that means defining the target audience should follow the competitive analysis). Consider the following questions (discussed in some detail in Chapter 2):

- Who are the consumers?

- What motivates them to buy?

- What do they look for in a product?

- How do they look at life?

Identifying Consumers. We discussed several ways to delineate the target in Chapter 2 and you should review those. However, you will at least profile the audience in demographic terms. You want to indicate who uses the product in absolute and relative terms. Indicate how much of a product is consumed by various population segments, and how this usage varies depending on whether you are talking about light, medium, or heavy usage. Consider using data from all four columns in the *MRI* and *SMRB* volumes on product usage (that is, the A, B, C, and D columns). Feel free to interpret the index numbers for the reader. If the index number is 189, say that this demo uses "nearly twice as much of the product as the average consumer." Identify product usage both for the product category and the brand, if this information is available. If you can also delineate product usage with psychographic data, put that here. This section is another place where a chart can convey detailed information a lot easier than text.

Identifying Consumer Motivations. This section is tricky for students to write because it is hard to feel confident about what motivates people to buy, especially considering the limited amount of research students can access. Nonetheless, it is a good idea to go ahead and speculate about what consumers may think or feel about the product or brand. If the researchers or planners don't do this then the creatives will have to reach conclusions without any insight from the research. Just be careful how you present your ideas. For example, focus groups may or may not be representative of the target audience so what you uncover in this type of research may not be characteristic of the target audience.

Identifying Consumer Needs, Wants, Problems, and Interests. Why people buy is, of course, related to their needs, wants, and the problems they would like to solve. When presenting this information, remember to discuss needs, wants, and problems in terms of the degree to which they are important. Sometimes people just sort of want something. Try to convey, as carefully as you can, a realistic appraisal of what consumers think and feel. As is often the case, consumers may not *really* need something. If this is so, then evaluate whether the brand is something consumers can get interested in without any degree of difficulty. The information in this section should be based on your research, but some of your conclusions will most likely be intuitive in nature. Don't shy away from giving an opinion because you can't back it up with research findings. Simply be careful with how you phrase your opinions so the reader recognizes that your statement is based on personal judgment.

Identifying Consumer Values and Lifestyles. Consumers can be resistant to advertising. Copywriters and artists need detail and insight about the target audience so they can craft ads that motivate consumers. Little details about the target's values, their activities or hobbies, how the product fits into their lives, who influences them, may be the tiny aspect of an ad that makes the audience feel you are talking to them. If you have accumulated a great deal of information in this area, display it in a chart.

When you have completed the above, your analysis should provide a precise description of the important consumer segments in terms of demographic factors such as age, gender, income, education, marital status, and occupation. Because demographic profiles only provide part of the picture of a prospective target audience, you should also include any psychographic, lifestyle, and geodemographic data that are available to give a richer picture of how your brand fits into the audience's lives. These factors can be compared to product usage and media usage patterns to determine the characteristics of the prospective consumer targets for your campaign. You are looking for some insight into prospective buyers' behavior that you can effectively use as part of your strategy.

Market Analysis

The market analysis is an extension of the consumer analysis. As such, there may be some practical advantage to doing these two analyses together to avoid redundant information. This section should tell the reader where the consumers are—obviously. But to derive much value out of this information, planners (especially those in media) need to know more than simply the best markets for the brand; they need to know how much better one market is than another. Index numbers are a good way to show how one market compares to an average market. Be careful not to misuse index numbers. A high index number may indicate the market uses more of the brand than the average market. However, if the market is a small percentage of the overall market, it is important to point out that information as well.

The market analysis section should also include pertinent data on the size of the market in terms of sales, market share, and structural aspects of the market (such as distribution and your client's relationship with the trade.) This section should provide an overall sense of market potential, what the viable market segments might be, and where you should focus your marketing communications' efforts.

The geographic pattern of sales can be broken down by region, by major metropolitan markets, and by comparing rural, urban, and suburban purchase patterns. The market analysis should provide a clear picture of where your brand does best and its market potential in areas where it may not be doing as well as expected. Market potential is evaluated by calculating and reporting the product category development index (CDI) and brand development index (BDI) for the markets your brand competes in.

Student groups often have an especially difficult time with this section because they usually don't have access to the detailed market-by-market sales information professionals get from AC Neilsen, IRI, and Claritas. Regional product usage can be obtained from *SMRB* and *MRI*, but this information, although helpful, doesn't provide the local market sales data that planners use to determine which markets may need extra emphasis. One approach, albeit of limited value, is to use a local market as an example of the kinds of decisions the student group would make if they had access to local market data on a national basis. This type of information could go in this section or in the section on media.

Product Analysis

Although this may seem obvious to some people, the first thing to get straight is to use the correct terminology for this section. If the assignment is for a service or an issue advocacy campaign, then the title of this section should reflect this difference. If it is for a product, avoid the temptation to begin this section by describing the product. This may have some small value if you are preparing the plans book for someone other than the client. However, the product analysis section should be more than a descriptive presentation of the physical attributes of the product. Your client is more concerned with how consumers rate, evaluate, and perceive a product than what its tangible characteristics are. If this report goes to the advertiser, assume they already know product detail.

You can start off this section with an assessment of how the product qualities match up with what consumers want. Do this both qualitatively and quantitatively. Your research should have uncovered what consumers like and dislike about the product and, perhaps, what they think is missing. You'll also need to present how well the product sells and when. This point is also important to the competitive analysis and could instead be included in that section. An argument can also be made that since the client already knows this information, you don't really need to present it until you get to the media section where you might want to allocate media dollars on the basis of the seasonal variation in sales.

As we've already said, the client already knows a lot of this information. What the client may not quite know is what the brand has to offer to the consumer—something that will set it apart from the competition. Products exist on shelves. Brands exist in the minds of consumers. Here's where your analysis can provide some insight. Brands have images, personalities, and assets—even liabilities. Minute Maid orange juice is made from concentrate, unlike Tropicana which is not. It's an asset for Tropicana, but a liability for Minute Maid. Copywriters need this kind of information.

Give the client some idea of how much value there is in the brand name. Further, evaluate the opportunity to add value to the brand name—to determine whether it can become a "power" brand (see Chapter 5 for more information). End this section the way you began it—by stating what the brand has that addresses what is important to the target audience. Naturally, this means you have presented how the consumer perceives the brand. These consumer perceptions influence the essence of what the brand is. Be sure to point this out with some emphasis.

Competitive Analysis

The competitive analysis is an extension of the product analysis, and the two analyses should be coordinated to avoid overlap. The first step in this analysis is to address how the brand stacks up against the competition. To do that well, you have to identify who or what is the competition. Competition can come from companies within the product category, or from outside the category. Coca-Cola competes against other soft drinks; they also compete against any beverage consumers drink for refreshment. Kroger competes against McDonald's. If consumers spent less time at McDonald's, they might buy more groceries.

Notwithstanding, the most important comparisons should be provided on companies within the product category. Some of the information about the product such as price, distribution, and promotion, can be included here. What's important is not the information per *se,* but the evaluation of the comparison among brands. Comparisons of the advertising, including media expenditures, can be helpful to include in this section. This information can be useful in predicting how the competition may respond to your campaign. Marketing communications' strategy is developed specifically to compete against other brands in your category. It is important not only to know them well, but also to specifically point out exactly where they are weak or where they are strong.

Writing the Situation Analysis

There are several ways to make the situation analysis concise, to reduce its length.

1. Use Graphs, Charts, and Tables to Present Important Data. The many available and easy-to-use graphics software packages should make this task much easier than it had been in the past. Converting your data into pictures makes it easier to digest, and this will allow you to make reference to the data without having to describe it at great length in writing. Pie charts work well for illustrating market share, competitive media spending, product usage segments, and budgets. Bar graphs are ideal for comparing data as well as for indicating trends. Line graphs illustrate expenditure and sales trends.

Exhibit 11–1   Plans Book Table of Contents

*The primary research section may not be an official section, but a description of the methods you used to gather data should be included in the plans book. This section will appear in different places in different plans books depending on where the findings fit best. Primary research as an official section is usually placed before the consumer analysis as illustrated in this exhibit.
**The location of the budget can be located at various places in the plans book. We place it in the above position only to remind you of its importance early in the campaign process. In most instances, the budget will be located following the media or the marketing communication section.

2. Use Bulleted Lists to Highlight or Summarize Key Information. The following example shows how a bulleted list summarizes key findings on pet ownership in the United States.

Example
- More households own dogs than cats.

- Cat owners are more likely than dog owners to have more than one pet.

- Working couples are more likely to own a cat than a dog.

- Cat ownership is on the rise, and dog ownership levels remain constant.

This outline form of writing gives emphasis to important information while presenting it as concisely as possible.

3. Make Good Use of Heads and Subheads. Heads organize your information, and make it easier to find. Major (first level, primary) heads appear flush left in your table of contents. Subheads (second, third, and fourth level) further break down the information (provide detail) to your primary heads. These appear indented under the primary heads on your table of contents. Usually, only primary and secondary heads are listed in your table of contents. For example, your creative strategy is typically a subheading under your advertising strategy section. Note that it is indented on the table of contents in the figure. You can indicate the different levels of importance of your subheads through the use of capitalization, bold lettering, and underlining. Always give more emphasis to the major sections and successively less emphasis to each subsection in a hierarchical fashion. A quick perusal of this text will illustrate how subheads are used to organize the book's content.

It is not wise to overuse heads or subheads because it can impede the flow of your writing by making it appear choppy. Too many subheads can make the organization of your chapters appear unnecessarily complicated to the reader.

PROBLEMS AND OPPORTUNITIES

It is highly recommended that you set up a formal section for problems and opportunities because it provides a bridge from your situation analysis to your objectives and strategies. Your objectives and strategies will be based on problems and opportunities that you have uncovered in the situation analysis. This is a necessary part of your thinking whether or not you state the problems and opportunities formally. Stating your problems and opportunities is a good exercise in digging for that insight that will catapult your recommendations forward. Likewise, a good set of problems and opportunities demonstrates to the client how you got from your analysis to the objectives and strategies.

Problems are drawn from weaknesses that you found in your situation analysis. These problems can be derived from a particular piece of information or a set of findings. You may find them in any one or all sections of your situation analysis. Exhibit 11–2 illustrates how problems were deduced from various sections of the situation analysis.

Note that the problem statements in the exhibit are conclusions drawn from the situation analysis and state the weakness without offering a solution. Do not steal the thunder from the rest of your plan by presenting your solutions to the problems in this section— that subject belongs in your strategy section.

Exhibit 11–2   Deriving Problems from the Situation Analysis

Company Analysis

Company X has been changing advertising agencies at a rather frequent rate resulting in inconsistent advertising messages with no recurring and unifying theme. This example is similar to a situation Burger King found itself in for many years before developing quality campaigns in the late 1990s.

Problem

Company X's advertising messages are inconsistent with no recurring and unifying theme.

Consumer Analysis

Consumers in the product category perceive all the major brands to be relatively alike. They tend to buy when a brand is on sale, or they have a coupon, and then repurchase whatever other brand is on sale the next time they buy. Category usage is high but brand repurchase is low. The soft-drink category might exhibit these characteristics for many brands. Home delivered pizza is another example.

Problem

Consumers in category are not brand loyal.

Combined Market, Product, and Competitive Analysis

The company's current models are lagging the competition in technological sophistication. The company is presently working on new models but has to sell its existing inventory. Automotive and computer companies often have to work within the constraints of this type of problem.

Problem

Company X's models do not offer the most current technology available in the market.

As you analyze your marketing situation, your aim should be to find some *opportunities* in addition to problems. An opportunity is something that you discover in the situation analysis that you can take advantage of. This opportunity may be the result of a particular company or product strength or a weakness exhibited by the competition, or it could be an opportunity to take advantage of a trend or change in government regulations. Your client might be the first to incorporate something new into a product. There are many places to look for opportunities. The important thing to remember is that in analyzing your situation, you should look for opportunities as well as problems. Exhibit 11–3 illustrates how opportunities might be derived from the situation analysis.

Real opportunities translate into expanded sales. Typically, to increase sales you (1) strive to get new users, (2) get current users to use more of the product, or (3) find new uses for the product, thereby, increasing the likelihood that (1) and (2) will increase. You

Exhibit 11–2   Deriving Problems from the Situation Analysis—cont'd

Market Analysis

The product usage of some product categories and specific brands do especially well in some regions of the country and not well in others. Breakfast sausage in general, and Jimmy Dean's brand in particular, are examples of this situation.

Problem

Consumers are predisposed to prefer brands that have been historically identified with certain regions of the United States.

Product Analysis

The client is operating in a parity product category where there are differences between brands, but these differences are not known to consumers. Furthermore, it is not clear whether or not these differences are important criteria to the purchase decision. Over-the-counter drugs and personal-hygiene-products marketers have to be concerned about consumer understanding of brand differences in their categories.

Problem

Consumers perceive company X's brand to be the same as the competitors' brands.

Competitive Analysis

Company X was the first to enter the growing health-food market and established itself as the category leader. Since then, new competitors have made inroads, and this has altered company X's brand position in the market. These new competitors have also been successful in influencing consumer preferences for the types of foods offered in the category. As new categories grow and mature, consumer preferences for certain attributes and types of products often change. This can be a natural result of new competitors entering the category and offering new benefits to the consumer market.

Problem

Company X's brand has lost its position and image in the category due to changes in consumer preferences and new competition.

will run into situations where it is not clear whether you have found a problem or an opportunity. Many situations are actually hybrid cases where a problem can be turned into an opportunity. Don't assume, however, that you can simply restate any problem as an opportunity. Look, also, for genuine opportunities that the situation analysis presents apart from the problems you have found.

Your list of problems and opportunities should include only those areas that are relevant to the marketing communications' plan. A client may have problems, such as store location, that cannot be resolved by marketing communications; omit those problems from your plans book. If you present a SWOT analysis, handle the information much as suggested above. SWOT analyses lend themselves particularly well to the use of a chart or table.

Exhibit II-3   Deriving Opportunities from the Situation Analysis

---

Company Analysis

Company X has established a strong distribution system and has good trade relationships with its retailers. It would like to use this experience and positive image with the trade to support a new product introduction. This could be a fairly common advantage to a company wishing to extend its product line around an existing brand name.

Opportunity

Company X already has a strong distribution system and good trade relations.

Combined Consumer and Product Analysis

Company X has found that consumers want a particular product attribute that company X's brand has but that attribute has never been advertised. Consumers do not associate company X's brand with this attribute. This may appear to be too good to be true, but 7-Up found itself in this exact position regarding the caffeine in soft drinks. It never had caffeine in 7-Up and was able to take advantage of the fact that consumers were unaware of this.

Opportunity

Company X's brand contains a highly desired attribute that consumers are unaware of.

Combined Consumer and Market Analysis

The increase in two-wage-earner families and the aging of the population have made company X's experience in the service area the foundation for expansion of its business. Lawn and garden services, house painters, snow removal companies, and house cleaning firms are all benefiting from this current trend.

Opportunity

Company X's services are in more demand due to reduced leisure time for people to do chores and the inability of older consumers to do these household jobs.

TARGET MARKET PROFILE

This section of the plans book tells your client to whom your marketing communication campaign is going to be directed. It sets up the marketing and advertising objectives, in that the underlying assumption is that the objectives are to be achieved against this group.

The target market profile also tells your client where the resources and efforts of the company are going to be focused. The consumer and market analysis sections of your plans book set up the selection of the target market by analyzing the various potential market segments that might become the focus of your campaign. Therefore, the profile of the target market should come as no surprise.

The target market or target audience for a given brand or product is that segment whose needs and wants are best met by the product. This means that the target market for

Exhibit 11–3 Deriving Opportunities from the Situation Analysis

Product Analysis

Company X has been focusing on one particular use of its brand and in doing so had marketed to one market segment. Analysis of the product found that it offered other uses that appealed to different market segments. Some readers will recognize this as the classic Arm & Hammer baking soda case where they advertised the product for use as a deodorizer in kitty litter and the refrigerator among other things. The reality is that some companies miss opportunities because they only see their products from one perspective.

Opportunity

Company X's brand has multiple uses, most of which have yet to be marketed to the appropriate market segments.

Competitive Analysis

The analysis uncovered that existing competitors were upgrading their models and by doing so making them more expensive. Their move upward was leaving the lower end of the market open and ripe for entry by a new company willing to sell cheaper models. This has happened in the automobile industry, where companies that entered the market with cheap subcompact cars could not resist the temptation to build bigger and more expensive cars. Often the low end of the market has been abandoned, thus providing an opportunity for another manufacturer to enter the market.

Opportunity

There is no competition for company X in the lower end of the product category.

a brand may not always be the heavy-user segment in the category. Different brands in many consumer product categories meet different needs. Your situation analysis should provide the appropriate insight with which to select a target that will best respond to your product and marketing communication campaign.

Example: A Typical Target Market Profile for a Manufacturer of Canned Vegetables
Primary Market

- Heavy users (35% of the users and 65% of the total consumption) who normally stock large quantities of inexpensive food for their families

- Female homemakers

- Age 25 to 49

- Blue-collar occupation

- Household income $25,000 to $40,000

- Resides in size B and C counties

- High school education

- Family size 3+ skewing to 5+

- Eastern and Midwest regions

Secondary Market

- Trade

- Buyers for chain supermarkets and independent grocers who cumulatively represent a minimum of 65% of total canned vegetable sales

- Current brokers/wholesalers[2]

Note that in this example there is a secondary target market, the trade, which will have to be sold on carrying the product. These two targets complement each other. Usually, there will not be two or more consumer markets because it is difficult to design a marketing communication campaign that can communicate with equal effectiveness to more than one consumer target. However, as we saw in Chapter 8 on marketing communications, the trade is an important target if an advertiser hopes to gain distribution for the product advertised to the ultimate consumer.

Although it might be simplest to identify one target audience, there will be situations in which you will have to combine several submarkets into a group that is large enough to warrant your marketing communication effort. Or, you might be asked to develop a campaign for a large client that sells to more than one market segment. In these cases, you will find yourself defining more than one audience as the target of your campaign. When this occurs, it makes sense to determine which markets are primary and which secondary.

A short rationale should be provided for the selection of your target markets. Note that in the example some of this rationale concerning the size of the target markets has been built into the profiles. The rationale should be brief because you have spent some time and space in your consumer analysis supporting this choice.

MARKETING AND ADVERTISING OBJECTIVES

Usually, it is not the job of the advertising or marketing communication team to develop the marketing objectives. These are usually provided by the client. However, the marketing objectives are often restated here to demonstrate to your client how the proposed marketing communications' campaign supports its total marketing effort. Additionally, smaller clients may not have the sophistication to provide marketing objectives to you. In this case, you will have to make some estimate of your sales or share of market objectives. Estimating may not be as difficult as it sounds because smaller clients are likely to be retailers or local businesses for whom there is a much more direct link between marketing communication activities and sales.

Chapter 4 presented a detailed discussion of how to set objectives. (For example, remember: advertising objectives should include a message element—say, awareness, and a media part—say, reach 70% of the target audience.) Your job in the plans book is to present objectives that provide clear direction to your campaign. You should also demonstrate that you understand the interrelationship between the sales goals of marketing and the communications' goals of advertising and the other marketing communications' elements. You might find that you can skip setting communications and advertising objectives at this stage in favor of presenting them with the appropriate marketing communications' elements. This decision depends on how extensive your advertising, sales promotion, public relations, and direct marketing recommendations will be.

Setting advertising objectives at this stage assumes that your marketing communications' recommendations are simply the execution part of the plan. However, if you intend to give each marketing communications' element a major strategic emphasis, then you should defer your advertising and other objectives for the appropriate section.

BUDGET

There is some discretion as to where the campaign budget should be placed in the plans book. We include it here merely to cause you to think about this section early. Some clients and agencies like to put the budget directly following the marketing objectives so that expenditures can be compared easily to what they are going to achieve. Others (usually agency presenters) do not like to tell the client what a campaign is going to cost until after they have convinced the client's management team that the recommendations are really worth the costs involved. You will have to assess each situation to determine where it makes the most sense.

Another way to look at the budget is in terms of presenting the total figure broken down by major marketing communications' elements to illustrate the relative strategic emphasis given to each early in the plans book. Then the budget for each marketing communications' element can be further broken down in its section. We prefer to put the budget either after the media section or following the section on related marketing communications.

The other approach is to build toward the total budget by placing it at the end of the plans book. Although this approach makes it difficult for the client to remember how the budget relates to objectives and elements of the campaign, it does place the budget closer to the recommendations—the items the client is really paying for in the final analysis.

List all expenditures that will be incurred in the implementation of your campaign, including not only media but also research, production (optional—depending on the client), and contingencies. The budget presentation should be no more than a page or two and can be presented in both tabular and graphic formats. Tables can be used to break down the budget into all its important items, and pie graphs can be used to illustrate the major allocations. Remember to include a small percentage as a reserve, or contingency fund.

MARKETING COMMUNICATIONS' STRATEGY OVERVIEW

The key word in this section is *overview*. This section can be relatively brief. What you want to present here is an indication of how the various marketing communications' tools, such as advertising, sales promotions, direct marketing, and public relations will complement each other to achieve the campaign goals. This overview covers some major strategic decisions. Do not equate a brief section with one that is only of minor importance.

This is the section where you indicate how much money to allocate to the various communications' tools, such as advertising and public relations. You can present this information simply enough in a pie chart, table, or graph, but your rationale should be closely argued and well reasoned. Briefly explain how each of the marketing communication elements will fit together to accomplish the campaign objectives. Be sure that your strategies cover all your objectives and at the same time establish the direction for how you are going to use your marketing communications' elements.

Each strategy statement should have only one focus. It should state how you are going to employ some promotional element or combination of elements to achieve the campaign's objectives. Keep your strategies broad and directional. Do not let them become tactical. For example, state if you are going to use advertising to maintain the brand's image during peak sales cycles. But do not state what the ads will look or sound like or what the slogan will be. These explanations are reserved for the actual advertising part of your plan.

A short rationale should be provided for each strategy that links it back to your problems and opportunities, objectives, and key information that have been gleaned from the situation analysis. For example, if you found that there are certain times during the year when sales dip and have set an objective to achieve better sales during these periods, you should have a strategy that addresses that problem. Your short rationale should be able to provide the link between the strategy and objectives.[3]

Example
Promotion Strategy—Emphasize sales promotions during slow sales periods in July and August to build product categories in which company X is not realizing its full potential.
Rationale—The strategy is based on the realization that sales promotion is required to bolster sales during slow periods and for products that are not reaching their sales potential. Company X should continue to use advertising during peak sales seasons to maximize margins and profit when consumers are buying at higher rates.[4]

ADVERTISING STRATEGY

Your advertising strategy consists of two substrategies: one that addresses what will be said in the advertising messages and one that addresses how media will be used to deliver these messages with the greatest impact. These substrategies are the creative and media strategies that make up the heart of a typical marketing communications' campaign. This section should be very brief.

Creative Strategy

Creative Objectives and Strategy

The creative strategy section of your plans book tells the client how advertising messages are going to be used to achieve the campaign's objectives. The primary function of this section is to explain your creative objectives, strategy, and your tactics. You have some discretion as to whether you want to include your creative executions here, or instead put them into a special section at the end labeled "Creative Supplement."

You will probably want to restate the target audience, perhaps in creative terms (see Chapter 6). Next, present the objectives of your creative strategy—what you want the strategy to accomplish. These will be couched in communications' terms, such as awareness, comprehension, attitude, or image. Use action words with these objectives, such as to convince, to establish in teenagers' minds, to make aware, to remind, to educate, to persuade, to counter the impression, and to demonstrate how to use. Remember, the creative objective is the message (or content) part of the advertising objective. Think in terms of what you want the target audience's response to be. What do you want your target audience to think, feel, or do after being exposed to your ad?

Be ever mindful of what advertising can accomplish by itself. Do not set marketing or sales-oriented objectives here unless direct marketing is a key element and you expect to generate sales.

Consider also using subheads to explain the major components of your creative strategy, such as the message strategy itself, a big unifying idea, and/or how you want to position the product. Refer back to Chapter 6 for more details. Be sure when you discuss the message strategy that you point out how the strategy centers on a strategic focal point. Distill down to one or two sentences the essence of the message strategy. Do the same with your big unifying idea and your brand position. Write a paragraph or two to provide rationale for your strategic decisions.

Use subheads (as described above) and a paragraph of rationale for optional creative elements, such as a theme, slogan, or tactical focal points (also called key copy points). Other strategic elements you might want to include are discussions about the tone, attitude, or appeal (not discussed in this book) which are part of your message strategy.

Creative Tactics

Examples or prototypes of your creative executions should be included in the plans book. If these examples are numerous, you might consider including representative examples here and placing the rest in a creative supplement or an appendix. Print ads should be in a semicomprehensive layout form with illustrations and display copy sketched in. Body copy can be ruled in and provided on a separate copy sheet.

Television spots are best presented in storyboard form and radio commercials as scripts. Large-scale ads, such as outdoor and transit ads, should be scaled down but still maintain the proper proportions of the life-size posters. All executions should be copied so that they can fit into the plans book. Sometimes photographs of the ads in their media context can aid a client in seeing how they will look in their real environment. For example, a photograph of an outdoor board in place or transit card on a bus can supplement the scaled-down example of the ad.

To double check your executions, you may want to review the following three sections. If you feel comfortable in your knowledge about copy and layout, especially if you have taken a basic course, you may want to move on to the media section.

Points to consider when creating print ads

1. Does the headline attract attention and appeal to the reader's self-interest? Does it present news? arouse curiosity? offer a benefit? Is the headline believable?

2. Is the illustration or photograph in the advertisement relevant to the headline and the body copy? Does it work well with the headline to communicate the important part of the message?

3. Does the body copy expand on the headline? Does it substantiate or elaborate on what has been stated or implied in the headline? Does it identify the features of the product? Does it discuss the benefits of these features? Is the copy long enough? Is it easy to read?

4. Does the layout feature unity? harmony? Does it employ formal balance? informal balance? Does it employ proportion? Does it contain contrast? Do the physical elements lead the reader's eye from one area to another in a logical sequence?

Points to consider when creating radio commercials

1. Does the commercial convey the major selling idea?

2. Does the commercial focus on one idea?

3. Does the commercial register the brand name?

4. Can the listener visualize what has been presented (words and sounds)?

5. Does the commercial repeat key terms and/or brand name?

6. Is the choice of music appropriate for the spot?

7. Is the commercial interesting and arresting throughout? or, Does it contain weak spots? Does it end with a positive and suggestive statement? (In most cases, you want the consumer to respond to your commercial by purchasing the product.)

8. Is the commercial's message believable?

Points to consider when creating television commercials

1. Does the commercial focus on a major selling idea?

2. Does the commercial present a situation with which the target can relate?

3. Does the video show as well as tell the story?

4. Does the commercial demonstrate the product's benefits?

5. Are different shots, including close-ups, employed to help maintain interest?

6. Are scene transitions appropriate and not distracting? Are camera directions properly used?

7. Do certain scenes show the brand, package, and logotype clearly?

8. Is the commercial believable?

9. Does the product's promise reflect the product's characteristics?

Media Strategy

In your plans book, the media strategy can be divided into five subsections: (1) an introductory statement of key media implications to be drawn from the situation analysis and marketing communication strategy, (2) media objectives, (3) media strategy, (4) the media plan (that is, the tactics) and schedule, and (5) the media budget summary. Your media recommendations should be based on a thorough understanding of how media can be used to help achieve the campaign objectives. This requires a *brief* review of the situation analysis and marketing strategy with an eye toward identifying those problem areas that are really the concern of the media planner. The media planner should be looking most closely at data and information concerning the target audience, geographic markets, possible seasonal sales patterns, competitive spending levels, and the nature of the marketing communications' and advertising objectives. Here we are looking down the road a bit to get a sense of how difficult (or easy) it is going to be to put enough media exposure directed at the target audience at the right times and in the right places to meet your objectives.

Media Objectives

These objectives are set to provide direction and standards to be met for the media strategy. The criteria for media objectives are well established in the advertising business and reflect the availability of audience data with which they can be measured. The minimum requirements for media objectives are that they state how much reach, frequency, gross impressions, gross or targeted rating points the plan is expected to achieve. You will not need to incorporate all these measures of exposure into your objectives, so consider your selection carefully. If you use reach, than you will also want to use frequency. If you use impressions or rating points, you should indicate that you want to achieve these goals against the target audience (or against a specific demo). (For more information, see Chapter 7, pages 180–189.) Campaign continuity is also an important media consideration. Continuity is concerned with how constant your message exposure will be. Media planning is a game of trade-offs. On a given budget, you can expose your message to many different people (that is, emphasize reach) or expose it to fewer people more often (that is, emphasize frequency). Likewise, you can limit your media weight to short periods of time (flights) for impact, spread it out for continuity (but lose some impact), or combine some of each by varying media weight from one time period to the next (pulsing). You determine which of these patterns is best by comparing the alternatives to what the entire campaign has been designed to achieve.

Setting media objectives is no different from setting objectives for other parts of your campaign. They should always include a target audience, criterion to measure, and time limit in which they will be achieved. Generally, media objectives are written in terms of reach and frequency. At your option, you may also want to include qualitative media objectives as well (see Chapter 7, page 189).

Media Strategy Elements

There is a tendency in planning the media strategy to jump right in and start buying specific media vehicles, such as *Time*, *Newsweek*, and *Sports Illustrated*. Resist this temptation. First, consider the elements that make up a media strategy:

- **Target Audience**—Is this the same as the target for the campaign? If so, indicate that. If not, then briefly restate it.

- **Media Classes**—You need to indicate which media you select, and if you are not using some major medium sometimes it's also appropriate to indicate why.

- **Media Mix**—The amount of emphasis you place on each medium you select is a major strategic decision. It's not enough simply to show a pie chart for the media mix.

Explain how you determined the relative weight to place on the various media classes you chose.

*   **Media Timing**—Both the pattern you choose to deliver the messages and when you schedule them are major decisions.

Explain and support your decisions; support for your decisions can include both quantitative and qualitative factors.

Decision Criteria

The two primary quantitative criteria that you want to look at closely are the relative cost efficiency of each medium and its ability to deliver your message to the target audience. Some of these data are available in syndicated media-audience reference sources, some will have to be calculated, and some come from experience. At this point, your calculations or estimations are generalized. Specific information on the relative cost efficiency of the vehicles that you select should come later in the media section.

It is a good idea to rank order your media alternatives from best to worst in terms of their ability to deliver your audience in a cost-efficient manner. If you have access to a cost-estimating guide used by some of the major agencies (e.g., DDB Needham and Leo Burnett), estimating the relative cost efficiency of media is fairly straightforward. If you do not, then you will have to calculate costs for vehicles that are representative of the type you are likely to select for your plan. When you present your material consider indicating where the competition is spending its media dollars. Will your recommendations schedule the client in head-to-head competition or will your plan select media that the client can dominate without worrying about competitive activity?

Qualitative factors include creative message requirements, such as the use of sound, motion, product demonstrations, coupon offers, and/or color. The media environment should be evaluated in terms of its news value, entertainment value, and quality. You are trying to ascertain what the media environment might add or take away from the effectiveness of your ad. Controversial topics, for example, tend to frighten advertisers because they do not know how the controversy will rub off on their advertising. Some media, such as television and newspapers, have a built-in risk in this regard. Media that carry only advertising messages, such as outdoor ads and direct mail, do not possess this characteristic. Qualitative considerations are very important and come from experience with the media.

After you have evaluated the media alternatives, you should decide on the relative weight that is going to be given to each medium in the mix. Some of your media choices should be identified as primary because they are going to carry the major responsibility of delivering your audience; others will be support media. **Support media** typically add something special to the campaign, such as reaching more of the audience, adding synergy in terms of a different way to execute the creative message, providing a vehicle for delivering samples or coupons, or providing a special timing or placement advantage. For example, an owner of a local, upscale specialty shop might put most of the advertising budget into local media. But the owner might add a small-space ad in *The New Yorker* for image and status reasons because many of the shop's customers read that magazine. Consider also discussing how the media you select can enhance the message strategy. Review "Which Media Do It Best," Chapter 7, page 199.

For each media type selected, you should describe how it is going to be used. For example, what dayparts are you going to use for television and radio? Are there special programming considerations? If you are recommending newspapers, be sure to indicate the days of the week and newspaper sections you feel are best. If you are recommending outdoor advertising (be sure to refer to it as outdoor, not simply billboards) indicate the size showing or the GRPs you would like to see scheduled. If direct mail is recommended, how many pages will the mailing consist of? What about color? How many pieces will you printing?

Media Tactics

After you have made these tactical decisions, present the specific media vehicles that you are recommending. Obviously, vehicle selection should fit the strategy and rationale that have preceded these choices. You want to describe which TV programs, radio stations, magazines, newspapers, and other media you are including in your schedule. To support your decisions, present at least the cost efficiency of the vehicles you recommend. Simply presenting the CPMs next to the vehicles you select helps, but it is more helpful to show comparisons between the vehicles you recommend and the vehicles you do not. In the event you are recommending some vehicle with a relatively high CPM, discuss why it is a good choice.

The following statement is not generally considered a sufficient reason for choosing a vehicle: "This vehicle reaches more of our target than any other." You need to evaluate the reason in light of the vehicle's cost efficiency, especially its ability to deliver the target efficiently. Cost per thousand prospects is always a more powerful measure than a CPM based on total audience.

Media Calendar

Your media plan and schedule is easiest to visualize in the form of a media calendar or flowchart (also called a continuity schedule). The media calendar illustrates how you have scheduled your media over time and what weight you have given to your selections. Your scheduling and media mix strategies will be obvious from one look at this calendar. Figure 11–1 provides an example of a media schedule calendar. Note that each medium has its own symbolic code so that you can tell at a glance how each is scheduled.

Media Budget Summary

The last item that you want to include in your media strategy section is a media budget summary. Media budget summaries can take a number of different forms depending on those factors that are most important to your plan. If market coverage is important, then present how much money you allocated to each medium by market. Perhaps scheduling is the most important consideration. In this case, present the budget by each quarter of the campaign year. If product support is important, show how much money you have allocated to support each brand in a product line. If more than one factor is important, do not hesitate to provide more than one table to illustrate how the media budget has been allocated.

Figure 11–1 Advertising Campaign Strategy.

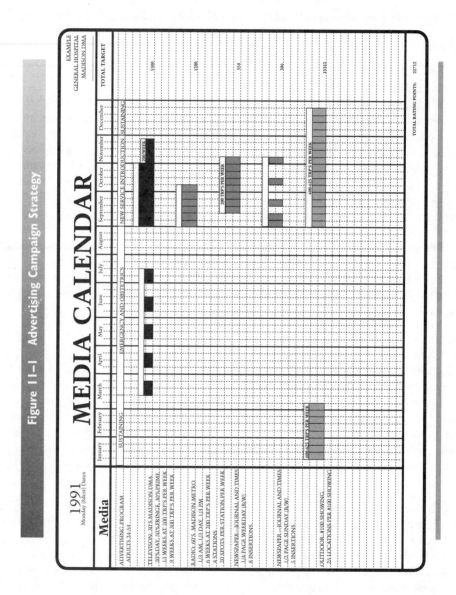

SALES PROMOTIONS, PUBLIC RELATIONS, AND DIRECT MARKETING STRATEGIES

Sales promotions, public relations, and direct marketing should be broken out into individual sections in the plans book. Each section should follow the general form of the media section. You should state specific objectives appropriate to what you want these marketing communications' elements to accomplish. Likewise, describe the strategies recommended and include the actual activities or techniques you have selected to implement these strategies. Include examples of your tactics, as you did in your creative strategy section. To illustrate how your entire plan fits together, provide a schedule of these activities in each section to demonstrate how they dovetail with your advertising media recommendations. Finally, a brief budget summary should demonstrate how you have allocated your marketing communication dollars to the recommended activities in each area. Pricing some of your recommendations, especially in the area of sales promotions, can be difficult for students. If you use estimates, be sure you label them clearly as such.

Not every plans book has a complete set (sales promotions, public relations, and direct marketing) of marketing communications' recommendations. How extensive these sections are will depend on the scope of the marketing communications' problem you have been asked to resolve.

CAMPAIGN EVALUATION

The purpose of a campaign evaluation plan is to provide a methodology for determining whether or not you are achieving your stated objectives. Because you have set objectives for your overall campaign and each substrategy, you have to decide how you want to measure your campaign results.

The nature of the evaluation plan will be influenced by how much money your client wants to invest in monitoring and evaluating the campaign. This plan can run from a simple before-and-after survey of communications' objectives (such as awareness, comprehension, attitude and image), to an expensive and elaborate controlled experiment (test market) in the marketplace. This plan should answer the question, Are we getting there?

You have at your disposal methodologies ranging from focus groups (with all their inherent external validity problems) to surveys to field experiments (which are very expensive). Many clients are removing from their agencies the responsibility for evaluative research. Nonetheless, you should be able to demonstrate to your client how you will judge whether or not the recommended campaign is being successful.

APPENDICES

You want your plans book to be a clear presentation of your analysis and recommendations unencumbered by unnecessary items. You also want your client to see that you have done your homework. The appendices of a plans book are good places to include research findings, media calculations, extra ad examples, and alternative strategies.

Do not allow your appendices to become catchall sections in which you indiscriminantly deposit material. Be sure that the appendices genuinely add something to the impression you want to make. They should serve a purpose.

Exhibit 11–4   15 Key Points for Writing Marketing Communication Recommendations

Develop an outline before writing.

Develop tables, graphs, and visual support before writing.

Make your situation analysis as concise and factual as possible.

Use primary research to support your consumer and product analysis.

Make sure your problems and opportunities reflect each section of your situation analysis.

Be sure your analysis is analytical, not merely descriptive.

Keep all objectives to one sentence.

Aim objectives at a specific target audience. Write objectives that are specific, and measurable, to be achieved within an established time frame.

Make sure strategies describe how objectives will be achieved.

Make sure your advertising and other marketing communication recommendations are on target and on strategy.

Create disruptive ads.

Make sure your media plan will deliver the reach, frequency, and media weight necessary for your campaign to achieve its objectives.

Integrate all promotional recommendations into a unified campaign.

Propose how you plan to measure your results.

Be clear and concise. Not brief.

KEY POINTS TO WRITING THE PLANS BOOK SUMMARIZED

Exhibit 11–4 lists 16 points to remember when writing your plans book. These tips also follow the general logic of campaign planning from your situation analysis through your plans for executing the substrategies of marketing communications. The arrangement of the plans book follows a logical flow. Within this framework you can adjust and adapt to the specific marketing communications' problem confronting you.

Advertising and marketing communications demand creative and innovative solutions formed within the discipline demanded by carefully set objectives and strategic thinking. A creative approach to showcase a technique or a special effect will not help you to achieve your objectives because often these type of ads are created without regard for the target audience or an understanding of what has to be communicated to them for a campaign to succeed.

The plans book should be a clear presentation of your analysis of the marketing situation, problems and opportunities, objectives, strategies, recommended tactical executions, and evaluation of results. The marketing communications' plan should be efficient and effective. Although the process you undertake to put this plan together is dynamic, the final plan should be a carefully crafted set of recommendations that are easy to understand and that push for closure in terms of solving the client's problem.

THE COVER

Once you've completed your writing tasks, you can attend to details that will enhance the impression of the plans book. Consider a professional-looking cover. Be sure it contains all the pertinent information, including (1) the client's name; (2) your agency's name (in a student competition this should be your school's name); other information optional in a university setting, such as (3) the course name, and (4) the competition name. The cover is the first place that sells your campaign. Consider how to make it stand out from the competition. Do not leave your creativity behind after you've completed your campaign work. Extend colors, design approaches, and themes to your plans book cover. Most cover designs incorporate the client's colors and logo at a minimum.

Consider going beyond this minimum standard for the cover in special situations such as the AAF/NSAC competition or new business pitch. However, ask your instructor or supervisor if putting more effort into the design of the cover is appropriate. In any competitive activity it is better to put in a little extra effort, but the cost of doing so might outweigh the benefits. Your instructor (or supervisor) is the best person to guide you in this regard. If you decide to put a little more into your plans book cover, the next three paragraphs are for you.

The plans book is considered a companion piece to the campaign presentation. It should be designed to look like the presentation. Use similar graphics on the cover and section dividers to establish a team identity. This shared look will help campaign judges and clients make a quick association between your team and the plans book once the presentation is over.

Computer technology and the availability of color laser printers and photocopiers have added a great deal of flexibility in designing and printing full-color covers for plans books. This type of design might not be necessary for most class or routine agency projects but has become close to a necessity for the AAF National Student Advertising Competition.

Take into consideration how many copies of your plans book are necessary to produce. If you need to make a lot of copies, color graphics and other fancy technological frills will be expensive to reproduce. You might decide to make full-color and comprehensive plans books for judges, instructors, and clients while providing black-and-white copies for others. Once again, you will have to assess your situation and the importance of the use of color in your plans book.

THE TITLE PAGE

The first page inside your plans book should be a title page. Once again, the content of the title page has some optional elements. The title page can include more information than the cover because cover design considerations typically do not have to be considered. Most title pages include (1) the client's name, (2) the agency's name, (3) agency team members' names and titles, (4) advisor or instructor's name, (5) course title, (6) school name, (7) appropriate dates, and (8) acknowledgments. There is a lot of discretion in how to set up your title page. The best advice is to keep it simple and clean.

You can carryover some of the content from the cover onto the title page. Campaign themes, slogans, and logos can add to the continuity of the plans book as you move the reader from the cover to the inside.

TABLE OF CONTENTS

Once you complete the writing of the plans book, it's time to create a table of contents, which should be the second page of your book. List the major headings in your plans book in chronological order, and then indicate the page location of each along the right-hand margin of the page. A typical table of contents is illustrated in Exhibit 11–1.

The general form for a table of contents reflects the outline of a marketing communications' plan, as shown in Chapter 1. These are the basic elements of a plans book. These headings will be given different emphases as the marketing and advertising problems you are confronted with change from project to project. Your instructor might ask for a slightly different order, or the client's problem could require other areas to be included. For example, the outline in Exhibit 11–1 does not include a section for a test market. If your client's problem requires a test market, then you will include it in a section in your plans book (and in the table of contents).

THE EXECUTIVE SUMMARY (OPTIONAL)

The first one to three pages of your plans book should include a brief version of the entire marketing communications' plan, called the executive summary. This summary should hit the highlights of your campaign recommendations. Your client is most interested in knowing what you plan to do and what it is going to cost. The key elements of an executive summary should include (1) the central thrust of your campaign; (2) who you are targeting; (3) how much it will cost, or the total budget; (4) the creative strategy; (5) any key elements that will encapsulate the campaign, such as the theme, product position, or slogan; (6) which media you are recommending; and (7) the scheduled time period in which it is going to run. Write this summary after the rest of the plans book has been completed. This will help you know your recommendations in detail and you will be better prepared to write a summary highlighting what you have actually put in the plans book.

The executive summary should be clearly written and organized so that the client's management team can understand the recommendations without having to distill them from the detailed presentation inside the book. Clients can and will look inside the plans book for verification and details to support the recommendations, but typically do not want to read the plans book in depth from cover to cover.

Notes and References

[1]Baumgardner, R. L. (1998). Writing plans and recommendations. In American Association of Advertising Agency Committee on Client Service (Eds.), *What every account executive should know about writing plans and recommendations* (pp. 7–8). New York: American Association of Advertising Agencies.
[2]Hiebing, R. G. Jr., & Cooper, S. W. (1991). *The successful marketing plan: A disciplined and comprehensive approach.* Lincolnwood, IL: NTC Business Books, p. 100.
[3]Hiebing & Cooper, *The successful marketing plan*, pp. 114–115.
[4]Hiebing & Cooper, *The successful marketing plan*, p. 115.

Chapter 12

Preparing a Winning Presentation

Are you ready for a show? You should be. Presentations are serious business, but they *are* also performances. As intimidating as they may be to beginners, they can be quite rewarding and intensely satisfying. However, many beginners spend 90% of their time doing research and 10% or less putting together the oral presentation. They are often dismayed when others who do less research, win the account or get a better grade. This happens because they underestimated the power of a good presentation. If you are unable to present your ideas orally, no one will understand and appreciate them. Does this mean that substance is less important than style? Certainly not. In today's business world, both are necessary to excel, and the same is true in the classroom.

No matter how hard you've prepared for the presentation, it's natural to feel nervous and concerned. Still, if your nervousness shows, it's probably more apparent to you than it is to the audience. It's best not to worry excessively about things mostly beyond your control. Relax and enjoy yourself.

PRELIMINARY PREPARATIONS

As you begin putting your presentation together, there are four questions you should answer:

1. To whom will you be presenting?

2. Where will you give your presentation?

3. How will you present your material?

4. What is the one thing you want your audience to remember when the presentation is over?

It is important to have answers to these questions before you prepare for your "show."

This chapter has been developed and written in part by Dr. Lynda M. Maddox, a professor of marketing and advertising at The George Washington University. Her students have competed in numerous advertising competitions sponsored by the American Advertising Federation. She is former chair of the Academic Division of the AAF. In 1998, The George Washington University won the AAF national competition.

Understanding the Audience

Knowing your audience can give you insight on what you should emphasize and what you might cover quickly. We'll look at three basic types of audiences: clients, review panels, and faculty.

Clients and Panels

Typically, clients and panel members are working professionals. They can, however, differ considerably in the way they will evaluate your presentation. Find out as much as you can about their backgrounds, especially if they have a particular expertise or interest in the area of advertising and marketing.

Generally, clients tend to be much more interested in how you can help them solve their problems. Panels, although they can vary widely, want to see quality advertising. For clients, getting a well-balanced campaign is nice, but getting something that addresses their problems directly is likely to have a higher priority. A key to satisfying many clients is to do a good job of identifying their problems. This puts them at ease and helps them be receptive to your analysis and ideas. Later, if you can show them how they can solve their problems and, even better, how they can capitalize on some unanticipated opportunities, this is mostly all they want.

If this is a high-level panel or a very competitive presentation, you need a strong presentation with no weaknesses. The creative, however, is generally where campaigns are won and lost. Naturally, you should have great strategy and big ideas. But do not underestimate the value of impressing the panel with *quantity*. It shouldn't make a difference if you have a great strategy—but only a small number of very good ads. Here's why having quantity can work (even though you are unlikely to get a professional to agree with this point). Winning a creative shootout can be like a crapshoot. Some of it is luck—or at least a matter of differing opinions. Consider the annual surveys of the best and worst ads: some campaigns are frequently cited in *both* categories!

Even though you emphasize the importance of strategy, some clients still get captivated by executions. By providing numerous executions, the panel is likely to quickly gloss over the ads they don't like until their eyes catch one they do. If they only have a few to look at, they'll look at all—good and bad—in detail. How many ads should you present? At least three or four more than the other teams have, and at least two or three more than the panel has time to carefully consider.

Faculty

Just as with a client, think hard about what your instructors may have said—in class and in all the courses they teach. Do they teach creative, media, or management courses? If you are not sure about their expectations, ask their advice. It's no more a good idea for you to surprise your instructor with your work than it would be for a copywriter to show an ad directly to a client. Professionals show their work first to a supervisor—at least, to an account executive. Most instructors naturally have personal biases. One might be strongly impressed with primary research. Another might be impressed with research, but may be skeptical about your data-gathering methods. In the creative area, it helps to know the relative value faculty place on professional-looking executions versus strategic ideas. The best advice we can possibly give you is to get advice—not once, but twice. The first time to get the information, and the second time to see if you are interpreting it correctly. (A third time wouldn't hurt either.)

Evaluating the Presentation Location

The location of the presentation is very important because it will influence the context in which your ideas and information will be received. A small intimate boardroom lends itself to a warmer more casual environment than a large classroom. This can influence the style of your presentation. In smaller rooms, clients like to ask questions. Knowing this in advance can help you prepare for answers. You will want to check out the site physically, if possible. Later, on page 355, we'll give you some tips on what to check out on the day of the presentation. At this point, you want to evaluate how the site will enhance or limit your presentation options. For example, if you ask clients if they are equipped to handle PowerPoint presentations at their facility, be sure you check out what they mean by "equipped." You want to be sure that their idea of a PowerPoint presentation isn't viewing it on a 25-inch TV set while what you have in mind is projecting on a six-by-eight-foot screen.

Choosing the Presentation Medium

There are several media from which you can choose to deliver your presentation. However, your selection will mostly likely come down to one of the following:

- Computer-based media
- 35mm slides

- Overhead transparencies

- Presentation boards and flipcharts

Computer-Based Media

Desktop computers have ushered in new electronic methods that allow users to produce professional-quality slides, overheads, and handouts. The main difference is that computers require materials to be converted or created in a digital format before they can be edited and assembled. Once assembled, users can choose to output their materials in the form of traditional 35mm slides, overhead transparencies, or print media. They can also choose to deliver their multimedia presentations via the computer itself (using either a monitor or a projector interface). Most multimedia software allow you to incorporate audio and video, and to choose to operate the presentation manually or automatically. Users can also create interactive buttons that allow viewers or presenters to jump, in a nonlinear manner, to other slides with related material. The information can also be linked to the World Wide Web.

Many of the media elements used in computer presentations can be created by the multimedia software itself. All of the applications discussed below have word-processing capabilities, along with some drawing or illustration tools. Some also include graphing tools and spreadsheets, or are they available in packages that bundle them with other similar "office" functions. Users can also paste or import elements created in other compatible software packages. Scanners can be used to import print-media images, photographs, illustrations, and even text (with the aid of optical character recognition [OCR] software). And digital cameras can be used to capture original photographic compositions.

Users need to be mindful that digital elements can be saved in dozens of different formats. Almost all software allows users to save files in more than one format. A scroll-down menu of available formats usually appears as part of a dialogue box when you use the "save as" command (other format choices are available if you choose the "export" command). Not all formats are compatible with all software applications. Different multimedia software applications may not be able to open or import some formats. Compatibility problems may arise if you use one software application to create, scan, or edit a media element, and a different software program to "open" or "import" your already prepared presentation. In these cases, you need to know the limitations of your multimedia presentation software, and to use only those applications that are compatible. Adobe Photoshop is capable of opening many different kinds of images and converting them to the format preferred by most other presentation software programs.

Consistency in color is especially difficult to predict or control when using more than one software application to create a presentation. The appearance of colors can also shift when you use different computers, monitors, printers, or operating platforms. While some presentation software can be used in cross-platform situations (that is, they operate on both a Macintosh and a PC), specific elements, including color, may not appear the same in all instances. Unless you are familiar with trouble-shooting these kinds of compatibility issues, it is best to create your entire presentation using a single multimedia application.

Attempts to discuss specific software applications are always problematic because technology is always changing. Emerging technologies, software upgrades, and fierce competition create a chaotic playing field where businesses are constantly being bought, sold, or going out of business. Software purchases should be based on performance (what can the software do), compatibility (will it work with your existing computer, scanner, and printer), and difficulty (how easy is the application to use).

Microsoft PowerPoint

- **Performance**—By far, this is the most widely used presentation software. When bundled with Microsoft Office, PowerPoint has the ability to execute word processing, spreadsheets, graphs, tables, and illustrations within the application. It can also import specific formats of pictures, movies, and sounds with the click of a mouse. Animation, interactivity, transitions, and narration can be applied automatically. Annotation allows the presenter to draw on the slide during the presentation (notes disappear as soon as you select the next slide). Users can choose from a variety of output formats— on-screen slide shows, 35mm slides, color overheads, handouts, and Web pages.

- **Compatibility**—PowerPoint is available for both Macintosh and PC. "Pack and Go" command allows you to save your presentation as a slide show and play it back on any computer with the free PowerPoint Viewer software.

- **Difficulty**—No scripting or programming is required. PowerPoint comes with dozens of predesigned slide and page templates. Pull-down menus add custom animation to text and graphics. Pop-up messages appear automatically to provide tips to new users.

Astound

- **Performance**—Astound got an early jump on PowerPoint by being first to include built-in templates that automatically program animation, sound, and video clips. It uses drag-and-drop technology to import and assemble specific formats of pictures, text, graphs, movies, and sounds. Users can create and customize their own music, narration, and sound effects. Speaker notes can be incorporated into the presentation. Interactivity allows users to link slides, create customized buttons, or turn any graphic or text into interactive links.

- **Compatibility**—Astound is available for both Macintosh and PC. It can also import presentations from Microsoft PowerPoint and Lotus Freelance Graphics for Windows.

- **Difficulty**—No scripting or programming is required. Built-in templates and drag-and-drop assembly for animation, 3D, and Web-presentation make Astound easy to use.

Lotus Freelance Graphics

- **Performance**—When accompanied by Lotus Notes, Freelance has the ability to execute word processing, graphs, and illustrations.

- **Compatibility**—Freelance is available only for Windows. However, it can open PowerPoint and Harvard Graphics files. "Save and Go" feature allows files to be saved as a presentation and as a mobile slide show so users without Freelance Graphics application can receive and play these files.

- **Difficulty**—Freelance Graphics has a conversion assistant to guide users through the process of converting files for Web output and easy-to-use content suggestions tools.

Harvard Graphics

- **Performance**—Harvard Graphics can create charts, slides, and multimedia presentations. It includes drag-and-drop access to clip art and text from other applications and easy incorporation of sounds and ready-made animation.

- **Compatibility**—Available for Windows only. Harvard Graphics can export presentations to the Web and to Lotus Freelance.

- **Difficulty**—Harvard Graphics comes with predesigned presentations. An advisor gives step-by-step guidance at the click of a mouse and a design checker identifies problems and fixes them automatically.

Macromedia Director

- **Performance**—By far, the most powerful and complex multimedia software available. Unlike the others, Director is a true multimedia authoring program. It has too many attributes to list—it is capable of programming almost any trick you desire. Special effects allow 360° rotation, horizontal/vertical flipping, object transparency, and blending.

- **Compatibility**—Director can output to either platform, Macintosh or PC. Presentations can be converted for use on the Web or on CD-ROM.

- **Difficulty**—The learning curve for Director is much steeper than for the others. It uses object-oriented scripting (lingo), some of which can be accessed via menus. It has familiar drag-and-drop functions and automated "behaviors" for some events. Director has the power to give professionals a definitive edge, and to virtually humiliate amateurs.

35mm Slides

The use of slides has largely been supplanted by computer-based presentations. Still there are a few good reasons why you might want to use this medium. Colors, especially for photographs, are sharp and clear. You may consider using slides to set yourself apart from the competition, most of whom will likely be using a computer-based presentation. Of course, you run the risk that you will be considered old-fashioned, but a slide presentation done well still looks very good

Overhead Transparencies

Although often slighted, transparencies or overheads are easy to make, inexpensive, portable, and flexible. You can write on them. They also command audience attention. On the downside, the colors are not as clear or the type as crisp as with other media unless you use a good laser printer. Probably, the biggest disadvantage to using transparencies is that the audience may not think you're as sophisticated as another group that uses a more technologically advanced method. However, if you do use transparencies consider the following tips:

- **Use frames for holding the transparencies in place.** If you need to use tape, don't make it masking tape; instead use drafting tape.

- **Lightly pencil in cues or tips for your presentation on the frame borders of each transparency.** These tips can remind you of script points, or to remind you to smile or to hold your hands at your sides.

- **Label each of your transparencies.** This is important because you don't want to have to turn on lights to check just which transparency you are showing.

Presentation Boards and Flipcharts

Boards and flipcharts shorten the psychological distance between you and the client. You can write on them, handle them, and move them closer. They seem more real and exciting to the client, and are dependable because they have no mechanized parts that can break down as some machinery tends to do at the most inopportune times. If you choose to use presentation boards and flipcharts, consider the following tips:

- **Use bold magic markers to write.** Create contrast with the background.

- **On a flipchart, use all capital letters.** Don't be afraid to add or delete on the pads and charts as you present them. Lightly pencil in cues for yourself on the back of the pad or chart.

- **Staple a blank sheet behind each page so that bleeding or fuzzy lettering doesn't show through. If you're concerned about the quality of lettering or art, go to the Yellow Pages or other source for traceable images.** Clip-art books, rub-on letters, and children's coloring books are also helpful.

Creating a Lasting Impact

Professional presenters know that the audience will not remember much of what they say. But this fact is often disheartening to students who may have spent the better part of a semester collecting information to present. After you've assessed your audience, your venue, and your presentation medium, you're ready to answer an important question. If your audience remembers only one thing about your presentation, what would you want that to be? This is often difficult to answer, especially if you are presenting the work of a team. You must all agree on this one point to make a successful presentation. Usually, the answer to this question is that you want the client to remember your solution to his or her problem.

Make the solution the "hero" of your presentation. Too often, students focus on all the research they have collected. In a client presentation, this is not as important as showing your ideas, your solution to the problem. Develop a theme to your presentation that brings the listeners back again and again to your main idea. If you want your audience to remember your key point, we believe they should hear it at least four times.

PLANNING THE PRESENTATION
Determining the Order of the Presentation

Much of the discussion about the order in which to present the various areas in the campaign focuses on how to showcase the creative section. Clearly, the ads and the message strategy are the highlights of impressive campaigns. The following are some options:

SA → CS → ADS → MP → RMC → RMCE → B
SA → MP → RMC → B → C → AD → RMCE
SA → CS → MP → RMC → B → ADS → RMCE
CT → SA → CS → CT → MP → B → RMC → B → ADS → RMCE

Key

SA = situation analysis   CS = creative strategy
   ADS = advertising examples   MP = media plan
   RMC = related marketing communications   CT = creative teasers
   RMCE = related marketing communication examples   B = budget

Is there a preferred order in the above options? Not really. The order in which you deliver your presentation depends a lot on what you think of your creative. It is important to remember that when people leave presentations, they don't usually talk about the media; they talk about the message strategy and/or the ads. All of the approaches, even the fourth one, basically start out with the situation analysis. The logic of this approach assumes that the analysis forms the foundation upon which subsequent strategy and executions are based.

The first option is fairly straightforward and mostly follows the outline of the book. Its advantage is that it is fairly logical. Its disadvantage is that once the ads are shown anything shown afterward can be anticlimactic. One way to minimize this limitation—don't show much in the way of media or other communication ideas. In the business world, this approach works fine. In a competition or a class situation, the judging criteria will usually militate against taking this direction.

The second option is sometimes appropriate for established brands for which the media plan is fairly well assumed. The idea here is to get the analysis and the media out of the way and then devote most of the presentation to the creative. The advantages and disadvantages here are similar to the above in that what works well in the business world may not go so well out of it.

The third option is highly recommended. You get to talk about your strategy and ideas early, but you still save the executions for the end of the presentation where you hope you will "wow" the audience. By saving your executions until the end, you hope that the last thing the audience remembers about your presentation are the things that are likely to leave the most favorable impression. Although we put the marketing communication examples after the ads, don't take that position literally. You can also consider mixing the marketing communication examples in with the ads. For example, if you had a radio or television spot with music, you might want to put that execution at the end—to leave people humming.

The fourth option is the most fluid and potentially creative of all the options. It won't work very well, however, unless there is something in the creative plan to weave a thread of excitement throughout the presentation. The idea is to build excitement for the creative ideas by hinting or teasing at what it might be. For example, you could start your presentation off by announcing, "On January first, in the year 2000, Brand X will introduce its advertising idea for the new millennium." Of course, once you have the audience hooked you have to deliver on your promise. The new idea could be something serious such as a product promise, or a new warrantee. It could also be something less than serious such as a new trade character like a lizard or a chihuahua. A variation of this option is to show ads and use them as examples of specific points you want to make in the presentation.

Determining the Content of the Presentation

Depending on the order in which you present your material, what you present can vary considerably. As you go through the plans book, consider the following tips regarding what to present:

Company Analysis

- Keep this section brief. Avoid covering material that could be covered in the product analysis.

- Very quickly let the client know you understand their problems.

- Tell the client how you will improve sales or profits.

- Find a gap between what is and what could be.

- Let the client know that you will be telling them how to close the gap.

- Do more than simply identify the problem, expand the client's knowledge of it.

- Use the client's values to understand why they should care about their problems.

- Lay the foundation for your campaign by identifying opportunities your campaign will later address.

- Be sure to relate what is going on with the company to the industry or economy in general.

Consumer Analysis

- Establish who is using both the brand and other products in the generic category.

- At a minimum, delineate users with demographic variables, using other criteria as available.

- Describe usage with terms such as heavy, medium, light, above average, and so on. Indicate index numbers to give an indication as to what these terms mean.

- If you have done primary research, indicate very briefly a description of what you did, including your methodology.

- Include only the key findings that provide insight into how consumers think or feel about the brand and generic category.

- Indicate what consumers want either from your brand or this type of product.

- Indicate the degree to which consumers might be interested in either the brand or the category.

- Briefly, sketch out the consumers' lifestyle, brand loyalty, and other factors that may influence consumers' thoughts or feelings about the brand.

- Provide a detailed understanding of the consumer's buying decision process.

Market Analysis

- Briefly indicate the relative geographical dispersion both of users and product usage across the United States.

- Indicate the quantity of users with raw numbers or percentiles and the type of usage (i.e., heavy, medium, or above average) with index numbers on a selective basis.

- Indicate how brand usage compares to usage in the generic category.

- Use brand development index (BDI) and category development index (CDI) numbers if available, but be sensitive to the audience's understanding of these terms.

- If available, indicate whether usage varies with county size.

Product Analysis

- Tell what the product has that addresses what consumers want. Avoid merely describing the product.

- Indicate advantages and limitations.

- Include in your appraisal of the product an evaluation of the brand's distribution, price, and past advertising—being careful not to merely describe this information.

- Indicate whether the consumer's perception of the brand reflects real product characteristics or whether it is a result of cultural trends, advertising, competitive efforts, or past experiences with the brand.

- Show how consumers feel about the brand, apart from the way they feel about the product's physical characteristics. How much brand equity does the product have? What is the brand's market position?

- Evaluate the opportunity to build the brand. Can it be a power brand? Give the client hope, but don't overpromise.

Competitive Analysis

- Evaluate the competition similar to what was done in the product analysis. Avoid simply describing the competition, both direct and indirect.

- Be sure to indicate where the competition does well.

- Evaluate briefly (no more than a few sentences) the competition's advertising.

- Indicate competitive media expenditures if available.

- Show where your brand falls on a perceptual map vis-à-vis the competition.

Problems and Opportunities

- If you haven't already discussed problems and opportunities at the end of each analysis, sum them up here.

- In your summary, indicate the difference between major and minor problems and opportunities.

- At some point in this section, your discussion of problems and opportunities should converge on your conclusion of the opportunity to expand sales.

- Is there an opportunity to expand sales by getting new users? by getting current users to use more of the product? by promoting new uses of the product?

- Consider a SWOT analysis to summarize problems and opportunities.

- Consider turning problems into opportunities. Even a skeptical client can be converted by optimism.

Profiling the Target Audience

- Upon completion of the previous section, inform the audience that the decision about whom to target comes only after considering the entire situation analysis carefully.

- State the target as simply as possible. Indicate who they are and where they are located. It shouldn't be necessary to provide any justification.

- Prioritize multiple target markets by indicating your rationale for selecting primary, secondary, and tertiary markets.

Objectives

- If you have been given marketing objectives, restate them here.

- If you can set realistic marketing objectives, state them here (students generally do not have enough information to do a good job here).

- If you don't have marketing objectives, indicate your sales expectations in a general way, probably without putting them on a slide (or other medium).

- List your campaign objectives. Indicate you will later break down these objectives further in the other sections.

Campaign Budget

- We recommend you put the budget near the end of the presentation with the section on evaluation. However, if you prefer to put it here, show the budget at least two different ways: in percentages allocated to specific items, such as advertising, public relations, and sales promotions; and in terms of the dollar amounts allocated for each item.

- It's not necessary to read every number that appears in front of the audience. Give highlights and round off big numbers.

- If you offer this material at the end of the presentation, tie the budget to the achievement of objectives.

Marketing Communication Strategy Overview

- If you present anything from this section, keep it very brief. You may not even want to put anything in a visual aid. If you do, consider a pie chart indicating the break down of money spent on the various marketing communications' tools.

- Briefly tell how all the marketing communications' tools will complement each other to achieve campaign objectives.

- Present strategy and rationale throughout the presentation.

Advertising Strategy

- Remember, in many people's eyes, advertising strategy and the message strategy are the same thing. So if you want to say anything about media here, keep it very brief.

Creative Strategy

- Whatever you show or say, it has to be both special and different. Your visuals, speech, and manner should all convey the feelings of pride, confidence, excitement, and even . . . the love (there we've said it !) that your team has toward the ads.

- Consider quickly reminding the audience of the target audience, perhaps restated in creative terms (see page 140).

- If you present creative objectives on a visual (although you may not want to) do so briefly. Resist the urge to read full sentences.

- Summarize your creative strategy in a simple statement. Consider putting the statement on a visual.

- Present other major elements of your message strategy, such as a big unifying idea or your brand position. Consider visuals for these elements, too.

- Consider presenting other elements of the message strategy, such as the theme, slogan, or tone, but discuss these as you present your executions. Use them to tell the client why the ads will work.

- If you have mounted examples of print ads, take them off the easel and bring them to the client. Show just how special you think they are.

- Read the headline in your print ads. Describe the copy, but don't read all the ads unless the client requests it.

- For television, don't read anything the audience can see. If they can't see your storyboards, briefly describe them.

- When reading the audio for television or radio, inject enthusiasm and personality into each reading. Make it a performance.

- If two females read a spot written for a male and a female, have one lower her voice. If two males read a spot written for male and female, use your judgment.

- If presenters are free to move about, consider moving closer to the client and audience to give them a close look. Use the opportunity to make a more personal connection with the audience.

Media Strategy

- Move quickly into the media presentation. Media is becoming more and more important and creative. Show original thinking and integrate non-traditional media.

- If you present your media objectives on a visual, don't read them verbatim. If you read your media objectives, don't put the full text on a visual. (Present objectives in terms of reach, frequency, impressions, and rating points.)

- Briefly discuss the major elements of your strategy: the media choices, the media mix, and the timing.

- You can discuss media choices by presenting pictures of media vehicles each selected along with your rationale.

- The media mix can be communicated easily with a pie chart.

- You may want to talk briefly about media timing. You can show a continuity schedule (i.e., a media calendar) after you have discussed media tactics.

- When presenting media vehicles, group them according to media categories and provide both quantitative and qualitative reasons for selecting them.

- Remember, cost per thousand prospects (CPMP) is usually more relevant than a simple CPM. Provide CPMs for vehicles you did not select to compare.

- Graphs or maps are quick ways to show how media dollars are allocated on a geographical or seasonal basis.

- End this section with a media calendar and a budget.

Sales Promotion, Public Relations, and Direct Marketing

- Briefly state objectives, indicating how they tie into campaign goals.

- Briefly state strategy in a few sentences and be ready to move quickly into your promotion examples.

- Be sure promotional ideas integrate with and complement your advertising.

- Execute prototypes of your promotional ideas. Show them on your slides.

- Talk about the role of promotions in accomplishing your objectives.

- Small ideas that will probably get rejected by the client are no big deal in this area, especially if you preface your ideas by saying, "Here are some additional ideas for you to consider."

- Develop a calendar for your ideas.

- Try to give the impression you are a source of unlimited ideas.

- Include promotions in your budget.

- Indicate how the public relations' program will complement the other marketing communications' activities.

- Tie PR objectives in with campaign goals.

- Briefly state strategy and give examples of your PR ideas.

- Indicate when the PR activities will take place. Talk about costs.

- Give examples of public relations.

- If you are using direct marketing in the campaign, indicate how it fits in with other marketing communication tools.

- Very briefly state objectives and strategy. Show or pass around examples of what you plan to use in the program.

- Very briefly indicate your costs and a calendar.

Evaluation

- Indicate how you will evaluate the campaign's effectiveness. Include examples of benchmarking surveys, focus groups, or other research.

- If this is the last item in the presentation, use the last tip to segue into a closing statement where the account executive will . . .

Conclusion

- . . . ask for the account.

Important Advice for Planning the Presentation

The tips discussed above are only advice. Campaigns are different and so are agencies. Customize your presentation to fit your team and the situation. Moreover, if you are in a competition with other schools and they have read this book, you will want to avoid looking like them. This book has been used by approximately 80 schools in the United States and about 100 schools worldwide. Retain the important principles, but be different.

Presentation Goals for the Individual Presenters

As you think about the individual role you will play in the overall team presentation, there are five points (goals) to keep in mind.

1. Understand the Presentation. As you plan your own individual role in the overall presentation, be careful not to lose sight of the team's presentation goals. The team should discuss specifically what impressions they want to leave with the client and the audience.

Campaigns are like a product. Telling consumers a product is special for multiple reasons makes them less likely to remember what is *really* special about the product. Determine what is special about your campaign. Then be sure everyone keeps that in mind when they plan their own parts.

2. Get and Keep Attention. Whatever you say or show in the presentation will be meaningless unless your audience is paying attention. Thus, the second goal for individuals is to find ways to keep the audience involved. Consider a few surprises at the outset and along the way, the kind that raise eyebrows and pique one's attention. You should also give long and hard consideration to the beginning and end of the presentation. A presentation is like a horse race; it's the beginning and end that count. Possible openings for the beginning of your presentation are featured later in this chapter.

3. Bond with the Audience. You need to find common ground with the client. You want them to feel you're on their side, with their best interests at heart. Part of that common ground relates to the personal connection you make with the client. There's nothing wrong with friendliness throughout the presentation, but it's especially important at the beginning. Think of how you can establish some common ground with the client to better promote your ideas.

4. Establish Credibility. Product success, reputations, brand equity, and certainly money is at stake for the client, and so doubts inevitably surface. One key doubt relates to your credibility. Your presentation plan should include pointed strategies for eliminating that doubt.

5. Be Persuasive. Plan your presentation so the client feels you are sincere and trustworthy. Project those traits. With your presentation, hook into the prospective client's wish list of needs and wants. What you say and show requires alignment with those needs and wants.

Overall, these five goals should guide your presentation. Consider them as you make the hard decisions centered on what to say and show.

Writing the Presentation

Some people suggest you literally write out everything you say in a presentation. If you will be presenting in a set period of time, say 20 minutes, there is some merit to this idea. If time is somewhat flexible, it is usually more spontaneous to present from an outline. This spontaneity helps develop credibility as the client sees you that understand the material and are not simply reading from a script. A common suggestion is that you memorize only the beginning and end, and then rely on key words or concepts to guide you through the presentation's middle. It depends somewhat on how you feel most comfortable and confident. But be aware that complete memorization can break down and leave you speechless. It's often better to have a firm grip on the flow of the presentation, with key terms and concepts memorized.

Still, scripting has benefits. Ambitious presentations are often storyboarded in the planning stage in the same way storyboards are used to guide the production of commercials or movies. (Yes, movies. Alfred Hitchcock, for example, used highly detailed storyboards before beginning filming, and referred to them constantly during filming.) It can be especially helpful to storyboard ideas using PowerPoint software. You can use the sort option to arrange and rearrange slides until you feel comfortable with the sequence of the points you plan on covering in the presentation.

Decide on Governing Messages or Themes. An advertising presentation usually contains more than one message. Typically, there is a range of information provided, spanning topics such as creative and media. To link together these topics or information, a few governing themes should be threaded throughout the presentation. The themes unify all that you say and show, and they serve to anchor the client's internal responses in a meaningful, easily understood context. The messages presented through the script attach themselves to that theme. Typically, this theme will involve something with the message strategy, but it could center on some new opportunity such as a new product launch.

Unify and Coordinate Sections. Governing themes help unify and coordinate the diverse sections of the presentation, but are not enough by themselves. Within each section, such as creative, media, and promotion, you should strive for consistency of format and structure.

Be consistent with the use of words and terms. Tighten your language to cut down on the amount of material the client is expected to decode or remember. For example, if your creative is introduced through objectives and strategies, then consider introducing all of your media and promotion the same way. This consistency provides symmetry between the sections and makes it easier for the client to follow your presentation, even though you may be moving quickly from one part to another.

In a similar way, keep your wording of terms consistent from one part to another. For example, if you use the word *objectives* in the creative part of the presentation, consider this usage in the media and promotion parts. All language should be consistent.

Keep a Consistency in the Style of Presenting Visual Aids. As you plan visuals, such as slides and charts, keep what is said about them in the script consistent with what is portrayed on them. There is nothing wrong with saying aloud what is also shown on a slide. (Just don't read every word.) Repeating key words or terms from slide to slide or presentation section to section can help unify and coordinate the presentation.

Structural Integrity. View the presentation both as a whole and as parts and sections within the whole. The structural integrity of the presentation means you give each part and section a strategic and pointed emphasis, rather than giving all of them equal weight.

In the presentation, you will have a limited amount of time to make your case. How much time should you devote to the beginning? the middle? the end? to the research? to the creative or media? In the National Student Advertising Competition (NSAC), the creative section generally receives the most time and is placed closer to the beginning of the presentation than to the end.

As you consider the steps and tips in planning your presentation, be aware that your presentation structure will likely be refined over time.

Think Beginning, Middle, and End

Think of your presentation as having three distinct parts: a beginning, middle, and end. Each of these parts should be tied together, in much the same way that you would tie together the specific sections of the presentation.

The Beginning. The beginning and end are considered the most important parts of your presentation. Some professional presenters believe you should design the end of your presentation first, before the beginning. We'll take the traditional approach and plan the beginning first. Either way, plan these two parts before you work on the middle.

A good beginning quickly gets the audience's attention and develops an interest in what will follow. As you write the beginning, consider the following points about how a beginning should function.

- It should grab attention.

- It should preview the subject by introducing the main messages or themes.

- It clarifies and emphasizes what's in it (the benefit) for the prospective client.

- It establishes you as a credible source.

By considering these points, you should have an idea about what to say or even what to show at the presentation's beginning. You know, for instance, that before the beginning blends into the presentation's middle or body, the audience should be riveted, clear about the presentation's focus and benefit, and confident in your credibility. The question is, how do you do achieve these desired results? The following techniques are some of the tried-and-true methods:

- **Ask a question**—This rivets and focuses audience attention.

- **State an unusual fact**—This raises eyebrows, especially when the fact is in some way central to the client's needs, wants, or problems.

- **Give an illustration, an example, or a story**—This pulls your audience into the presentation.

- **Give a quote**—Why not quote directly from the prospective client or someone the client knows or respects?

- **Tell what's common between you and the client**—If, for example, both your agency and the client were central to furthering a certain business practice or perspective, make that known.

- **Use humor**—Be careful if you decide to inject humor into your presentation because what's funny to one person is not necessarily funny to another. Finally, make certain your humor relates to the client's general business or the situation at hand. Local libraries have books that you can use that contain humorous anecdotes for all occasions and situations.

- **Tell why you're credible**—The key here is understatement and subtlety, not overstatement and boldness.

The Middle. To be effective, this section often requires a lot of information. This can lead to tedium, if not boredom You can keep the client interested by embedding the script with elements similar to some of the points we have already discussed in other sections. They include the following:

- Keep words and terms alike or similar.

- Tie concepts to the main messages or themes.

- Get personal. Be sure to use the pronoun *you* in your presentation.

- Simplify complex data or information.

- Summarize frequently.

- Embed minor diversions for strategic purposes. If you have flooded the client with a great deal of information, take a breather and inject some humor or a brief anecdote.

- Avoid "jargon" or confusing concepts without explanations. Don't assume that all clients are familiar with some of the more technical advertising terms. However, assume that they may be able to intuitively figure out some terms, like cost per thousand.

The End. Like the beginning, the presentation's end, or close, is significant, simply because it will be the last thing the audience will remember about you and your agency. This is why care needs to be taken with the ending. Overall, you should seek to reinforce the presentation's goals and to consolidate the main points around the governing themes that have acted as glue for your presentation. Consider the following possible presentation endings.

- **The happy ending**—End on a positive note. Be upbeat and optimistic.

- **The funnel ending**—Here, you distill numerous points made in the presentation down to a few main points, often centered on the governing themes.

- **The "we're here to help" ending**—Position yourself as a genuine, sincere, and constructive solution to the client's problem.

- **The predict-the-future ending**—Make projections of how your proposal will have an impact on the client's future, obviously in a positive way.

- Emphasize the enthusiasm of your agency for the account.

At the very end, write a note to yourself: "ASK FOR THE BUSINESS."

Improve Writing Style

Once you've determined the structural integrity and content of the presentation's main parts and sections, concentrate on stylistic improvements in the script. Consider the following stylistic tips:

- **Write in a conversational tone**—Write like you talk, but with some elaboration at key points.

- **Use action verbs**—Action verbs breathe life into the writing and speaking. They stimulate the listener to imagine and construct scenes, emotions, and meanings. Use action verbs such as *propel, surge, advance*, or *stimulate*.

- **Vary the sentence pacing**—Sound out your script by reading it aloud. If reading it aloud results in a singular rhythmic drone of words, then changes are needed.

- **To add variety to the rhythm, vary sentence lengths**—If you have two long sentences together, then think about following them with a short sentence or phrase. It will help a sentence stand out.

- **Write short paragraphs**—The presenter finds short paragraphs easier to remember and less intimidating. Short paragraphs also force the scriptwriter to focus on organization and embed more transitions.

- **Explain and repeat difficult or knotty concepts**—If a certain concept seems particularly difficult or knotty for the client, elaborate it, perhaps by use of analogy or example.

Designing and Using Visuals

Visual aids reinforce and help explain the points you cover while making the presentation. People tend to trust what they see. Moreover, visuals can liven up a presentation.

Although certain principles might change as you move from boards to slides to transparencies, essentially the foundation of basic design principles remains the same.

Using Type in Visual Aids

- **Keep it simple**—Use discretion when emphasizing a point; only stress the most important point.

- **Put words near the top**—Words near the top of the enclosure or page lift the viewers' eyes and are easier to read. So, with flipcharts as well as slides or transparencies, place words or images in the top two-thirds of a page.

- **Limit the number of words**—Don't expect the audience to read too much. Use only key words, especially when the visual field is crowded, as with lists or a number of items.

- **Use uppercase and lowercase letters**—You can use all caps on flipcharts, otherwise use uppercase and lowercase letters which is what people are generally accustomed to reading.

- **Use large letters**—Don't be misled by how easy something is to read when you're right on top of it. Assume a safe distance from the visual field, and then judge how large the letters should be.

- **Use sans-serif fonts**—Maintain a consistent choice and size of typeface or lettering. Try to keep the lettering consistent with that used in your plans book. Remember to display words without serifs in your visuals to make reading easier and reduce eye strain.

- **Use only one method of emphasis**—If you use boldface, then don't underline. Avoid italics which read better in print than on visuals.

Using Graphics in Visual Aids

- **Use a single orientation**—Choose either a landscape (horizontal) or portrait (vertical) format for your visuals, not both. As much as possible, you should stick with one orientation or format. Only when you cannot apply that orientation should you change.

- **Color can offer emphasis, mood, distinction, associations**—As with advertising generally, color adds considerable attention-grabbing potential to your visuals. Particularly with slides, color can be used to lead the viewer from one line of words down or up to another. One of the most common of all slide treatments is to highlight in color the item or line of words the presenter is addressing. A rule of thumb is not to use more than three colors. You need to make strategic decisions about the actual choices of color. Contrast works best here, with an understanding that black type or images on a yellow ground shows up well for reading, although the yellow can be a visually nervous color. You may want to consider a cool-color background, such as blue, which tends to recede and not advance. Then your words or images would be a hot color, such as yellow, which tends to advance and not recede. And color choice like your other choices should be consistent and continuous throughout.

- **Keep visuals simple and singular**—Don't be tempted to cram as much as humanly possible on one slide or flipchart. Limit what you include, trying to keep each visual enclosure limited to one core idea or concept.

- **Condensation is important in your visuals**—Highlight key words or terms and don't feel obliged to abide by rules of grammar, particularly in respect to complete sentences.

- **Use bullets and graphic flourishes**—Consistency is important. If you start with one type of graphic element such as a bullet or a checkmark, you should continue with it.

- **Condense complex numbers into pie charts and bar graphs**—Simplify numbers so that they can be understood in a glance.

- **Reduce the number of curves on a graph to no more than three**—Limit the curves you show on each graph. Simplicity leads to clarity and comprehension.

- **Use charts, graphs, and diagrams appropriately**—Charts, graphs, and diagrams serve various functions. Use bar charts to show comparisons. Use pie charts to show relationships of parts to a whole. Use graphs to show changes and trends. And use diagrams to show complex ideas or concepts. Make simple associations, not clichés.

- **Keep maximum screen time to one minute**—Audiences can get into a rhythm. If a slide remains on-screen longer than a minute, the audience's rhythm can be disrupted.

Visuals for Data and Numbers

A variety of visuals can help you convey data and numbers quickly to the client. All of them can be created on a computer, then enlarged for display or photographed for slides. Sandra Moriarity and Tom Duncan suggest the following use of visuals for quantitative material:[2]

- **Tables**—Tables are good for showing extensive data and numbers, but these kinds of detail can drag down a presentation. However, tables may serve your purpose if you need to explain some information in detail. You can always highlight some of the data by using boldface or color.

- **Line graphs**—Line graphs work on two dimensions, showing time horizontally and volume or amounts vertically. Line graphs are effective for showing trends or changes over time.

- **Bar graphs**—Bar graphs show units and are effective for making comparisons. They can also be shown three dimensionally, creating depth in the visual image and thus highlighting key comparisons.

- **Flowcharts**—One of the most popular uses for a flowchart is to show media uses over time.

- **Pie charts**—Pie charts show the relationship of parts to a whole and are generally appropriate for showing percentages. An interesting and arresting visual adaptation of pie charts is to have them explode, separating one wedge or piece from the others.

- **Diagrams**—Diagrams often are effective for showing how something works. They can also be used to show cross sections or even the flow of one element to another.

- **Pictographs**—Pictographs lend visual excitement to data because the data are captured in an arresting visual field. For example, if you were pitching an automobile manufacturer, you might be inclined to show data inside the outline of a particular car model.

These data displays shown in Figure 12–1 all simplify within a glance what could be complex data to explain in words.

Reinforcing Visuals Aids

Another way to add extra interest to the presentation is to give the audience something to look at other than a screen or the presentation. It gives people a momentary rest, especially if they have been watching more than one presentation. Consider the following reinforcements for comprehensives (comps).

- Create comps of actual ads and sales promotion materials. Despite the visual power of slides or transparencies, nothing quite beats comps where clients can lay their hands on the real thing. Comps can also be brought closer for inspection, creating involvement on the part of clients.

- Use acetate overlays for a glossy finish.

- Letter in headlines and subheads. Body copy should be neatly ruled.

- Present comps on boards. Use an easel or wall background.

- Board sizes should be 18 inches, and the type size approximately 60 points if the viewing distance is 12 feet. If the viewing distance is 14 feet, the board size should be 24 inches and the type size approximately 72 points. If the viewing distance is 16 feet, the board size should be 36 inches and the type size 120 points.

Consider using props; they can be valuable for breaking down the walls between you and the client and for creating involvement. Your choice of props might include the following: miniversions of your client's product, product packaging, and product displays.

Rehearsing the Presentation

Everybody understands the value of rehearsing. However, it's not only about the amount of time you devote to rehearsing, but the quality of time as well. Consider the following tips to help you rehearse.

- **Be serious about practice**—There's an old saying in sports that applies here. If you practice bad, you'll play bad.

Figure 12–1   Displays of Data

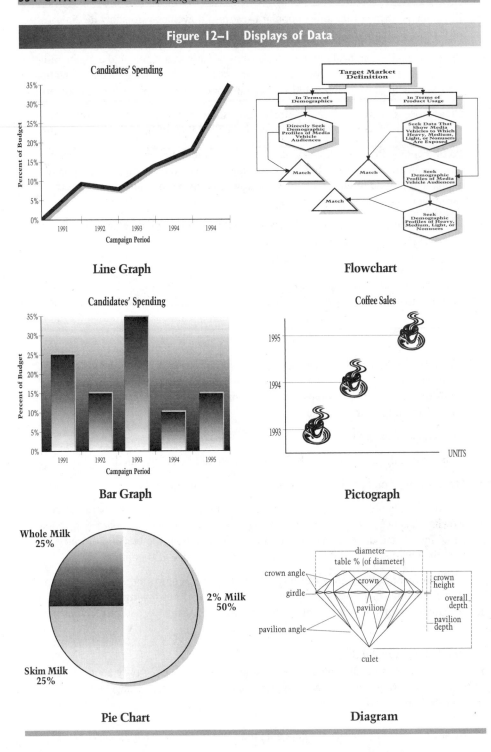

Line Graph

Flowchart

Bar Graph

Pictograph

Pie Chart

Diagram

- **Be prepared**—If there are stumbling blocks during rehearsal, they are only going to be bigger obstacles when the time comes to make the final pitch. Knowing your information inside and out can prevent a bad case of the "um's," ("the, um, target audience, um . . .")

- **Attitude**—You may be worn out from producing the campaign. Professionals don't let it show. Be enthusiastic. Sell yourself during the presentation. Vocal resonance, body language, and eye contact can communicate excitement as well as confidence better than anything you say. Practice enthusiastically.

- **Visual aids**—Aids are in the presentation to help you. If they are distracting or irrelevant, than reevaluate their place in your presentation. Simplify wherever you can.

- **Nervous quirks**—While it's natural to be fidgety, when presenting in front of a group, nervous mannerisms can undermine your ability to persuade the audience (or client) of your good ideas. When rehearsing, be on the lookout for wringing hands, holding elbows, and biting nails.

- **Physical appearance**—It's natural to want to practice in casual clothes. Consider dressing in the type of clothes you will wear in the presentation at least once. (It's called a dress rehearsal.) Practice at the site if possible or create a close simulation.

FINAL CHECKING AT THE SITE

It's always a good idea to do a final check on the sight before your presentation. Develop a checklist consisting of the following points.

- Know the room necessities for making a presentation. Know all about lights, temperature, chairs, and tables. BE certain they are ready to operate for your benefit.

- Know who to call for help. Wherever you are presenting, the owners or managers are certain to have staff people to help. Know who they are and how you can reach them in a hurry.

- Know the building's facilities and equipment. Your presentation room will be in a building. You should know where certain facilities and operations are in that building. For example, know where the restroom is, where the stairs and elevators are, and where the copy machine is.

- Check the equipment. Do tests on lecterns, easels, overhead projectors and computers.

- Check chairs and tables for positioning and stability. If permitted, arrange the chairs and tables to suit your presentation's purposes. For informality, avoid lecterns or tables separating you from the client. Leave room to stroll. Check lighting and light switches. Know how to work the dimmers, for instance.

MAKING THE PRESENTATION

A lot can go wrong with your presentation. Machinery can break down. The lighting may not be right. Heads can get in the way. All sorts of disastrous and sometimes unimaginable things can happen. It's your job to make sure they don't. The following tips are organized according to two primary concerns, your visual aids and you as a presenter. These tips should guide you in making certain everything goes according to plan.

Presenting Visuals

- Don't block the audience's view. Take pains to clear the viewing area before starting. Be certain about audience placement so that heads and arms don't obstruct the view.

- Direct audience attention. The audience is watching you. If you cast your eyes to the visual, the audience's eyes will follow. At key words use a pointer, especially for emphasis.

- Round off big numbers. Though you may be speaking of millions of dollars, don't be tempted to show the entire figure. Abbreviate and round off big numbers so that they are easily read and understood.

- Use circles, arrows, and other directional devices. Help your audience direct its attention by use of such devices.

- Keep transparencies in a binder and slides in a carousel. Avoid shuffling your visuals about or keeping them loose.

- Project images straight on the screen. Before you begin the presentation, make certain slides and transparencies are aligned properly on your screen.

- Show and remove visuals at the right time. The general formula is to introduce, show, and comment. For example, introduce the slide, show it, and then comment on it.

- Cover parts of some visuals at times. You can cover all but one line on a flip chart or transparency, then show each of the next lines one at a time. You can highlight certain lines on slides with color. Progressively disclosing information helps control what the audience is watching and thinking.

- Begin and end with lights full bright. Don't upstage yourself with a visual. You take the lead and direct the audience, and when your use of a visual is over, take the lead again.

- Use visuals to help other parts of the presentation. As mentioned previously, keep cues or notes on transparency frames or on flipcharts (front or back). Write key words from the script lightly on the palm of your hand.

- Make certain the first of everything is in place and in working order. Stretch a rubber band around the flipchart pad.

- Check the equipment. Check the sound level if you're using audio. Clean fingerprints from overheads. Check of the focus on slide and overhead projectors.

- Bring spare everything. Bring as much as you can to the presentation—not that you'll use it—that can bail you out of a jam: binders, extra flip-chart paper, magic markers, pens, a screwdriver or good Swiss army knife, and an extension cord. Make a checklist before leaving for the presentation, and then check off the items as they're readied for transport.

YOU AS PRESENTER

Many items on the previous two lists go beyond the use of your visuals. They begin to move into another sensitive area in your presentation's success: you. All the best visuals will come to nothing if you don't present well. Consider the following tips to help you do a winning presentation:

- Rehearse. Rehearse. Rehearse—as a team and alone.

- Leave cues in handy places. Leave them around the presentation area and on your own hand

- Make eye contact. This is one of the most important considerations in nonverbal communication. Look for one person first, then make eye contact every three to five seconds with different people. Or, make eye contact in a Z direction around the room.

- Smile. A smile helps put your audience at ease. Draw happy faces on your notes or in secret places to remind you to smile.

- Don't drink before a presentation (especially the stuff that is supposed to make you relax; it won't). Drinking any liquid may make things more difficult for you. If you need to refresh yourself, moisten your mouth or lips or use Vaseline. Try biting your tongue.

- Use talcum powder. Talcum powder will help keep you dry. As the saying goes, "Never let them see you sweat."

- Face your audience head on. This will suggest your confidence and sincerity.

- Practice gestures beforehand. Make pointed gestures during highlights in the presentation. Don't cross your arms. Keep your arms and hands at your side, but use them for emphasis when the time is right.

- Vary the distance and movement in relationship to the audience. Don't just stand in one place. Move around. Be comfortable. At key points shorten the distance, literally and figuratively, between you and the audience.

- Practice vocal tone, pitch, and pace variations. Use pauses to emphasize key points. Deepen your pitch by speaking from the diaphragm. Punch certain words or concepts. Vary your volume and rate of speaking, so you speed up in some places and slow down in other places.

- Lean forward, not backward, and hold yourself erect. By leaning forward you'll seem eager and enthusiastic. By holding yourself erect you'll seem confident and sure.

- Coordinate with the team the entrance and exit of the presentation. These can be the two most unorganized times (getting things set up or cleaned up), but they are also the most remembered moments. In fact, coordinate as much as possible with team members.

- Relax. This Should Be Fun.

AFF PRESENTATIONS

Dr. Lynda Maddox was asked to specifically give her impressions about what it takes to create a winning presentation at the AAF presentations. Her remarks follow.

Each year, participants at approximately 140 American Advertising Federation affiliated colleges and universities participate in an annual "rite of passage" for students interested in advertising. For over 25 years, AAF's National Student Advertising Competition (NSAC) has been the testing ground for advertising student knowledge, insight, and creative problem-solving in a real-world environment. Arguably the most prestigious, difficult, and comprehensive of all student advertising competitions, the NSAC features a different corporate sponsor each year. Competing teams solve a case study developed by the client. Each team produces a 40-page plans book and a 20-minute oral presentation that includes all aspects of an advertising and integrated marketing communications' plan.

Winners at the 15 AAF regional competitions compete at "Nationals" for the coveted first place prize. The judges for both the plans books and the presentations include distinguished persons from the sponsoring company as well as advertising agencies and the media. They are consistently amazed and impressed at the quality of the student presentations, likening them to major ad agency pitches. Moreover, AAF-sponsoring clients actually use the students' ideas and may even hire some team members.

This author has been involved with the American Advertising Federation's National Student Advertising Competition for most of its 25-year history, both as a student and faculty advisor. My students at the George Washington University have consistently placed in the top three at our District 2 competition, and in 1998 won in both our district and the Nationals. A key component of winning presentations at the NSAC and in the "real-world" is a professional presentation. The following tips are similar to what has been presented above, but are especially relevant for a winning presentation at the national competition.

Getting Started

- Start thinking early about the presentation. You should spend at least as much time putting the presentation together as you spent collecting the information. Many teams wait until the plans book is finished to begin thinking about it. This is too late. Read the presentation score sheet so you get a handle on the relative importance of various aspects. Remember that the judges will be using this to score you.

- Take pictures throughout the semester to include in your presentation. Record each stage of the campaign. For example, take pictures of your focus groups or of one of your team members conducting a survey. These pictures will add clout and interest to your presentation.

- Include some humorous shots. One year the GW team went on a road trip to conduct surveys in another city. On the way, they got a speeding ticket. The picture with the team members posing with the Pennsylvania State policeman brought a chuckle from the judges and expressed the dedication of this team! You'll also find that these pictures bond the team and are cherished memories after everything is finished.

- Before you begin writing the presentation, ask yourself, "If there was only one thing that the judges could remember after my presentation, what would I want that to be?" Be sure the team agrees on this point, since it will serve as the theme or focal point of the presentation. It will help you to organize large amounts of information.

- Reread the case and your plans book to be sure you know what to communicate. Set objectives and build your presentation around them. Do not think, "What can I say in

20 minutes?" Think, "What do I need to say?" You can edit your speech once you have included all that you need to express.

Selecting Presenters

- Throughout the semester, schedule various interim presentations to allow each class member to practice presenting. Sometimes an individual who does not think he or she is a good presenter will become the star after receiving feedback from the class and the advisor.

- Develop a procedure for selecting presenters. Set criteria early so that each student in the class has a chance to develop the skills necessary to be selected as a presenter. This helps to improve learning and maintain fairness. It reduces the chance that the selecting of presenters will become a popularity contest.

- Some teams opt to use formal auditions, and this can certainly work. At GW, each team member will have had at least three "auditions" throughout the semester since each student participates in interim presentations.

- It is usually best to select presenters who have been intimately involved in the development of the campaign *and* who have developed excellent presentation skills. A skilled presenter without an emotional attachment to the material will sound stilted and unconvincing. This is especially important since presenters must also perform well in the all-important Question and Answer session.

- To give each student an opportunity to learn and to meet advertising professionals, the GW team usually opts to have the maximum five presenters. Judges respond well to this format, but it requires careful choreography.

- Each team member also has a "coach." The coach's job is to encourage and support the presenter and to work with them one on one. If need be, the coach is fully prepared to step in and become a presenter.

Crafting the Presentation

- Know who your judges are and remember your objectives as you begin writing your presentation. Learn as much as you can about the judges ahead of time. This will help you feel more comfortable and help you connect with them when you get to the presentation.

- Make *your ideas* the hero of your presentation. The judges do not want to hear each team regurgitate the information the company gave to you. They are there to hear the fresh, creative, insight that can only come from unbiased creative thinkers like you.

- Start fresh when crafting your presentation. Do not follow the linear format of the plans book. As you make your ideas the focal point of the presentation, use your primary and secondary research, as well as the information from the case, as the supporting rationale.

- Your creative executions are usually the most impactful part of your presentation. Build your presentation around your creative ideas. Show your strategic thinking.

- Answer the question, "Why does this ad work?" Demonstrate that you believe in your creative, and tell the judges the supporting research. Let them know that you are proud of your work and even that you have favorites among your ads.

- Show ads on the screen and on storyboards. Display promotional ideas on slides and create prototypes. The more the judges can see and interact with the creative executions, the more they will remember them.

- Remember that oral speech differs from written. Since you have a strict 20-minute time limit, it is too dangerous to speak extemporaneously. You must script your presentation and memorize it, but you should do this so well that you will seem as if you are speaking to the judges one on one.

- Script the presentation, then edit and rewrite it until it is short, concise, and conversational.

- Be creative in your presentation style and format. Be sure your presentation has an element of surprise that makes it stand out. This can mean using a different audio visual aid, unique slides, or presentation styles. Avoid standing behind podiums and robotic-type presentations.

- Make it easy for the judges to follow your presentation. Provide an agenda and follow it. Remind judges periodically throughout the presentation about where you are on your agenda.

- Give your team an identity. Name your "agency" and be sure to repeat your name throughout the presentation. The name of your agency and the name of the client should be on every slide.

- Slides should be interesting and creative. Intersperse text, photographs, graphs, charts, and other visuals. Interact with your visuals. Do not operate in the dark. The judges want to see you as well as your visuals.

- Have a point of view and stick with it. Your campaign theme should connect all aspects of your presentation.

- Each presentation should have a strong introduction and a strong close. Tell the judges what you will present and why it is important. At the end, summarize what you have presented, tell how it accomplishes the goals of the assignment, and ask for the business.

- Practice, practice, practice. Practice in front of friends, classmates, and faculty. Consider criticisms constructive even if they sometimes seem harsh. Watch facial expressions as you present. The feedback you receive at this point will allow you to craft an excellent presentation.

- Practice until you sound natural and conversational. Practice until you do not need notes. Practice gestures, intonation and timing. You should run through your presentation at least three times exactly the way you want it to be before the big day.

Making the Presentation

- Above all, remember that your judges are the audience you should be addressing. As you stand on the stage facing an audience, you may be tempted to talk to the room. Resist this temptation and talk to the people who matter—the judges.

- *Connect* with the judges. Talk to them in a conversational style. Shake their hands. Make eye contact. Come out from behind the podium. Get down off the stage. Walk up to them. Show them your work. Feed off their reactions. Smile with them. Tell them your names. Wear name tags. Make them like you as individuals, and as a team.

- Be sure the judges remember the key aspects of your presentation. Think back to the one thing you want them to remember. Keep in mind that in order for a judge to re-member something you've said, he or she must see or hear it at least four times. So say it, say it again in another way, show it, and then repeat it again. You will not bore the judges. You will make your point.

- Do not worry too much about your randomly selected order of presentation. You can-not do anything about it. If you try to use a particular slot to your advantage, this may backfire on you since the judges are concerned about fairness.

- If you're first or immediately after lunch, keep in mind that it takes the judges a minute or two to warm up. Pay special attention to greeting them and acclimating them to your presentation format. If you're toward the end, be especially careful not to repeat the case information since many teams before you will have already done this.

- Show the judges that you are a team and that you enjoy working together. This is not easy to fake, so work on building team spirit and camaraderie throughout the project. Research shows that wanting to work with a team is the number one criterion for se-lecting an agency.

- Show the judges that you work and think well together. Feed off one another in a conversational style throughout the presentation. When a team member is speaking, nod affirmatively to support key ideas. Do not fidget or look bored. Let the personal-ity of the team members and the team shine through.

- Ask for the business. At the end of the presentation, tell the judges why the campaign will work and why you're the best team to work with.

- Confidently invite the judges to ask you questions.

Doing Well on the Q&A Session

- If you've done a good job on your presentation, the judges will have a lot of ques-tions! Welcome them. Students often think that judges ask questions to trip them up, and they respond defensively. This is rarely the case.

- Judges want to know more about your thinking and want to see how committed you are to your ideas. They are not looking for right or wrong answers. Use this as an op-portunity to connect with the judges and to show them how well you can work to-gether as a team. The Q&A session is often where the competition is won or lost.

- Prepare for the Q&A session ahead of time by having team members and others ask questions. Rehearse answers to questions just as you rehearse your presentation.

- Address any controversial issues in the regular presentation where you have control of it. Never assume that you will answer a major question only if it comes up in Q&A.

- The Q& A session is a good opportunity for you to "roll up your sleeves" with the judges. They will often ask you to move toward them or to sit down. You may want to do this at the beginning of the Q&A. At the Nationals for Hallmark, University of Texas received high marks for pulling up their chairs to the judges' table and looking them in the eyes.

- If you do not know the answer to a question, let the judges see you think. Often if one team member begins, another can elaborate. Use your research and your insight to show the judges that you can think on your feet.

- Answer the questions clearly and succinctly. Although it is a good idea to feed off one another, do not "overanswer" a question. Since judges have only 10 minutes of Q&A, they want you to answer concisely so they can have all of their questions answered.

Conclusion

- Good presentations do not just happen. They are carefully planned and orchestrated performances that affect whether the information is remembered, retained, and believed.

Steve Doyal, Vice President of Public Affairs and Communications for Hallmark, talked about what made George Washington University's presentation a winning one. He said, "GW came down off the stage and made a direct connection with the judges. It was just like a discussion between an agency and client." Doyal also stressed that "outstanding creative captivates the viewer, but it's strategic relevance and insight that make a winner, and GW had both." Doyal also offered that the best teams told the judges something not found in the plans book and they guided the judges through their thinking.

Mary Ellen Woolley, Senior Vice President/Education Services from the AAF, who has seen many winning teams in her nine-year tenure at AAF echoed Doyal's thoughts. She said that "a winning team is natural, confident, persuasive and energetic." Woolley added that judges, like real-world clients, always ask the question, "Do we really want to work with these people?"

Doyal and Woolley offered a few "don'ts" as well:

- Don't look memorized.

- Don't repeat the information from the case.

- Don't simply regurgitate your plans book.

- Don't act. Connect.

Instead:

- Engage with the audience.

- Make a personal and emotional connection.

- Come down off the stage and from behind the podiums.

- Support one another with nods and by looking interested.

- Above all, link your strategic insight with your executions.

One Final Note: For many advertising students, a presentation in a campaigns class is one of the last academic assignments you will have. Look forward to doing it. Doing it well. And enjoying it.

Notes and References

[1] Some material in this section is based on Joyce Kupsh & Pat R. Graves, *High Impact Business Presentations.* Lincolnwood, IL: NTC Books, 1994, pp. 27–48.
[2] Duncan, T., & Moriarity, S. (1989). *How to create and deliver winning advertising presentations.* Lincolnwood, IL: NTC Business Books, pp. 62–72.

Index